# Introduction to Quantitative
# Political Science

# Introduction to Quantitative Political Science

LEONARD CHAMPNEY
*University of Scranton*

HarperCollins*CollegePublishers*

Editor-in-Chief: Marcus Boggs
Project Editor: Diane Williams
Design Manager: Lucy Krikorian
Cover Design: John Callahan
Manufacturing Manager: Willie Lane
Electronic Page Makeup: Interactive Composition Corporation
Printer and Binder: RR Donnelley & Sons Company
Cover Printer: RR Donnelley & Sons Company

INTRODUCTION TO QUANTITATIVE POLITICAL SCIENCE

Library of Congress Cataloging-in-Publication Data

Champney, Leonard.
    Introduction to quantitative political science / Leonard Champney.
      p. cm.
    Includes index.
    ISBN 0-06-501032-9
    1. Political science—Statistical methods.     I. Title.
JA73.C47   1995
320'.072—dc20                                                    94-5006
                                                                 CIP

94 95 96 97 9 8 7 6 5 4 3 2 1

# Contents

## PART 2    PROBABILITIES AND INFERENCES   89

## CHAPTER 5   INTRODUCTION TO STATISTICAL INFERENCE   91

## CHAPTER 6   INFERENTIAL STATISTICS FOR SINGLE VARIABLES   103

## CHAPTER 7   INFERENTIAL STATISTICS FOR RELATIONSHIPS
         BETWEEN VARIABLES   111

# Preface

*Introduction to Quantitative Political Science* is designed for use in the first quantitative research methods course taken by undergraduate students in political science and related disciplines such as public administration, legal studies, and international studies. The text introduces students to the computation and interpretation of statistics and to the key concepts of social scientific inquiry (e.g., operational definitions, validity, reliability, independent and dependent variables, and research design). Our explicit assumption is that the former cannot be properly understood in isolation from an understanding of the latter. Hence, statistical analysis is treated as a logical outgrowth of precisely defining research problems and systematically solving those problems.

In a sense, then, this is both a research methods text and a statistics text. More precisely, it is an *applied political science statistics* text, designed to expose students to the variety of ways in which statistics are used by political scientists, policymakers, and lawyers. To that end, it is often "cookbook" in its approach. But to that same end, the text demonstrates the application and interpretation of the cookbook computations not only to the academic research problems of political scientists across a wide range of disciplinary subfields (from mass and elite political behavior in the United States to comparative and international politics), but also to current real-world uses of statistics in the policy and legal communities. It does so on the assumption that students should take two things away from their quantitative methods courses: first, an understanding of how political scientists do research; and second, an ability to evaluate the results of statistical analysis that they all will surely encounter later in their careers—as public servants, politicians, lawyers, or whatever.

In advancing this purpose, the text demonstrates how the results of statistical computations are interpreted in actual research situations, and how statistics serve as tools that may contribute to a clearer understanding of specific policy problems, through the use of supplementary research articles, research reports, and news reports reprinted as appendixes. About a dozen selections are reprinted, and the text provides extended commentary on each.

The book is better than it would otherwise have been, if not for the generosity of many colleagues. Janice Ballou of the Eagleton Institute of Politics at Rutgers University, Stephen Chilton of the University of Minnesota at Duluth, and several anonymous reviewers read and commented on the entire manuscript, some more than once. Ken Dautrich of the Eagleton Institute of Politics at Rutgers University, Joe Camaranno of

Syracuse University, Barbara Salmore of Drew University, and David Baldus of the University of Iowa Law School read and commented on portions of the manuscript. Reviewers were Stephen C. Brooks, University of Akron; Michael Corbett, Ball State University; David Dabelko, Ohio University; Terri Susan Fine, University of Central Florida; Michael Munger, University of North Carolina–Chapel Hill; Richard Rich, Virginia Polytechnic Institute; and Robert Y. Shapiro, Columbia University. Lauren Silverman, formerly of HarperCollins, encouraged the project and was patient in seeing it off the ground. Others at HarperCollins, including Marcus Boggs, Diane Williams, and Jennifer Goebel, have been similarly encouraging and patient.

LEONARD CHAMPNEY

# Numbers and Descriptions

# Chapter

# 1

# Why Numbers?

*P*olitical scientists, who study political phenomena and teach the principles of politics to their students, routinely rely on numbers to perform these tasks. Moreover, political practitioners, such as elected officials, bureaucrats, interest group representatives, and attorneys, routinely rely on numbers to discharge their responsibilities and advance their political objectives. This textbook introduces numbers as *tools* used to learn about politics and to act on that knowledge.

## THE IMPORTANCE OF QUANTITATIVE ANALYSIS

Fundamentally, numbers are tools used to learn about the world in which we live. Whereas natural scientists, such as physicists, chemists, and biologists, employ these tools to describe and explain the physical world, social scientists, such as economists, sociologists, and political scientists, employ them to describe and explain the human social condition. Political scientists and political practitioners focus on the politically significant aspects of this condition.

The most popular numerical tools employed by political scientists and practitioners are *statistics,* which *combine and summarize numbers* in ways that aid understanding of politically significant aspects of the social world. For example, if you were to divide the gross national product (total dollar value of all goods and services produced in one year; GNP) of the United States by its population, it would produce a statistic, a *ratio* termed "per capita gross national product," that combines GNP and population. This statistic is most likely politically significant, in that nations with low per capita GNPs probably display different political characteristics than nations with high per capita GNPs.

As another example, consider the total family income of each student in your quantitative research methods class. Add these together and divide by the number of students, producing a statistic termed the *mean*, which combines and summarizes the individual numbers represented by each student's family income. This statistic is likely politically significant as well, in that classes with lower mean family incomes probably possess different political attitudes and behaviors than classes with higher mean family incomes.

Statistics are widely used by political scientists and political practitioners. Indeed, although statistical analysis is now common in biology and chemistry, virtually dominates research in psychology, and has recently become fashionable in theoretical physics, the origin of statistics actually lies in political science! According to the *Oxford English Dictionary*, the term "statistics," derived from "state," was first used in a 1770 British publication to indicate a method of ascertaining the strength of the states of Europe and the political arrangements prevailing in them. A 1787 publication referred to statistics as the "branch of political science dealing with the collection and classification of facts bearing on the condition of a state." The term gained wide currency throughout nineteenth-century Europe to refer to strategies for measuring the characteristics of populations.

Political scientists and practitioners use a wide range of statistical tools because the precise summaries they generate greatly aid efficient communication. The more precise a definition (per capita GNP; mean income), the easier it is for people to *communicate* with one another when discussing the significance of political phenomena. *Statistics is a language,* routinely observed in communication regarding political affairs. When economic policy is under discussion, we hear references to the "unemployment rate," the "consumer price index," the "rate of inflation," the "prime interest rate," and so forth. Each of these terms carries a specific meaning upon which all the communicators (elected officials, bureaucrats, interest group representatives) agree. For example, the unemployment rate is defined as the total number of people seeking employment divided by the sum of the total number of people seeking employment and the total number of people currently employed. If the unemployment rate is 4.6 percent, that single number carries a precise meaning derived from the agreed-upon definition.

Moreover, precision promotes informed judgments and informed actions. Precision is extremely important to a political candidate using past patterns of electoral turnout and vote preferences to assess her chances of victory, to a public administrator using corporate hiring practices to assess the success of affirmative action programs, to a political scientist attempting to determine if differing levels of economic development influence politics among nations.

The candidate cannot rely on her casual impressions of what sorts of people are likely to vote and for whom; she needs precise data on the characteristics of the electorate in order to deploy her campaign resources intelligently and efficiently. For example, if running for the United States House of Representatives in one of the 435 electoral districts containing approximately half a million constituents, she may wish to invest $50,000 or so in a survey of a thousand or so randomly selected individuals in the district. By asking questions directly relevant to the campaign (whether the individuals recognize her name, what issues they believe are most important, their party identification, and their vote intention) and questions about individual characteristics (race, level of income, level of education, etc.), she can determine what sorts of folks are most and least likely to vote for her, and why. She may then concentrate her campaign resources accordingly.

The public administrator cannot rely on anecdotal evidence of employment discrimination; he must have hard statistical data on workforce composition. For example, an official of the United States Equal Employment Opportunity Commission investigating charges of discrimination against blacks at a major corporation might wish to separate the job descriptions at that corporation into those for which employee recruitment is concentrated in the local community of the corporation headquarters (clerical, secretarial, janitorial) and those in which recruitment is national (upper-level management). He may then consult census data to determine "pool availability" of blacks with the appropriate qualifications locally and nationally. Pursuing such a strategy permits comparisons of the proportions in the pool to proportions at the corporation.

And the political scientist studying foreign affairs cannot simply assume that the newer nations of Africa and Asia are economically underdeveloped, while the older nations of Western Europe are developed. She must establish a precise definition of economic development, such as per capita GNP, and apply it consistently to categorize each nation. We see such a process unfold in the following section.

## ARRIVING AT NUMBERS: THE MEASUREMENT PROCESS

Agreement that certain *concepts* symbolize certain real-world phenomena is the first step toward precise and efficient communication. As a result, definitions of concepts must be agreed upon among those using the terms. In discussing the various possible causes and consequences of current political developments with teachers and students in your college classes, you have no doubt heard the admonition, "define your terms!" This is particularly important in quantitative analysis, since such analysis is based on very precise definitions. A precisely defined concept *classifies*.

For example, the concept "party identification" classifies individual people in the United States as Democrats or Republicans or something else. The classification is politically significant. Democrats and Republicans likely display differences in their political behavior. Similarly, the concept of economic development classifies nations as developed or underdeveloped.

The observable evidence of an abstract concept permitting classification is termed an *indicator*. As an indicator of party identification, ask fellow students in your quantitative research methods class to identify themselves as either a Democrat or a Republican. As an indicator of economic development, record the per capita GNP of each nation in the world. For some concepts, *multiple indicators* are appropriate. A combination of dollar income and years of education might be used to indicate "socioeconomic status" for individual people in the United States. Similarly, area in square miles and population might be employed to indicate the "size" of states in the United States.

An *operational definition* constructed on the basis of carefully chosen indicators contains a detailed set of instructions outlining with precision the manner in which objects are classified. A complete operational definition establishes categories, specifies the procedures by which objects are placed into these categories, and assigns numbers to the categories. For example, in an operational definition of economic development, the categories are High and Low. Nations with per capita GNPs of $5,000 or less are classified as Low and those above $5,000 as High. The low category is assigned the number (1) and the high category the number (2).

For an example a bit more complex, consider an operational definition of socio-economic status, using multiple indicators: The categories are Low, Medium, and High. Individuals without a college degree who make $40,000 or less per year are classified as Low. Individuals with a college degree who make over $40,000 per year are classified as High. Everyone else is classified as Medium. The low category is assigned the number (1), the medium category the number (2), and the high category (3).

Once objects are classified on the basis of a carefully constructed operational defin-ition, the concept is measured, resulting in a *variable,* a set of *cases* (the objects classi-fied) that vary across the categories produced by the operational definition. Cases are also referred to as *units of analysis.* The cases vary, in that they take on different values, or *scores,* by virtue of the fact that they fall into different categories, as established by the operational definition, on any given variable. Many different sorts of cases may be classified, depending on the research question; for example, voters from the eligible population in the United States (cases) vary across the party identification (variable) cat-egories of Democrat and Republican; United States senators (cases) vary across the age (variable) categories of 42, 45, 49, 50, 51,. . . ; universities (cases) vary across the average Scholastic Aptitude Test scores of entering freshmen (variable) categories of 900, 920, 950, 1,000, 1,110,. . . ; cities (cases) vary across the percentage of minority population (variable) categories of 0, 1, 2, 3, 4, 5,. . . .

The cases are the points at which the measures are taken—the points at which the values of the variable are assigned. As a result, each case takes on one of the values, or scores, associated with one of the categories of the operational definition. In the exam-ples just mentioned, each senator takes on a two-digit score for age, each university a three- or four-digit score for average SAT, and so forth. For party identification, de-pending on how the operational definition was constructed, a case might take on a value of (1) for Democrat, (2) for Republican, or (3) for other.

## REFINING NUMBERS: THE LEVELS OF MEASUREMENT

The simplest and most basic level of measurement is the *nominal* level, from the Latin for "name." The numbers assigned to the categories, and used as the measure of each case in that category, serve simply as names for those categories and cases. Employing an operational definition for gender that would place students (the cases) in your quan-titative research methods class into the categories (1) Female and (2) Male provides an example. Term the women either "Females" or (1)s and the men either "Males" or (2)s. The names and numbers are interchangeable. This is a *qualitative* level of measure-ment—the numbers simply distinguish among cases that possess different qualities; for example, male versus female for students or developed versus underdeveloped for na-tions. Mathematically: $1 = 1$ and $2 = 2$ and $1 \neq 2$.

Obviously, at this level of measurement, assigning numbers to the categories seems unnecessary. Yet, it is done for several reasons. First, a complete operational definition, as previously noted, calls for the assignment of numbers to the categories. Similarly, the measurement process requires that values, or scores, be assigned to each category, so that each case takes on one of these values. Second, as we shall observe later, managing a large body of data, even at the nominal level, frequently requires computer assistance. Computer analysis requires "coding" cases with numerical values.

Some variables may be measured at the *ordinal* level. Here, the categories may be placed in *order* and the numbers assigned to the categories reflect that order. A particular category is "more or less" than another category or "bigger or smaller" than another category; therefore, specific cases may be compared to one another on the basis of their position on the ordered scale of scores, as determined by the categories into which the cases fall. In the example of socioeconomic status, with categories of (1) Low, (2) Medium, and (3) High, an individual (the case) scoring (1) is lower on the scale of socioeconomic status than an individual scoring (3). Similarly, any case found in category (3) has "more" socioeconomic status than any case found in categories (1) or (2). Mathematically, state: $3 > 2, 2 > 1, 3 > 1, 1 < 2, 2 < 3, 1 < 3$. State no more than this.

Public opinion polls commonly request respondents (the cases) to indicate their agreement or disagreement with statements about the success of public policies or the evaluation of public officials or candidates. Frequently, the respondents are asked if they: (1) Strongly Disagree, (2) Disagree, (3) Have No Feeling One Way or the Other, (4) Agree, or (5) Strongly Agree; they may then be placed in the appropriate category. Termed a *Likert scale*, this variable is ordinal.

In select instances, variables may be measured at the *interval* level, permitting the establishment of precise *distances* between categories, and between the cases in those categories, by using an actual *unit of measurement*. At this level, we may discuss "how much" more or less or "how much" bigger or smaller one category is than another and identify the exact distance between any two categories and any two cases within the categories, using the units of measurement to establish the distance. For example, an interval level classification of individual people (the cases), based on their yearly income, assigns each case a precise number, employing dollars as the unit of measurement. A person falling in the category of $40,000 a year makes $2,000 more than a person falling in the category of $38,000 a year—$2,000 is the interval. There is a distance of $2,000 between the two scores.

Or measure the level of political participation in the states in the United States, using turnout in the presidential election of 1992 as the indicator. A state (the case) with a turnout of 47 percent falls 5 points below a state with a turnout of 52 percent. There is an interval of 5 between these two cases; the percentage point is the unit of measurement. The distance between the two cases, and the distance between the two categories in which the cases fall, is 5 percentage points.

While interval level variables may take on negative values, a *ratio* level variable is defined by an *absolute zero*, below which no cases may fall, nor categories be defined. Fahrenheit temperature is a popular example from the natural sciences of a variable which, while interval, is not ratio. If the high was 10 degrees yesterday, and is 20 degrees today, it is 10 degrees warmer today. Twenty is a distance of 10 degrees from 10. However, it is *not* twice as warm! To make such a statement, we would need an absolute point of reference at 0. At the interval level, we may make statements based on the principles of addition and subtraction. For example, 5 degrees below 0 is 15 degrees less than 10 degrees; –5 plus 15 is 10. But we cannot make statements based on the principles of multiplication and division with a measure that has an arbitrarily set 0 along a continuum containing both positive and negative values. Twenty-five degrees is 15 degrees more than 10 degrees. But this does not permit the conclusion that 25 degrees is twice as much as –5 degrees. Such statements may only be made at the ratio level.

Political scientists and political practitioners are seldom concerned with the distinction between interval and ratio, since they rarely, if ever, encounter variables with negative values. Dollar income, years of education, area in square miles, size of population, percentage of minority population, percentage of turnout, gross national product, and so forth, either take on a positive value or take on the value of absolute zero. *Therefore, in this text, we refer to any interval or ratio variable simply as interval.*

Indeed, both the earlier income and participation examples are actually ratio rather than simply interval. For example, $10,000 is 10,000 units above 0 and $20,000 is 10,000 units above $10,000; this *does* mean we can multiply $10,000 by two and get $20,000. Similarly, a state with a turnout of 30 percent has a turnout of half as much as a state with 60 percent.

There are at least two very important points to remember about levels of measurement. First, a properly constructed operational definition at the nominal or ordinal level of measurement produces categories labeled by both names and numbers, while a properly constructed operational definition at the interval level produces categories labeled only by numbers. Note the following four examples of variables containing categories on the basis of which cases classify. The first is nominal, the second ordinal, and the third and fourth interval:

### Religion of people:

1. Protestant
2. Catholic
3. Jewish
4. Other

### Size of states:

1. Very small
2. Small
3. Large
4. Very large

### Per capita GNP of nations in U.S. dollars:

170
920
1,112
5,200
6,300

7,100

8,600

.

.

.

## Age of students in your class:

18

19

20

21

22

An interval level variable may, in principle, have as many categories as cases. Conceivably, each of 175 nations could achieve a distinct score on per capita GNP, or each of several hundred individual people could have a different yearly income, each case having its own category, because each case has a unique score. For this reason, distributions on interval level variables are not normally presented as they have been here, since the number of categories can be unmanageably large. Chapter 2 considers in detail the manner in which distributions are presented.

Second, levels of measurement are *cumulative* or *hierarchical.* Nominal is the crudest or simplest level; interval is the most sophisticated, or highest powered level. Nominal classifies by creating categories in which to place cases. Ordinal not only classifies, but also orders the categories, thereby achieving order among the cases. Interval classifies, orders, and establishes distance between categories and the cases in those categories. Ordinal is nominal plus order. Interval is ordinal plus distance. Therefore, a variable measured at the ordinal level is also measured at the nominal level and a variable measured at the interval level is also measured at the ordinal and nominal level.

In the Likert scale example, we might choose to recategorize the cases, simply using (1) Disagree and (2) Other. By breaking this ordinal variable down into two categories (termed a dichotomy), we loose the ordered array, in effect producing a nominal variable. Similarly, any interval array may be broken down into discrete categories. A list of per capita GNPs for each nation in the world might, by choice, be recategorized into (1) Low, (2) Medium, (3) High, or simply divided into a dichotomy at some middle point.

However, some variables are only nominal, such as the religion of people in the example given earlier. Gender is another example. There is no choice; there is no order, no distance. Similarly, some variables are only ordinal or nominal. Most common among these are operational definitions designed to measure attitudes and opinions. Although it is possible to employ Likert scales indicating degree of agreement or disagreement on selected issues, no unit of attitudinal measurement permits establishment of precise distances or intervals.

## IDENTIFYING "GOOD" NUMBERS: VALIDITY AND RELIABILITY

The question of *validity* is conceptual and definitional. It asks, "How good is the 'fit' between the concept to be measured and the indicator(s) chosen?" and "Do the categories constructed out of the indicators make distinctions among the cases that are reasonable in light of the concept?" For example, is it reasonable to employ income and education as indicators of socioeconomic status? Do these indicators "get at" commonly agreed upon meanings of socioeconomic status? Similarly, is it reasonable to use area in square miles as an indicator of size of states? Or does this indicator leave out something important about the meaning of size? Operational definitions, like any other definitions, are neither correct nor incorrect, they are only more or less *convenient and reasonable*. If most researchers agree that the indicators chosen measure the concept of interest, we deem our operational definition valid.

Different researchers often use different operational definitions for the same concept. Perhaps one researcher decides to use per capita GNP as an indicator of the economic development of nations, while another decides to use per capita consumption of electricity. Do not say one has chosen the correct definition and the other has chosen an incorrect definition. Both definitions are reasonably valid for the concept of economic development, and both would likely produce similar categorizations of nations. Similarly, do not say that using a per capita GNP of $5,000 as the cutoff point to determine economic development is incorrect and that only a cutoff point of $8,000 would produce the correct categorization. Again, it is a matter of definition. And definitions involve human choices.

The question of *reliability* is technical and procedural. It addresses the precision, accuracy, and care with which data are collected after the operational definition is constructed. Would exactly the same classification of cases result if two different researchers applied the same operational definition? Insuring reliability is the primary reason operational definitions must be detailed and precise. For an operational definition to be reliable, *different* researchers must be able to repeat the application of the *same* definition with the *same* result. Once an operational definition is constructed, there should be no room for judgment in applying it to classify cases. Most reasonable people agree that income and education are valid indicators of socioeconomic status. But the resulting classification of cases is not reliable if the researcher is sloppy in collecting the data or careless in classifying the cases. Clearly, reliability is a question of degree, since no measure is perfectly accurate. For example, recording the population of states in the United States using census data is extremely reliable. Yet, even here, complete reliability is unattainable, as these populations change constantly.

Validity and reliability must be evaluated separately. An operational definition may produce a valid, but unreliable categorization scheme. Classifying the students in your research methods class into "social background" categories, using family income as the indicator, and "guessing" each income by looking at the manner of dress, provides an example. Income is a reasonably valid indicator of social background, but categorizing by "guessing" is highly unreliable—both imprecise and inaccurate. This example demonstrates that the distinction between validity and reliability is sometimes tricky. Take care to note that income is the indicator here, not manner of dress. An attempt is made to establish the value of income through a guessing process that includes evaluating the manner of dress. If manner of dress were the indicator for the concept of social background, instead of income, the measure would be invalid rather than unreliable.

Alternately, an operational definition may produce a reliable, but invalid, measure. Classifying the nations of the world into categories of economic development, using the amount of money each spent on social welfare programs for their citizens as an indicator, provides an example. While the nations may be very carefully categorized based on very accurate and precise data for levels of spending, few reasonable people agree that level of social welfare spending is a valid indicator of economic development. Clearly, other indicators provide a tighter "fit" with the concept, such as per capita GNP. Of course, carefully constructed operational definitions produce measures that are both valid and reliable.

## ORGANIZATION OF THE TEXT

Once variables are measured, a wide variety of statistical techniques may be employed to summarize the resulting quantitative information; some are very simple and some are highly complex. All the techniques, however, are defined by three basic distinctions. First, different statistical techniques are appropriate at each level of measurement discussed earlier: nominal, ordinal, and interval. Second, statistics are either descriptive or inferential. Third, they are either univariate, bivariate, or multivariate.

*Descriptive* statistics depict the pattern of variation in measures for a given set of cases. For example, the mean family income of students in your class depicts the "average" income for a given set of cases, the students. Similarly, a survey of 1,000 randomly selected voters in a congressional district (the set of cases) may depict that 35 percent of them are registered Democrats. Means and percentages are both descriptive statistics.

*Inferential* statistics establish the likelihood that descriptions for a given set of cases are characteristic of, or generalizable to, all cases. Is the mean family income of students in your class the same as the mean family income of all students at your college? Is it the same as the mean family income of all college students in the United States? If 35 percent of a randomly selected sample of 1,000 voters in a congressional district are Democrats, may we conclude that 35 percent of *all* voters in the district are Democrats? Inferential statistics are designed to answer these questions. They are most commonly employed in situations such as the latter, when surveys and public opinion polls based on *samples* of cases are conducted.

*Univariate* statistics summarize the pattern of variation in single variables. Mean family income is a univariate statistic because a single variable, family income, is summarized. Univariate statistics may be descriptive (the mean itself) or inferential (the likelihood this mean is characteristic of all cases).

*Bivariate* statistics are designed to determine if two variables "vary together." Are students from families with higher incomes (first variable) more likely to consider themselves Republicans (second variable)? Are voters in a congressional district who are registered Democrats (first variable) more likely to consider themselves "liberals" (second variable)? Bivariate statistics may be descriptive (do the two variables vary together for a given set of cases?) or inferential (what is the likelihood the two variables vary together for all cases?)

*Multivariate* statistics are designed to determine if additional variables influence bivariate relationships. Are students from higher-income families more likely to consider themselves Republicans regardless of whether they are white, black, or something else? Are registered Democrats more likely to consider themselves liberal regardless of whether they are Catholic, Protestant, Jewish, or something else? Just as with univariate and bivariate statistics, there are multivariate descriptive statistics and multivariate inferential statistics.

The text is organized around the three basic distinctions: level of measurement of variables; descriptive and inferential statistics; and univariate, bivariate, and multivariate statistics. Chapter 2 discusses descriptive statistics for single variables at each level of measurement. Included are averages, such as the mean, and summaries of dispersion around the average on a single variable for a given set of cases, such as the standard deviation. Chapters 3 and 4 discuss the importance of bivariate descriptive statistics for the study of political phenomenon and detail the most common statistical techniques employed. These range from the very simple, such as percentages at the nominal level, to the more complex, such as regression analysis at the interval level.

In Chapters 5, 6, and 7 the focus is shifted to inferential statistics. We discuss the importance of "random sampling" and an understanding of the "normal curve" for sound inferential analysis, as well as the "population parameter" for variables described by samples. In addition, we discuss the most commonly employed bivariate inferential statistics, with particular emphasis on chi square.

Chapters 8 and 9 focus on the importance of multivariate statistics in the study of political phenomenon and detail the most common statistical techniques employed, including multiple regression. Chapter 10 discusses survey research and public opinion polling in more detail, examines other methods of data collection, and introduces time-series analysis, an advanced multivariate statistical technique.

The following matrix depicts the three basic distinctions. Each cell of the matrix contains a different statistical technique. As we move through the text, discussing the various statistics, we will be "filling out" the cells of the matrix.

|  | Descriptive | | | Inferential | | |
|---|---|---|---|---|---|---|
|  | Univariate | Bivariate | Multivariate | Univariate | Bivariate | Multivariate |
| Nominal | Chap. 2 | Chap. 4 | Chap. 9 | Chaps. 5, 6 | Chap. 7 | Chap. 9 |
| Ordinal | Chap. 2 | Chap. 4 | Chap. 9 | Chaps. 5, 6 | Chap. 7 | Chap. 9 |
| Interval | Chap. 2 | Chap. 4 | Chap. 9 | Chaps. 5, 6 | Chap. 7 | Chap. 9 |

## A WORD ON MATHEMATICAL NOTATION

The mathematical operations introduced in this text are quite simple and straightforward; however, some of these operations involve several steps and some involve very small or very large numbers. Use an inexpensive calculator to assist with your computations. In addition, a basic familiarity with simple mathematical notation, which instructs us to perform certain mathematical operations, substantially aids comprehension. Before proceeding, therefore, let us outline the most commonly encountered symbols.

Everyone is familiar with the basic symbols that instruct us to add, subtract, multiply, or divide. As you may also know, there is more than one such symbol for multiplication and more than one such symbol for division. An instruction to multiply $P$ times $Q$ may take any one of the following forms:

$$P \times Q$$

$$P \cdot Q$$

$$(P)(Q)$$

In this text, we use all three forms of notation.

An instruction to divide $P$ by $Q$ may take any one of the following forms:

$$P \div Q$$

$$P / Q$$

$$\frac{P}{Q}$$

In this text, we use either the second or third form of notation.

You also know that multiplying a negative number by a positive number yields a negative number, multiplying a negative number by a negative number yields a positive number, and dividing a negative number by a positive number yields a negative number:

$$(^-2)(3) = {}^-6$$

$$(^-2)(^-3) = 6$$

$${}^-6 / 2 = {}^-3$$

This text does not call for mathematical operations more sophisticated than taking a square root, denoted by $\sqrt{P}$. As you know, the square root of $P$ is the number that, multiplied by itself, yields $P$. If $P$ is 900, the square root of $P$ is 30. A calculator puts square roots at your fingertips.

Variables for a set of cases are symbolized by letters. The most common are $X$ and $Y$; we speak of the "$X$ variable" and the "$Y$ variable." Another very common symbol, $\Sigma$, the summation sign, instructs us to "add up." For example, if we have an $X$ variable for five cases and the value of the first case is 2, the second case 3, the third case 4, the fourth case 5, and the fifth case 6, $\Sigma X$ instructs us to add these values up, resulting in 20. $\Sigma(X^2)$ instructs us to square each value first, then add them up, resulting in 90. $(\Sigma X)^2$ instructs us to add the values up first, then square the result, yielding 400.

This brings us to the importance of parentheses in mathematical equations. Always approach parentheses "inside out," performing the operations contained in the parentheses most deeply embedded in the equation first, and work your way out to the parentheses enclosing the largest number of operations. With $\Sigma(X^2)$, we squared $X$ first, then added, since $X^2$ was in parentheses. With $(\Sigma X)^2$, we added first, then squared the result, since $X$ was in parentheses. Suppose we had $[\Sigma X + (\Sigma X)^2]$. We would take the summation of $X$, square it, then add the result to the summation of $X$. Test your knowledge by solving the following equation, using the five cases on the $X$ variable described earlier:

$$100{,}000 - [(\Sigma(X^2) \cdot 10)/5] \;/\; \left[ [(\Sigma X \cdot (\Sigma X)^2) - 200]\,[5] \right]$$

Your answer should be approximately:

$$99{,}820 / 39{,}000 = 2.56$$

*Chapter*
# 2

---

# *Descriptive Statistics for Single Variables*

$M$any of the methods commonly employed to combine numbers are very simple to work with, such as percents, rates, and ratios. Frequently, operational definitions of concepts in political science employ these numerical combinations to produce more valid measures than otherwise possible. For example, the amount that individual states in the United States spend on education, as an indicator of their "commitment to education," is invalid. Large states such as New York and California, with large total budgets, obviously spend more money on education than other states, even if education is a relatively low budget priority; therefore, total money spent on education more likely indicates the size of the state rather than "commitment." Resolution of this difficulty requires adjusting the indicator; for example, computing per capita education expenditures or computing percent of the total budget devoted to education.

## PERCENTS, RATES, AND RATIOS

### Percents

To compute *percent* of total budget devoted to education, divide total budget into education budget and move the decimal two places to the right. For example, if a state has a budget of $900 million and spends $175 million on education: 175 / 900 = .194 = 19.4

percent; 175 is 19.4 percent of 900. And 250 is 100 percent of 250: 250 / 250 = 1 = 100 percent. In the same way, 30 is 300 percent of 10: 30 / 10 = 3 = 300 percent. Percent means "per 100." In the first example, $19.4 per $100 are spent on education. Moving the decimal two points to the right is equivalent to multiplying by 100. This transforms the result of the division into "per 100."

In measuring politically significant phenomena, computation of *percent change* across time is also common. For example, to calculate the percent change in the population of a state from Time 1 ($T1$) to Time 2 ($T2$) perform the operation: $(T2 - T1) / T1$. Suppose population was 10.2 million in 1980 and 11.5 million in 1990: $(11.5 - 10.2) / 10.2 = 1.3 / 10.2 = .127 = 12.7$ percent change. If no change: $(10.2 - 10.2) / 10.2 = 0$. Or a decline: $(9.5 - 10.2) / 10.2 = -.7 / 10.2 = -.068 = -6.8$ percent.

When dealing with change across time for quantities themselves measured as percents, always take care to distinguish between percent change and *change in percentage points*. For example, suppose the unemployment rate changes from 5 percent at Time 1 to 10 percent at Time 2, obviously a change of 5 percentage points, from 5 to 10. But it is a 100 percent change!: $(10 - 5) / 5 = 5 / 5 = 1 = 100$ percent. Keep an eye on politicians when they deal with percent change over time. An aspiring officeholder choosing to paint a bleak picture argues that unemployment doubled! A politician defending her record as an incumbent during the period from Time 1 to Time 2 says no, it only changed 5 percentage points!

## Rates

When measuring the threat of violence in cities of the United States, an operational definition relying simply on the number of murders committed in a year is invalid. Again, larger cities have more murders simply because they have more people. Correcting by taking the number of murders committed in a year as a percentage of the number of people in the city produces an extraordinarily small number. For example, 1,000 murders in a city of 1 million people yields a murder percent of .1. Computation of a murder *rate*, based on the number of murders per 100,000 people, serves as an alternative. Simply multiply the result of the division of people into murders by 100,000 instead of 100, resulting in movement of the decimal point five places to the right instead of two: $(1,000 / 1,000,000) \times 100,000 = .001 \times 100,000 = 100$ murders per 100,000 people, "per 100,000" instead of "per 100." Similarly, when there are 620 murders in a city of 1,204,500 people: $(620 / 1,204,500) \times 100,000 = 51.5$ murders per 100,000. A rate is just like a percent with the exception that the base is no longer 100. Indeed, some indicators expressed as percents are, in common usage, referred to as rates. For example, in computing the unemployment rate, researchers take the number of those looking for work as a percent of all working plus all looking for work.

## Ratios

Note that with percents and rates, the division is always performed on equivalent units. In the budget example it is: dollars / dollars. In the population example it is: people / people. In the murder example it is: number of people murdered / total number of people. *Ratios,* on the other hand, are computed by dividing with nonequivalent units. Per capita gross national product is a ratio of money to people. If the gross national product of the United States is $4 trillion and the population is 230 million, the ratio is: 4 trillion / 230 million = $17,391 per person. To define the "agriculturalness" of states in the United States, construct a ratio of acres in farming to square miles. If a state has 20,000 acres in farming and 9,000 square miles, it has 2.2 acres per square mile: 20,000 / 9,000. If a state has 20,000 acres in farming and 40,000 square miles, it has .5 acres per square mile: 20,000 / 40,000. Note that these expressions are fundamentally different from expressions such as "$19.4 per $100" or "51.5 murders committed per 100,000 people." Acres and square miles are nonequivalent units, as are money and people in the gross national product example. A choice to divide acres into acres produces a percent or a rate, rather than a ratio.

## DISTRIBUTIONS, GRAPHS, AND CHARTS

After measuring a concept with a carefully constructed operational definition that categorizes a set of cases, the result for that set of cases may be visually summarized in distributions, graphs, and/or charts. *Frequency distributions* summarize cases categorized at the nominal or ordinal level. These distributions simply list the numbers and the names of the categories produced by the operational definition, record the number of cases falling into each category, and record the percent of cases falling into each category. We offer two examples from a set of data containing the characteristics and attitudes of approximately 400 University of Scranton students. The data were gathered from responses to a questionnaire distributed through the mail during the spring semester, 1987. (We discuss the technique by which the data were collected in more detail in Chapter 10.)

|     | Gender | No. of respondents | Percent | Cumulative percent |
|-----|--------|--------------------|---------|--------------------|
| (1) | Male   | 207                | 51      | 51                 |
| (2) | Female | 199                | 49      | 100                |
|     |        | 406                | 100     |                    |

|     | Ideology | No. of respondents | Percent | Cumulative percent |
|-----|----------|--------------------|---------|--------------------|
| (1) | Very conservative | 5        | 1.3     | 1.3                |
| (2) | Conservative      | 75       | 18.8    | 20.1               |
| (3) | Moderate          | 212      | 53.1    | 73.2               |
| (4) | Liberal           | 97       | 24.3    | 97.5               |
| (5) | Very liberal      | 10       | 2.5     | 100.0              |
|     |                   | 399      | 100     |                    |

*Note:* The gender distribution contains 406 cases, while the ideology distribution contains 399 cases. Such discrepancies are not uncommon when distributions are constructed from survey results, since some questions elicit more complete responses than others. Obviously, everyone is capable of a response when asked their gender; however, some may be unable to respond when asked their ideological orientation, as a result of incomplete understanding of the concept, or unwillingness to commit themselves.

The gender variable is nominal and the ideology variable is ordinal. In both instances, University of Scranton undergraduates are the cases. Of 406 students, 207 or 51 percent, are Male. Ten of 399 students, or 2.5 percent, are Very Liberal. The first column gives the actual number of respondents in each category. The first set of percents presents the number of respondents as a percent of the total number. The second group of percents are termed "cumulative percents" and report the percent of cases in and above the category in which they are reported. For example, 100 percent of 406 students are either Male or Female. Of 399 students, 73.2 percent are either Very Conservative, Conservative, or Moderate.

Frequency distributions must be *exhaustive* and *mutually exclusive.* An exhaustive distribution contains a category for every case in the set of data. For example, if displaying a frequency distribution of religious affiliation for a sample of the general population in the United States, the categories of (1) Protestant, (2) Catholic, and (3) Jewish are insufficient. To ensure exhaustiveness, the category, (4) Other, must be added to cover Buddhists, Muslims, and so on, as well as another category, (5) None.

In a mutually exclusive distribution, no case may fall into more than one category. Pursuing the religion example, an array laying out (1) Protestant, (2) Catholic, (3) Jewish, (4) Baptist, (5) Other, and (6) None, contains a flaw. Baptists are also Protestants; the array is not mutually exclusive, since a Baptist case could be placed in either category (1) or category (4), or both. The rule for frequency distributions: Every case in the set of data fits one, and only one, category.

Frequency distributions seldom display interval level variables. Since these variables often contain a large number of unique scores, such distributions are unmanageable, with many categories containing only one case. For example, percent of state budget devoted to education and percent change in population in the states, both interval level variables, may, in principle, contain 50 different scores for the 50 different states. To list each score, and place a "1" next to it, to indicate one case, makes little sense. Exceptions apply when interval level variables are "rounded." For example, individual incomes rounded to tens of thousands of dollars: $10,000, $20,000, $30,000, $40,000, $50,000.... Exceptions also apply in select instances where the range of variation in scores is limited. For example, the array of student ages contained in Chapter 1, although interval, may be placed in a frequency distribution, since the range of variation is restricted to between 18 and 22.

Moreover, interval data appears as *grouped* or *ungrouped.* Nominal and ordinal distributions are grouped by definition; the cases are placed into clearly defined categories. Interval level data, for the reasons already noted, are not grouped by definition. For example, a list of the rate of crime per 100,000 people in the largest cities of each state in the United States[1] follows. Of course, we could put a "1" to the right of each score, indicating that one case fell in that category, but this would be inefficient.

| | | |
|---|---|---|
| 5,369 | 9,155 | 12,318 |
| 5,628 | 9,192 | 12,768 |
| 5,753 | 9,353 | 13,065 |
| 5,966 | 9,916 | 13,648 |
| 6,150 | 10,033 | 13,904 |
| 6,407 | 10,235 | 13,975 |

| | | |
|---|---|---|
| 6,977 | 10,251 | 14,054 |
| 7,030 | 10,280 | 14,832 |
| 7,043 | 10,501 | 15,671 |
| 7,317 | 10,594 | |
| 7,340 | 10,660 | |
| 7,531 | 11,071 | |
| 7,542 | 11,625 | |
| 7,665 | 11,773 | |
| 7,869 | 11,972 | |
| 8,152 | 11,987 | |
| 8,474 | 12,002 | |
| 9,089 | 12,156 | |
| 9,122 | 12,309 | |

However, such data may be grouped many ways, depending on researcher preferences. For example:

| Crime Rate | No. of Cases |
|---|---|
| Under 6,000 | 4 |
| 6,000–7,999 | 11 |
| 8,000–9,999 | 8 |
| 10,000–11,999 | 12 |
| 12,000–13,999 | 9 |
| Over 13,999 | 3 |
| | 47 |

But once so grouped, the variable becomes *ordinal,* a consequence extremely important to bear in mind. Make *absolutely certain* you understand why this is now an ordinal variable. The only situation in which a grouped interval level frequency distribution remains interval after grouping is when variation is restricted; for example, student age. Another example: grades given in a course, expressed as quality points:

| Quality Points | Grade | No. of Cases |
|---|---|---|
| 0 | F | 2 |
| 1 | D | 5 |
| 2 | C | 10 |
| 3 | B | 8 |
| 4 | A | 6 |
| | | 31 |

Of course, grade points could be listed individually, as in the crime-rate example. However, this too would be inefficient, since the range of variation is restricted and each case does not have a unique score. Again, make *absolutely certain* you understand why the grade distribution is interval, while the *grouped* crime rate distribution is ordinal.

Nominal and ordinal data appear in summary form in graphs and charts, as well as in frequency distributions. Bar graphs display the frequency of occurrence of cases in the categories of nominal and ordinal distributions by constructing "bars" drawn proportional to the number of occurrences. Figures 2.1 and 2.2 display bar graphs for the student gender and ideology distributions. Note that such graphs may be vertical or horizontal. The gender bars are vertical, with categories listed along a horizontal plane and the incidence of each gender indicated by the height of the bars. The ideology bars are

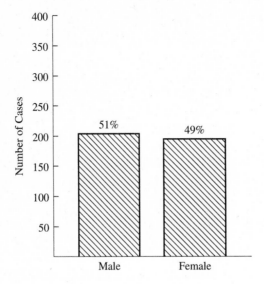

**Figure 2.1**

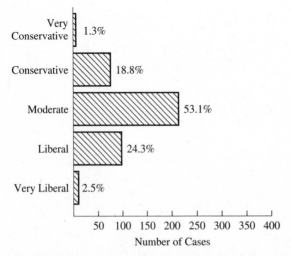

**Figure 2.2**

horizontal, with categories listed along a vertical plane and incidence of each ideology indicated by the length of the bars.

Pie charts are also common. Figure 2.3 displays proposed receipts and outlays in the federal budget submitted to Congress by the Bush administration for fiscal year 1991. Obviously, they are quite easy to read; for example, the outlay chart simply indicates the percentage of dollars going to each area, from a total budget of approximately $1.23 trillion ($1,230 billion).

There are two cautions, however. First, program outlays may be combined in a number of different ways—the chart is constructed from one among many possible operational definitions. Therefore, the five categories simply represent one grouping strategy among a virtually unlimited number of possibilities. And definitions, as we know, involve human choices. For example, the 43 percent figure for "direct benefit payments for individuals" obscures the fact that approximately $433 billion of the $530 billion in this category goes to social security and medicare, to which all retired citizens over the age of 65 are automatically entitled, whether needy or not. Therefore, only about $97 billion of the total budget, or about 8 percent, actually goes to programs designed specifically to benefit the poor. In addition, approximately 75 percent of the total federal budget is devoted to social security, medicare, defense, and interest on the debt. Any attempt to cut spending and balance the budget must take this fact into account.

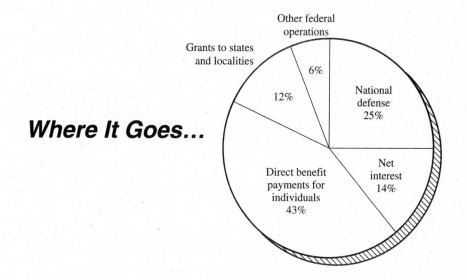

*Where It Goes...*

Receipts, Outlays, Deficit/Surplus Under the President's Proposed Policy
(in billions of dollars)

|  | 1989 | 1990 | 1991 | 1992 | 1993 | 1994 | 1995 |
|---|---|---|---|---|---|---|---|
| Receipts | 990.7 | 1,073.5 | 1,170.2 | 1,246,4 | 1,327.6 | 1,408.6 | 1,486.3 |
| Outlays | 1,142.6 | 1,197.2 | 1,233.3 | 1,271.4 | 1,321.8 | 1,398.0 | 1,476.9 |
| Surplus or Deficit ( + / − ) | − 152.0 | − 123.8 | − 63.1 | − 25.1 | +5.7 | +10.7 | +9.4 |

**Figure 2.3**

*Source*: Budget of The United States Government, Fiscal Year 1991. 101st Congress, 2nd Session. House Document No. 101-102.

Second, pie charts, unlike frequency distributions and bar graphs, are difficult to evaluate from the perspective of "variables and cases." Clearly, the frequency distribution and bar graph for ideology is easily interpreted in this regard: (1) Very Liberal, (2) Liberal, (3) Moderate, (4) Conservative, and (5) Very Conservative are the categories of the variable; students the cases. In the budget pie chart, direct payments, interest, defense, state/local transfers, and other are the categories. However, dollars are the cases! The United States is *not* the case. If we had pie charts for several nations in the world, we could make the categories into variables and the nations cases; for example, we could score each nation on the percentage of its budget devoted to defense.

## MEASURES OF CENTRALITY: MODE, MEDIAN, AND MEAN

Recall that statistics summarize numbers by combining them in ways that aid understanding of politically significant aspects of the social world. Statistics summarizing the pattern of variation in a single variable are termed *univariate descriptive statistics*. Univariate means "one variable." A variety of statistics are useful in managing the complexity of a large body of data by summarizing the pattern of variation of cases across the categories of a single variable; for example, large bodies of data such as attitudes and characteristics of students, crime rates of cities, or budgets of nations. Since statistical summaries often take the form of a single number, they are convenient to work with. Univariate descriptive statistics identifying the central point of a distribution are termed *measures of centrality*, or, more commonly, *averages*. Different measures of centrality are appropriate at different levels of measurement.

### Mode

At the nominal level, compute the *mode*, or the most commonly occurring score in a frequency distribution. It is the category containing the most cases. In the gender example, Male or (1) is the mode because 207, or 51 percent, of the 406 cases are males. This permits the statement that male is the "average" gender in the distribution. Obviously, the mode is a very crude average since the nominal level of measurement is a very simplistic level. In the ideology example, Moderate or (3) is the mode, because 212, or 53.1 percent, of the 399 cases are moderates. Two hundred and twelve is the largest number of cases appearing in any category; 53.1 percent is the largest percentage in any category; (3) is the most frequently occurring score.

Avoid a common error: In the following frequency distribution, contrived for illustrative purposes, Protestant or (1) is the mode; *50 is not the mode.*

|     | Religion   | No. of Respondents | Percent |
|-----|------------|--------------------|---------|
| (1) | Protestant | 100                | 40      |
| (2) | Catholic   | 50                 | 20      |
| (3) | Jewish     | 50                 | 20      |
| (4) | Other      | 30                 | 12      |
| (5) | None       | 20                 | 8       |

The mode is the *category* with the most cases in it. The mode is *not* the number of cases appearing most frequently; it is the score, or characteristic, occurring most frequently.

Note that some distributions display more than one mode. This contrived example is *bi-modal,* with modes of (2) Catholic and (3) Jewish:

|     | Religion   | No. of Respondents | Percent |
| --- | ---------- | ------------------ | ------- |
| (1) | Protestant | 50                 | 17      |
| (2) | Catholic   | 100                | 33      |
| (3) | Jewish     | 100                | 33      |
| (4) | Other      | 25                 | 8       |
| (5) | None       | 25                 | 8       |

One hundred is the largest number of cases appearing in any category; yet, this highest number of cases appears twice. Conceivably, a distribution might have three modes, or even more; but this is unusual.

Finally, avoid another common error: Do not incorrectly conclude this is an interval level distribution because "there are twice as many Jews as Protestants" and "33 percent is twice as much as 17 percent," and so on. Level of measurement is determined by the nature of the *numbers placed on the categories, not the number of cases that fall into the categories.* If nations were the cases, and the United States was 33 percent Catholic, while Poland was 90 percent Catholic, the variable, "level of religion," would be interval. The numerical measure is always a characteristic of the case. A nation can be a "33 percent" on Catholicism, a person cannot. Individuals can only be a Catholic, or some other religion.

# Median

At the ordinal level, compute the *median,* the value of the middle case in a distribution. It is the *category the middle case occupies.* The median is termed a *partition value* because it partitions the cases into two groups, with an equal number of cases in each group. To compute the median, a distribution must be at least ordinal, since "middle" makes no sense unless the distribution reflects an ordered array in which notions of "more and less" and "higher and lower" achieve relevance. The nominal level, with only categories, limits us to mere identification of the most frequently occurring category; at the ordinal level, knowledge of *ordered* categories permits computation of a more sophisticated average.

Consider the following three examples.

|     |        |   |
| --- | ------ | - |
| (1) | Small  | 5 |
| (2) | Medium | 3 |
| (3) | Large  | 5 |

In the first, Medium or (2) is the median. With 13 cases, the seventh occupies the middle (6 above and 6 below). If we count down from the top, we hit the seventh case in the Medium category. With 5 cases in the Small category, the Medium category contains the sixth, seventh, and eighth cases in the array of 13.

|     |        |    |
| --- | ------ | -- |
| (1) | Small  | 3  |
| (2) | Medium | 3  |
| (3) | Large  | 10 |

In the second example, with an even number of cases, no true middle case exists. However, if there were a true middle case, it would fall between the eighth and ninth cases in this array of 16. It would fall into Large or (3); therefore, this category is the median category.

Finally, note an array with an even number of cases where the two middle cases occupy two different categories contains *no true median*:

| | | |
|---|---|---|
| (1) | Small | 8 |
| (2) | Medium | 5 |
| (3) | Large | 3 |

Here, the eighth case in the array of 16 occupies category (1) and the ninth case occupies category (2). If there were a true middle case, it would fall between categories (1) and (2); therefore, there is no median category. Statisticians sometimes split the difference, citing (1.5) as the median—poor practice at the ordinal level, an issue addressed in more detail a bit later.

To compute the median with an *odd* number of cases, first count down to the $(N + 1)/2$ case, where $N$ is the total number of cases, to identify the middle case. In the first contrived distribution, $(13 + 1)/2$ equals the seventh case. Then identify the category in which this case falls—the median.

To compute the median with an *even* number of cases, first identify the two middle cases, at $N/2$ and $(N/2) + 1$. In the second contrived example, $16/2$ equals the eighth case and $(16/2) + 1$ equals the ninth case. If both cases fall into the same category, that is the median category. Employ the *odd* method to identify the median in our student ideology distribution: $(399 + 1)/2 =$ the two hundreth case. Counting down, the two hundreth case falls into the Moderate or (3) category. Note also that the cumulative percentages may be used to identify the median. Simply move down these percentages until hitting the category exceeding 50 percent. Here go from 20 percent in category (2) to 73 percent in category (3)—the median category.

We may compute a mode with both nominal and ordinal distributions, since clearly defined categories provide sufficient information for the computation. We may compute a mode and a median with both ordinal and interval distributions, since ordered categories provide sufficient information for the computation. Indeed, interval level data enjoys the most common application of the median. For example, we frequently see references in government publications, and hear references by government officials, to phenomena such as *median income* and *median age* in various states and locales, or in the nation as a whole. Returning to crime rates, 10,033 is the median since 23 cases fall below 10,033 and 23 cases fall above 10,033. Dropping the first case, creating an array with an even number of cases, renders no true median value since the middle case, if there were one, would then fall between 10,033 and 10,235. Common practice dictates marking the median at 10,134, half the distance between these two scores—a more acceptable strategy at the interval level, where distance achieves relevance, since we can conceive of the possibility that a case might take on the value of 10,134. This was poor practice in the ordinal example of (1) Small, (2) Medium, and (3) Large, with no possibility for a case to take on the value of 1.5, half the distance between 1 and 2—distance makes no sense at the ordinal level.

Some violate this principle in computing medians for interval level data grouped into the ordinal level, such as the crime rate distribution:

| Crime Rate | No. of Cases |
|---|---|
| Under 6,000 | 4 |
| 6,000–7,999 | 11 |
| 8,000–9,999 | 8 |
| 10,000–11,999 | 12 |
| 12,000–13,999 | 9 |
| Over 13,999 | 3 |
| | 47 |

Since the median case is the twenty-fourth case, it lies "at the beginning" of the fourth category (the twenty-third case lies at the end of the third category). This prompts the suggestion that the median is 10,000, since 10,000 marks the beginning of the category and the twenty-fourth case is the "first case" of the category. If the case were "halfway through" the category, the suggestion would be that the median is half the distance between 10,000 and 11,999. This is poor practice, however, since we do not know the precise value of any of the 12 cases in the fourth category. Distance between cases has no meaning. A proper evaluation dictates only that the fourth category, "10,000–11,999" is the *median category*. A caution: It is tempting to conclude that this is an interval distribution, since each category is defined by "an interval of 1,999." Resist the temptation.

The median is not the only partition value. Others include quartiles, deciles, and percentiles. The median is the value of the single case that divides the distribution into two equal parts; quartiles are the values of the three cases that divide the distribution into 4 equal parts; deciles are the values of the 9 cases that divide the distribution into 10 equal parts; percentiles are the values of the 99 cases that divide the distribution into 100 equal parts. Note, with the ungrouped crime rate distribution, the quartiles lie at 7,531, 10,033, and 12,002. These partition the distribution into 4 segments of 11 cases each. Of course, the second quartile lies at the median, as does the fifth decile and the fiftieth percentile. Depending upon the total number of cases, and the divisibility of this total number by the number of segments to be partitioned, the computation of these values can be rather complex. We need not get into these computations. But be certain you understand the general idea behind partition values, and their interpretation.

Standardized test scores are almost always reported as percentiles. Scores for a very large number of cases, usually in the thousands, are partitioned into 100 equal segments. If you lie at the tenth percentile, you scored higher than 10 percent of the cases and lower than 90 percent. If you lie at the sixty-eighth percentile, you scored higher than 68 percent of the cases, and lower than 32 percent. If you lie at the fiftieth percentile, you lie at the median.

## Mean

When we think of averages, we usually think of the *mean*, computed at the interval level by adding together each score and dividing by the total number of cases. If the data is ungrouped, as with crime rates, use the simple formula: $\overline{X} = \Sigma\, X / N$. $X$ denotes the values of the variable; here, crime rate. $N$ denotes number of cases. Therefore, add up all

47 values of crime rate ($\Sigma$ $X$) and divide by 47 ($N$) to get the mean: 465,724 / 47 = 9,909.

In uncommon instances of grouped interval level frequency distributions, such as course grades, employ a slightly altered equation: $\overline{X} = \Sigma [f(X)] / N$, where $f$ denotes frequency of occurrence of each score, or the number of cases appearing in each category. The categories for grades are 0, 1, 2, 3, and 4. In the grade distribution previously displayed, 2 cases appear in category 0, 5 in category 1, 10 in category 2, 8 in category 3, and 6 in category 4; before "summing up," lay out the results of a number of multiplications, $f(X)$, equal to the number of categories:

| X | f | f(X) |
|---|----|-----|
| 0 | 2 | 0 |
| 1 | 5 | 5 |
| 2 | 10 | 20 |
| 3 | 8 | 24 |
| 4 | 6 | 24 |
|   | 31 | 73 |

The summation of $f(X)$ = 73; therefore, $\overline{X}$ = 73 / 31 = 2.35. There are 31 cases, or students. The summation of $f(X)$ provides a shorthand method of adding each of the 31 grades together. Note the unacceptability of such a strategy when an interval level variable is grouped in such a way that the categories become ordinal, such as grouping crime rates into ranges. The categories are defined by no specific single scores by which to multiply. However, multiplication is perfectly legitimate in the grade example, since each individual score lies along an interval scale—0 is 1 point less than 1, 4 is twice as much as 2, and so forth. Indeed, individual students' grade point averages are normally reported as specific values along a scale from 0 to 4, such as 2.35.

This again reminds us that while we have only categories at the nominal level; we have both categories and order at the ordinal level; and categories, order, and distance at the interval level. Compute a mode with categories; compute a median with order; compute a mean with distance. At the interval level, compute modes, medians, and means. At the nominal level, compute only modes; at the ordinal level, only modes and medians. The mean is the most sophisticated average, taking advantage of the most information about a distribution—information about distance between cases, available only at the most sophisticated level of measurement. To test your knowledge, identify the mode and the median in the grade distribution.

The statistical definition of the mean requires knowledge of distance: The mean lies at the point in a distribution around which the cases form a "balanced deviation." The sum of the total distance from the mean of all cases below the mean equals the sum of the total distance from the mean of all cases above the mean. Mathematically, $\Sigma (X - \overline{X})$ = 0. Subtracting the mean from every case below the mean and adding up the result yields a negative number equal to the total distance from the mean of all cases below the mean. Subtracting the mean from every case above the mean and adding up the result yields a positive number equal to the total distance from the mean of all cases above the mean. Since the total distance from the mean of all cases below the mean equals the total distance from the mean of all cases above the mean, these distances together add up to 0.

For a manageable illustration, take only five crime rates:

5,369

7,531

10,033

12,002

15,671

The mean: $50,606 / 5 = 10,121.2$.

The balanced deviation:

| X | $(X - \bar{X})$ |
|---|---|
| 5,369 | -4,752.2 |
| 7,531 | -2,590.2 |
| 10,033 | -88.2 |
| 12,002 | 1,880.8 |
| 15,671 | 5,549.8 |
| | 0 |

The same result occurs in laying out all 47 cases, and subtracting 9,909. Of course, with a grouped interval level frequency distribution, the definition of the balanced deviation becomes $\Sigma [f (X - \bar{X})] = 0$:

| X | f | $\bar{X}$ | $(X - \bar{X})$ | $f(X - \bar{X})$ |
|---|---|---|---|---|
| 0 | 2 | 2.35 | -2.35 | -4.7 |
| 1 | 5 | 2.35 | -1.35 | -6.75 |
| 2 | 10 | 2.35 | -.35 | -3.5 |
| 3 | 8 | 2.35 | .65 | 5.2 |
| 4 | 6 | 2.35 | 1.65 | 9.9 |

The last column does not add exactly to 0, because of rounding error. The mean is closer to 2.355 than 2.35. But such error is tolerable.

## MEASURES OF DISPERSION: MEAN DEVIATION, STANDARD DEVIATION, AND z SCORES

While measures of centrality identify central points, measures of dispersion indicate the manner in which cases vary around central points. At the nominal and ordinal level, frequency distributions and bar graphs crudely indicate dispersion. In the student gender distribution, although male is the "average" or "central point," not all cases take on the average value—nearly half (49 percent) take on the nonmodal value of female. There exists considerable dispersion. In the student ideology distribution, although Moderate is both the mode and the median, not all of the cases are Moderate—again, nearly half (about 47 percent) take on other values, indicating considerable dispersion. Visually inspecting frequency distributions and bar graphs gives a quick, general indication of dispersion at the nominal and ordinal levels.

At the interval level, however, measures of dispersion take on much greater significance since the average *distance* of all cases from a central point may be specified precisely. The *mean deviation* and *standard deviation* illustrate this. The standard deviation is most common because, as we shall see, it possesses important statistical properties. Yet, these properties are more easily understandable with knowledge of the mean deviation.

## Mean Deviation

The mean deviation is simply the average distance from the mean of all the cases in a distribution—both distances above and distances below the mean. For ungrouped interval data: $\Sigma|X - \bar{X}| / N$. The symbol | | denotes *absolute value,* meaning simply that, for each case, we subtract the mean from the value of the case and drop the sign if the value is negative. Therefore, negative distances (those below the mean) take on positive values, as do distances above the mean. For the simplified ungrouped crime rate example:

| $X$ | $\bar{X}$ | $\lvert X - \bar{X} \rvert$ |
|---|---|---|
| 5,369 | 10,121.2 | 4,752.2 |
| 7,531 | 10,121.2 | 2,590.2 |
| 10,033 | 10,121.2 | 88.2 |
| 12,002 | 10,121.2 | 1,880.8 |
| 15,671 | 10,121.2 | 5,549.8 |
| | | 14,861.2 |

The mean deviation is 14,861.2 / 5 = 2,972.2. The "average case" in this distribution is 2,972.2 units from the mean.

Again, the formula is a bit different for grouped interval data: $\Sigma \left[ f \lvert X - \bar{X} \rvert \right] / N$.

| $X$ | $f$ | $\bar{X}$ | $\lvert X - \bar{X} \rvert$ | $f \lvert X - \bar{X} \rvert$ |
|---|---|---|---|---|
| 0 | 2 | 2.35 | 2.35 | 4.7 |
| 1 | 5 | 2.35 | 1.35 | 6.75 |
| 2 | 10 | 2.35 | .35 | 3.5 |
| 3 | 8 | 2.35 | .65 | 5.2 |
| 4 | 6 | 2.35 | 1.65 | 9.9 |
| | | | | 30.05 |

The mean deviation is 30.05 / 31 = .97. The average case is .97 units from the mean.

Mean deviations report *original units,* meaning the units initially employed to measure the variable. Crime rate was measured in crimes per 100,000 people; therefore, the average case is 2,972.2 "crimes per 100,000 people" away from the mean number of crimes per 100,000. Grades were measured in grade points. Therefore, the average case is .97 grade points away from the mean grade point.

The mean deviation indicates whether the cases are relatively close to the mean or relatively far away from the mean. It indicates whether the cases are, on the whole, similar to one another or, on the whole, different from one another. If all cases have the same value, the mean deviation is 0. The further from 0 the mean deviation, the less similar the cases are to one another. These principles become clearer with discussion of the standard deviation.

## Standard Deviation

Like the mean deviation, the standard deviation measures the average distance from the mean of all the cases in an interval level distribution. However, rather than employing the absolute value of the difference between $X$ and $\bar{X}$, the standard deviation relies on the squared distance between $X$ and $\bar{X}$. It is the square root of the sum of the squared deviations from the mean. Note: Squaring transforms all distances to positive values, whether above or below the mean, since multiplying a negative number by a negative number yields a positive number.

$$\sigma = \sqrt{\frac{\Sigma\left[(X - \bar{X})^2\right]}{N}}$$

| $X$ | $\bar{X}$ | $X - \bar{X}$ | $(X - \bar{X})^2$ |
|---|---|---|---|
| 5,369 | 10,121.2 | − 4,752.2 | 22,583,404 |
| 7,531 | 10,121.2 | − 2,590.2 | 6,709,136 |
| 10,033 | 10,121.2 | −    88.2 | 7,779 |
| 12,002 | 10,121.2 | 1,880.8 | 3,537,408 |
| 15,671 | 10,121.2 | 5,549.8 | 30,800,280 |
| | | | 63,638,007 |

Take the square root of 63,638,007 / 5, or 12,727,601, which is 3,567.
For grouped interval level data:

$$\sigma = \sqrt{\frac{\Sigma\left[f(X - \bar{X})^2\right]}{N}}$$

| $x$ | $f$ | $\bar{X}$ | $X - \bar{X}$ | $(X - \bar{X})^2$ | $f(X - \bar{X})^2$ |
|---|---|---|---|---|---|
| 0 | 2 | 2.35 | −2.35 | 5.53 | 11.06 |
| 1 | 5 | 2.35 | −1.35 | 1.82 | 9.1 |
| 2 | 10 | 2.35 | −  .35 | .12 | 1.2 |
| 3 | 8 | 2.35 | .65 | .42 | 3.36 |
| 4 | 6 | 2.35 | 1.65 | 2.72 | 16.32 |
| | | | | | 41.04 |

Take the square root of 41.04 / 31, or 1.32, which is 1.15.

In the equation for the standard deviation, the sum of the squared distance between each case and the mean, $\Sigma (X - \bar{X})^2$, is termed sum of squares or total variation. The total variation divided by the number of cases, $\Sigma (X - \bar{X})^2 / N$, is termed variance.

The standard deviation is the square root of the variance. Like the mean deviation, the standard deviation is relatively large if the cases are widely dispersed about the mean. If all cases take on the same value, the standard deviation is 0.

As a rule of thumb, a standard deviation greater than a mean indicates considerable spread. The *coefficient of variation* evaluates the proportionality between a mean and a standard deviation; it is simply the standard deviation divided by the mean. If the coefficient of variation is 0, there is no variation. If the coefficient is 1, the standard deviation is as large as the mean, indicating a good deal of variation. In our crime rate example, the coefficient of variation is 3,567 / 10,121.2, or .35, indicating moderate variation in the distribution. In our grade example, the coefficient of variation is 1.15 / 2.35, or .49, indicating similarly moderate variation.

Recall that univariate descriptive statistics summarize many numbers by combining them into single numbers. As such, they render large bodies of data more manageable. Obviously, it would be rather tedious to scrutinize 50 different crime rates for the 50 largest cities in each state in an attempt to determine the general rate of crime in the states. Yet, with two statistics, the mean and standard deviation, we have two summary pieces of information that alert us to the general nature of the data. Similarly, in our class grade distribution, the average grade is a bit better than C, and variation around this grade is moderate; grades vary around the mean less than a full letter grade. If all the grades were As and Fs, the value of the standard deviation would approach the value of the mean.

## z Scores

The standard deviation is an extremely important statistic, upon which many higher-order statistics are based. A familiarity with the link between the standard deviation and "standard scores" is essential to understanding such statistics. The *z score* indicates the distance of a particular case from the mean in standard deviation units: $(X - \bar{X}) / \sigma$. If a case falls above the mean, its $z$ score takes on a positive value; if below, a negative value. In our simple crime rate example, the $z$ score for the case with a value of 12,002 is 1,880.8 / 3,567. This case lies .53 standard deviation units above the mean. In our grade example, those five students with Ds each have a $z$ score of $-1.35 / 1.15$. They lie 1.17 standard deviation units below the mean.

If all cases in a distribution are transformed into $z$ scores, we have a new variable, also called *standard scores*, based on a new unit of measurement, standard deviation units. The grade scores may be transformed out of grade points into $z$ scores:

| X | f | $\bar{X}$ | $X - \bar{X}$ | $\sigma$ | z |
|---|---|---|---|---|---|
| 0 | 2 | 2.35 | −2.35 | 1.15 | −2.04 |
| 1 | 5 | 2.35 | −1.35 | 1.15 | −1.17 |
| 2 | 10 | 2.35 | − .35 | 1.15 | − .3 |
| 3 | 8 | 2.35 | .65 | 1.15 | .56 |
| 4 | 6 | 2.35 | 1.65 | 1.15 | 1.43 |

Note that this transformation does not change the position of the cases *relative to one another* in the distribution. For example, using grade points, 0 is 2 units from 2 and 2 is

2 units from 4—the same relative distance. Similarly, using $z$ scores, $-2.04$ is 1.74 units from $-0.3$ and $-0.3$ is 1.73 (rounding error) units from 1.43—the scores for the Fs, Cs, and As are still the same relative distance from one another. We are measuring exactly the same thing, just with different units of measurement—all we have done is divide through by a constant, the standard deviation.

Take the analogy of kilometers and miles. A mile is 1.609 kilometers; therefore, to convert kilometers to miles, divide through by 1.609. One hundred kilometers is 62.15 miles. Obviously, two points that are 62.15 miles apart are also 100 kilometers apart; the actual distance between them does not change just because we use a different unit of measurement! While the initial measurement is in "original units," $z$ scores are termed *standard units*. The C grade is 2 original units (grade points) below A. It is 1.74 standard units (standard deviations) below A. And note, because standard scores retain their sign, that the $z$ scores of a distribution will always add up to 0, by virtue of the balanced deviation. Just as the sum of $(X - \overline{X})$ is always 0, so too is the sum of $(X - \overline{X}) / \sigma$. You may demonstrate this in the grade distribution, but be sure you multiply each $z$ score by $f$ first, and tolerate rounding error.

Note finally that, while the mean and standard deviation are characteristics of an entire distribution, $z$ scores are characteristics of single cases. In the grade array, $\overline{X}$ and $\sigma$ take on the same value all the way down the column, whereas the $z$ scores take on unique values.

The use of $z$ scores permits comparison of the relative positions of a single case in two distributions that employ different original units of measurement. For example, suppose we have measured education in years and income in dollars for a sample of several hundred individuals in the population. Suppose one individual is three years above the mean on education and \$15,000 above the mean on income. For which variable is the individual closer to the mean? This is indeterminate because years and dollars are not comparable units of measurement. Yet, if the individual has a $z$ score of 2.1 on education and 1.5 on income, we have the answer. She is only 1.5 standard units from the mean on income, but 2.1 standard units from the mean on education.

As another example, suppose you scored 1,050 on the Scholastic Aptitude Test, required for entrance to most colleges and universities. Suppose you decided to go to law school upon graduation, took the Law Scholastic Aptitude Test and scored 30. Did you do better on the LSAT than the SAT? This is indeterminate, since the SAT is based on a possible total of 1,600 points, and the LSAT on 48 points. However, if your $z$ score was 1 on the SAT and 0 on the LSAT, you scored at the mean LSAT for all individuals having taken it when you did, and scored 1 standard unit above the mean on the SAT for all individuals; you could "compare" your test results to each other.

Normally, standardized test scores are reported as percentiles. In any large group of cases scored on an interval level variable, approximately 68 percent of the cases fall within 1 standard deviation of the mean and approximately 95 percent of the cases fall within 2 standard deviations of the mean. Obviously, a $z$ score of 0 lies at the mean, or at the fiftieth percentile. Therefore, approximately 68 percent of the cases fall between the case with a $z$ score of $-1$ and the case with a $z$ score of 1; approximately 95 percent between $-2$ and 2. Therefore, a case with a $z$ score of $-1$ lies at about the sixteenth percentile, and a case with a $z$ score of 1 lies at about the eighty-fourth percentile. Similarly, a case with a $z$ score of $-2$ lies at about the second or third percentile, and a case with a

$z$ score of 2 lies at about the ninety-seventh or ninety-eighth percentile. This is depicted graphically as:

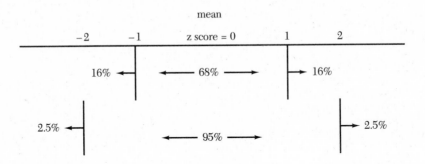

Obviously, if you score 1 standard deviation above the mean on a standardized test, you have done quite well; at 2 above the mean, you have done outstandingly in comparison with the others who took the test at the same time.

Remember: The mean and standard deviations are relative measures, used to locate positions in a distribution relative to the distribution as a whole. Your position in a standardized test distribution is dependent on the position of everyone else. Obviously, in the unlikely instance that everyone taking the LSAT on the same day you did received the same score, everyone would have a $z$ score of 0 and lie at the fiftieth percentile!

Interval level data arrays are very simply summarized referring to the mean and standard deviations. A statistician can tell a great deal about the nature of a distribution using only these two pieces of summary information. Moreover, knowing the $z$ score of any particular case permits us to envisage quickly the position of that case in a distribution.

## INTRODUCTION TO THE NORMAL CURVE

The 68 percent and 95 percent rules discussed previously hold when an array of interval level data is "normally distributed." Data that are normally distributed form bell curves, such as those depicted in Figure 2.4. The value of the variable is arrayed along the horizontal axis, while the proportion of cases taking on a particular range of these values is listed along the vertical axis. The curve tracks the proportions and the bell curve is formed in situations where the highest proportion of cases clusters in the middle of the distribution, around the mean, and the lowest proportion of cases is found on the "tails" of the distribution—near the lowest score in the distribution and near the highest score in the distribution. Clearly, such a situation is consistent with the 68 percent and 95 percent rules—very few cases lie beyond 2 standard deviations from the mean. The majority of cases are within 1 standard deviation of the mean.

Almost any large group of cases scored on an interval level variable results in a normal distribution. For example, the following data array, upon which Figure 2.4 is based,

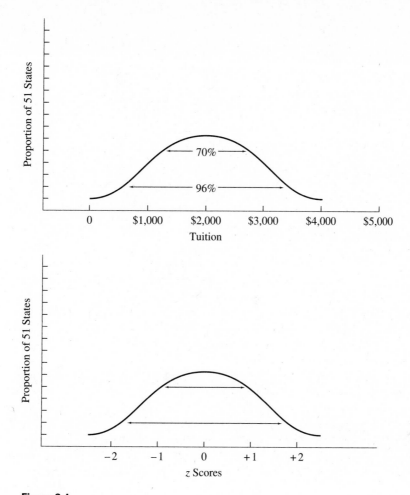

**Figure 2.4**

shows the average tuition and fees at public four-year institutions of higher education in the 50 states and Washington, D.C., during 1990 and 1991[2]:

| | | | |
|---|---|---|---|
| $664 | $1,444 | $1,823 | $2,313 |
| $986 | $1,478 | $1,854 | $2,317 |
| $1,112 | $1,518 | $1,880 | $2,465 |
| $1,148 | $1,524 | $1,906 | $2,580 |
| $1,189 | $1,543 | $1,919 | $2,622 |
| $1,220 | $1,553 | $1,927 | $2,635 |

| $1,279 | $1,569 | $1,930 | $2,691 |
| $1,290 | $1,587 | $1,951 | $2,860 |
| $1,337 | $1,592 | $2,067 | $2,910 |
| $1,340 | $1,593 | $2,216 | $3,110 |
| $1,382 | $1,680 | $2,263 | $3,401 |
| $1,409 | $1,733 | $2,287 | $4,092 |
| $1,418 | $1,791 | $2,311 |  |

Computation of the mean of this distribution yields approximately $1,888, and computation of the standard deviation yields approximately $656. Therefore, those cases lying within 1 standard deviation of the mean take on values between $1,232 and $2,544. There are 36 such cases—about 70 percent of the distribution. Those cases lying within 2 standard deviations of the mean take on values between $576 and $3,200. There are 49 such cases—about 96 percent of the distribution. But note that, although the distribution is generally normal, it is a little "skewed" toward the high end. No cases fell below 2 standard deviations, while two cases fell above 2 standard deviations. These two cases are very large in relationship to the mean—the largest is $2,204 above the mean (compared to the smallest case, which is only $1,224 below the mean). This pulled the mean toward the high end, skewing the distribution a bit.

Nonetheless, the normality of the distribution is reflected in the fact that the cases tend to cluster around the mean. Moreover, those cases on the tails of the distribution are further away from one another than those cases near the mean. The two cases closest to the mean are, respectively, $8 and $18 from the mean; the bottom two cases are $322 from one another; the top two cases are $691 from one another.

This brings us to the statistical definition of the normal curve—in an interval level distribution that is perfectly normal, the mean, median, and mode take on the same value. The peak of the distribution contains the most cases (mode), there is an equal number of cases on either side of the peak (median), and each side slopes downward in conformity with the principle of the balanced deviation (mean). While not perfectly normal, our distribution conforms quite well to these criteria. There is no mode in the distribution, since no two cases have exactly the same value. The median is 1,791, which is 97 below the mean. Again, this is because the distribution is skewed upward a bit, as a result of the extreme scores on the upper tail. Inspect Figure 2.4 carefully, and be certain you understand why the distributions conform generally to this statistical definition of a normal curve.

The distribution is not perfectly normal because we only have 51 cases. The more cases, the more normal the distribution. In those instances where we have thousands of cases scored on an interval level variable, or even hundreds of cases, perfect normality will be closely approached. Almost exactly 68 percent of the cases will fall within ±1 standard deviation of the mean and almost exactly 95 percent of the cases will fall within ±2 standard deviations of the mean. The mean and the median will be almost exactly the same. You may wish to take the array of 47 crime rates listed earlier in this chapter, compute the mean, compute the standard deviation, and determine, as we did with the tuition and fees data, whether the array is normally distributed.

# APPLICATION OF UNIVARIATE DESCRIPTIVE STATISTICS

In most states in the United States, the largest proportion of public money used to finance elementary and secondary public schools comes from local school districts and is collected through local property taxes. Therefore, affluent suburban districts frequently enjoy much higher per-pupil expenditures than poorer urban or rural districts. As a result, the executive and legislative branches in some states, New Jersey among them, are currently under state court order to equalize spending among districts. And, on January 10, 1991, suit was filed against the state Department of Education and the governor of Pennsylvania by 128 school districts, challenging the state constitutionality of unequal expenditures. Of course, in order to equalize expenditures, information must be gathered on the extent of the disparity and policy decisions must be made regarding the appropriate standards of equalization.

On June 5, 1990, the New Jersey Supreme Court ruled unanimously that the state must ensure that the poorest districts spend as much as the richest districts, and ordered the state legislature to provide the money to raise levels of spending in poorer districts to levels permitting "thorough and efficient" education.[3] It ordered that funding be equalized across districts by 1995. It argued that, although the districts in New Jersey taken together spend at one of the highest levels in the nation, there is considerable variation from district to district in per-pupil expenditures. In other words, although mean expenditures are high, there is also considerable deviation about this mean. The court cited 1984–1985 per-pupil expenditures, noting that richer districts, on average, spent 40 percent more than poorer districts—the mean per-pupil expenditures for several of the richest was $4,029 and for several of the poorest, $2,861. The court also noted that the disparity was not as pronounced in the middle, an indication that many students are "packed in around the mean." This suggests the probability of a small standard deviation in per-pupil expenditures in New Jersey, although there exist students in districts that are "extreme outliers" in the distribution, both on the rich and poor ends.

Literally within hours of the New Jersey Supreme Court decision, Governor James Florio, who had been working on equalization formulas in anticipation of the court decision, was meeting with legislators to negotiate the content of an appropriate formula that would distribute state money among districts in such a way that equalization could be achieved. One legislative negotiator noted that "if the right statistics were used," the state could allocate more money to rich and poor districts alike. In other words, it is possible to develop formulas that would not only equalize spending, but also be politically attractive to all school districts, by giving them all more state money.

The result was passage of the Quality Education Act, which attempts to achieve equalization by channeling large chunks of state money into poorer districts and capping spending in richer districts. The legislation is highly controversial and has been amended several times over the past two years. As of July 1992, the quantitative evidence suggested that no progress was being made toward equalization; in fact, the gap between the poorest and richest districts had increased. The 30 poorest districts in the state were back in court, this time challenging the Quality Education Act.

Not surprisingly, the New Jersey Supreme Court left the legislature considerable latitude in quantitatively defining equalization. It did not specify exactly what "spending as much as richer districts" meant in statistical practice, and left room for latitude by indicating that its decision could be complied with if enough money were available in all districts for "thorough and efficient" education. If richer districts on average only spend 20 percent more, would that be acceptable? Or would it have to be 10 percent? Or 5 percent? These are political judgments and political judgments are always controversial.

In the Pennsylvania suit, the 128 districts also addressed gaps in district spending and the necessity for equalization formulas. They argued that, in 1974–1975, the school district at the ninetieth percentile spent $1,074 per pupil, or 47 percent more than the district at the tenth percentile, spending $732. In 1988–1989, the differential increased to 66 percent—the ninetieth percentile district spending $4,174 and the tenth percentile district spending $2,520.

Formulas developed by legislatures to alleviate such inequities are extremely complex and there are virtually an unlimited number of ways to structure them, depending on the political preferences of the policymakers. The quote from the New Jersey legislator reflects this reality. Again, data are always presented and analyzed on the basis of definitions, and definitions involve human choices. In the public policy process, these choices are political.

But most important for our purposes, in structuring these formulas, the policymakers must understand univariate descriptive statistics. They must understand exactly what a per-pupil spending ratio is, grasping the nature of the cases under scrutiny. New Jersey policymakers are working with pupils as the cases. In other words, if per-pupil expenditures in district A are $1,500 and district A contains 5,000 students, then $1,500 will be entered into the calculation of statewide per-pupil expenditures 5,000 times. Those who filed the suit in Pennsylvania, on the other hand, cited the 501 districts as the cases—the analysis was based on a list of 501 per-pupil expenditures. Percentile rankings were offered for districts, rather than pupils.

Of course, conclusions reached about spending disparity may differ, depending on whether districts or pupils are the cases. The extent of difference depends on the size of districts. If poorer and richer districts have very large numbers of students, while districts spending in middle ranges have very few students, analysis with districts as cases produces less disparity than analysis with pupils as cases. If poorer and richer districts have very few students, while districts spending in middle ranges have very large numbers of students, analysis with districts as cases produces more disparity than analysis with pupils as cases. Only with such understanding is it possible for policymakers to grasp the significance of measures of centrality and measures of dispersion to arrive at definitions of equality and inequality of expenditures on the education of our citizens.

Important for our purposes also is that the school funding controversy exists, in part, as a result of considerable quantitative evidence that school finance systems are inequitable. Appendix A reprints an article by Cynthia A. Cronk and Gary P. Johnson, titled "An Equity Analysis of Pennsylvania's Basic Instruction Subsidy Program, 1977–80," which appeared in the Spring 1983 issue of the *Journal of Education Finance*.

Cronk and Johnson endeavor to determine whether or not per-pupil expenditures devoted to instruction in Pennsylvania are equally distributed and whether the distribution changed over the three-year period under consideration.

The portion of the article most instructive for our purposes is the univariate analysis of the variable AIE (actual instructional expense), the average "dollars per pupil" each district in the state spends. The 504 districts are the cases in the analysis; an individual average dollar amount is recorded for each district. To determine the extent of equality in district spending the authors compute six measures of dispersion. In other words, they compute six measures that indicate how "spread out" the average expenditures are—how much inequality there is among the districts. We focus on three of these measures.

The range is simply the difference between the highest-spending district and the lowest-spending district. The range increased from 1,133 to 1,541 over the three-year period, indicating increasing inequality. The restricted range is the difference between the expenditures of the district at ninety-fifth percentile (spending more than 95 percent of the districts) and the expenditures of the district at the fifth percentile (spending more than only 5 percent of the districts). The restricted range is often preferred since it is less influenced by "extreme scores." The restricted range increased from 537 to 719 over the three-year period, indicating increasing inequality.

They report the coefficient of variation as a percentage. It increased from .1676 to .1762, which they report as 16.76 and 17.62. When reported as a percentage, the coefficient of variation indicates the percentage of the mean that the standard deviation constitutes. Recall that, in most distributions containing a large number of cases, about 68 percent of these cases will fall within ±1 standard deviation of the mean. Since the coefficient of variation tells us what percentage of the mean the standard is (here about 17 percent), if we increase the mean by 17 percent and decrease the mean by 17 percent, about two-thirds of the districts will fall in that expenditure range.

This discussion of the Pennsylvania school finance system is also interesting for the lessons it offers about the manner in which governments transfer money to one another. The federal government frequently transfers funds through what are known as block grants or formula grants. Similarly, the state governments use formula grants to transfer money to local governments, including school districts. Pennsylvania enters variables such as proportion of low-income children, local tax effort, and population density into their equations. Similarly, a federal jobs-training block grant program might enter variables such as unemployment, median income, population density, and the like. Obviously, legislative and executive officials at all levels of government must have some facility with basic statistical methods in order to discharge their responsibilities in these areas.

# SUMMARY

Statistics combine and summarize numbers. Political scientists and political practitioners frequently employ simple combinations, such as percents, rates, and ratios, to measure politically significant phenomenon. Budget analysts might concentrate on percent of total expenditures devoted to selected policy areas; researchers in the criminal justice area might deal with measures for rates of crime per 100,000 people; foreign affairs experts studying economic development might consider per capita gross national product—that is, ratio of population to total dollar value of goods and services produced in a nation.

Univariate descriptive statistics summarize large bodies of data assembled on the basis of carefully constructed operational definitions. These summaries include measures of centrality, or averages, and measures of dispersion, indicating variation around averages. Different measures of centrality and different measures of dispersion are appropriate at different levels of measurement.

The mode, as an average, identifies the category with the most cases in it. We need only categories to compute the mode. The mode is simply qualitative, or categoric; at the nominal level, we have categories, but no more. Therefore, the mode is the only appropriate measure of centrality at the nominal level.

The median is an average appropriate to the ordinal level. It is the value of the case which has an equal number of cases below that value and above that value. We need both categories and order (or knowledge of "more" and "less") to compute the median. At the ordinal level, both modes and medians may be computed.

The mean is appropriate at the interval level. It is computed by adding the values of cases together and dividing by the number of cases. We need categories, order, and a specific unit of measurement to compute the mean. Without a specific unit of measurement, we cannot perform the arithmetic functions on the values of the cases, such as addition and division, necessary to compute the mean. At the interval level, modes, medians, and means may be computed. Recall that levels of measurement are hierarchical—a statistic computed with categories may also be computed with ordered categories and with ordered categories for which distances may be identified; a statistic computed with ordered categories may also be computed with ordered categories for which distances may be identified.

At the nominal and ordinal level, measures of dispersion normally take the form of visual displays, such as frequency distributions, graphs, and/or charts. These simply display the categories of a distribution and indicate the number of cases falling into each category. As such, they give a general notion of the proportion of cases that do not take on the average values represented by the mode and/or median. At the interval level, with a unit of measurement permitting statements about distances between categories and between the cases in those categories, more sophisticated measures of dispersion, taking advantage of this information, are possible. The mean deviation is the average distance of all cases from the mean (both above the mean and below the mean) in original units. For an income variable, the mean deviation is expressed in dollars; for a crime rate variable, in crimes per 100,000 population; for a variable showing a distribution of percent spent by states on education, in percentage points.

The standard deviation is the square root of the average squared distance from the mean (both above and below) of cases in a distribution. It is a much more common measure of dispersion than the mean deviation and it has important statistical properties employed widely in interval level analysis. The $z$ scores are characteristics of cases in interval level distributions: the distance of a case from the mean in original units divided by the standard deviation. Therefore, a $z$ score is the distance of a case from the mean in standard units; it takes on a positive value if the case is above the mean and a negative value if the case is below the mean. And $z$ scores indicate the relative distance of cases from the mean in different distributions.

These scores, also referred to as standard scores, assist us in understanding the behavior of normal distributions. Any large number of cases scored on an interval level variable will form a bell curve when the proportion of cases along the distribution is graphed, with most of the cases clustered near the mean and increasingly spread out further away from the mean. Approximately 68 percent of the cases fall within 1 standard deviation of the mean (between the standard scores of 1 and −1), while approximately 95 percent of the cases fall within 2 standard deviations of the mean (between standard scores of 2 and −2).

Political scientists and political practitioners widely employ univariate descriptive statistics to describe the social and political conditions of people, cities, states, and nations. Many other sorts of cases may be described as well, such as universities, bureaucracies, interest groups. The list goes on.

A political candidate running for mayor of a large city certainly finds it useful to ascertain the characteristics of the citizens, using public opinion surveys, census data, or some combination of the two. What is the modal party identification? What is the median income? A political scientist studying global economic inequality certainly finds it useful to determine the distribution of wealth. What is the mean per capita GNP for the approximately 175 nations of the world? What is the dispersion about that mean? Is the standard deviation close to 0, indicating relative equality among nations? Or is the standard deviation much larger than the mean, indicating severe inequality? And, as we have seen, the policymakers responsible for reducing the disparity in per-pupil spending in the school districts of their states must first discover the precise extent of that disparity. Carefully constructed operational definitions and carefully chosen univariate descriptive statistics are essential for precision.

# NOTES

1. Bureau of the Census, United States Department of Commerce, *City and County Data Book,* 10th ed., 1983, Washington, D.C. The rates are based on serious crimes known to police for 1981. Data are incomplete for three states; therefore, the distribution contains only 47 cases. Bridgeport, Connecticut, had the highest rate: 15,671; Sioux Falls, South Dakota, the lowest: 5,369.
2. "The Nation," *Chronicle of Higher Education Almanac,* August 26, 1992, p. 7
3. The information contained in this paragraph, and the next several paragraphs, is taken from: "New Jersey Ruling to Lift School Aid for Poor Districts," *New York Times,* June 6, 1990: A1, B4; "Trenton Seeks to Tailor Florio School Plan to Court Order," *New York Times,* June 7, 1990: B1; "Education Cutbacks Arouse Barrage of Complaints," *New York Times,* September 6, 1992: XIII: 1, 15; "Pa. Enters the School Funding Fray," *The Philadelphia Inquirer,* January 13, 1991: 3-G.

*Chapter*

# 3

# The Comparative Method and Political Science

$S$tatistical analysis entails more than just precision of definition, efficiency of communication, and quantitative descriptions of politically significant phenomena. It is linked intimately to *science*, which carries many meanings. For the social sciences in general and political science in particular, the term "science" is most productively defined as a research *method*, or working procedure, employed to answer questions about politically significant aspects of the social world. Statistics are among the most important tools of this method. Indeed, statistics courses in the social sciences are frequently referred to as *methods* courses.

## SCIENTIFIC METHOD

The scientific method is empirical, logical, comparative, probabilistic, and tentative, and seeks to generalize. *Empirical* methods answer the question: What really exists? This entails not only precise descriptions, but also *causal explanations*. Indeed, a primary reason for precise, quantitative descriptions is the assistance these offer in building causal explanations.

For example, classifying individuals on the basis of their socioeconomic status yields interesting descriptive insights into the character of the population. Yet, the description itself is not the only reason for the classification. Rather, socioeconomic status may be an important explanatory factor in determining the likelihood that an individual will vote and in determining for which candidate they are most likely to vote in a given election. Similarly, the level of economic development of nations of the world is frequently measured on the assumption that other variables play a role in determining levels of development. An additional assumption is that high development is "good" and low development "bad."

Social scientists frequently distinguish empirical questions from *normative* questions. The former ask what really exists, or what "is." The latter, what should exist, or what "ought to be." Empirical statements offer facts; normative statements offer opinions. A researcher might assemble empirical evidence supporting the proposition that people of lower socioeconomic status are less likely to vote than people of higher socioeconomic status. He may also draw the normative conclusion that it is just as well that people of lower socioeconomic status vote less frequently, since they are unlikely to possess the requisite skills needed for informed electoral judgments. Similarly, a researcher may assemble empirical evidence indicating that half the population of the world is undernourished, using a carefully constructed operational definition of undernourishment. She may go on to advance the normative proposition that this is not good. She may even then go on to pursue additional empirical research designed to determine the causes of widespread undernourishment, so that solutions might be found.

The scientific method permits the test of ideas about what actually exists, and why. It is a very rigorous method, allowing confrontation of hunches and suspicions with evidence and facts from the real world. Although a very powerful method, science has limitations. Chief among these is that it cannot answer normative questions. Science guides a determination of what does and does not exist; it offers no counsel on what is good and bad.

The scientific method is not only rigorous, but also *logical* and *comparative.* Science compares. In testing ideas against reality, the method adheres to rules of comparison and to common sense. Normally, the ideas are posed as hypotheses. An *hypothesis* seeks to explain the factual existence of one variable by reference to the factual existence of another variable. It poses $Y$ as a function of $X$. $Y$ is the *dependent variable,* or object of causation. $X$ is the *independent variable,* or agent of causation. We hypothesize that $X$ causes $Y$. Four examples follow.

1. Whites are more likely to vote than blacks. Race is the independent variable. Likelihood of voting is the dependent variable. People are the cases.
2. States with higher median incomes spend a larger proportion of their budgets on education than states with lower median incomes. Median income is the independent variable. Proportion of budget devoted to education is the dependent variable. States are the cases.
3. Corporations that receive federal government contracts enjoy higher profit margins than corporations that do not receive such contracts. Receipt of government contracts is the independent variable. Profit margin is the dependent variable. Corporations are the cases.

**4.** Nations with unequal income distributions are less likely to be democracies than nations with more equal income distributions. Income distribution is the independent variable. Democracy is the dependent variable. Nations are the cases.

Each of these hypotheses may be tested logically by comparing cases. Compare the proportion of whites who vote to the proportion of blacks who vote. Divide states into those with high median incomes and those with low median incomes; determine the average proportion of budget spent on education among those with high median incomes to the average proportion among those with low median incomes. In the third hypothesis, compare corporations to corporations; in the fourth, nations to nations.

Science is also *probabilistic and tentative.* No hypothesis is completely and unconditionally true. At best, hypotheses *tend toward confirmation.* To suggest all whites vote and all blacks do not is empirically untenable. It may well be, however, that whites are *more likely* to vote than blacks—if white, then probably vote; if black, then a lower probability of voting. The logic applies with equal force to any set of cases under empirical investigation—states, corporations, nations, or whatever.

Indeed, some hypotheses turn out to be completely untrue. During World War II, with quantitative social science in its infancy, a group of scholars headed by Samuel Stouffer cooperated with the U.S. Army in applying statistical tools to aid the war effort. They conducted research on, among other things, the causes and consequences of morale in the military services. In one study, Stouffer hypothesized that soldiers (cases) in the Army Air Corps view the promotion process as more fair (dependent variable) than soldiers in the Army Military Police. His hypothesis was reasonable, since promotion rates in the Air Corps were far higher than in the Military Police. Yet, he discovered precisely the opposite of what he hypothesized: Soldiers in the Military Police viewed the promotion process more favorably than soldiers in the Air Corps!

As a result, he reevaluated the reasoning leading to the initial hypothesis. Out of these efforts, and the efforts of others doing similar research about the same time, *reference group theory* emerged: Individuals evaluate their success not on the basis of any objective standard, but rather on the basis of their condition in reference to their immediate environment. Air Corpsmen, although more likely as individuals to enjoy promotions, were in an environment where they routinely viewed others receiving promotions. Therefore, their standard of success was much higher. Military police, on other hand, were not in an environment where promotions were taking place. Therefore, they did not feel unfairly treated as individuals.[1]

Of course, all scientific knowledge is tentative and subject to revision on the basis of continuing empirical research. For example, until the age of Copernicus and Kepler in the sixteenth and seventeenth centuries, everyone "knew" that the sun revolved around the earth. Subsequently, everyone "knew" the earth revolved around the sun. Yet, in the twentieth century, counseled by Einstein's theory of relativity, we are not now even sure of this. Perhaps they sort of revolve around each other, depending on the relative position of observer and observed.

Therefore, hypotheses are never judged true. Rather, they are presented only as *testable and falsifiable*—stated in such a way that they may be tested against empirical facts and are capable in principle of being proven false. Repeated tests against reality and repeated failures to falsify an hypothesis build confidence in the acceptability of the hypothesis, but never permit unequivocal statements of truth. Scientists never argue truth; they only argue that existing empirical knowledge does not contradict currently accepted hypothetical relationships between variables.

The four hypotheses listed earlier in this chapter are all testable and falsifiable. Gathering data on the proportion of whites who vote and the proportion of blacks who vote permits a test of the first; gathering data on median income and education expenditures in the states permits a test of the second. When tested, these hypotheses can in principle be falsified; we may find that whites and blacks do not differ in their voting behavior or that states do not differ in their education expenditures.

Finally, science *seeks to generalize.* The method deals in general categories rather than specific instances. For example, a social scientist interested in studying the impact of gender on attitudes toward social welfare expenditures would no doubt choose to divide her cases into male and female to determine, in general, whether females in the aggregate are more or less likely to support increases in such government expenditures than males in the aggregate. She would not be interested in a detailed examination of how any single individual male or female felt, and why. While a clinical psychologist might intensively study a single individual's attitude formation, a social scientist seeks patterns in large aggregates of cases.

Indeed, there are two major routes to the accumulation of knowledge. On the one hand, it may be accumulated by detailed examination of all causes producing a particular effect. The clinical psychologist, in attempting to treat an individual patient, adheres closely to this strategy, attempting to identify all the causal mechanisms contributing to the state of the individual psyche. On the other hand, knowledge may be accumulated by comparing the frequency of occurrence of selected characteristics to determine if they are statistically related. The social scientist in our example compares a large group of cases to determine if being a female is statistically related to support for social welfare expenditures.

Moreover, these differing approaches, the *particularlistic* and the *generalized,* are among the primary features distinguishing the discipline of history from the social sciences. Asking an historian for the causes of revolution likely elicits a response specific to particular revolutions. He might distinguish the French Revolution from the Russian Revolution, and the Russian Revolution from the American Revolution, arguing that a full understanding of the causes of each requires intensive and detailed examination of a virtually unlimited number of specific and time-bound factors. Asking a social scientist for the causes of revolution likely elicits a general response, in the form of statistically testable hypotheses. She might identify selected economic, social, and religious factors; measure each; then classify a large number of cases on these variables to compare nations that have undergone revolutions to nations that have not. The particularlistic approach usually considers the interaction of a very large number of variables for one case; the generalized approach considers the interaction of a few variables for a very large number of cases.

# COMPONENTS OF A "GOOD" HYPOTHESIS

In political science, hypotheses are (1) politically interesting, (2) plausible, (3) positive and nontautological, (4) addressed to a single set of cases, and (5) addressed to more than one case. Many disciplines in and out of the social sciences work with hypotheses. For example, we might hypothesize that lower-income people likely prefer Crest toothpaste and higher-income people likely prefer Colgate. This is a legitimate hypothesis, containing an independent variable (income), a dependent variable (toothpaste preference), and a set of cases (consumers). Indeed, such hypotheses are common in market research and corporations spend a good deal of money testing them. The point: This is not a politically interesting hypothesis; therefore, it is irrelevant to political science. Indeed, social scientists and political analysts sometimes refer sarcastically to market research as the "toothpaste polls," in spite of the fact, of course, that market research addresses a very broad range of consumer behavior— not just toothpaste preferences!

We could hypothesize that rural, agricultural states in the United States are more likely to have state universities with top 20 NCAA football teams than are urban, industrial states. This is a legitimate hypothesis, containing an independent variable (rural or urban), a dependent variable (top 20 or not), and a set of cases (states)— indeed, the hypothesis may very well tend toward confirmation. Yet, again, this hypothesis is of no interest to a political scientist; therefore, it is not a "good" political science hypothesis. Note that it may, however be a "good" hypothesis for someone studying the sociology of sport.

Second, hypotheses must be plausible. For example, the suggestion that blacks are more likely than whites to vote for Democratic candidates makes a good deal of sense; the suggestion that people with brown hair are more likely to vote for Democratic candidates than people with blonde hair makes no sense. The former hypothesis is plausible because it can be supported by reasonable theories about how people behave. Historically, Democrats enjoy the popular perception that they are the "party of the little guy," while Republicans have long been associated in the public mind with the wealthy and with business interests. Similarly, Democrats are viewed as "big spenders" of tax dollars—tax dollars spent, in part, to initiate and maintain social welfare programs. Blacks, for a variety of complex reasons, not the least of which is a legacy of slavery and racial discrimination, are, as a group, less economically well off than whites and more in need of government assistance. In brief, we are able to draw on historical insight and *theoretical reasoning* about the relationship between economic conditions and political behavior. Obviously, no such insight or reasoning finds relevance in the hair-color hypothesis.

Similarly, we may plausibly suggest that states with higher median incomes are likely to spend a higher proportion of their budgets on education; it is implausible that states with a higher number of trees per capita spend a higher proportion of their budgets on education. In the former instance, theoretical insight again plays a role. Citizens of higher income usually are also of higher education. These citizens likely place high value on good schools for their children. In a democracy, those things the citizens value presumably translate into public policy on occasion. No such plausible reasoning may be developed in the "tree" hypothesis.

Third, hypotheses must be "positive" and "nontautological." By positive, we mean simply that, as a matter of technical style, they must be stated as propositions rather than asked as questions. "Are blacks more likely to vote Democratic?" is a question. "Blacks are more likely to vote Democratic" is an hypothesis. We posit a relationship between variables and then test the relationship against empirical reality.

A tautology is a statement that is true by definition; it suffers from circular reasoning. "Rich people have more money than poor people" is a tautology because the amount of money people have is part of the definition of being rich. The explanation for having money is circular: People have more money because they are rich and they are rich because they have more money and they have more money because. . . . "Belligerent nations are more likely to go to war than peaceful nations" is a tautology because going to war must be part of the definition of belligerence. To explain war-making by reference to belligerence is to engage in circular reasoning. Rather, we need to identify those variables that lead nations into belligerent warring behavior.

These examples are obvious tautologies. However, we must guard constantly against slipping into more subtle forms of tautological reasoning. A 1982 book-length study illustrates. Edward Handler and John Mulkern, in the second chapter of *Business in Politics: Campaign Strategies of Corporate Political Action Committees* (Lexington Books), develop a "typology of corporate PACs" that differentiates the "pragmatic" from the "ideological" on the basis of several quantitative indicators. Chief among these indicators is the proportion of corporate PAC money contributed to incumbents in Congress as opposed to challengers (contributing to incumbents is deemed pragmatic and to challengers, ideological) and the proportion of corporate PAC money contributed to Republicans in Congress as opposed to Democrats (contributions to Republicans is deemed ideological and to Democrats, pragmatic). PACs with incumbency contributions below 59 percent and Republican contributions above 63 percent are defined as ideological and the rest as pragmatic—these are the mean values of each percent measure for all corporate PACs.

At the end of Chapter 2 of their book, after some additional statistical analysis, Handler and Mulkern emphasize the conclusion that "examination of contribution strategy reveals no pattern to which PACs uniformly adhere. Instead, two mainstreams of PAC giving are discernable" They continue:

> Some observers of the PAC phenomenon have speculated that the momentum of corporate-PAC growth presents a new kind of threat of corporate dominance of the political process. The evidence of a lack of single-mindedness in corporate PAC-giving, however, points to the existence of at least one limitation on the potential for such dominance.

What's the problem here? Handler and Mulkern *choose to define* two basic categories of PAC giving by dividing their quantitative indicators at the mean value for all PACs, ensuring that some PACs are *defined* as ideological and some as pragmatic. They then conclude that there are two kinds of PAC giving, and argue lack of evidence for singlemindedness. But there is no evidence one way or the other; they have fallen into the tautological trap. They use their data to create two categories and then say "Hey, look, we found two categories." Their "conclusion" is true by definition. Even very careful and well-respected analysts must guard constantly against the tautological trap.

Of course, hypotheses must be positive and nontautological in order to satisfy the testability and falsifiability requirements. Hypotheses posited as statements can be tested against reality to determine if they hold up. Moreover, tautologies are not capable of being proven false since a statement that is true by definition cannot be contradicted by empirical evidence. Therefore, such a statement cannot be tested scientifically.

Fourth, the independent and dependent variables contained in an hypothesis must classify the same set of cases. For example, testing the hypothesis that corporations with government contracts enjoy higher profit margins than corporations without such contracts requires that a single set of corporations be classified on both variables. If 500 corporations are grouped on the basis of whether or not they have contracts, these same 500 corporations must be grouped on the basis of their profit margins. Otherwise, the hypothesis cannot be tested by comparing the profit margins of contract corporations to those of noncontract corporations. Such a comparison is not possible if, for example, 500 corporations were classified on the basis of their profit margins and 500 *other, different* corporations were classified on the basis of whether or not they had contracts.

Fifth, hypotheses must encompass more than one case and the cases must fall into more than one category on the independent variable. The hypothesis that the rise of Hitler in Germany altered the course of world history cannot be tested comparatively and scientifically because it encompasses only one case. Obviously, we cannot compare several worlds where Hitler rose to several worlds where he did not rise to determine which worlds possessed altered courses of history! This is *not* to say that the hypothesis cannot be tested—it can, and has, using a particularistic approach. It is only to say that it cannot be tested comparatively and scientifically.

Hypothesize that college students are more likely to be conservative in their political outlook than noncollege students from the general population. To test the hypothesis, ask the students in your quantitative research methods class whether they consider themselves liberal, conservative, or something else. If 90 percent consider themselves conservative, is the hypothesis confirmed? No! This hypothesis cannot be tested by inquiring only of the students in your class, because this produces a situation in which all the cases fall into one category of the independent variable. To test the hypothesis, both students and nonstudents are necessary. Only then can you *compare* student responses to nonstudent responses. Even in the unlikely situation that 90 percent of the students considered themselves conservative, you might empirically observe that 95 percent of the nonstudents considered themselves conservative, and conclude the hypothesis was not confirmed!

Finally, always bear in mind that a variable may be independent in some hypotheses and dependent in others. In political science research, individual characteristics such as race, income, and education are almost always independent variables. Yet, research in sociology or economics may, in some hypotheses, treat income levels and education levels as dependent variables. Indeed, even race, which obviously can never be a dependent variable in social research, is a dependent variable for biologists doing research in genetics.

Moreover, some variables may be treated both as dependent and independent within the discipline of political science. Hypothesize, for example, that whether a state is predominantly agricultural or predominantly industrial determines the party composition of its legislative branch, and whether the legislative branch is dominated by Republicans or Democrats determines the proportion of the state budget allocated to social welfare programs. Here we have two hypotheses. In the first, party composition is the dependent variable; in the second, it is the independent variable. Economic base causes party composition, which in turn causes expenditure patterns.

As a second example, hypothesize that income level determines a person's likelihood of identifying with the Democratic party and party identification determines likelihood of voting for the Democratic candidate in a presidential election. Party identification depends on income; voting depends on party identification. We call these patterns *causal chains*. Any given variable is likely caused by other variables and likely the cause of still others.

## SUMMARY

The scientific method employs precise descriptions to arrive at general explanations. Take the most famous equation of the twentieth century: $E = mc^2$. If mass is transformed to energy, the amount of energy equals the mass multiplied by the speed of light squared. Each of these variables may be measured very precisely to demonstrate that the general relationship contained in the equation holds under specified conditions. Mass may be precisely measured with a variety of techniques, most based on a proportionality between weight and volume. Energy may also be precisely measured in a variety of ways, some based on temperature release, and others on acceleration. The speed of light squared is a constant designed to achieve standardization between the measures of mass and energy. It is a very large constant, indicating that very small quantities of mass may be transformed into very large quantities of energy. To the best of our knowledge, an atom smashed anywhere in the universe results in a release of energy directly proportional to the atom's mass.

Obviously, social science is neither physics nor chemistry. Political scientists are never in a position, for example, to state unequivocally anything like $P = ie^2$: Participation in politics equals income multiplied by education squared! There are at least two reasons for this. First, given the ever-present problems of validity and reliability for social and political indicators discussed in Chapter 1, precise, continuously stable, and universally accepted definitions of participation, income, and education are likely impossible.

Second, the social sciences, in comparison to the natural sciences, are *very* probabilistic and tentative. While some uncertainty will always exist on the universality of equations in natural science, such as Einstein's, the relationships they express hold much more completely and consistently than relationships between race and voting, wealth distribution and democracy, and so forth. Human behavior is simply less predictable than the behavior of chemicals, molecules, and atoms. Humans exercise free will, and often alter behavior in response to unidentified factors. Even if we found that $P = ie^2$, people would get upset at their predictability and defy us by changing their behavior! Quite simply, *there are too many independent variables in the study of human behavior; it is extremely difficult, if not impossible, to identify and measure all these variables.*

This is not to say that the scientific method cannot be productively employed to shed light on human behavior. Although the method here suffers more constraints than in the natural sciences, its application to politics and society nonetheless yields interesting insights. In the following chapters, we see just how useful the method can be in helping to answer a wide range of research questions in political science.

# NOTE

1. Earl Babbie, *The Practice of Social Research*, 5th ed., Belmont, CA: Wadsworth, 1989, pp. 416–420.

# Chapter
# 4

# Descriptive Statistics for Relationships Between Variables

$S$tatistics that combine numbers from two different variables in order to summarize the degree to which the variables do or do not "vary together" are termed *bivariate descriptive statistics*. (Bivariate means "two variables.") These statistics describe the mutual pattern of variation in two variables; therefore, they are used to perform quantitative tests of politically interesting hypotheses. As with univariate descriptions, different statistical procedures are appropriate for bivariate descriptions, depending upon the level of measurement of the two variables. Very simple statistical procedures are employed if both variables are nominal, more sophisticated procedures if both are ordinal, and the most sophisticated if both are interval.

## THE NOMINAL LEVEL: CONTINGENCY TABLES AND PERCENTAGING

Hypothesize that economically underdeveloped nations are more preoccupied with maintaining a strong military than they are with other policy objectives, such as health, education, and social welfare. The hypothesis is plausible. Economically underdeveloped nations likely experience more internal unrest since their citizens are likely displeased with economic disadvantages; therefore, political elites may use a strong military as one strategy to ensure internal order. Moreover, political elites in nations with serious internal problems may seek to divert attention from these problems by emphasizing the existence of external threats to "rally" their citizens. Finally, nations in an economic "squeeze" sometimes attempt to conquer less powerful neighbors in a bid to expand their resource base.[1]

In August 1990, Iraq invaded Kuwait in an attempt to expand Iraqi control over Middle Eastern oil reserves. Although in dire economic straits, Iraq, with one of the largest standing armies in the world, devotes considerable resources to its military. Kuwait, a small oil-rich neighbor, is much more economically developed, but not as militarily powerful: Iraq took Kuwait in less than 12 hours. Our hypothesis that economically underdeveloped nations are more preoccupied with maintaining a strong military than they are with other policy objectives is a politically interesting and plausible one; economic development is the independent variable, preoccupation with a strong military is the dependent variable, and nations are the cases.

Use per capita gross domestic product (GDP) as an indicator of economic development and proportion of budget devoted to military expenditures as an indicator of military preoccupation. Further, create two simple dichotomous variables. Nations with per capita GDPs of $5,000 or below are (1) Underdeveloped, and those with per capita GDPs of over $5,000 are (2) Developed. Nations devoting 10 percent or less of their yearly budgets to the military are (1) Low Military Commitment, and those devoting over 10 percent are (2) High Military Commitment.

Gross domestic product is the total value of all goods and services produced within the geographic boundaries of a nation, differing from gross national product in its inclusion of foreign investment in the host nation's product, rather than in the product of the investing nation. Therefore, using per capita GDP as an indicator of economic development may pose a slight validity problem. Countries in which there is heavy foreign investment have gross domestic products exceeding their gross national products. Therefore, using this indicator, scores for poorer nations serving as hosts for heavy foreign investment are inflated somewhat.

Categorizing nations on the basis of a reliable source, *The Statistical Abstract of the United Nations*, permits us to determine if these two variables "vary together." Be reminded, however, that no operational definition is ever perfectly reliable. First, the economic and budgetary data collected by the United Nations are frequently estimated on the basis of previous years and/or on the basis of information volunteered by the governments of the nations. Second, although the yearbook was published in 1988, not all data were available for a single year. The per capita GDP data were taken for either 1985 or 1986. While most of the budgetary data were taken for 1983 or 1984, some go back as far as 1980. For these reasons, any single score for either variable will be somewhat unstable, a common situation in research of this nature. The problem is mitigated by collapsing the scores into two broad categories for each variable.

A *contingency table* or *cross-tabulation* combines two frequency distributions of nominal data, as shown in Table 4.1. The table "cross-tabulates" the two variables for the purpose of determining if the dependent variable is "contingent" on the independent variable. It contains data on 64 cases, chosen to be generally representative of the

|                  | Underdeveloped | Developed |       |
|------------------|----------------|-----------|-------|
| Low Expenditure  | 20<br>45.5%    | 14<br>70% | 34<br>53.1% |
| High Expenditure | 24<br>54.5%    | 6<br>30%  | 30<br>46.9% |
|                  | 44<br>68.8%    | 20<br>31.2% | 64  |

Table 4.1

nations of the world, but also, of necessity, chosen on the basis of availability of data. Nineteen of the cases are European nations and non-European English-speaking nations, 12 are Asian and Near Eastern, 13 are African, 13 are Latin American, and 7 are Middle Eastern. Thirty-four, or 53 percent of the cases, score Low on military expenditures, while 30, or 47 percent, score High. Forty-four, or 69 percent of the cases, are Underdeveloped, while 20, or 31 percent, are Developed.

In constructing a contingency table to determine if the two variables are statistically related, follow four rules. First, *list the independent variable across the top of the table*, and divide the cases into the categories of the independent variable. In Table 4.1, level of economic development is listed across the top of the table; 44 cases are Underdeveloped and 20 cases are Developed.

Second, *list the dependent variable down the side of the table and fill in each of the cells of the table* by recording the number of cases in each of the categories of the dependent variable that fall into each of the categories of the independent variable. In Table 4.1, 34 cases score Low on military expenditures, 20 are Underdeveloped, and 14 are Developed. Thirty cases score High on military expenditures, 24 are Underdeveloped and 6 are Developed. This strategy permits "description of level of military expenditures in terms of level of development" and "comparison of the incidence of Low and High levels of expenditures within the categories of High and Low levels of development." It permits us to determine if levels of expenditures are contingent upon levels of development.

Third, to assess contingency, *compute percentages down the column* and enter these percentages into the cells of the table. Twenty is 45.5 percent of 44 and 24 is 54.5 percent of 44; therefore, 45.5 percent of the Underdeveloped nations have Low Military Expenditures and 54.5 percent have High Military Expenditures. Fourteen is 70 percent of 20 and six is 30 percent of 20; therefore, 70 percent of the Developed nations have Low Military Expenditures and 30 percent have High Military Expenditures.

Fourth, *compare the percentages across the rows*. Compare 45.5 percent to 70 percent. Compare 54.5 percent to 30 percent. Forty-five percent of the Underdeveloped nations have Low Military Expenditures, while 70 percent of the Developed nations have Low Military Expenditures. Fifty-five percent of the Underdeveloped nations have High Military Expenditures, while 30 percent of the Developed nations have High Military Expenditures. These differences carry the message of the table: Underdeveloped and Developed nations differ in their expenditure patterns. The independent variable has an impact on the dependent variable. Underdeveloped nations are more likely to spend high. Developed nations are more likely to spend low.

Don't forget—list the independent variable across the top, compute the percentages down the columns, then compare the percentages across the rows.

## A Second Example

As a second example, hypothesize that students majoring in a business-related discipline, such as marketing or accounting, are more likely to consider themselves to be Republicans, while students majoring in a humanities discipline, such as history or philosophy, are more likely to consider themselves Democrats. The hypothesis is plausible. Students interested in a career in business are likely to be more sympathetic to the political party identified in the public mind (although not always accurately) with deregulation and reduced taxation. Students interested in the humanities are likely less concerned with "making money," and perhaps more concerned with the "people issues" identified in the public mind (although, again, not always accurately) with the Democratic party. The cases are students, the independent variable is major, and the dependent variable is party identification.

Table 4.2 is constructed, on the basis of the four rules, from the student survey described in Chapter 2. Across the top, disciplines are listed: Business, Natural Science, Social Science, Humanities. Down the side, party identification is listed: Democrat, Republican, Other. This example demonstrates two related points that are important to bear in mind. First, contingency tables may be of any size, depending on the number of categories contained in the variables. While the previous example was of a "2 × 2" table, this table is "3 × 4." Second, not all nominal variables are simple dichotomies. Here, discipline of major is nominal, but has four categories. Party is also nominal, but has three categories.

As a result, the column percentages in this example are compared across three rows. Those majoring in the Humanities are, in fact, more likely to consider themselves Democrats than are Business majors, by a margin of 47.8 percent to 33.6 percent. Natural Science comes in at 32.9 percent, and Social Science at 43.8 percent. And those

| | Business | Natural Science | Social Science | Humanities | |
|---|---|---|---|---|---|
| **Democrat** | 42<br>33.6% | 46<br>32.9% | 49<br>43.8% | 11<br>47.8% | 148<br>37% |
| **Republican** | 59<br>47.2% | 60<br>42.9% | 32<br>28.6% | 5<br>21.7% | 156<br>39% |
| **Other** | 24<br>19.2% | 34<br>24.3% | 31<br>27.7% | 7<br>30.4% | 96<br>24% |
| | 125<br>31.3% | 140<br>35% | 112<br>28% | 23<br>5.8% | 400 |

Table 4.2

majoring in Business are more likely to be Republicans than those majoring in the Humanities, by a margin of 47.2 percent to 21.7 percent. Natural Science comes in at 42.9 percent and Social Science at 28.6 percent. Finally, those in the Humanities are more likely to consider themselves "Other" than those in Business, by a margin of 30.4 percent to 19.2 percent. The independent variable has an impact on the dependent variable, and the hypothesis is confirmed.

## The Lambda Statistic

In employing bivariate statistics to determine if variables vary together, *prediction* takes on central importance. If the value of the dependent variable can be predicted from knowledge of the value of the independent variable, the variables are statistically related.

In Table 4.1, assume knowledge only of the frequency distribution for level of military expenditure and guess whether a particular nation, chosen at random, is (1) Low or (2) High. Guess Low. *Over the long run,* or over repeated guesses for randomly selected nations, we will guess correctly 53.1 percent of the time. Now assume knowledge of whether the randomly selected nation is (1) Underdeveloped or (2) Developed, and assume knowledge that 54.5 percent of the Underdeveloped nations are High on expenditures, while 70 percent of the Developed nations are Low on expenditures. If Underdeveloped, guess High. If Developed, guess Low. Over the long run, we now enjoy a 54.5 percent success rate in 68.8 percent of the cases (underdeveloped) and a 70 percent success rate in 31.2 percent of the cases (developed). This produces a success rate of 59.3 percent [(.688 × 54.5) + (.312 × 70)]. The rate of success in predicting the value of the dependent variable increases from 53.1 percent to 59.3 percent—it increases by 11.7 percent. About 6 percentage points, but 11.7 percent. Remember? The variables are statistically related. If the variables were not statistically related, about 53 percent of both Underdeveloped and Developed nations would score Low on military expenditures, the proportion for all 64 cases. Knowledge of the independent variable would confer no advantage in guessing the value of the dependent variable.

In the second example, the best guess of the value of the dependent variable, in the absence of knowledge of the value of the independent variable, is Republican, producing a success rate of 39 percent over the long run. With knowledge of the value of the independent variable, the best guess is Republican for Business and Natural Science, but Democrat for Social Science and Humanities. The success rate rises to 44.8 percent [(.313 × 47.2) + .35 × 42.9) + (.28 × 43.8) + (.058 × 47.8)]. This is a 14.9 percent increase; the variables are statistically related. If the variables were not statistically related, the column percentages within each row would be very similar to one another—about 37 percent across the Democratic row, 39 percent across the Republican row, and 24 percent across the Other row. Ability to guess the party identification of cases, even with knowledge of major, would not rise above 39 percent.

If the success rate rises to 100 percent, the relationship between the two variables is perfect. In the first example, this would mean all of the Underdeveloped countries had High expenditures, and all the Developed countries had Low expenditures. In the second example, it would mean all Business and Natural Science majors were Republicans and all Social Science and Humanities majors were Democrats. In each instance, the value of the dependent variable could always be predicted perfectly from knowledge of the value of the independent variable—a perfect statistical relationship.

The preferred method of statistically evaluating predictive success is to determine the proportion by which errors in prediction are reduced rather than, as previously, determining the proportion by which correct predictions are increased. This method is termed PRE, *proportional reduction in error.*[2] In the first example, the rate of prediction error using only the frequency distribution for the dependent variable is 46.9 percent. The rate of error using the independent variable is $[(.688 \times 45.5 \text{ percent}) + (.312 \times 30 \text{ percent})] = 40.7$ percent. Obviously, this is the inverse of predictive success, which was, respectively, 53.1 percent and 59.3 percent. Here, error is reduced by 6.2 percentage points, just as success increased by 6.2 percentage points. PRE is expressed as:

$$\frac{E1 - E2}{E1}$$

where $E1$ is the amount of error produced by guessing the value of the dependent variable from knowledge only of the frequency distribution of the dependent variable, and $E2$ is the amount of error produced by guessing the value of the dependent variable from knowledge of the value of the independent variable. The difference between $E1$ and $E2$ divided by the original amount of error $(E1)$ produces the proportional reduction in error. Here, $(46.9 - 40.7) / 46.9 = 6.2 / 46.9 = .133$. Reduction in error is 13.3 percent. Note this differs from the increase in predictive success given previously, because it reports 6.2 as a proportion of 46.9 rather than as a proportion of 53.1. Note also that if the variables are not related, $E1$ will equal $E2$ and PRE will equal 0; alternatively, if $E2 = 0$ because all error has been eliminated, PRE will equal 1 for a reduction in error of 100 percent.

Most statistical analysts prefer to employ a shortcut in computing PRE that produces the same result and is termed *lambda:* Compute the sum of the largest frequencies in each column of the table. Subtract from that the largest frequency in the frequency distribution of the dependent variable. Divide the result by the difference between the total number of cases in the table and the largest frequency in the frequency distribution of the dependent variable. Here:

$$\frac{(24 + 14) - 34}{64 - 34}$$

$$= \frac{38 - 34}{30}$$

$$= .133$$

Note that we are still dividing original error (30 incorrect guesses) into the difference between original error and error produced by using the independent variable. Here, using the independent variable gives us 4 more correct guesses than just using the dependent (38 instead of 34). Note also that if the number of correct guesses is the same under both rules the variables are not statistically related and lambda is 0. If use of the independent variable eliminated all errors, all 64 of the cases would be predicted correctly, the numerator in this example would be 30, and lambda would be 1.

In the second example (Table 4.2) lambda is:

$$\frac{(59 + 60 + 49 + 11) - 156}{400 - 156}$$

$$= \frac{179 - 156}{244}$$

$$= .09$$

Error is reduced by 9 percent.

The central importance of prediction necessitates listing the independent variable across the top, computing the column percentages, and comparing these percentages across the rows. If these rules are violated, trouble may follow. For example, in Table 4.3, seek to determine if Jewish people are more likely to consider themselves to be Democrats than are members of the general population. Assume 540 Democrats and 420 Republicans; among them, 60 Jews and 900 other people. Note that, unlike the genuine data in Tables 4.1 and 4.2, these data are contrived to illustrate a point.

In Table 4.3(a), party identification, the dependent variable, is incorrectly listed across the top. The column percentages show that 7 percent of the Democrats are Jews and 5 percent of the Republicans are Jews. As these two percentages are quite similar to one another, we might conclude that whether or not a person is Jewish has no impact on party identification. Wrong!

(a)

|  | Democrat | Republican |  |
|---|---|---|---|
| Jewish | 40<br>7.4% | 20<br>4.8% | 60<br>6.3% |
| Not Jewish | 500<br>92.6% | 400<br>95.2% | 900<br>93.7% |
|  | 540<br>56.3% | 420<br>43.7% | 960 |

(b)

|  | Jewish | Not Jewish |  |
|---|---|---|---|
| Democrat | 40<br>66.6% | 500<br>55.5% | 540<br>56.3% |
| Republican | 20<br>33.3% | 400<br>44.5% | 420<br>43.7% |
|  | 60<br>6.3% | 900<br>93.7% | 960 |

Table 4.3

Ethnic background must be the independent variable. We are not interested in whether or not Democrats are more or less likely to be Jews. We are interested in whether or not Jews are more or less likely to be Democrats. Similarly, in Table 4.1, we were interested in whether or not Underdeveloped nations spent more or less on defense. In Table 4.2, we were interested in whether or not Business majors were more or less likely to be Republicans. Of course, the reason that the 7 percent is so similar to the 5 percent in Table 4.3(a) is that Jews make up such a small proportion of the population that they will make up a small percentage of Democrats and of Republicans. Table 4.3(b), correctly constructed, demonstrates that 66.6 percent of Jews are Democrats, while 55.5 percent of the other people are Democrats.

## Contingency Tables and the Comparative Method

Clearly, the logic of contingency table analysis is embedded in the logic of the scientific method, as described in Chapter 3. A properly constructed table indicates whether or not there is a statistical relationship between an independent and dependent variable, at the nominal level. If the column percentages differ substantially when compared across the rows, such a relationship exists; if they do not differ substantially, such a relationship does not exist. The existence of a statistical relationship is a necessary condition for the argument that the independent variable causes the dependent variable. If level of economic development is causing patterns of defense expenditure, nations at different levels of development will display different patterns of expenditure. If student major plays some causal role in determining party identification, students in different majors will display different identification patterns.

Contingency table analysis is fundamentally comparative—it is based on a comparison of the cases in different categories of the independent variable. In Table 4.1, about half of the Underdeveloped countries spend Low and about half spend High. One might conclude, therefore, that underdevelopment plays no role in expenditure pattern. One would be wrong to conclude that, however. Comparisons must be made. Only in comparing Underdeveloped nations to Developed nations can a proper conclusion be drawn. While about half of Underdeveloped nations spend Low, 70 percent of Developed nations do.

Contingency tables display patterns that are probabilisitic and tentative. Table 4.2 does not demonstrate that all Business majors are Republicans and that all Humanities majors are Democrats. It only demonstrates that there is a tendency for Business majors to be Republicans and Humanities majors to be Democrats. Business majors are more likely to be Republicans than are Humanities majors. If a Business major, then more likely a Republican; if a Humanities major, then more likely a Democrat.

Finally, contingency tables permit generalizations to certain classes of phenomena; they do not permit predicting with certainty the behavior of any single case. Indeed, in the first example, the United States had the highest per capita gross domestic product, at approximately $16,300, and one of the seven highest levels of defense expenditures, at approximately 25 percent. Similarly, Sri Lanka was extremely low on both variables—a per capita GDP of only about $360 and defense expenditures of only about 2 percent. There are always individual exceptions to statistical generalizations, since these generalizations apply only to the behavior of the cases in the aggregate.

To demonstrate this point in another way, consider the second example, in which there are 400 cases. The removal of any single case from the table would not alter the aggregate pattern of relationship at all. Indeed, the removal of several dozen cases probably would not alter the pattern. A single case will not influence a statistical relationship; these relationships are always the product of general tendencies among a large number of cases.

## Application of Contingency Tables and Percentaging

The *Star-Ledger*/Eagleton Poll is a periodic survey of public opinion in the state of New Jersey sponsored jointly by the *Newark Star-Ledger* newspaper and the Eagleton Institute of Politics at Rutgers University. Appendix B contains a press release distributed by the Poll on November 1, 1992, in the days immediately preceding the presidential election. This press release illustrates the practical application of contingency table analysis, since the Background Memo, beginning with the description of the manner in which the sample was drawn, contains eight pages of cross-tabulations.

The body of the press release states that, among likely voters,* Clinton leads with 42 percent, Bush has 30 percent, Perot 18 percent, and 9 percent are undecided. It also states Clinton has stronger partisan support than Bush—87 percent of the Democrats intend to vote for Clinton and 67 percent of the Republicans intend to vote for Bush. Focus on the statistical evidence for these conclusions (page 186).

First, note that the contingency tables violate our rule requiring the listing of the independent variable across the top. Rather, the dependent variable, vote choice, is listed across the top and the independent variables (party, age, race, gender, etc.) are listed down the side. This is done for ease of presentation: There is only one dependent variable and several independent variables. Note also that the percentages add to 100 percent across the rows (excepting rounding error) rather than down the columns. If the independent variable is listed across the top, the percentages must be computed down the columns; but if the dependent variable is listed across the top, they must be computed across the rows. These percentages indicate proportion of voters within the various categories of the independent variables that intend to vote for Clinton, Bush, and Perot—the information required.

The lesson: It is not unusual to encounter carefully constructed contingency tables that do not follow "our rules." The key: Carefully study any table encountered to determine the direction in which the percentages are adding to 100 and use that information to confirm which of the variables is independent and which dependent. And transform,

---

*Those conducting survey research use a variety of techniques to identify the "likely voters" in their sample. Normally, the term is confined to those in the sample who are registered to vote, who say they intend to vote, and who express a high degree of interest in the electoral contest.

|  | Republican | Independent | Democrat |  |
|---|---|---|---|---|
| Clinton | 21<br>10% | 116<br>35% | 199<br>87% | 336<br>43% |
| Bush | 143<br>67% | 83<br>25% | 9<br>4% | 235<br>30% |
| Perot | 30<br>14% | 96<br>29% | 9<br>4% | 135<br>18% |
| Undecided | 21<br>10% | 34<br>10% | 12<br>5% | 67<br>9% |
|  | 215<br>28% | 329<br>42% | 229<br>30% | 773 |

Table 4.4

on the basis of our rules, a carefully constructed table into our format. Table 4.4 does so for the relationship between party identification and vote intention in the press release. This transformation is possible with knowledge of the number of cases falling into each category of the independent variable and knowledge of the percentage of those cases choosing each of the alternatives on the dependent variable. Note, however, that the transformation does not precisely replicate the proportions of the entire sample of 801 choosing each candidate, since only 773 of these reported their party identification.

Finally, consider the implications of this sort of statistical analysis for allocation of campaign resources by political candidates. Virtually all candidates for national and statewide offices now conduct opinion surveys as a routine part of their campaign strategy. Note, for example, that 9 percent of the New Jersey electorate sampled was undecided at the end of October. This percentage rises to 12 percent among females and to 13 percent among independent females. Such differences can often be substantial, and are frequently employed by candidates to determine which subgroups of the electorate to "target" in their campaigning.

Finally, note that the press release (pages 182–183) and the Background Memo (pages 187–188) examine when respondents made up their minds for whom to vote and the extent to which respondents are certain in their choice; such questions are employed to determine if support for a candidate is "firm" or "soft." Clearly, this variety of information can be extremely useful in conducting a political campaign.

## THE ORDINAL LEVEL: GAMMA, A RANK-ORDER STATISTIC

In Table 4.5, imagine an independent variable ordered 1, 2, and 3, from Low to High and a dependent variable ordered 1, 2, and 3 from Low to High. Both examples are contrived to illustrate the difference between a statistical relationship that is ordered (Table 4.5[a]) and a statistical relationship that is not ordered (Table 4.5[b]). In the former in-

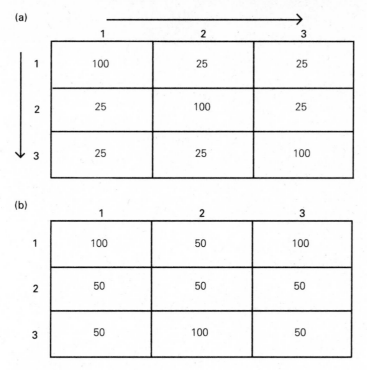

(a)

|  | 1 | 2 | 3 |
|---|---|---|---|
| 1 | 100 | 25 | 25 |
| 2 | 25 | 100 | 25 |
| 3 | 25 | 25 | 100 |

(b)

|  | 1 | 2 | 3 |
|---|---|---|---|
| 1 | 100 | 50 | 100 |
| 2 | 50 | 50 | 50 |
| 3 | 50 | 100 | 50 |

Table 4.5

stance, the cases tend to *concentrate along the diagonal* from the upper left to the lower right. The 1s on the independent variable tend to 1s on the dependent variable; 2s on the independent variable tend to 2s on the dependent variable; 3s, 3s. In the latter instance, although there is a relationship, it is not ordered. Here, 1s on the independent variable tend to 1s on the dependent variable, but 2s on the independent variable tend to 3s on the dependent variable, and 3s tend to 1s. The vectors accompanying Table 4.5(a) help us to envisage the nature of an ordinal relationship—movement from 1 through 2 to 3 on the independent variable tends to movement from 1 through 2 to 3 on the dependent variable.

Evaluating *pairs of cases*, determine the degree to which a *statistical relationship is ordered.* Mr. *P* is a case scoring 1 on the independent variable and 1 on the dependent variable; he is located in the cell in the extreme upper left-hand corner of the table. Ms. *Q* is a case scoring 3 on the independent variable. Under what conditions will this constitute a *same-ordered pair*? If Ms. *Q* scores either 2 or 3 on the dependent variable, this pair (*P* and *Q*) orders the same way on both the independent and dependent variables:

      either      *P*(1,1)      or      *P* (1,1)

              *Q* (3,2)             *Q*(3,3)

*Q* is higher than *P* on the independent variable and *Q* is higher than *P* on the dependent variable. *Q* and *P* are ordered the same way on each of the two variables.

There are four other kinds of pairs. Those that are different-ordered:

$P$ (1,2)

$Q$ (3,1)

Those that "tie" on the independent variable:

$P$ (2,2)

$Q$ (2,1)

Those that "tie" on the dependent variable:

$P$ (1,3)

$Q$ (2,3)

Those that "tie" on both variables:

$P$ (2,3)

$Q$ (2,3)

If tied on the independent variable, both cases locate in the same column of the table. If tied on the dependent, both locate in the same row. If tied on both variables, both cases locate in the same cell of the table.

Table 4.6 is contrived to illustrate three extreme possibilities. In Table 4.6(a), all pairs of cases are either same-ordered or tie on both variables, displaying a perfect ordinal relationship—the vectors again help us envisage the pattern. Computation of the column percentages produces three values of 100 percent along the upper left to lower right diagonal. Table 4.6(b) displays an equal number of same- and different-ordered pairs, and a considerable number of ties. No ordered relationship here exists; indeed, no relationship exists at all. Computation of the column percentages produces 33.3 percent in each cell—1s on the independent variable are equally likely to be 1s, 2s, or 3s on the dependent variable. So are 2s on the independent variable; and 3s. In Table 4.6(c), all pairs are either different-ordered or tie on both variables. This too is a perfect ordinal relationship, the mirror image of Table 4.6(a). All 1s on the independent variable are 3s, all 2s are 2s, and all 3s ares 1s. Think vectors.

The *gamma statistic* is one of a number of rank-order statistics that analyze pairs of cases to determine if ordered relationships exist. Gamma "throws out" all ties and calculates, among the remaining pairs, the proportion of same- to different-ordered pairs. If all the remaining pairs are same-ordered, there is a *perfect positive relationship* between the two variables, as in Table 4.6(a). If all the remaining pairs are different-ordered, there is a *perfect negative relationship,* as in Table 4.6(c). If there are an equal number of same- and different-ordered pairs among the remainder, there is *no ordinal relationship,* as in Table 4.6(b).

Gamma is a *correlation coefficient*, which may take on any value between −1 and +1. If −1, there are different-ordered pairs, but no same-ordered pairs. All cases fall on the upper right to lower left diagonal. If +1, there are same-ordered pairs, but no differ-

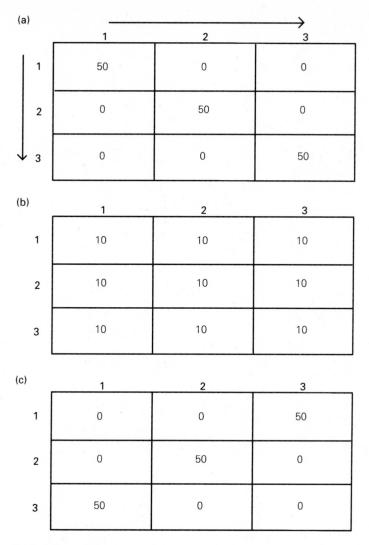

Table 4.6

ent-ordered pairs. All cases fall on the upper left to lower right diagonal. If 0, there are an equal number of same- and different-ordered pairs. There is no concentration of cases along either diagonal. Think vectors. A preponderance of same-ordered pairs produces a positive coefficient. A preponderance of different-ordered pairs produces a negative coefficient. In Table 4.5(a), the preponderance of pairs are same-ordered. But some are also different-ordered. Gamma takes on a value above 0 and below +1. As a rule of thumb, .3 is generally considered a moderate positive relationship and −.3 a moderate negative relationship. A coefficient of .5 is generally considered a strong positive relationship and −.5 a strong negative relationship. A coefficient of .7 is considered to be very strong positive; −.7 very strong negative.

## Computation of Gamma

Any cross-tabulation of ordinal level data likely contains a very large number of pairs of cases. The formula for computing number of pairs among a set of cases is:

$$\frac{N(N-1)}{2}$$

where $N$ is the number of cases. Two cases form 1 pair. Three cases form 3 pairs. Six cases form 15 pairs. Three hundred cases form 44,850 pairs! In a table containing 300 cases, it would be extremely time-consuming to pull out every one of 44,850 pairs to determine whether each is same- or different-ordered. Use a shortcut.

To compute gamma, use only the number of same-ordered pairs ($Ns$) and the number of different-ordered pairs ($Nd$). To compute $Ns$, first identify every cell in the table that has cells *below it and to the right*. Not just below. Not just to the right. Below *and* to the right. Every case in each of these cells forms a same-ordered pair with every case below and to the right. Therefore, as a second step, perform a series of multiplications equal to the number of cells having cells below and to the right—multiply the number of cases in the cell by the total number of cases in the cells below and to the right. In Table 4.5(a), four cells have cells below and to the right:

$$100 \times (100 + 25 + 25 + 100) = 25{,}000$$

$$25 \times (25 + 100) = 3{,}125$$

$$100 \times (100) = 10{,}000$$

$$25 \times (25 + 100) = 3{,}125$$

Third, add the products to arrive at the number of same ordered pairs: $Ns = 41{,}250$.

To compute $Nd$, first identify every cell in the table that has cells *below it and to the left*. Not just below. Not just to the left. Below *and* to the left. Every case in each of these cells forms a different-ordered pair with every case below and to the left. Therefore, second, perform a series of multiplications equal to the number of cells having cells below and to the left; multiply the number of cases in the cell by the total number of cases in the cells below and to the left. In Table 4.5(a), four cells have cells below and to the left:

$$25 \times (100 + 25 + 25 + 25) = 4{,}375$$

$$25 \times (25 + 25) = 1{,}250$$

$$100 \times (25) = 2{,}500$$

$$25 \times (25 + 25) = 1{,}250$$

The number of different-ordered pairs is 9,375.

Finally, determine the proportion of same- and different-ordered pairs (ties are not considered) by employing the simple formula for gamma:

$$\frac{Ns - Nd}{Ns + Nd}$$

$$\frac{41{,}250 - 9{,}375}{41{,}250 + 9{,}375} = .63$$

This is a strong positive ordinal relationship.

If all pairs are same-ordered, the equation produces a gamma of 1; if all pairs are different-ordered, the equation produces a gamma of −1; if there are an equal number of same- and different-ordered pairs, the equation produces a gamma of 0. Employing the formula, confirm that the Table in 4.6(a) produces a gamma of 1, that the Table in 4.6(b) produces a gamma of 0, and the table in 4.6(c) produces a gamma of −1.

## Example 1

Returning to genuine data, hypothesize that upperclasspeople in our student sample are more likely to consider themselves to be of "liberal" political ideology, while underclasspeople are more likely to consider themselves to be of "conservative" political ideology. The hypothesis is not unreasonable. Students of college age are at a critical point in the formation of political beliefs. Therefore, they are particularly susceptible to influence from various "agents of political socialization" in their environment. Agents of socialization are institutions that communicate political lessons and political beliefs: family, church, workplace, school. The university is a strong agent of socialization.[3] Moreover, university professors are more likely to be liberal in their outlook than conservative.[4] Therefore, university professors likely play a role in "socializing" their students in the liberal direction. Students, as they move from freshman to senior year, likely become increasingly liberal.

Table 4.7 lists Freshman, Sophomore, Junior, and Senior across the top and Conservative, Moderate, Liberal down the side. The data derive from direct questions to the students in our sample about their year in school and with which of the three ideological categories they identify most closely. Note three aspects of this example.

First, both variables are ordinal. Students are arrayed from Freshman (lowest) to Senior (highest). They are also arrayed from Conservative to Liberal, with Moderate

|  | (1) Freshman | (2) Sophmore | (3) Junior | (4) Senior |  |
|---|---|---|---|---|---|
| (1) Conservative | 14<br>13.7% | 20<br>20.6% | 18<br>19.1% | 28<br>26.4% | 80<br>20.1% |
| (2) Moderate | 62<br>60.8% | 50<br>51.5% | 51<br>54.3% | 49<br>46.2% | 212<br>53.1% |
| (3) Liberal | 26<br>25.5% | 27<br>27.8% | 25<br>26.6% | 29<br>27.4% | 107<br>26.8% |
|  | 102<br>25.6% | 97<br>24.3% | 94<br>23.6% | 106<br>26.6% | 399 |

Table 4.7

falling "between" Conservative and Liberal. Second, the table is set up in such a way that confirmation of the hypothesis produces a positive gamma—if movement from Freshman to Senior produces movement from Conservative to Liberal, gamma falls between 0 and 1. Third, in this table, there is no perfectly symmetrical diagonal. This presents no difficulties. Simply think concentration of cases in the "upper left and lower right" of the table. Conservatives should cluster in the lower years and Liberals in the higher years.

In evaluating a hypothesized ordinal relationship, always analyze the column percentages first. Here, first trace the column percentages across the Conservative row to determine if the proportion of Conservatives declines with movement from Freshman to Senior. It does not; it rises. Second, trace the column percentages across the Liberal row to determine if the proportion of Liberals rises with movement from Freshman to Senior. It does not; it remains highly stable. Apparently, the hypothesis is flawed. Computation of gamma should confirm this—gamma is likely very close to 0, or negative.

$$
\begin{aligned}
Ns:\ 14 \times (50 + 51 + 49 + 27 + 25 + 29) &= 3{,}234 \\
20 \times (51 + 49 + 25 + 29) &= 3{,}080 \\
18 \times (49 + 29) &= 1{,}404 \\
62 \times (27 + 25 + 29) &= 5{,}022 \\
50 \times (25 + 29) &= 2{,}700 \\
51 \times (29) &= \underline{1{,}479} \\
&\phantom{=}\ 16{,}919
\end{aligned}
$$

$$
\begin{aligned}
Nd:\ 28 \times (62 + 50 + 51 + 26 + 27 + 25) &= 6{,}748 \\
18 \times (62 + 50 + 26 + 27) &= 2{,}970 \\
20 \times (62 + 26) &= 1{,}760 \\
50 \times (26) &= 1{,}300 \\
51 \times (26 + 27) &= 2{,}703 \\
49 \times (26 + 27 + 25) &= \underline{3{,}822} \\
&\phantom{=}\ 19{,}303
\end{aligned}
$$

$$
\frac{16{,}919 - 19{,}303}{16{,}919 + 19{,}303} = \frac{-2{,}384}{36{,}222} = -.07
$$

The hypothesis is not confirmed. No ordinal relationship exists; upperclasspeople are not more likely to be Liberal than underclasspeople.

## Example 2

Return to our economic development and military expenditure example, now using the indicators to construct two ordinal variables. If per capita GDP is less than $2,000, eco-

| | (1) Low Develoment | (2) Medium Development | (3) High Development | |
|---|---|---|---|---|
| **(1) Low Expenditure** | 6<br>15.8% | 3<br>27.3% | 2<br>13.3% | 11<br>17.2% |
| **(2) Medium Expenditure** | 22<br>57.9% | 6<br>54.5% | 12<br>80% | 40<br>62.5% |
| **(3) High Expenditure** | 10<br>26.3% | 2<br>18.2% | 1<br>6.7% | 13<br>20.3% |
| | 38<br>59.4% | 11<br>17.2% | 15<br>23.4% | 64 |

Table 4.8

nomic development scores (1) Low; if it is between $2,000 and $8,000, inclusive, it scores (2) Medium; if over $8,000, (3) High. If proportion of budget devoted to military is less than 5 percent, expenditure scores (1) Low; if it is between 5 percent and 15 percent, inclusive, it scores (2) Medium; if over 15 percent, (3) High.

Since the hypothesized relationship is that more-developed nations spend less, expect movement from Low to High on development to produce movement from High to Low on expenditures in Table 4.8. In other words, expect concentration of cases in the "upper right and lower left" of the table. Think vectors. Although an inspection of the column percentages across the Low Expenditure row does not conform to such a pattern, an inspection across the Medium and High rows does. Increasing incidence of Medium Expenditures accompanies movement from Low to High Development, and there is a clear pattern of decreasing incidence of High Expenditures with movement from Low to High Development. Computation of the gamma statistic should confirm at least a moderate negative relationship. Remember—the hypothesized relationship was negative: High Development, Low Expenditures; therefore, a moderately negative gamma tends toward confirmation of the hypothesis. Test your knowledge by computing gamma for Table 4.8.

## Important Points to Remember About Ordinal Analysis

The central importance of prediction in statistical analysis is evident at the ordinal level, as at the nominal level. Gamma indicates the success enjoyed in randomly selecting pairs of cases from a table, after ties have been thrown out, and guessing whether or not they are same- or different-ordered. If gamma is 0, there are an equal number of same- and different-ordered pairs. Predictive success, over the long run, achieves a level of 50 percent. Fifty percent is simply random success, like flipping a coin. There is no ordinal relationship.

Twice as many same-ordered as different-ordered pairs produces a success rate of 66.6 percent, since guessing same-ordered over the long run is correct two times out of three. And 66.6 percent is a 33.3 percent increase over 50 percent. Gamma is .33 if same-ordered pairs outnumber different-ordered pairs by 2:1. Four times as many different-ordered pairs as same-ordered pairs produces a success rate of 80 percent, since guessing different-ordered pairs over the long run is correct four times out of five. And 80 percent is a 60 percent increase over 50 percent. Gamma is −.6 if different-ordered pairs outnumber same-ordered pairs by 4:1. If all pairs are either same-ordered or different-ordered, gamma is either 1 or −1. In either instance, predictive success increases by 100 percent, from 50 percent to 100 percent.

The preferred PRE method also applies. In the case of twice as many same-ordered as different-ordered pairs, error is reduced by 16.6 percentage points, from 50 percent to 33.3 percent; 16.6 divided by the original error of 50 percent equals .33. In the case of four times as many different-ordered pairs as same-ordered pairs, error is reduced by 30 percentage points, from 50 percent to 20 percent. Thirty divided by the original error of 50 percent equals .6. With gamma, the proportion by which predictive success is increased will always be equal to the proportion by which predictive error is reduced, since we begin in both computations with a base of 50 percent—half same-ordered pairs and half different ordered pairs.

Recall that nominal classifies, while ordinal classifies and orders. Therefore, any statistical analysis performed at the nominal level may also be performed at the ordinal level. With an ordinal cross-tabulation, always compute the column percentages first, and evaluate what these indicate about the relationship. Then compute and evaluate the gamma statistic. Use both column percentages and gamma to draw conclusions about the hypothesis.

Recall also that ordinal analysis is not performed on nominal variables, since nominal only classifies. Returning to Table 4.2, do not compute the gamma statistic. Discipline of major and party identification are not arrayed along a continuum from low to high. It makes no sense to "move from Business through Natural Science and Social Science to the Humanities." It is not possible to evaluate same- and different-ordered pairs because the measurements contain no sense of order.

## Application of Gamma

Appendix C reprints Chapter 2 of Richard F. Fenno, Jr., *Home Style: House Members in Their Districts*. The chapter, "Home Style: Allocation of Resources," demonstrates application of the gamma statistic in research by a political scientist. Throughout this text, as already evident, we review quantitative research in the form of book chapters, scholarly articles, and research reports. We do so systematically, identifying the basic elements of the work: (1) What is the general research question the author attempts to answer? (2) What are the specific hypotheses the author tests in this attempt and what is the reasoning behind these hypotheses? (3) What are the independent variables, dependent variables, and cases? (4) Do the operational definitions present any validity or reliability problems? (5) What are the results of the quantitative tests and what do these results imply for acceptance of the hypotheses? Consider each of these five elements as you analyze Fenno's work.

Fenno is interested in determining what U.S. congresspeople do in their home districts and why. In the material presented in Appendix C, he is interested in determining how they allocate the political resources of time and staff in their home districts. He advances a number of hypotheses: Those in electoral jeopardy will spend more time at home. Those in office longer will spend less time at home. Those whose districts are farther from Washington will spend less time at home. Those whose districts are farther from Washington will put more staff at home. Those in electoral jeopardy will put more staff at home.

Focus on the second hypothesis. It makes sense to hypothesize that those in office longer will spend less time at home, since they likely need to be less concerned with "pressing the flesh" to maintain political support. Those serving in the House of Representatives for extended periods enjoy ample opportunity to shower public largesse on constituents through federal spending in the district. They also have very high "name recognition" among these constituents. This logic is confirmed by the extraordinarily high rate of success among incumbents seeking reelection to the House. The independent variable is time in office, the dependent variable is time spent at home, and the cases are congresspeople.

Fenno creates two ordinal level variables, each with three categories. On the independent variable, one to three terms scores Low, four to seven terms scores Medium, and eight or more High. On the dependent variable, under 24 trips home per year scores Low, 24 to 42 scores Medium, and over 42 High. Measurement of the independent variable poses no validity nor reliability problems. Number of terms served is a direct indicator of time spent in the House and the information is readily available in reliable sources such as the *Congressional Quarterly's Guide to Congress*. The dependent variable is a bit trickier. Regarding validity, number of trips home is not the most direct measure of time spent at home. For example, some members may make frequent trips home but not stay very long on any single trip. Therefore, a little "slippage" exists between concept and indicator. Regarding reliability, Fenno notes on page 193 that "six students . . . conducted a survey by visiting every member's office and talking to his or her administrative assistant or personal secretary. The question about frequency of member trips home usually produced an educated estimate." The data are not completely reliable since the number of trips recorded for some members is not totally accurate.

On page 195, Fenno presents a cross-tabulation (Table C.2) that violates our rules by listing the dependent variable across the top (our record is not too good so far!). Note again, however, that he compensates by computing the percentages across the row. Also note the typographical error: 189 should be 109. Observe that "Low Frequency of Trips Home" increases in incidence with movement from Low to High seniority—22 percent to 48 percent. Observe further "High Frequency of Trips Home" decreases in incidence with movement from Low to High seniority—50 percent to 28 percent. This is consistent with Fenno's gamma of −.3—the cases concentrate in the upper right and lower left of the table. Movement from Low to High on seniority produces movement from High to Low on frequency of trips home. There is a moderate inverse relationship and the hypothesis is confirmed.

|  | High Seniority | Medium Seniority | Low Seniority |  |
|---|---|---|---|---|
| Low Trips | 52<br>48% | 43<br>28% | 34<br>22% | 129<br>31% |
| Medium Trips | 26<br>24% | 59<br>38% | 44<br>28% | 129<br>31% |
| High Trips | 31<br>28% | 52<br>34% | 78<br>50% | 161<br>38% |
|  | 109<br>26% | 154<br>37% | 156<br>37% | 419 |

Table 4.9

Finally, understand that this table can be "swung upward from the left," putting High, Medium, and Low seniority across the top and Low, Medium, and High frequency of trips down the side. Table 4.9 conforms to our rules. The cases concentrate in the upper left and lower right, producing a gamma of .3. The hypothesis is still confirmed—it is the same data! Movement from High to Medium to Low on seniority still produces movement from Low to Medium to High on trips home. However, the table is arranged in such a way that a positive gamma results. Think vectors.

In Table C.3, Fenno does not report the gamma statistic. He only reports percentages. Be certain you understand why.

Clearly, this sort of statistical analysis proves extremely helpful to political scientists attempting to understand the behavior of legislators and attempting to communicate this understanding to their students. Knowledge that senior members of Congress need to pay less attention to their home districts is fully consistent with knowledge that well in excess of 90 percent of incumbents seeking reelection to the House win. This may be one of the more interesting and significant dilemmas our representative democracy currently faces. Presently, there are proposals afoot to amend the Constitution to limit the number of terms congressional representatives and senators may serve.

## THE INTERVAL LEVEL: SIMPLE REGRESSION

Imagine six cases, each scored on an interval level independent variable, $X$, and an interval level dependent variable, $Y$. The first case scores 4 on $X$ and 40 on $Y$, the second 6 on $X$ and 60 on $Y$, and so forth:

| $X$ | $Y$ |
|---|---|
| 4 | 40 |
| 6 | 60 |
| 8 | 80 |
| 10 | 100 |
| 20 | 200 |
| 30 | ? |

If asked to guess the value of the sixth case on Y, the pattern clearly dictates the answer. The guess emerges from an implicit comparison of pairs of cases. Recall that the ordinal level of measurement provides knowledge of order, permitting discussion of same- and different-ordered pairs—whether or not a particular case is more or less than another case on the independent variable and more or less than another case on the dependent variable. At the interval level, knowledge of distance also exists, making it possible to discuss "how much" more or less. Consider a few pairs of cases in this example:

(10, 100)　(20, 200)　(4, 40)
(20, 200)　　(6, 60)　(30, ?)

In the left-hand example, 20 is twice as much as 10 and 200 is twice as much as 100. In the middle example, 6 is 30 percent of 20 and 60 is 30 percent of 200. In the right-hand example, if the proportional relationship between the two cases on the dependent variable is the same as the proportional relationship on the independent, guess 300.

The *Pearson's correlation coefficient* measures the extent to which an increase or decrease in one variable is accompanied by a *proportional* increase or decrease in another. Like any other correlation coefficient, Pearson's varies between −1 and +1 and the same rules of thumb apply in assessing the strength of a relationship between two interval level variables. Indeed, Pearson's is the "classic" correlation coefficient—when data analysts use the term "correlation" they almost always refer to Pearson's.

In the example just given, Pearson's correlation is a perfect +1, since any two pairs of cases predict perfectly the value of the dependent variable on one, with knowledge of the value of the dependent variable on the other, and knowledge of the value of both independent variables. Consider three more examples:

| X | Y | | X | Y | | X | Y |
|---|----|---|---|----|---|---|----|
| 1 | 15 | | 1 | 75 | | 1 | 15 |
| 2 | 30 | | 2 | 60 | | 2 | 30 |
| 3 | 45 | | 3 | 45 | | 3 | 45 |
| 4 | 60 | | 4 | 30 | | 4 | 30 |
| 5 | 75 | | 5 | 15 | | 5 | 15 |

In the first, Pearson's is 1, since Y increases 15 with an increase of 1 in X in a perfectly predictable pattern. In the second, Pearson's is −1 since Y decreases 15 with an increase of 1 in X in a perfectly predictable pattern. Both are perfect correlations. In the third, Pearson's is 0 since it is not possible to predict Y based on knowledge of X. Y goes up when X goes up for some pairs of cases, and Y goes down when X goes up for some pairs of cases. The pattern is not consistent.

## Computation of Pearson's Correlation Coefficient

At the interval level, data are not placed in cross-tabulations for obvious reasons. For example, record the *exact* per capita GDP for each of our 64 nations and the *exact* percentage each devotes to military expenditures. Unique values could appear for each nation on each variable, producing a contingency table with 4,096 (64 × 64) cells! Rather, list the values of the cases under an X and Y columns. Once this is done, employ the following formula to compute Pearson's correlation coefficient:

$$r = \frac{N\,[\Sigma\,(xy)] - [(\Sigma\,x)(\Sigma\,y)]}{\sqrt{[N\,\Sigma\,(x^2) - (\Sigma\,x)^2]\,[N\,\Sigma(y^2) - (\Sigma y)^2]}}$$

Lay it out for the first of the three examples listed at the end of the last section:

| X | Y | XY | X² | Y² |
|---|---|---|---|---|
| 1 | 15 | 15 | 1 | 225 |
| 2 | 30 | 60 | 4 | 900 |
| 3 | 45 | 135 | 9 | 2,025 |
| 4 | 60 | 240 | 16 | 3,600 |
| 5 | 75 | 375 | 25 | 5,625 |
| 55 | 225 | 825 | 55 | 12,375 |

$N$ is five, because there are five cases listed individually:

$$\frac{[5(825)] - [(15)(225)]}{\sqrt{[(5 \times 55) - 225]\,[(5 \times 12,375) - 50,625]}}$$

$$= \frac{750}{\sqrt{50 \times 11,250}}$$

$$= \frac{750}{750} = 1$$

Confirm that the second example at the end of the last section produces a Pearson's correlation of −1 and that the third example produces a Pearson's correlation of 0.

## An Example with Genuine Data

Hypothesize that rural agricultural states in the United States enjoy higher levels of voter turnout in presidential elections than urban industrial states. The hypothesis is not unreasonable. Voting is, at least in part, a function of "community spirit" and a belief that the individual can make a difference in the affairs of the community. Rural farming communities are generally more "closely knit" than urban neighborhoods, and farmers, more so than industrial workers and managers, are engaged in an occupation that likely gives them a greater sense of control over their environment.[5] Note here that type of state (rural farming or urban industrial) is the independent variable, level of voter turnout is the dependent variable, and states are the cases. Reference is made to individuals only as part of the reasoning behind the hypothesis.

Use thousands of acres of land in agricultural production per square mile to indicate the extent to which states are rural agricultural rather than urban industrial, and percentage of eligible voters casting a ballot in the 1984 presidential election to indicate turnout. Using thousands of acres per square mile in agricultural production as an indicator may pose some validity problems. While it is undoubtedly a good indicator of the degree to which a state is agricultural, some slippage exists on the rural dimension. States such as Nevada and Alaska, for example, while predominantly rural, are not particularly agricultural.

Proceeding nonetheless to categorize states on the basis of a reliable source, the Council of State Government's *Book of States*, we are in a position to determine if these two variables vary together. The agricultural data are taken from 1985 and the turnout data, obviously, from 1984. Each is scored at the interval level. The unit of measurement for the independent variable is thousands of acres, and the unit of measurement for turnout is the percentage point. In the following, we lay out the data for only 10 of the 50 states, to make the example more manageable, and hypothesize a positive Pearson's correlation coefficient. Of course, a proper analysis requires computation of the correlation for all 50 states. Note that the independent variable takes on decimal values only. For example, .21 thousand acres is 210 acres, .39 thousand is 390, and so forth. The reason for this definitional choice will be discussed a bit later.

| X | Y | XY | $X^2$ | $Y^2$ |
|---|---|---|---|---|
| .21 | 50.1 | 10.52 | .044 | 2510 |
| .23 | 42.2 | 9.71 | .053 | 1780.8 |
| .6 | 62.3 | 37.38 | .36 | 3881.3 |
| .26 | 51.4 | 13.36 | .067 | 2642 |
| .45 | 57.8 | 26 | .203 | 3340.8 |
| .13 | 56.9 | 7.4 | .017 | 3237.6 |
| .39 | 58.2 | 22.7 | .152 | 3387.2 |
| .15 | 40.1 | 6.02 | .023 | 1608 |
| .17 | 60 | 10.2 | .029 | 3600 |
| .36 | 50.4 | 18.1 | .123 | 2540.2 |
| 2.95 | 529.4 | 161.39 | 1.071 | 28,528 |

$$\frac{[10(161.39)] - [(2.95)(529.4)]}{\sqrt{[(10 \times 1.071) - 8.7][(10 \times 28,528) - 280,264]}}$$

$$= \frac{52.17}{\sqrt{2.01 \times 5016}} = .52$$

As it turns out, this result is rather different from the result achieved when the correlation is computed for all 50 of the cases. For these 10 cases, there is a strong positive relationship. For all 50, there is a weak positive relationship of .15. For all 50 cases, there is only a slight tendency for agricultural states to display higher voter turnout. The correlation is not strong enough to accept the hypothesis. This means that there are other variables that are much more important than "agriculturalness" in determining turnout. Perhaps median education or median income levels would produce higher correlations. Had the correlation for all 50 states achieved the level achieved for 10 states used in the example, the hypothesis would have been confirmed.

## Understanding Pearson's Correlation Coefficient

Statisticians and mathematicians derive formal proofs from first principles, demonstrating why Pearson's correlation must always vary between −1 and +1, and why the two extremes constitute perfect correlations in data arrays. Most political scientists (yours truly among them) are not so capable.However, consider two explanations, based on knowledge of the formula, that give a "feel" for the behavior of the coefficient. The first is very informal and casual; the second, a bit more technically complex.

Using the first two of the three extreme examples presented initially as reference points, note that if X and Y "get big together," the numerator is large, but if "Y gets small while $X$ gets big," the numerator is small. The first expression of the numerator produces this effect. The second expression "subtracts out" the relative magnitude of the units of measurement for both variables taken together, permitting a negative numerator in instances of inverse correlations. Therefore, if $X$ and $Y$ "go up together," the numerator is relatively large, producing a correlation above 0. If one goes up while the other goes down, the numerator is relatively small, producing a correlation under 0. The denominator standardizes this result, taking into account the relative magnitude of the units of measurement, producing a coefficient varying between $-1$ and $+1$. Note in this regard that these first two examples produce the same denominator, because the amount of variation in $X$ and $Y$ is the same in both examples; the only difference is the direction of that variation. While this explanation would unlikely impress a statistician, it does provide a general idea of what the equation accomplishes. The second explanation is a bit more impressive.

Recall from Chapter 2 that $z$ scores, or standard scores, defined as the distance of a case from the mean in standard deviation units, permit comparison of the position of a case, in relation to the mean, on two different interval level variables, even though those two variables are measured in different original units. Using the formulas for the standard deviation and $z$ scores contained in Chapter 2, transform original scores to standard scores. The result, in the first example:

| X | Y | z for X | z for Y |
|---|----|---------|---------|
| 1 | 15 | −1.42 | −1.42 |
| 2 | 30 | − .71 | − .71 |
| 3 | 45 | 0 | 0 |
| 4 | 60 | .71 | .71 |
| 5 | 75 | 1.42 | 1.42 |

Pearson's correlation reports the change in the $z$ scores of $Y$ produced by 1 unit of change in the $z$ scores of $X$. We know that Pearson's correlation here is 1, a perfect positive relationship. Observe that for every unit of change in the $z$ scores of $X$, the $z$ scores of $Y$ change 1 unit. If $Y$ is inverted, producing a Pearson's of $-1$, the $z$ scores for $Y$ invert also, permitting the observation that 1 unit of change in the $z$ scores of $X$ produce $-1$ units of change in the $z$ scores of $Y$. As Pearson's correlation weakens toward 0 from either of the extremes of 1 and $-1$, the amount of change in the $z$ scores of $Y$ attributable to one unit of change in the $z$ scores of $x$ progressively diminishes. At 0, there is no change in the $z$ scores of $Y$ attributable to change in the $z$ scores of $X$. There is no relationship between the two variables.

Indeed, an alternate method of computing Pearson's correlation coefficient is:

$$r = \frac{\Sigma \, [z(x) \, \cdot \, z(y)]}{N}$$

Simply transform the $X$ and $Y$ variables to $z$ scores, multiply the $z$ scores by one another for each case, sum the result, and divide by the total number of cases. Multiplying the $z$ scores by one another and dividing by the number of cases results directly in a determination of the amount of change in one set of $z$ scores associated with 1 unit of change in the other set. Confirm that this operation produces a Pearson's correlation of 1 in our example. Of course, using the formula for Pearson's correlation first advanced is more efficient than transforming data arrays into $z$ scores before performing the computations.

The example also demonstrates that any two variables displaying the same pattern of variation have the same $z$ scores. Cases scored 1, 2, and 3 have the same $z$ scores as cases scored 10, 20 and 30; and the same $z$ scores as cases scored 100 ,200, and 300; *ad infinitum*. As a result, any variable may be divided through by a constant without compromising Pearson's correlation coefficient. We did this with acres per square miles, dividing it through by 1,000. The correlation produced is exactly the same as if we had not divided through; if .21 had been left as 210, .39 as 390, and so forth. By dividing through, extraordinarily large numbers were avoided in completing the computation. In the section immediately following, we see more clearly the central role of $z$ scores for an understanding of interval level analysis.

## Evaluating the Form of an Interval Level Relationship

Pearson's correlation coefficient signals the strength and direction of a relationship between two interval level variables. Recalling our rules of thumb, −.3 is a moderate (strength) inverse (direction) relationship, −.5 is a strong inverse relationship, −.7 is a very strong inverse relationship, and −1 is a perfect inverse relationship. Similarly, 1 is a perfect (strength) positive (direction) relationship, .7 is a very strong positive relationship, .5 is a strong positive relationship, and .3 is a moderate positive relationship.

In interval level statistics, the *form* of a relationship is also evaluated. Form is the amount of change in original units occurring in $Y$ in response to 1 original unit of change in $X$. Pearson's correlation is based on change in $z$ scores; the form of relationship is based on change in the original scores from which those $z$ scores derive. Remember also that Pearson's correlation measures the extent to which an increase or decrease in one variable is accompanied by a proportional increase or decrease in another variable. The form of the relationship reports exactly what that proportion is. And recall that at the ordinal level it was possible to discuss strength and direction because we had knowledge of order. But it was not possible to talk about form because we had no knowledge of distance; we had no actual unit of measurement. At the interval level, we do.

Figure 4.1 displays graphically the three extreme examples presented initially. The graphs are termed *scatter diagrams* and they position each case in a field defined by the intersection of the $X$ variable, listed on a horizontal axis, and the $Y$ variable, listed on a vertical axis. In the first two examples, as depicted in Figure 4.2, a straight line may be drawn through all six cases. This *line of regression* has a *slope*, defined as the *rise over the run*. In the first example, if we "run from 2 to 4," we "rise from 30 to 60," rising a distance of 30 units while running a distance of 2 units. Don't forget—distance and units have meaning only at the interval level. The slope is 30 / 2 = 15. A right angle may be drawn from any two points off this line and the rise over the run will equal 15. Fifteen is the slope of the regression line. Fifteen is the form of the relationship. When $X$ goes up 1, $Y$ goes up 15. The proportional increase equals 15. Demonstrate that the slope in the second example is −15, using the dotted right angle as a hint and bearing in mind that the rise is negative.

Figure 4.3 displays graphically the 10 cases from the agriculture and turnout example. No line may be drawn upon which all cases fall, since this is not a perfect correlation like the two previous examples. However, a *best-fitting line* may be drawn that reflects a summary of the average amount of change in the original units of $Y$ for 1 unit change in the original units of $X$. The formula for the slope of the best-fitting line is:

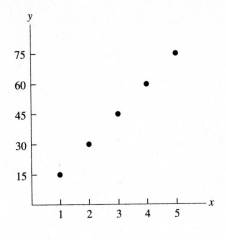

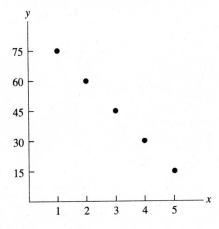

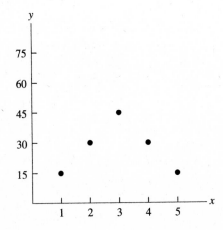

**Figure 4.1**

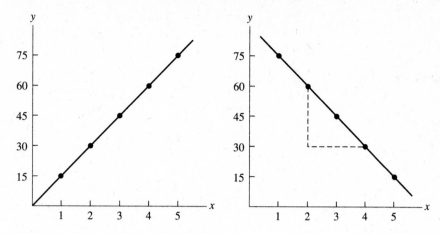

**Figure 4.2**

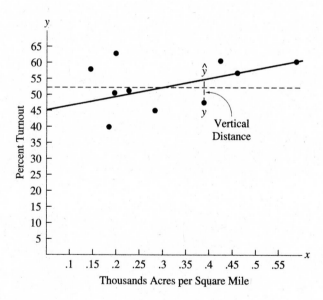

**Figure 4.3**

$$\frac{[N(\Sigma\, xy)] - [(\Sigma\, x)(\Sigma\, y)]}{[N(\Sigma\, x^2)] - (\Sigma\, x)^2}$$

Taking the numbers from the array used to compute Pearson's correlation:

$$\frac{[10(161.39)] - [(2.95)\,(529.4)]}{[(10 \times 1.071) - 8.7]}$$

$$= \frac{52.17}{2.01} = 26$$

For every 1,000-acre increase, there is an increase of 26 percentage points. (The actual slope for all 50 cases is 6.) Remember, while Pearson's correlation is based on change in standard units, the slope is based on change in original units. Therefore, the slope may take on virtually any value, depending upon the original units of measurement used, and on whether the correlation is positive or negative. Use this formula to confirm that the first example in Figure 4.1 produces a slope of 15.

The second step in drawing the best-fitting line is to compute the *Y intercept*, which is the predicted value of $Y$ when $X$ is 0. It is the point at which the best-fitting line intersects the vertical axis:

$$a = \overline{Y} - b(\overline{X})$$

$$= 52.94 - 26(.295)$$

$$= 45.27$$

Mark the $Y$ axis at 45.27 on the scatter plot. The third step is to use the equation for a straight line to identify a second point on the plot:

$$Y = a + b(X)$$

Choose any value of $X$. We'll use .5:

$$Y = 45.27 + 26(.5)$$

$$Y = 58.27$$

When $X$ is .5, the predicted value of $Y$ is 58.27. Mark this point, and connect it to the intercept with a straight line, the line of regression.

This is the best-fitting line, using the criteria of *least squares*. It provides the minimum squared distance from the line for all cases in the set of data. In other words, if you square the vertical distance from this line of each of the 10 cases and add the 10 squared distances together, you get a smaller number than that produced, using the same method, by any other line—the least squared distance.

It is now possible to demonstrate the central role of $z$ scores in correlation analysis from another perspective. Recall that Pearson's correlation reports the change in the $z$ scores of $Y$ produced by a change of 1 in the $z$ scores of $X$. Therefore, the slope of a set of $z$ scores must equal the Pearson's correlation coefficient produced by the original data.

Now lay out the $z$ scores for the 10 states. Compute the slope to confirm that it equals .52. Your task is eased by the fact that the sum of a set of $z$ scores is always equal to 0. Therefore, the summation of $X$ and the summation of $Y$ are both 0. (Rounding error may result in slightly different values, but you should use 0s in the equation.) In addition, confirm that the "$z$ score formula" for Pearson's correlation also produces a .52.

| X | Y |
| --- | --- |
| −.592 | −.4 |
| −.452 | −1.51 |
| 2.122 | 1.31 |
| −.244 | −.22 |
| 1.079 | .686 |
| −1.148 | .56 |
| .661 | .74 |
| −1.009 | −1.81 |
| −.87 | 1 |
| .452 | −.36 |

## Development and Expenditure Example

Now lay out genuine data for 12 of our 64 nations, leaving per capita GDP and percentage devoted to military in their original interval level scores, and hypothesizing a negative Pearson's correlation coefficient. Note that per capita GDP is reported in thousands of dollars, for the same reason this strategy was used in the agricultural example. Twelve cases are used to make the example more manageable. Of course, the correlation should properly be computed on all cases for which data are available.

| X | Y |
| --- | --- |
| .957 | 10.8 |
| 1.297 | 12.0 |
| 1.656 | 10.7 |
| .491 | 6.0 |
| .509 | 11.8 |
| 1.112 | 26.3 |
| .064 | 3.2 |
| 6.886 | 5.0 |
| .590 | 14.5 |
| .360 | 2.3 |
| 1.135 | 10.6 |
| 2.788 | 6.2 |

As it turns out, the result obtained in computing Pearson's correlation for these 12 cases is almost exactly the same as the result achieved when the correlation is computed for all 64 cases. Compute the Pearson's correlation for this example and interpret what it tells you about the interval level relationship between the two variables. In addition, compute the slope, interpret its meaning, compute the $y$ intercept, and draw the line of regression. Be careful! The slope will be negative. Therefore, $a = \overline{Y} - b(\overline{X})$ will produce a double negative that will turn into a positive. Also, $Y = a + b(X)$ will actually end up as $Y = a - b(X)$ since $b$ is negative.

If Pearson's correlation is positive, the slope is positive. If Pearson's correlation is negative, the slope is negative. If Pearson's correlation is 0, the slope is either 0 or undefined. If the numerator of the equation for $b$ ("rise") takes on the value of 0, the slope will be 0 and the line of regression will be perfectly horizontal. If the denominator of the equation for $b$ ("run") takes on the value of 0, the slope will be undefined and the line of regression will be perfectly vertical.

Figures 4.4 and 4.5 illustrate graphically the connection between Pearson's correlation and the slope. It is worth emphasizing that the slope tells nothing about the strength of a relationship. Very weak relationships may have slopes as great in magnitude as very strong relationships. Figure 4.4(a) shows a negative relationship that is very strong because the cases are clustered very tightly around the line of regression. Figure 4.4(b) shows a negative relationship that is very weak because the cases are spread out away from the line of regression. As cases spread out farther and farther away from the

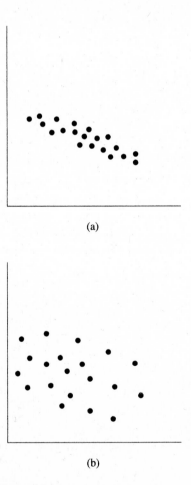

(a)

(b)

**Figure 4.4**

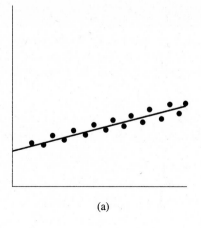

(a)

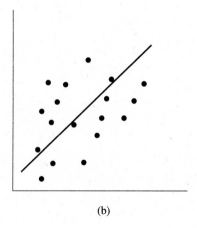

(b)

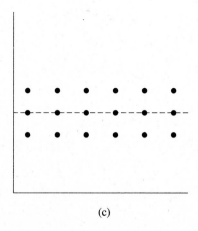

(c)

**Figure 4.5**

line, Pearson's approaches 0. But both would have the same slope because the line of regression would be the same.

Figure 4.5(a) shows a positive relationship that is very strong because the cases cluster tightly around the line. Figure 4.5(b) shows a relationship that is weaker because the cases are spread out away from the line. But the slope in 4.5(b) is greater in magnitude than the slope in 4.5(a), because the line of regression is steeper. Do not confuse form with strength—big slopes do not necessarily mean strong relationships!

Figure 4.5(c) shows a situation in which there is no relationship. Pearson's correlation and the slope both take on the value of 0. This is the only situation in which Pearson's correlation and the slope will certainly be the same. There is no correlation: Pearson's is 0. When $X$ changes 1 unit, $Y$ does not change: The slope is 0.

## Prediction

In simple regression, the value of $Y$ is predicted based on knowledge of the value of $X$. The more predictive success enjoyed over the long run, the stronger the correlation. The line of regression is the predictor. $Y = a + b(X)$ is the prediction. If all cases fall on the line of regression, all values of $Y$ may be predicted exactly from knowledge of the value of $X$. There is a perfect correlation. Predictive success reaches 100 percent. The slope of the line of regression provides a prediction rule. Pearson's correlation indicates how successful the application of that rule is over the long run.

Pearson's correlation squared ($r^2$), with the decimal moved two places to the right, indicates *the percentage of the variation in Y explained by X*. At +1 and −1, 100 percent of the variation is explained; at .5, 25 percent; at .3, only 9 percent; at 0, none. If Pearson's correlation is 0, the best guess, over the long run, of the value of $Y$ on randomly selected cases is $\overline{Y}$. This guess puts us closer to the exact value of $Y$ than any other guess. The total amount of "error" (the squared difference between the guess and the actual value) is minimized. This is analogous to guessing the value of a case on a nominal level dependent variable from the frequency distribution of that variable, choosing the average (mode), as previously discussed. If $X$ is correlated with $Y$, however, the best guess becomes $Y = a + b(X)$. In the absence of a correlation, this equation predicts $\overline{Y}$. If there is no correlation, $b$ is 0. Therefore, $a = \overline{Y} - b(\overline{X})$ produces $a = \overline{Y}$. And then $Y = a + b(X)$ produces $Y = \overline{Y}$. This is portrayed graphically by the dotted horizontal lines in Figure 4.3 and Figure 4.5(c), which track at $\overline{Y}$.

Recall from Chapter 2 that the sum of the squared difference between the value of each case and the mean is termed the "total variation." Here that would be $(Y - \overline{Y})$. Total variation in simple regression is $E1$ because it is the total amount of error produced when using $\overline{Y}$ to predict $Y$. If $X$ is correlated with $Y$, less error is produced by using $Y = a + b(X)$ as the predictor. This is $E2$, again analogous to the nominal level PRE situation in which the dependent variable is predicted from knowledge of the independent variable. Therefore, the proportion by which $E1$ is reduced when shifting to the line of regression as the predictor is:

$$\frac{E1 - E2}{E1}$$

$E2$ is less than $E1$ if $X$ is correlated with $Y$. The difference between $E1$ and $E2$ is the amount of error eliminated—the amount of variation explained by $X$. Dividing by the initial amount of error produces the proportion of variation in $Y$ that $X$ explains. It produces $r^2$. $E1$ is the total variation. $E1 - E2$ is the "explained variation." $E2$ is the "unexplained variation."

Returning to the example of turnout in the states, first record the squared difference between $Y$ and $\bar{Y}$ for each case, add it up, and term it $E1$. Then use the line of regression as predictor, employing $Y = 45.27 + 26(X)$ to arrive at $\hat{Y}$ for each case. For example, the first case is $\hat{Y} = 45.27 + 26\,(.21) = 50.73$. Taking the squared difference between $Y$ and $\hat{Y}$ for each case and adding it up produces $E2$. Then demonstrate that

$$\frac{E1 - E2}{E1} = .27$$

Pearson's correlation coefficient is .52; $r^2$ is .27. Twenty-seven percent of the variation in $Y$ is explained by $X$. Therefore, the operation must produce a .27.

| $Y$ | $\bar{Y}$ | $(Y - \bar{Y})^2$ |
|---|---|---|
| 50.1 | 52.94 | 8.07 |
| 42.2 | 52.94 | 115.35 |
| 62.3 | 52.94 | 87.61 |
| 51.4 | 52.94 | 2.37 |
| 57.8 | 52.94 | 23.62 |
| 56.9 | 52.94 | 15.68 |
| 58.2 | 52.94 | 27.67 |
| 40.1 | 52.94 | 164.87 |
| 60 | 52.94 | 49.85 |
| 50.4 | 52.94 | 6.45 |
| | | 501.54   ($E1$) |

| $Y$ | $\hat{Y}$ | $(Y - \hat{Y})^2$ |
|---|---|---|
| 50.1 | 50.73 | .4 |
| 42.2 | 51.25 | 81.9 |
| 62.3 | 60.87 | 2 |
| 51.4 | 52.03 | .4 |
| 57.8 | 56.97 | .69 |
| 56.9 | 48.65 | 68.1 |
| 58.2 | 55.41 | 7.8 |
| 40.1 | 49.17 | 82.3 |
| 60 | 49.69 | 106.3 |
| 50.4 | 54.63 | 17.9 |
| | | 367.80   ($E2$) |

$$\frac{501.54 - 367.8}{501.54} = .226$$
(rounding error)

Observe that if all cases fall on the line of regression, $E2$ takes on the value of 0 and the equation produces the value of 1—100 percent of the variation is explained. If Pearson's correlation is 0, $\hat{Y} = \overline{y}$. Under those circumstances, $E1 = E2$ and the equation produces the value of 0, because none of the variation is explained.

## Application of Simple Regression

Appendix D is a reprint of a scholarly article by John Fenton, titled "Turnout and the Two-Party Vote," which appeared in the February 1979 issue of the *Journal of Politics.* It demonstrates the application of simple regression in research by a political scientist. Fenton, who is interested in determining whether or not Democrats benefit from higher voter turnout in U.S. elections, tests two separate, but related, hypotheses.

The first hypothesis is: In elections won by Republicans, the victory margin will be negatively correlated with voter turnout. The second hypothesis is: In elections won by Democrats, the victory margin will be positively correlated with voter turnout. These two hypotheses make sense, in that citizens of lower socioeconomic status (education and income) traditionally identify with the Democratic party; moreover, citizens of lower socioeconomic status are less likely to vote than citizens of higher socioeconomic status. When turnout is low, those least likely to vote in the first place are probably the ones staying home. There is an old saying based on this conventional wisdom: "Republicans pray for rain on election day." When the weather is bad, turnout is low. When turnout is low, Republicans enjoy an advantage. Fenton puts the conventional wisdom to an empirical test.

In testing each hypothesis, Fenton employs interval level variables. In each hypothesis, percentage turnout is the independent variable and margin of victory (the percentage point difference between victor and vanquished) the dependent variable. Take care to note that presidential elections between 1828 and 1976 are the cases. Voters are not the cases, nor states, as in previous examples. The cases are always the "points" at which the measures of the variables are taken. Here, each presidential election is scored on each variable.

Since each variable may be measured directly, validity is not a big problem. Note, however, that in elections conducted before 1856, the major alternative to Democratic is classified as Republican. Reliability is a bit trickier. Historical statistics are less reliable as we move farther back in time, since the procedures for collecting and recording such data were less sophisticated in times past. Therefore, data from the nineteenth century are probably a bit less reliable than data from the twentieth century.

Figure D.1 shows the scatter for the 18 Republican elections, and it is apparent that there is an inverse relationship, as hypothesized, since the cases slope downward. Higher levels of turnout are associated with lower Republican margins of victory. He reports a slope of −.584: On average, a rise of 1 percentage point in turnout produces a decline of .58 percentage points in Republican margin. He reports a Pearson's correlation of −.78 and an $r^2$ of 61 percent. This is a very strong negative correlation. Sixty-one percent of the variation in victory margin is explained by turnout. The first hypothesis is confirmed.

Figure D.1 may be used to estimate the actual values used and construct the equation for the line of regression. The estimates are:

$$\overline{Y} = 11$$

$$\overline{X} = 67$$

$$a = 11 - (-.584)67$$

$$a = 50$$

$$Y = 50 - .584(X)$$

This is the rule for predicting the values of $Y$, based on knowledge of the value of $X$, in original units, which here are percentage points. Plugging in a turnout rate of 40 percent, for example, yields a predicted margin of victory of 27 percent. Consider this: Since the predicted $Y$ is 50 when $X$ is 0, movement from 0 to 40 on $X$ (the run) produces movement from 50 to 27 on $Y$ (the rise). The rise is negative: $-23 / 40 = -.58$. Sound familiar? Caution: If you wish to draw the line of regression on Figure D.1, score the $X$ axis proportionally beginning with 0 rather than 48. If you do not, weird things will happen. Pearson's correlation tells us that this line of regression is a very good predictor. Over the long run, this predictor will permit us to explain 61 percent of the variation in $Y$.

However, Fenton's second hypothesis is not confirmed. For Democratic election victories, the correlation is also negative! The slope is $-.363$ and Pearson's is $-.45$. Situations in which empirical evidence does not support a hypothesis are frequently encountered. When this happens, it is necessary to revise the reasoning behind the hypothesis. Fenton does so. He speculates that perhaps higher turnout always goes along with lower victory margins, no matter the victor. Perhaps the electorate is able to anticipate when a contest will be close and this anticipation brings them out to vote. In effect, maybe perception of a close race is causing the turnout—maybe turnout should be the dependent variable!

Indeed, voter turnout as a dependent variable has recently occupied the attention of policymakers in the United States. Therefore, the sort of statistical analysis Fenton performs and the sort of analysis we performed earlier with turnout in the states can be extremely useful to these policymakers. Indeed, on May 11, 1993, the Senate passed legislation, which had earlier passed in the House of Representatives, to standardize nationwide voter registration. The application, renewal, or change of address for a driver's license or vehicle registration would automatically register one to vote. A partisan battle over this legislation had been going on in Congress since 1989, prompted by statistical evidence that one of the primary, if not *the* primary, factors determining levels of turnout in the states is the stringency of voter registration requirements.[6] President Clinton signed the legislation, which will take effect in 1995.[7]

## SUMMARY

Bivariate statistics are employed to determine if correlations exist between two variables—to determine if the variables vary together. As such, they are widely employed to conduct quantitative tests of politically interesting hypotheses in order to arrive at conclusions regarding the degree to which an independent variable influences patterns of variation in a dependent variable. Correlation is synonymous with prediction. If the value of a dependent variable can be predicted based on knowledge of the value of an independent variable, the variables are correlated.

If both variables in an hypothesis are measured at the nominal level, contingency tables and percentaging are the only appropriate statistical tests. At the nominal level, only categorization is possible. Therefore, conclusions may be drawn regarding the tendency for cases in a particular category of the independent variable also to fall into a particular category of the dependent variable. Comparisons are made between the proportions falling into various categories. The researcher must judge whether the differences in the proportions are large enough to warrant the conclusion that the variables are related and, if so, to determine the strength of that relationship. If one were to take the square root of the lambda statistic, the result could be interpreted generally as a nominal level correlation coefficient. It is probably more prudent, however, to simply exercise judgment in evaluating the proportion of cases in each category of the dependent variable falling into each category of the independent variable.

If both variables in an hypothesis are measured at the ordinal level, the direction of the relationship is evaluated along with the strength of the relationship. Since knowledge of order exists, conclusions may be drawn regarding whether the relationship is positive ("higher" values of the dependent variable produced by "higher" values of the independent variable) or whether it is negative ("lower" values of the dependent variable produced by "higher" values of the in dependent variable). Gamma is a rank-order statistic, signaling both the strength and direction of the relationship. Since it varies between −1 and +1, it is a correlation coefficient. Specific rules of thumb are employed to establish the strength of the relationship signaled by a correlation coefficient.

If both variables in an hypothesis are measured at the interval level, it is possible to talk not only about the strength and direction of a relationship, but also about its form. Since an actual unit of measurement exists, conclusions are drawn not only about whether a dependent variable gets "larger" or "smaller" when an independent variable is "larger," but also about "how much" larger or smaller. Pearson's correlation coefficient, taking on values between −1 and +1, reports the strength and direction of an interval level relationship. The slope of the line of regression reports the form of the relationship: the number of units of change in the dependent variable produced by 1 unit of change in the independent variable. Pearson's correlation coefficient and the slope are two among many statistics falling under the rubric of *simple regression.*

Any hypothesis that may be tested with interval level statistics may also be tested with ordinal level statistics. Ordinal statistics only require knowledge of order. At the interval level, we have knowledge order and we have a unit of measurement. Of course, the interval level data would need first to be recategorized into ordinal level data before they could be placed in a contingency table. Any hypothesis that may be tested with ordinal level statistics may also be tested with nominal level statistics. Nominal level statistics only require categories. At the ordinal level, we have categories and order. Indeed, in evaluating an ordinal level contingency table, the column percentages are always computed before the gamma. But you cannot use simple regression with ordinal and nominal data, because there is no unit of measurement at the ordinal and nominal level.

And you cannot use gamma at the nominal level because there is no knowledge of order at that level.

Political scientists and political practitioners employ bivariate statistics widely. Political scientists, such as Fenno and Fenton, do so to test politically interesting hypotheses. Political candidates do so to determine their chances of electoral success and make informed judgments about how to deploy their campaign resources. Public officials do so to determine the effects of public policies and reach conclusions regarding the desirability of altering those policies.

# NOTES

1. In 1983, the *International Studies Quarterly* devoted an entire issue, containing six scholarly articles, to the relationship between internal economic conditions and external belligerency among nations. "Special Issue: The Economic Foundations of War," *International Studies Quarterly*, 27:4, December 1983.
2. This formulation was introduced by John Mueller, Karl Schuessler, and Herbert Costner in *Statistical Reasoning in Sociology* (Boston: Houghton Mifflin, 1977).
3. Richard Dawson and Kenneth Prewitt, *Political Socialization* (Boston: Little, Brown, 1969), remains the classic statement on the agents of political learning. Prewitt and Dawson devote an entire chapter to the issue of lifelong political learning from early childhood through adulthood and another entire chapter to the role of formal education in political learning.
4. Herbert McCloskey and Alida Brill, *Dimensions of Tolerance: What Americans Believe about Civil Liberties* (New York: Russell Sage Foundation, 1983), compares, among other things, the attitudes of college professors to those of the general public and to those of other community "opinion leaders." On page 268, they state, "The libertarian attitudes of college professors seem to be part of a larger syndrome of consistent support for all liberal values." And "The Nation," in *Chronicle of Higher Education Almanac* (September 5, 1990), reports that 57 percent of professors interviewed at 306 colleges and universities in the United States in February 1989 consider themselves to be liberal.
5. In American political science, the question of who votes and for whom has probably received more attention than any other single question. We cite only one example from the literature addressing the question under consideration: Raymond Wolfinger and Steven Rosenstone, *Who Votes* (New Haven: Yale University Press, 1980), point out on page 30 that "there is considerable controversy about whether people who live in the country are less likely to vote than city residents" and on page 31 that in 1974, farmers had the highest turnout rate of any occupational group. They cite the farmers' high level of self-reliance as one explanatory factor.
6. In a large body of literature this was discussed recently by Peverill Squire, Raymond Wolfinger, and David Glass, "Residential Mobility and Voter Turnout," *American Political Science Review* (81:1, March 1987).
7. Richard Sammon, "Senate Kills Filibuster Threat, Clears 'Motor Voter' Bill," *Congressional Quarterly Weekly Reports*, 51:20, May 15, 1993, p. 1221.

# Probabilities and Inferences

*Chapter*

# 5

# *Introduction to Statistical Inference*

$D$escriptive statistics are the everyday tools of political scientists and political practitioners. These statistics describe patterns of variation in data generated from carefully constructed operational definitions of single variables (univariate descriptive statistics). They also describe the degree to which data generated for two different variables "vary together," permitting tests of hypotheses designed to determine if one variable explains, or causes, another (bivariate descriptive statistics).

These statistical strategies of description and explanation are scientific in that they employ the logic of comparison. In comparing the values of variables on sets of cases, tentative conclusions may be reached about the underlying structure of political reality. Remember also, however, that the scientific method seeks to generalize.

In pursuing the importance of generalization, recall the examples from Chapter 2 and Chapter 4. Of 400 University of Scranton students, 27 percent considered themselves liberal. Business majors were more likely to consider themselves Republican than Humanities majors. The survey was conducted, however, to learn about the characteristics of all 3,500 University of Scranton students. What, then, is instructive about the characteristics of the 400 interviewees? In fact, *nothing* is instructive about their characteristics *unless* we can *generalize* from the 400 to the 3,500. The 400 make up a *sample* and the 3,500 make up the *population*. *Inferential statistics* permit us to determine if generalizations from the sample to the population are warranted.

For example, they permit us to determine how good an *estimate* 27 percent is for the proportion of all 3,500 students that consider themselves liberal; they permit us to determine the likelihood that had we interviewed all 3,500 students, Business majors would in fact have been proportionally more Republican than Humanities majors. They permit us to assess the quality of our generalizations, or inferences, from samples to populations.

For the most part, use of inferential statistics is confined to instances in which the cases are people rather than cities, or states, or countries. If analyzing states in the United States, for example, we have only 50 cases. There is no need to draw a sample; 50 is the entire population of states. If analyzing countries in the world, we have only about 175. There is little need to draw a sample; collecting data for the entire population of 175 countries is normally manageable. Therefore, inferential statistics are encountered most commonly when dealing with the results of *surveys* of people, or *public opinion polls*. The quality of surveys and public opinion polls always hinges directly on the quality of the inferences that may be made from samples to populations. The quality of these inferences hinges directly on *statistical probabilities*.

# INTRODUCTION TO PROBABILITY AND SURVEY SAMPLING

The probability that event $A$ will occur ($PrA$) is equal to the number of times we expect it to occur ("outcomes"; $n$) divided by the number of times there exist the conditions making its occurrence possible ("tries"; $N$). For example, the probability that the event "heads" will occur when we flip a coin is .5. If we flipped a coin 100 times ($N$), each time creating a condition under which it is possible for heads to occur, we would expect heads 50 times ($n$). $PrA = n / N$. $PrA = 50 / 100 = .5$. If we mix up 200 marbles in a bowl, 30 of which are black and 170 of which are white, and select 1 marble blindly from the bowl (a condition under which it is possible for black to occur), the probability that the marble will be black is $30 / 200 = .15$. Probabilities always take on a value between 0 and 1. The probability of flipping a head is .5, or 50 percent. The probability of selecting a black marble is .15 or 15 percent.

Think "cases" and "variables." The number of flips ($N$) is the number of cases; each case may take on the value of either heads or tails; the numerator of the equation ($n$) equals the number of cases we expect to take on the value of heads on the variable. The number of times we select a marble is the number of cases; each may take on the value of either black or white; the numerator of the equation equals the number of cases we expect to take on the value of "black" on the variable for any given number of cases (blind selections).

## Random Selection and Representative Samples

Blind selection may be restated as *random selection* and defined by reference to the principles of probability outlined above: A marble is randomly selected from a bowl if, and only if, each marble in the bowl has an equal probability of being selected. In our example, each marble has a probability of $1 / 200$ of being selected (.005 or .5 percent). Since there are 30 individual black marbles, and each individual marble has a .005 chance of being selected on a single try, the probability of selecting a black marble on that try is $30 \times .005 = .15 = 15$ percent. And if, on each try, there is a 15 percent chance of selecting a black marble, then, over 100 separate random tries, we would expect about 15 black marbles: .15 × 100. This will only occur, however, if each try is random; if each individual marble, whether that individual marble is black or white, shares an equal probability of being selected on each try.

Probabilities are essential to understanding survey research and public opinion polling because they are crucial to the representativeness of the sample. *If a large enough sample is selected from a population, and if the sample is selected randomly, the sample will be representative of the population.* To select a sample randomly from a population, we must create the conditions under which each person in the population shares an equal probability of ending up in the sample.

Suppose we wish to randomly sample 1,000 people from the population of approximately 150 million people over 18 years of age (voting age) in the United States for the purpose of soliciting their political opinions. If we are able to create the conditions under which each of these people has an equal chance of being selected, then every time an individual is selected, each member of the population has a probability of 1 / 150 million (.0000000066 or .00000066 percent) of being the individual selected. If a sample of 1,000 people is randomly selected, each member of the population shares a probability of 1,000 / 150 million (.0000066 or .00066 percent) of ending up in the sample.

This has interesting implications, since national public opinion samples are usually based on about 1,000 respondents. Suppose the Gallup poll has been sampling 1,000 people a day every day you have been alive (of course, they do not sample that often). Assuming you are 20 years old and that your parents have lived in the United States for the entire 20-year period, what is the probability that a parent of yours would have been selected as part of one of these samples? One thousand (respondents) × 7,300 (days) = 7.3 million chances / 150 million = .05 = about a 5 percent probability. We frequently hear people remark "I've never been called by the Gallup poll," suggesting that somehow the Gallup poll is selecting samples incorrectly. Of course, if one of these people had been called by the Gallup poll two or three times, *that* would more strongly indicate incorrect selection. It is a simple matter of probabilities.

Why will a random sample be a representative sample? Suppose that 76 million people, or 51 percent of the 150 million in the population, are female. Each time a single person is selected, the probability of that person being female is 76.5 / 150, or .51. It is just like the marbles! As a result, by the time 100 people are selected, about 51 of them will be female (100 × .51); by the time 1,000 are selected, about 510 will be female (1,000 × .51). It is all a matter of probabilities. Of course, precisely the same logic applies to virtually any population characteristic, such as race, religion, candidate preference, and so forth.

Purely random samples are seldom possible. For example, most national public opinion surveys are now conducted over the telephone. Therefore, they cannot be based on random samples of the entire population, since not everyone has a telephone. Those without a telephone share a 0 percent probability of selection; those who have telephones share a non-0 percent probability. In order to select a pure random sample, *a list* containing the names of every person in the population needs to be available, to "throw into a jar and select blindly." This is almost never possible; however, as we shall investigate more thoroughly in Chapter 10, a variety of very sophisticated techniques is available to create conditions approaching pure randomness.

Samples that are not purely random are not completely representative. To the extent a sample is not representative because it is influenced to some degree by nonrandom factors, it is *biased*. Nonrandom factors create a situation in which the individuals in the population do *not* all share an equal probability of selection. In national telephone surveys, the results are biased toward respondents who have telephones; those who do not have telephones *are not represented in the sample*. While it is usually impossible to eliminate all bias, attempts must be made to eliminate it to the fullest reasonable extent by selecting samples that approach randomness insofar as possible.

A brief example illustrates. Suppose you wish to select a random sample of approximately 300 students at your college. The population is all the undergraduate students at the college; the sample is the approximately 300 you select; if you select randomly, the 300 will be generally representative of the entire population of undergraduate students at the college. Suppose further that there are about 300 students in the other classes in which you are enrolled; for the sake of convenience, you select these as your sample by simply distributing a questionnaire when you attend class. This sample is biased because it is not random. Those undergraduate students in your classes have a 100 percent chance of selection (except those that "cut class" frequently!), while those undergraduate students not in your classes have a 0 percent chance. What is the direction of the bias? If you are a political science major, taking a lot of political science classes, the sample is biased toward political science majors and *underrepresents* other majors. If you are a senior, taking a lot of upper-division classes, the sample is biased toward upper-classpeople and *underrepresents* first-year students and sophomores.

Suppose, to address these difficulties, you "intercept" every third student entering the campus library one afternoon until you have your sample of 300. Any problems here? Could they be resolved by "intercepting" both in front of the library and the student center? How about the library, the student center, and the local bar?

## Size and Representative Samples

Obviously, random samples are not representative samples unless they are also sufficiently *large*. A random sample of one person is certainly insufficient! So is a random sample of 5 people or 10 people or even 100 people. To illustrate the significance of sample size, think about flipping coins and selecting marbles again. The following principles may be demonstrated mathematically, as presented in Chapter 6. They may also be confirmed in practice by getting a whole lot of people together to flip coins and select marbles for a few days! But you probably have better things to do! Therefore, simply think logically about the principles as they are described and convince yourself they make good sense.

Imagine 1,000 people participating in 6 coin-flipping demonstrations. First, each flips a coin 10 times; second, each flips a coin 100 times; third, 500 times; fourth, 1,000; fifth, 3,000; sixth, 5,000. For each of the demonstrations, recording the number of times each of the individual "flippers" gets heads permits observation of a phenomenon critical to understanding probability. Almost exactly 95 percent of the 1,000 flippers fall into these ranges:

| Flips | Number of Heads | Percentage of Heads |
|---|---|---|
| 10 | 2–8 | 20–80 |
| 100 | 40–60 | 40–60 |
| 500 | 225–275 | 45–55 |
| 1,000 | 470–530 | 47–53 |
| 3,000 | 1,440–1,560 | 48–52 |
| 5,000 | 2,425–2,575 | 48.5–51.5 |

Focus on the extremes. Flipping 10 times, expect to get heads pretty close to 5 times. Obviously, do not expect to get heads exactly 5 times, although that outcome will occur more than any other single outcome; the probability of getting heads 10 times or 0 times in 10 flips is extremely slight, but will occur once in a while. In fact, there is about a 5 percent probability that an individual flipping a coin 10 times will get heads 0 times, 1 time, 9 times (same probability as one time), or 10 times (same probability as 0 times). Therefore, with 1,000 people flipping coins 10 times each, about 50 of them will fall *outside* the range of 2–8 heads. Obviously, the probability of getting heads 5,000 times in a row, or not at all, when flipping a coin 5,000 times is vanishingly small to the point of nonexistent. The vast majority of 1,000 flippers will be clustered in a relatively restricted range around 2,500 heads.

Of course, the most significant feature of these patterns is found in the percentages to the right. There is a 95 percent chance that any one flipper will get heads between 20 percent and 80 percent of the time in 10 flips. In 5,000 flips, there is a 95 percent chance of getting heads between 48.5 percent and 51.5 percent of the time. Think like a gambler with lots of common sense. If I tell you I will pay you $10 if I get heads less than 40 percent of the time or more than 60 percent of time in a series of flips, and give you the choice of whether I should flip 10 times or 5,000 times, what is your choice? If you have any common sense, your choice is 10 flips. You probably will not get the $10 although you might. In 5,000, you certainly would not get the $10.

Now imagine a huge jar, with 150 million marbles in it. Of these, 22 million, or 15 percent, are black. The rest are white. Although the coin flippers are dazed, and want to go home, we make them stay for several more days to select marbles randomly. We run five sequences of random selections (100, 500, 1,000, 3,000, 5,000), recording the number of black marbles for each "selector." We discover that almost exactly 95 percent of the selectors fall into the following ranges:

| Draws | Number of Black Marbles | Percentage of Black Marbles |
|---|---|---|
| 100 | 8–22 | 8–22 |
| 500 | 60–90 | 12–18 |
| 1,000 | 130–170 | 13–17 |
| 3,000 | 405–495 | 13.5–16.5 |
| 5,000 | 700–800 | 14–16 |

The logic is precisely the same applied to the coins; convince yourself the patterns make logical sense. *In random sampling from a population (here, 150 million marbles), the percentage of a characteristic appearing in the sample (here, black marbles) will move closer to the true population percentage (here, 15 percent) the larger the sample.*

You have no doubt recognized the significance of these patterns for survey sampling and public opinion polling. With 150 million people over the age of 18 in the United States, and 15 percent of them black, selecting a random sample of 10 people creates a fairly good chance the percentage of blacks in the sample will be a considerable distance from 15 percent. But selecting 1,000 people randomly creates a very good chance that *very close* to 15 percent of the sample will be black.

Further, the principle of *diminishing returns* operates in these patterns. Remember diminishing returns from your economics class? For the surveyor who wishes to employ the principles of randomness to ensure a representative sample, it makes a whole lot more sense to select a sample of 1,000 people than to select a sample of 100 people, because in so doing the range of error around a population characteristic of 50 percent will be reduced from ±10 percent to ±3 percent. But does it make any sense to increase the costs of conducting the survey five-fold (by going from a sample of 1,000 to a sample of 5,000) in order to reduce the error parameter from ±3 percent to ±1.5 percent? Probably not. Investing more resources in sample sizes beyond about 1,000 or so produces "returns" in reduced error parameters at a significantly diminishing rate. Doubling the sample from 500 to 1,000 produces an additional 2 percentage points of reduction on each end of the error parameter at twice the cost. Tripling the sample from 1,000 to 3,000 produces only 1 additional percentage point at triple the cost.

This may be the most widely misunderstood aspect of public opinion polling. We frequently hear people complain, "How can you tell what 150 million citizens think by only interviewing 1,000 of them?" The answer is contained in the previous paragraphs. A sample of 1,500 is much better than a sample of 100. A sample of 3,000 is somewhat better than a sample of 1,500. A sample of 10,000 makes no sense and its costs cannot be justified. Most public opinion surveys interview around 1,000 people, producing a parameter of about ±3 percent. More on this later.

We sometimes also hear the claim, "if there are 150 million people over 18 years of age in the United States and the Gallup poll can determine their opinions by interviewing 2,000 people (.001 percent of 150 million), then determining the attitudes of the 7 million people over 18 years of age in Pennsylvania only requires interviewing about 70 people (.001 percent of 7 million)." Wrong! Reflect on the absurdity. Pursuing this logic, determining the attitudes of 3,500 undergraduates at the University of Scranton requires interviewing less than one of them!

Imagine a jar with 18 million marbles instead of 150 million. Would the above parameters change? No. Imagine a jar with 8 million marbles. Would the parameters change? No. A representative sample of the United States requires about 1,000 randomly selected people; a representative sample of the population of New York State requires about 1,000 randomly selected people; a representative sample of the population of New York City requires about 1,000 randomly selected people. *The size of the population does not alter the required sample size; the parameters outlined earlier are absolute, regardless of population size.* Of course, this rule is relaxed for very small population sizes, those under about 5,000. For example, the parameters would change a bit in sampling the opinions of residents in a town with a population of less than 5,000, or sampling the opinions of students in a college with less than 5,000 enrolled.

An historical example illustrates the importance of size of sample rather than size of population. In the 1936 presidential race, a *Literary Digest* poll predicted that Landon would defeat Roosevelt by a landslide. This prediction was based on a sample of more than 2 million voters, but it was not selected randomly; rather, it was drawn from automobile registration lists! At the same time, George Gallup began random sampling techniques and was able to successfully predict the outcome of the election by selecting only about 1,000 respondents.[1]

## THE NORMAL CURVE REVISITED

The parameters outlined in the coin and marble examples result from the behavior of random probabilities and must be understood by reference to the normal curve, discussed in Chapter 2. Imagine 1,000 people, each flipping a coin 20 times. Obviously, different numbers of people get heads different numbers of times. More people get heads 10 times than get heads any other number of times, although a majority do not get heads 10 times. Very few people get heads 0 times or 20 times. In fact, we can graph the expected proportion of times each outcome occurs among the 1,000 people: 0 heads, 1 head, 2 heads, 3 heads, 4 heads, . . . , 20 heads. As displayed in Figure 5.1, approximately 18 percent of the 1,000 people get heads 20 times, approximately 16 percent get heads 9 times, approximately 16 percent get heads 11 times, approximately 12 percent get heads 8 times, approximately 12 percent get heads 12 times, and so on. Note that the probability of getting heads 9 times is the same as getting heads 11 times (which is the same as getting tails 9 times). Note also that on the "tails" of the curve (under 5 heads, over 15 heads) the probabilities are very small.[2]

Of course, the proportion of people getting different numbers of heads seldom conforms exactly to the percentages recorded. Yet, *over the long run*, they are very close; in other words, the more people flipping, the closer they are. Moreover, the most useful interpretation of these percentages lies in the "ranges." Approximately 50 percent of the

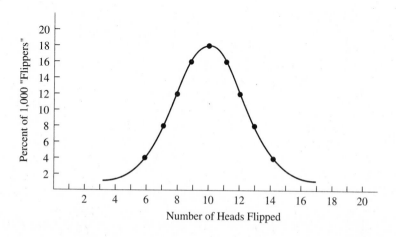

**Figure 5.1**

1,000 people get heads between 9 and 11 times, approximately 74 percent get heads between 8 and 12 times, and so on. Of course, 100 percent get heads between 0 and 20 times.

This, too, may be proven mathematically or demonstrated by getting a whole bunch of people together to flip coins. Again, however, simply think about this normal distribution logically and convince yourself that it makes good sense. Those desiring a more mathematically rigorous, yet clear, explanation of the behavior under discussion may consult the book by Michael Malec mentioned in Note 2.

This example also presents the opportunity to observe a clearer illustration of the statistical definition of the normal curve offered in Chapter 2. Placing the results of the 1,000 people flipping coins 20 times each into a frequency distribution results in something like:

| | | |
|------|-----|------|
| (0)  | 0   | |
| (1)  | 0   | |
| (2)  | 0   | |
| (3)  | 0   | |
| (4)  | 2   | .2% |
| (5)  | 8   | .8% |
| (6)  | 40  | 4 % |
| (7)  | 80  | 8 % |
| (8)  | 120 | 12 % |
| (9)  | 160 | 16 % |
| (10) | 180 | 18 % |
| (11) | 160 | 16 % |
| (12) | 120 | 12 % |
| (13) | 80  | 8 % |
| (14) | 40  | 4 % |
| (15) | 8   | .8% |
| (16) | 2   | .2% |
| (17) | 0   | |
| (18) | 0   | |
| (19) | 0   | |
| (20) | 0   | |

The people flipping the coins are the cases and the number of times each person gets a head is the variable (varying from 0 to 20). This is a normal distribution because, when graphed as in Figure 5.1, it forms a bell-shaped curve. It is also a normal distribution because the mode, median, and mean all take on the same value: 10. Ten occurs most frequently, category 10 contains the five-hundredth and five-hundred-first cases (counting up or down) and computation of the mean results in the value 10. Observe that the pattern of deviation from the mean is the same both above and below the mean. In a normal distribution, the peak of the curve contains the most cases (mode), there is an equal number of cases on either side of the peak (median), and each side slopes downward in conformity with the principle of the balanced deviation discussed in Chapter 2 (mean). The closer the mode, median, and mean, the more normally distributed a variable. When the mode, median, and mean are identical, the distribution is perfectly normal.

What would happen to the shape of the curve in Figure 5.1 if each person flipped a coin 200 times instead of 20 times? What would happen to the shape of the curve if each person were flipping a coin 10 times instead of 20 times? Reflect on the answers to these two questions and consider the implications of the answers for a "sample" of 10 flips, a "sample" of 20 flips, and a "sample" of 200 flips.

## THE SAMPLING DISTRIBUTION

Public opinion surveys, such as the New Jersey survey discussed in Chapter 4, commonly ask respondents to "rate" public officials. Suppose we wish to survey the population of California for the purpose of determining the popularity of Governor Wilson. Suppose that among all the residents of California, 60 percent feel that he is "doing a good job." Of course, the only way of actually knowing what proportion of a population holds a given opinion would be to interview everyone in the population; these proportions are always estimated with survey techniques. But assume for a moment that the *true* percentage holding this opinion in California is 60 percent.

Now suppose 1,000 different polls of 20 randomly selected residents of California are conducted. Sound familiar? If each of the 1,000 pollsters selected their 20 citizens randomly and asked each citizen if they thought Wilson was doing a good job, and if the percent were recorded for each of the 1,000 pollsters, the result would look something like Figure 5.2. This is referred to as a *sampling distribution*. The result would be very predictable because random probabilities behave in a very predictable fashion. Again, the interpretation lies in the ranges. Approximately 75 percent of these polls would produce a percentage between 50 and 70, approximately 91 percent would produce a percentage between 45 and 75, and so forth.

Now suppose each of these 1,000 pollsters interviewed 1,000 randomly selected residents. The normal curve would "pull in" around 60 percent, as indicated in Figure

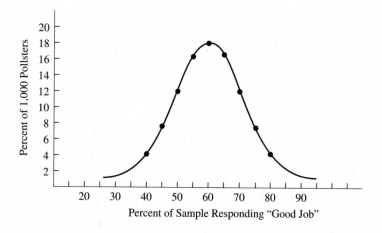

**Figure 5.2**

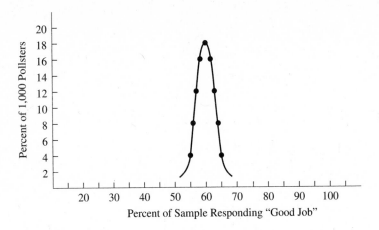

**Figure 5.3**

5.3. The larger the sample of respondents, the taller and narrower the curve; the smaller the sample of respondents, the shorter and flatter the curve. Logic and common sense dictate that larger samples yield less variation around the true population percentage, while smaller samples yield more variation.

Figure 5.4 presents a clearer way of illustrating this phenomenon. The 1,000 pollsters are the cases and the percentage approving of the job the governor is doing are the values of the variable. Suppose each value of the variable in Figure 5.3 was transformed into a $z$ score, discussed in Chapter 2. The standard deviation of the recorded sample percentages is approximately 1.5. Therefore, the $z$ score of 1 lies at about 61.5 percent and the $z$ score of 2 lies at about 63 percent; the $z$ score of −1 lies at 58.5 percent and the $z$ score of −2 lies at 57 percent. Recall from Chapter 2 that approximately 68 percent of the cases (here polls) fall within ±1 standard deviation of the mean (here 60 percent, the true population percentage) and approximately 95 percent of the cases fall within ±2 standard deviations of the mean. Therefore, 68 percent of the polls taken produce approval ratings of between 58.5 and 61.5, while 95 percent of the polls taken produce approval ratings of between 57 and 63. *The probability that any one poll of 1,000 randomly selected respondents is within ±3 percent of the true population percent (here, 60 percent) is 95 percent.*

## SUMMARY

Inferences, or generalizations, from samples to populations are frequently employed by political scientists and political practitioners engaged in survey research and public opinion polling, in which the samples are typically drawn from very large populations. If a large enough sample of cases is selected randomly from a population, that sample will be representative of that population. If the sample is representative, generalizations to the population are warranted. If the sample of cases is not selected randomly, or is too small, the sample is biased and generalizations to the population are unwarranted.

Beyond a certain point, the advantage of sample size is lost. While it makes a great deal of sense to randomly select 1,000 people from a population instead of 100 people,

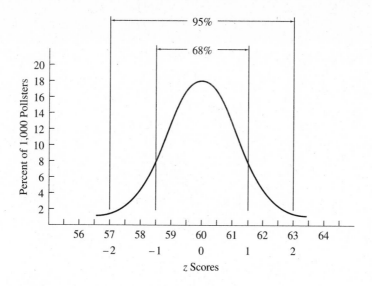

**Figure 5.4**

it makes little sense to randomly select 10,000 instead of 1,000. These principles hold, regardless of population size. A random sample of 1,000 people from a population of 150 million people will be just as representative of those 150 million people as a random sample of 1,000 drawn from a population of 10,000 will be of those 10,000.

For a sample to be random, each of the cases in the population must have an equal chance of ending up in the sample. While selecting a purely random sample is usually not possible, very sophisticated techniques are currently available that create conditions approaching randomness. And, in any event, an understanding of the behavior of random probabilities is essential to an understanding of the inferential statistics employed to assess the quality of generalizations from samples to populations.

When random samples are drawn repeatedly from a population, and the percentage of the cases in each sample sharing a given characteristic (gender, race, religion, party identification, issue position, etc.) is recorded, those recorded percentages form a normal distribution around the true population percentage for that characteristic. Of course, repeated samples are never actually selected, and these sampling distributions never actually charted. However, this phenomenon permits estimation of the standard range of error likely in a sample percentage for any single sample, if selected randomly. We now apply these principles to the computation of inferential statistics for single variables.

## NOTES

1. See Earl Babbie, *Survey Research Methods,* Belmont, CA: Wadsworth, 1973, pp. 74–75.
2. This particular example, including Figure 5.1 and the frequency distribution on page 98, is adapted from Michael Malec, *Essential Statistics for Social Research,* Philadelphia: Lippincott, 1977, pp. 62–68.

# Chapter
# *6*

# *Inferential Statistics for Single Variables*

*J*ust as descriptive statistics may be computed for single variables, so too may inferential statistics. Univariate inferential statistics are commonly employed to evaluate measures of centrality computed in samples of cases: percentages in nominal and ordinal frequency distributions, and means in arrays of interval data. These univariate inferential statistics contain three elements: a sample statistic, a population parameter, and a level of confidence.

The *sample statistic* is the measure of centrality computed for the sample data: percentages or means. The *population parameter* is the range of estimated potential population variation from the sample statistic; the probability that the population statistic (percentage or mean) falls within that range may be precisely specified. This probability is the *level of confidence*. Most political scientists and political practitioners employ the 95 percent level of confidence—meaning that there are 95 chances in 100 that the population statistic falls within the parameter. This is also referred to as the ".05 level of confidence," indicating 5 chances in 100 that the population statistic does *not* fall within the parameter. Each of these three elements may be illustrated by drawing on the subjects covered in Chapter 5.

# POPULATION PARAMETERS FOR PERCENTAGES AND MEANS

When a random sample is selected from a population, measures computed for the sample will be different from the true population values. For example, the percentage of people in a random sample identifying with the Democratic party will be different from the percentage of Democratic identifiers in the population from which the sample was selected; the mean income of the people in a random sample will be different from the mean income of the people in the population from which the sample was selected. In other words, using the sample statistic as an estimate of the true population value always results in error. However, the behavior of random probabilities is such that, over "the long run," or over repeated selections of random samples from the same population, the average amount of error is predictable— there is an ordinary amount of variation from the true population value, referred to as *standard error*.

## Estimating Percentages

Employ the following equation to build a population parameter, at the .05 level of confidence, around a percentage computed in a random sample:

$$\sqrt{\frac{P\,(Q)}{N}} \times 2$$

$P$ is the sample percentage, $Q = 100 - P$, and $N$ is the number of cases in the sample.

For example, suppose we wish to estimate the percentage of New York State residents identifying with the Democratic party from a random sample of 1,500 residents. Suppose 50 percent of our sample, or 750, identify themselves as Democrats:

$$\sqrt{(50)\,(50)\,/\,1500} = \sqrt{1.6}$$

$$= 1.3 \times 2 = 2.6$$

The range of error around 50 percent is 2.6 percent. Therefore, we are 95 percent confident that, had we interviewed *the entire population* of New York State residents, between 47.4 percent and 52.6 percent of them would have identified themselves as Democrats.

Use the equation to confirm that in a random sample of only 100 people (50 percent of whom are identified as Democrats), the population parameter is 40 percent to 60 percent. And confirm that in a random sample of 5,000 people, the population parameter is 48.6 percent to 51.4 percent. Obviously, the principle of diminishing returns is operative. With a sample statistic of 50 percent, the population parameters produced by various sample sizes are:

| | |
|---|---|
| 100 | 40%–60% |
| 1,500 | 47.4%–52.6% |
| 2,000 | 47.8%–52.2% |
| 5,000 | 48.6%–51.4% |

In fact, $\sqrt{P\,(Q)\,/\,N}$ is the standard deviation of the sampling distribution around a population percentage of $P$. As we know, the percentage of respondents considering themselves Democrats recorded for repeated random samples from a population in which 50 percent consider themselves Democrats will form a normal distribution around 50 percent. The mean of these recorded percentages is 50 percent. In addition, computing the standard deviation of these recorded percentages produces $\sqrt{P\,(Q)\,/\,N}$. Recall that, in a normal distribution, 95 percent of the cases (individual polls in a sampling distribution) fall within ±2 standard deviations of the mean of the distribution. Although repeated samples are never actually selected, and sampling distributions never actually graphed, we know that any single random sample (poll) has a 95 percent chance of falling within ±2 standard deviations of the true population percentage.

This is why $\sqrt{P\,(Q)\,/\,N}$ is multiplied by 2 then subtracted and added to the sample percentage. If it was not multiplied by 2, the resulting parameter would be narrower, but only capture about 68 percent of all random samples; if it were multiplied by 3, the parameter would be wider and capture 99 percent of all random samples. In the latter instance, the level of confidence is .01. We multiply by 2 since the accepted level of confidence among political scientists and political practitioners is .05. We want to be 95 percent certain the population percentage falls within the range of standard error. The principles are precisely those reflected in the coin and marble examples given in Chapter 5. Indeed, this equation was used to generate the error parameters in those examples.

Obviously, the primary determinant of the range of error in a random sample is the size of that sample. Recall that, as sample size increases, the normal distribution around the true population percentage becomes tighter and narrower. In the "PQ equation," as the denominator (sample size) becomes larger, the resulting parameter becomes smaller.

A second determinant is the size of the sample statistic. Sample statistics close to 50 percent produce wider population parameters; those closer to 0 percent or 100 percent, smaller parameters. Note how the numerator of the equation becomes smaller (making the resulting parameter smaller) with sample percentages further away from 50 percent:

$$50 \times 50 = 2{,}500$$

$$40 \times 60 = 2{,}400$$

$$30 \times 70 = 2{,}100$$

$$20 \times 80 = 1{,}600$$

$$10 \times 90 = 900$$

This effect occurs because there is less room for error when the population percentage is very small or very large—when there is a high degree of homogeneity in the population; in other words, when a very large proportion of the population shares the characteristic under consideration.

For example, suppose we asked 1,000 randomly selected citizens over 18 years of age in the United States whether they believed Saddam Hussein was doing a good job as the leader of Iraq. Suppose 4 percent said yes:

$$\sqrt{(4)\,(96)\,/\,1,000} = \sqrt{.4}$$

$$= .6 \times 2 = 1.2$$

The potential range of error from the four percent is 1.2 percent. We would be 95 percent certain that, had we interviewed all citizens over 18 years of age, between 2.8 and 5.2 percent would have said Saddam was doing a good job. Quite simply, the range of error for very small or very large percentages is restricted since there is less room for variation along the sampling distribution. A percentage "squeezing up against" 0 or up against 100 does not have as much of a range in which to diverge as a percentage near the middle of the distribution. For example, had the sample statistic been 40 percent here, the parameter would have been 3 percent instead of 1.2 percent.

Finally, note that the equation for computing population parameters for percentages is *binomial*—it evaluates individual sample percentages against the standard of 100 percent by multiplying the individual percentage, $P$, by $Q$ $(100 - P)$. The sum of $P$ and $Q$ is always 100. Therefore, the equation may be used to evaluate any individual percentage, even if the nominal or ordinal variable under consideration has more than one value. For example, suppose we conduct a public opinion poll on the presidential preferences of 700 randomly selected citizens in September, 1992, with the following result:

| Perot | 15% |
|-------|-----|
| Bush | 30% |
| Clinton | 45% |
| Undecided | 10% |

The binomial equation may be used to evaluate any one of these individual percentages: A population parameter may be constructed around Perot's 15 percent, around Bush's 30 percent, and around Clinton's 45 percent. Indeed, a population parameter may be constructed around the percentage of undecided:

$$\sqrt{(10)\,(90)\,/\,700} = \sqrt{1.3}$$

$$= 1.1 \times 2 = 2.2$$

We would be 95 percent confident that between 7.8 percent and 12.2 percent of all citizens were undecided at the time the survey was conducted.

## Estimating Means

Employ the following equation to build a population parameter, at the .05 level of confidence, around a mean computed in a random sample:

$$\frac{\text{sample } \sigma}{\sqrt{N}} \times 2$$

The numerator is the standard deviation of the interval level variable in the sample, the mean of which is being evaluated. $N$ is the number of cases in the sample.

For example, suppose we wish to estimate mean yearly household income in the state of Pennsylvania. We select a random sample of 400 households and compute the mean and standard deviation of income for that sample, discovering the mean is $31,500 and the standard deviation is 1,500:

$$\frac{1,500}{\sqrt{400}} \times 2 = \frac{1,500}{20} \times 2$$

$$= 75 \times 2 = 150$$

The range of potential error around 31,500 is 150. Therefore, we are 95 percent confident that, had we collected data for all households in Pennsylvania, the mean income would have been between $31,350 and $31,650

Use the equation to confirm that, in a random sample of only 100 people (with the same mean and standard deviation), the population parameter is $31,200 to $31,800. And confirm that, in a random sample of 5,000 people, the population parameter is $31,458 to $31,542. Obviously, the principle of diminishing returns is operative here, as well.

The behavior of this equation is very similar to the behavior of the equation for percentages, since this equation is equal to the standard deviation of the sampling distribution around a population mean, which also forms a normal curve. Again, the primary determinant of the range of error in a random sample is the size of that sample. In the previous equation, as the denominator (sample size) becomes larger, the resulting parameter value becomes smaller.

A second determinant is, again, the homogeneity of the population for the variable under consideration, as measured here by the standard deviation of that variable in the sample. If the standard deviation were 0, there would be no error, because all the cases in the sample would take on the same value on the variable. Obviously, if we selected 400 households randomly and every one of them had an income of $31,500, there is an extremely high probability that every household in the population has an income of $31,500! This is equivalent to getting 0 when multiplying $P \times Q$ in the equation for percentages, resulting when the sample percentage is either 0 or 100. For either equation, a numerator of 0 indicates the likelihood of complete homogeneity in the population.

## APPLICATION OF UNIVARIATE INFERENTIAL STATISTICS

Recall that Appendix B contains a press release distributed in New Jersey by the *Star Ledger*/Eagleton Poll on November 1, 1992. Recall also the Background Memo begins with a description of the manner in which the sample was drawn, stating a random sample of 801 respondents was interviewed between October 23 and October 29. It states, "The figures in this release are based on the sample size of of 801 likely voters and are subject to a sampling error of about ±3.5 percent. . . " Of course, many questions were asked in this survey and percentages for many different population characteristics are reported (sex, race, occupation, party, vote intention, etc.).

Conventionally, sampling error is reported as if the sample statistic were 50 percent since, as previously demonstrated, this produces the widest parameter. The actual error parameter for any given sample percentage will, as we also know, be dependent on the sample percentage's distance from 50 percent. Yet, it will never be larger than the parameter for 50 percent. Therefore, in this random sample of 801, the *most* that the sampling error will be for any given population characteristic is 3.5 percent.

The memo also states, "Sampling error is the probable difference in results between interviewing everyone in the population versus a scientific sample taken from that population." In other words, there is a certain probability that the percentages reported in the press release will be different from the percentages that would have resulted from interviewing the entire population. Here, there is a 95 percent chance that any percentages reported for this sample will be no more than 3.5 percent above or 3.5 percent below the true population percentage.

The memo also states, "In addition, some results are presented for 580 'probable voters.' These are likely voters who have the greatest probability of actually voting on election day. The sampling error for this group is about ±4 percentage points." This is a very important statement, in that it alerts us to the fact the number of cases used to compute the sampling error for a "subpopulation" in a random sample must be the number of cases in the subpopulation rather than in the entire sample. Here, although 801 were interviewed, only 580 were probable voters. For example, in using this sample to estimate the percentage of Democrats in New Jersey, 801 would be employed in the equation. However, in using this sample to estimate the percentage of Democrats among *probable voters* in New Jersey, 580 would be employed.

As another example of this very important principle, note on page 186 that 654 of all respondents are white and 127 are nonwhite. Thirty-eight percent of the whites indicated an intention to vote for Clinton and 64 percent of the nonwhites indicated such an intention. Estimating the sampling error for whites employs 654, producing a parameter of about 3.8 percent (34.2 percent to 41.8 percent of whites intend to vote for Clinton). Estimating the sampling error for nonwhites employs 127, producing a parameter of about 8.5 percent (55.5 percent to 72.5 percent of nonwhites intend to vote for Clinton). This parameter is much wider since it is based on a random sample of only 127 nonwhites.

In those instances where survey researchers and public opinion pollsters select very large random samples of several thousand respondents, it is usually because they wish to analyze subpopulations. For example, a random sample of 7,000 New Jersey residents would likely result in inclusion of about 1,000 nonwhites. The 1,000 could then be used to construct parameters for nonwhites. Another strategy for analyzing subpopulations is to "oversample" those subpopulations. One might interview 1,000 people randomly, including about 150 nonwhites, then select a separate random sample of 500 nonwhites (this sample would be drawn only from the population of nonwhites). Characteristics of the entire population would be based on the 1,000 only; characteristics of nonwhites would be based on 650 respondents (the original 150 plus the 500 from the oversampling). This would be less costly than randomly sampling 7,000 people. Of course, either strategy is rather costly; therefore, analysis of subpopulations is not normally undertaken.

As noted in Chapter 4, virtually all candidates for national and statewide office now conduct opinion surveys as a routine part of their campaign strategies, and the information these surveys generate is extremely useful in conducting these campaigns. Of course, the information is useless unless the sample of respondents interviewed is selected randomly and thereby representative of the entire population. Therefore, an understanding of probabilities, the sampling distribution, and the equations employed to make inferences to the population is essential to informed campaign research, as well as any other variety of survey research or public opinion polling.

Further, the principles outlined, and the equations discussed, apply regardless of the actual questions asked by surveyors. They apply to virtually *any* population characteristic. For example, the *El Paso Times,* on January 5, 1986, reported the results of a "Texas Poll" conducted by the Public Policy Resources Laboratory at Texas A&M University, designed to determine Texans' favorite football team![1] The article stated:

> This Texas Poll is based on telephone interviews conducted in November of 1,000 adults around the state. The sample of telephone numbers called was selected by a computer by Survey Sampling of Westport, Conn., from a complete list of telephone exchanges in Texas. In each household contacted, one resident was selected randomly for an interview.
>
> In theory, in 19 cases out of 20, the results based on the samples will differ no more than 3 percentage points in either direction from what would have been obtained by interviewing all adult Texans.

A random sample was selected of all adults in Texas, and the sampling error at the 95 percent level of confidence was reported (19 out of 20). Again, the sampling error was computed using a sample statistic of 50 percent, to produce a conservative estimate for all the percentages reported. Eighty-two percent of the sample said the Dallas Cowboys were their favorite team and 14 percent named the Houston Oilers. Therefore, in January 1986, there was at least a 95 percent chance that the Dallas Cowboys were the favorite team of between 79 percent and 85 percent of all adult Texans and that the Houston Oilers were the favorite of between 11 percent and 17 percent of all adult Texans.

The article also reported that 51 percent of the sample from the Houston–Gulf Coast area indicated the Cowboys were their favorite and 43 percent, the Oilers. However, the article neglected to point out that the sampling error is much larger for these percentages, since, in a random sample of 1,000 Texans, only about 110 would be from the Gulf Coast area, which contains about 11 percent of the state population. Indeed, Dallas support in the Houston area could be much lower than indicated, and Oiler support much higher. This is a flaw in the manner in which the data were reported.

# SUMMARY

When a random sample is selected from a population, the univariate descriptive statistics computed for the sample (percentages or means) will be different from the true population values. However, there is a predictable amount of variation from the true population value over repeated selections of random samples. Univariate inferential statistics employed to estimate this variation are comprised of three elements: a sample statistic (the univariate descriptive statistic computed for the sample of cases), a population parameter (the range of estimated variation constructed around the sample statistic), and a level of confidence (the probability that the population value falls within the parameter). The .05 level of confidence, or 95 percent probability, is conventionally used.

The population parameter at the .05 level of confidence is wider (more error) for small samples and narrower (less error) for large samples. However, the principle of diminishing returns applies. Larger samples result in narrower parameters at an increasingly diminishing rate. In addition, the number of cases used to compute the sampling error for a "subpopulation" in a random sample must be the number of cases in the subpopulation rather than the total number of cases randomly selected. For example, the parameter for some opinion or characteristic of the black population in a random sample of U.S. citizens (a subpopulation of whom is black) must be based on the number of blacks in the sample, not the total number of people selected.

The principles outlined only apply when the sample of respondents is selected randomly and is thereby representative of the entire population. And they apply regardless of the actual questions asked by surveyors. While survey research and public opinion polling is obviously used frequently by candidates for public office and by the media reporting on electoral politics, their most common use currently is probably by corporations conducting what is referred to as "market research." Large corporations continually conduct extensive surveys of individuals in selected markets to determine their preferences for various sorts of consumer products. It only appears that the media do most of the surveying of the population, since they always report the results of their polls—they survey to make news. Market research is always done "in house" and the results are proprietary, so the general public never sees them.

Further, survey research is now very commonly conducted by government agencies at both the state and national level for the purpose of determining citizen needs in selected policy areas and for the purpose of determining whether or not various policies are achieving their objectives. For example, it might be conducted to determine what proportion of the eligible population is actually receiving all of the social security benefits they are entitled to, or to determine the incidence of alcohol or drug abuse in a selected population. We discuss the policy applications of survey research in more detail in Chapter 9 and Chapter 10.

# NOTE

1. The *El Paso Times,* January 5, 1986, p. 2-D.

# Chapter
# 7
# Inferential Statistics for Relationships Between Variables

*J*ust as descriptive statistics may be computed for relationships between variables, so too may inferential statistics. Bivariate inferential statistics are commonly employed to evaluate statistical relationships between variables in samples of cases: contingency tables for nominal and ordinal data, and Pearson's correlation coefficient for arrays of interval data. They are employed to determine the likelihood that statistical relationships found in a sample exist in the population from which the sample was selected.

Suppose, for example, we have a random sample of 1,000 citizens over 18 years of age in the United States and have uncovered a number of statistical relationships in the sample by constructing several contingency tables and computing several Pearson's correlation coefficients. Suppose we discover, in one of our contingency tables, that blacks more likely consider themselves Democrats than whites (by a margin of 80 percent to 50 percent). We also discover, in one of our Pearson's correlations (a coefficient of .4), that the older a person is, the more times he or she has voted within the last two years. Bivariate inferential statistics permit us to determine the likelihood that, had we interviewed everyone over 18 years of age in the U.S. population, blacks would in fact have been more "Democratic" than whites (a difference in percentages between the races) and older people would in fact have voted more within the last two years (a positive correlation coefficient).

# ESTIMATING DIFFERENCES OF PROPORTIONS: CHI SQUARE

For contingency tables of nominal or ordinal data computed from random samples of cases, bivariate inferential statistics are employed to evaluate differences in percentages, or *differences in proportions.* In our example, is there, *in the population from which the sample was selected,* a difference in the proportion of the blacks identifying Democratic and the proportion of whites identifying Democratic? Understanding the computation of bivariate inferential statistics for differences of proportions again necessitates understanding statistical probability.

## Probability Revisited: Special Multiplication Rule

Recall that the probability event *A* will occur (*PrA*) is equal to the number of times we expect it to occur ("outcomes"; *n*) divided by the number of times there exist the conditions making its occurrence possible ("tries"; *N*). The probability "heads" will occur in a coin flip is .5. Flipping a coin 100 times (*N*), each time creating a condition under which it is possible for heads to occur, leads to the expectation of 50 heads (*n*). *PrA* = 50 / 100 =.5 or 50 percent. Flips (*N*) is the number of cases; each case takes on the value of either heads or tails; the numerator of the equation (*n*) equals the number of cases expected to take on the value of heads.

If event *A* and event *B* are *statistically independent,* the probability that *both* will occur equals $Pr(A) \times Pr(B)$. Event *A* and event *B* are statistically independent if the occurrence of *A* does not alter the likelihood of *B* occurring, and vice versa. For example, the probability of flipping heads twice in a row is .5 × .5 = .25 = 25 percent. The outcomes of the flips are statistically independent; the probability of heads on the second flip is .5, regardless of the outcome on the first flip.

The probability of drawing an ace randomly from a deck of cards is 4 / 52 = .075 = 7.5 percent. The probability of drawing a black card randomly is 26 / 52 = .5 = 50 percent. Think of cards as cases; think of values and color as variables. Predict the likelihood that a randomly selected case takes on the value ace and the color black. Predict .075 × .5 = .0385 = about 4 percent. Value and color are statistically independent—the aces in the deck are as likely to be black as red and black cards in the deck are as likely to be aces as any other single value. Of course, we know here that the probability of randomly selecting a black ace is 2 / 52 without using the special multiplication rule, because we know there are two black aces in the deck. However, the most important applications of this rule are employed in the absence of such complete knowledge.

Consider two other examples. Suppose 51 percent of the population of the United States is female and 15 percent is black. The probability of randomly selecting one black female from this population is .15 × .51 = .076 = about 8 percent. Race and gender are statistically independent in the population: blacks are not more or less likely to be males than females; females are not more or less likely to be blacks than whites. Now suppose 40 percent of the population lives in urban areas and 15 percent of the population is black. Is the probability of randomly selecting one black urban dweller .15 × .4 = .06 = 6 percent? Probably not. Why? Because place of residence and race are probably not statistically independent in the population. Blacks more likely live in urban than rural areas (the probability of living in an urban area is likely dependent on whether one is black). Therefore, *more* than 6 percent of the population is both black and urban; indeed, if all blacks lived in urban areas, the probability of being both black and urban would be 15 percent because the additional criterion of being urban would not screen out any blacks.

## Computation and Interpretation of Chi Square

Chi square is the bivariate inferential statistic employed to evaluate differences of proportions in contingency tables—it is a statistic used to determine whether or not differences of proportions in a random sample indicate similar differences of proportions in the population from which that sample was selected. The computation of chi square is based on comparison of the proportions (percentages) in a contingency table constructed from a random sample we would *expect* to find under the *assumption of statistical independence* in the population (expected values) and the proportions (percentages) we actually *observe* when we construct the contingency table from our sample of cases (observed values).

For an understanding of expected values, consider again the example of race and gender, consulting Table 7.1. In a random sample of 1,000 people, 490 or 49 percent of whom are male, 510 or 51 percent of whom are female, 150 or 15 percent of whom are black, and 850 or 85 percent of whom are white, how many would we *expect* to be black and male, white and male, black and female, white and female? We would expect about 74 of the 1,000 to be black males (49 percent of 150) and about 417 of the 1,000 to be white males (49 percent of 850); if race and gender are statistically independent, and 49 percent of the population is male, then 49 percent of the black population will be male and 49 percent of the white population will be male. We would expect about 76 of the 1,000 to be black females (51 percent of 150) and about 433 of the 1,000 to be white females (51 percent of 850); if race and gender are statistically independent, and 51 percent of the population is female, then 51 percent of the black population will be female and 51 percent of the white population will be female.

To compute expected values for each cell in a contingency table, multiply the total number of cases in the column by the total number of cases in the row and divide the result by the total number of cases in the table. In Table 7.1, the expected number of black males = (150 × 490) / 1,000 = 73.5; white males = (850 × 490) / 1,000 = 416.5; black females = (150 × 510) / 1,000 = 76.5; white females = (850 × 490) / 1,000 = 433.5.

When expected values are very close to observed values, the chi square statistic is close to 0, indicating little likelihood that any difference of proportions found in the

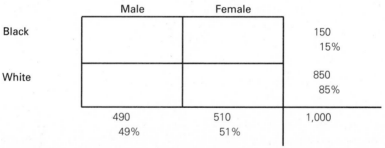

Table 7.1

sample also exists in the population. The further away the expected values are from the observed values, the further away chi square is from 0, indicating an increasing likelihood that any difference of proportions found in the sample also exist in the population.

Consider Table 7.2: Suppose we randomly selected 200 people from the population to determine if females are more likely to consider themselves Democrats than are males. Suppose further, for simplicity, that the random sample contains 100 Democrats and 100 Republicans as well as 100 males and 100 females. Imagine, as in Table 7.2(a), that 52 percent of the males are Republicans, compared to 48 percent of the females. What is the likelihood that this difference between 52 percent and 48 percent (comparing across the rows) in the sample indicates a difference between male and female party identification in the population from which the sample was selected—that these two variables (gender and party identification) are statistically related in the population rather than statistically independent? Alternately, imagine, as in Table 7.2(b), that 80 percent of the males are Republicans, compared to 20 percent of the females. What is

**(a)**

|  | Male | Female |  |
|---|---|---|---|
| Republican | 52<br>52% | 48<br>48% | 100<br>50% |
| Democrat | 48<br>48% | 52<br>52% | 100<br>50% |
|  | 100<br>50% | 100<br>50% | 200 |

**(b)**

|  |  |  |
|---|---|---|
| 80<br>80% | 20<br>20% |  |
| 20<br>20% | 80<br>80% |  |
|  |  | 200 |

**(c)**

|  |  |  |
|---|---|---|
| 50<br>50% | 50<br>50% |  |
| 50<br>50% | 50<br>50% |  |
|  |  | 200 |

Table 7.2

the likelihood that this difference indicates a difference in the population? Table 7.2(c) displays the expected values for each example—50 cases in each cell.

The equation for chi square is:

$$\Sigma \left( \frac{(f_o - f_e)^2}{f_e} \right)$$

For each cell in a contingency table of observed values constructed from a random sample, square the difference between observed $(f_o)$ and expected $(f_e)$ values, then divide each result by the expected value. Next, sum the overall cell results—the number of expressions summed equals the number of cells.

For Table 7.2a:

$$(52 - 50)^2 / 50 = 4 / 50 = .08$$

$$(48 - 50)^2 / 50 = 4 / 50 = .08$$

$$(48 - 50)^2 / 50 = 4 / 50 = .08$$

$$(52 - 50)^2 / 50 = 4 / 50 = \underline{.08}$$
$$.32$$

For Table 7.2b:

$$(80 - 50)^2 / 50 = 900 / 50 = 18$$

$$(20 - 50)^2 / 50 = 900 / 50 = 18$$

$$(20 - 50)^2 / 50 = 900 / 50 = 18$$

$$(80 - 50)^2 / 50 = 900 / 50 = \underline{18}$$
$$72$$

In instances where there are only four cells ($2 \times 2$ tables) it is not unusual for each expression in the computation of chi square to be identical. Each expression is .08 in the first example and 18 in the second example. In larger tables, this is often not the case, as we shall see.

As previously noted, when observed and expected values are similar, chi square is close to 0; when observed and expected values are dissimilar, chi square moves away from 0. Had Table 7.2(a) been the result of an actual random sample, the observed values would indicate little likelihood of differences between males and females in the population from which the sample was selected. There would not be that much deviation of what was observed from what would be expected "by chance." Had Table 7.2(b) been the result, it would indicate a high probability of differences in the population. The deviation of what was observed from what would be expected "by chance" would indicate that factors beyond "chance" were operating—that there was likely a relationship between the two variables in the population. Hence, chi square may be used to infer the likelihood that two variables are either statistically related or statistically independent in a population. More specifically, we may establish the "chance" that a particular value of chi square would result if two variables are statistically independent, or unrelated.

In order to precisely specify this chance, we must first establish the *degrees of freedom,* the number of additional pieces of information needed to fill in the cells of a contingency table if we know the row totals and the column totals. For example, in Table 7.1, we know the row totals are 490 (males) and 510 (females) and we know the column totals are 150 (black) and 850 (white). If we know that 74 cases are black males, then we *also* know that 416 cases are white males and then we know that 434 cases are white females, and 76 are black females. The entire table can be filled out with knowledge of the number of cases in one cell; the table has one degree of freedom. The equation for determining degrees of freedom is $(r - 1)(c - 1)$ where $r$ is the number of rows and $c$ is the number of columns. In a $2 \times 2$ table such as Table 7.1, degrees of freedom $= (2 - 1)(2 - 1) = 1$.

Once we know the degrees of freedom, we may evaluate the chi square statistic by consulting a *chi square table,* found in most statistics texts:

| df | .10 | .05 | .02 | .01 |
|---|---|---|---|---|
| 1 | 2.706 | 3.841 | 5.412 | 6.635 |
| 2 | 4.605 | 5.991 | 7.824 | 9.210 |
| 3 | 6.251 | 7.815 | 9.837 | 11.341 |
| 4 | 7.779 | 9.488 | 11.668 | 13.277 |
| 5 | 9.236 | 11.070 | 13.388 | 15.086 |
| 6 | 10.645 | 12.592 | 15.033 | 16.812 |
| 7 | 12.017 | 14.067 | 16.622 | 18.475 |
| 8 | 13.362 | 15.507 | 18.168 | 20.090 |

*Source:* Table is adapted from Fisher & Yates: *Statistical Tables for Biological, Agricultural and Medical Research,* published by Longman Group UK Limited, 1974. We are grateful to the Longman Group UK Ltd., on behalf of the Litrary Executor of the late Sir Ronald A Fisher, F.R.S. & Dr. Frank Yates F.R.S. for permision to reproduce from *STATISTICAL TABLES FOR BIOLOGICAL, AGRICULTURAL AND MEDICAL RESEARCH 6th/e (1974).*

*Levels of significance* are listed across the top. These are analogous to the levels of confidence discussed in Chapter 6. They indicate the probability that for a contingency table of a particular size (degrees of freedom) constructed from a random sample, the percentages for the population from which the sample was selected (when compared across the rows of a contingency table) would be different from one another. Again, we employ the .05 level of significance—we want to be 95 percent certain that if the contingency table was constructed for the entire population, there would be differences in percentages. At 1 degree of freedom, chi square must be at least 3.841 to be 95 percent confident of differences in the population.[*]

---

[*] The chi square statistic has a sampling distribution, just as single percentages have such a distribution. In repeated random samples for which there was *no* difference in proportions in a $2 \times 2$ table, 95 percent of those samples would generate chi square statistics under 3.841 and only 5 percent would generate chi square statistics over 3.841. Therefore, with any chi square over 3.841 for a $2 \times 2$ table we can be at least 95 percent confident that the variables are *not* statistically independent in the population—that there is a relationship between the variables.

Return to Table 7.2. In Table 7.2(a), chi square = .32. This value is very close to 0, indicating that the observed and expected values are not dissimilar and that there is little likelihood of differences in party identification between males and females in the population from which the sample was selected. Since chi square is less than 3.841, we cannot be 95 percent certain that such differences exist. The percentages in the table are very close to what we would expect to occur "by chance."

In Table 7.2(b), on the other hand, chi square = 72. This value is very large, indicating that the observed and expected values are very dissimilar and that it is very unlikely that this large a difference could have arisen by chance. Since the chi square is larger than 3.841, we can be at least 95 percent certain that such differences exist. Indeed, this chi square gives us confidence well beyond the .01 level; we are a good deal more than 99 percent certain of a relationship in the population.

## Two Examples

Recall from Chapter 4 that we randomly selected 400 University of Scranton undergraduates from a population of about 3,500. In Table 4.2, we discovered that, in the sample of 400, Business and Natural Science majors were more likely to consider themselves Republicans while Humanities and Social Science majors were more likely to consider themselves Democrats. Table 7.3 demonstrates computation of chi square to determine if these differences between majors in the sample may be inferred to the population.

Table 7.3(a) displays the expected values, computed from the row totals (148 Democrats, 156 Republicans, 96 Other) and the column totals (125 Business majors, 140 Natural Science majors, 112 Social Science majors, and 23 Humanities majors). For example, the expected number of Democratic Humanities majors (extreme upper right cell) is $(148 \times 23) / 400 = 8.5$. In other words, in a random sample containing 400 cases, 148 of whom are Democratic and 23 of whom are Humanities majors, we would expect, if major and party are statistically independent in the population, about 8 or 9 Democratic Humanities majors.

Table 7.3(b) contains the observed values: the actual distribution of data in the contingency table we constructed from our sample. We may now compute the chi square statistic by taking the difference between the expected and observed values for each cell, squaring it, dividing by the expected value, and adding the results together for all 12 cells. There are 12 expressions to be added together:

$$(11 - 8.5)^2 / 8.5 = 6.25 / 8.5 = .74$$

$$(49 - 41.4)^2 / 41.4 = 57.8 / 41.4 = 1.4$$

$$(46 - 51.8)^2 / 51.8 = 33.6 / 51.8 = .65$$

$$(42 - 46.3)^2 / 46.3 = 18.5 / 46.3 = .4$$

$$(5 - 9)^2 / 9 = 16 / 9 = 1.8$$

$$(32 - 43.7)^2 / 43.7 = 136.9 / 43.7 = 3.1$$

$$(60 - 54.6)^2 / 54.6 = 29.2 / 54.6 = .53$$

**(a)**

| | Business | Natural Science | Social Science | Humanities | |
|---|---|---|---|---|---|
| Democrat | 46.3 | 51.8 | 41.4 | 8.5 | 148 |
| Republican | 48.8 | 54.6 | 43.7 | 9 | 156 |
| Other | 30 | 33.6 | 26.9 | 5.5 | 96 |
| | 125 | 140 | 112 | 23 | 400 |

**(b)**

| | Business | Natural Science | Social Science | Humanities | |
|---|---|---|---|---|---|
| Democrat | 42 | 46 | 49 | 11 | 148 |
| Republican | 59 | 60 | 32 | 5 | 156 |
| Other | 24 | 34 | 31 | 7 | 96 |
| | 125 | 140 | 112 | 23 | 400 |

Table 7.3

$$(59 - 48.8)^2 / 48.8 = 104 / 48.8 = 2.1$$
$$(7 - 5.5)^2 / 5.5 = 2.25 / 5.5 = .4$$
$$(31 - 26.9)^2 / 26.9 = 16.8 / 26.9 = .62$$
$$(34 - 33.6)^2 / 33.6 = .16 / 33.6 = 0$$
$$(24 - 30)^2 / 30 = 36 / 30 = 1.2$$
$$\overline{\phantom{xxxxx}}$$
$$12.90$$

This table has 6 degrees of freedom; therefore, a chi square of at least 12.592 is necessary to infer the sample percentages to the population at the .05 level of significance. Since the chi square is 12.9, we can be 95 percent confident that such inferences are warranted. If we had data for the entire population of students, the percentages would very likely differ from one another when compared across the rows. The observed and expected values are dissimilar enough to create the likelihood of differences in the proportions of various majors identifying Democrat versus Republican—a statistical relationship in the population. Take Table 4.4 from Chapter 4 as a second example. Compute the expected values, compute chi square, and interpret the result.

## STATISTICAL VERSUS SUBSTANTIVE SIGNIFICANCE

Always take care to distinguish between statistical significance and substantive significance. *Substantive significance* entails a subjective judgment on the question of whether percentage differences in contingency tables constructed from samples of cases are large enough to be interesting to the researcher. *Statistical significance* entails an objective determination of the probability that percentage differences in contingency tables constructed from samples, regardless of their magnitude, exist in the population from which the sample was drawn.

### Examples

Consider Table 7.4. Suppose, in Table 7.4(a), we have constructed a contingency table for the relationship between gender and party identification from a random sample of 20 people. Sixty percent of the males consider themselves to be Republican and only 40 percent of the females. This is a substantively significant relationship because 20 percent is a rather striking difference. However, it is *not* a statistically significant relationship: A computation of the chi square statistic results in a value less than that required at the .05 level of significance.

Now suppose that, in Table 7.4(b), we have constructed a contingency table for the relationship between gender and party identification from a random sample of 10,000 people (of course, few surveys use samples this large). Fifty-one percent of the males consider themselves Republican and 49 percent of the females. This is *not* a substantively significant relationship because a difference of 2 percent is not very striking; other factors beyond gender must play a much larger role in determining party identification. However, it *is* a statistically significant relationship; computation of chi square results in a value sufficient to meet the .05 level of significance. There is a very high probability that differences between males and females exist in the population from which this sample was drawn. Obviously, the differences are small, but they very likely exist. Indeed, in a random sample of 10,000 people showing 51 percent of males Republican and 49 percent of females, probably *almost exactly* 51 percent of males in the population and 49 percent of females in the population are Republican. Ten thousand is such a large random sample that it would be almost perfectly representative.

Obviously, as with all inferential statistics, chi square depends primarily on sample size and secondarily on the magnitude of percentage differences in the sample. Note an interesting feature of Table 7.4(a). Computation of chi square results in a value of .8. However, if size of the sample doubles to 40 and the proportions remain 60 percent to 40 percent, chi square doubles to 1.6. If the size of the sample again doubles to 80, chi square again doubles to 3.2; if 160, 6.4, and so on. Work out these calculations for yourself.

Obviously, we seek relationships that are both substantively *and* statistically significant. Table 7.4(c) displays such a relationship. Although each example in Table 7.4 is

**(a)**

|  | Male | Female |  |
|---|---|---|---|
| Republican | 6<br>60% | 4<br>40% |  |
| Democrat | 4<br>40% | 6<br>60% |  |
|  |  |  | 20 |

**(b)**

| 2,550<br>51% | 2,450<br>49% |  |
|---|---|---|
| 2,450<br>49% | 2,550<br>51% |  |
|  |  | 10,000 |

**(c)**

| 200<br>66% | 100<br>33% |  |
|---|---|---|
| 100<br>33% | 200<br>66% |  |
|  |  | 600 |

Table 7.4

contrived for illustrative purposes, there has been a tendency, since the early 1980s, for women to be more likely than men to identify with the Democratic party and to vote for Democratic candidates. Table 7.5 reconstructs data on gender and vote intention from page 186 of the *Star-Ledger*/Eagleton Poll appearing in Appendix B, and discussed in Chapter 4. From a random sample of 801, 39 percent of the males intended to vote for Clinton, while 45 percent of the females intended such a vote; conversely, 53 percent of the males intended to vote for either Bush or Perot, while only 43 percent of the females intended such a vote. This is a statistically significant difference, popularly dubbed the "gender gap." Test your knowledge by computing the chi square statistic.

The concept of statistical significance also has applications to the public policy process and to litigation. For example, the Environmental Protection Agency may investigate claims that a toxic waste dump causes cancer among residents in nearby communities. One strategy for evaluating the claim is to compare the incidence of cancer among residents of these communities (e.g., number of cases per 100,000 population) to the incidence in the population of the United States for the purpose of determining if

|  | Female | Male |  |
|---|---|---|---|
| Clinton | 180 <br> 45% | 157 <br> 39% | 337 <br> 42% |
| Bush | 116 <br> 29% | 124 <br> 31% | 240 <br> 30% |
| Perot | 56 <br> 14% | 88 <br> 22% | 144 <br> 18% |
| Undecided | 48 <br> 12% | 32 <br> 8% | 80 <br> 10% |
|  | 400 <br> 50% | 401 <br> 50% | 801 |

Table 7.5

the differences are statistically significant. In Chapter 9 and Chapter 10, we discuss such public policy and legal applications more thoroughly.

## Statistical Significance and Hypothesis Testing

Hypotheses, such as those discussed in Chapter 3, are always *tested in steps.* The first step is to determine whether or not there is a substantively significant relationship between the independent and dependent variables of the hypothesis in the sample of cases with which the researcher is working. Bivariate descriptive statistics, such as those discussed in Chapter 4, are employed for this purpose. If the relationship is substantively significant, the next step is to determine if it is statistically significant. Bivariate inferential statistics are employed for this purpose. These steps are referred to as *"testing null hypotheses."* A null hypothesis is always the opposite of the research hypothesis. Therefore, we seek to *reject null hypotheses* in order to gain confidence in the research hypothesis. The more null hypotheses we can reject, the more confidence we have that the independent variable of the research hypothesis actually causes the dependent variable of the research hypothesis.

Suppose, for example, that we wish to test the hypothesis that whites are more likely to vote than blacks in presidential elections. We randomly sample 1,000 people, recording their race and recording whether or not they voted in the last presidential election. The research hypothesis is that race (independent variable) exerts a causal influence on propensity to vote (dependent variable). The first hurdle to overcome in seeking to confirm this hypothesis is to determine if, in our sample of 1,000, whites are in fact more likely to vote. The first null hypothesis is that they are *not* more likely to vote—that there is little or no difference in the proportions of whites and blacks in the sample that voted. Suppose we find that 60 percent of whites voted in the last presidential election compared to 40 percent of blacks. We thereby overcome the first hurdle by rejecting the first null hypothesis and gain some confidence in the research hypothesis.

The second hurdle to overcome is to determine the probability that there are differences in the proportions in the population from which the sample was selected. The second null hypothesis is that the chi square statistic is *not* significant at the .05 level. If the chi square statistic *is* significant at the .05 level, we may reject the second null hypothesis, gaining further confidence in the proposition that race exerts a causal influence on voting. Indeed, conventionally, the term "null hypothesis" is reserved for those instances in which researchers test to determine whether or not a statistically significant relationship exists between two variables. The null hypothesis is that it does not—that the variables are statistically independent in the population. We seek to reject the null hypothesis, accepting, with a high degree of confidence, the research hypothesis that the variables are in fact statistically correlated in the population.

Yet, it is still useful to think about a "series" of null hypotheses. What are the various alternatives to the research hypothesis that race somehow "causes" propensity to vote? The first is that there is not a relationship between race and voting; second, that the relationship is not statistically significant. But there are other hurdles as well. Perhaps race has nothing to do with voting. Perhaps income is the major determinant of propensity to vote—race and voting are statistically related only because whites tend to have higher incomes than blacks. Perhaps education is the major determinant of propensity to vote—race and voting are statistically related only because whites tend to have higher education levels than blacks. Perhaps. . . .

In other words, there are always an unlimited number of "counterexplanations" to research hypotheses; there are always an unlimited number of null hypotheses. The more null hypotheses we reject, the more confidence we gain in the research hypothesis. If we reject the first null hypothesis that the independent and dependent variables are not statistically correlated in the sample, and the second null hypothesis that the correlation is not statistically significant, and the third null hypothesis that income is the true causal factor, and the fourth null hypothesis that education is the true causal factor, we will have gained a great deal of confidence in our research hypothesis. But we will never have *complete* confidence because there will always be other possible "counterexplanations" that need to be tested. This is referred to as "controlling for third factors," discussed in more detail in Chapter 8 and Chapter 9.

Obviously, testing a research hypothesis by rejecting a series of null hypotheses is a very "negative" process. In other words, we never *prove* a research hypothesis, we only gain increasing confidence in it by repeatedly attempting to disprove it and failing each time. We keep attacking it, each time hoping the attack fails. But even as we pile success upon success with failing attacks, we recognize that, at some point in the future, a null hypothesis may be accepted, thereby destroying the research hypothesis. This approach is fully compatible with our observations in Chapter 3 that all scientific research is tentative and subject to revision on the basis of continuing empirical research. Therefore, hypotheses are never judged true, but only presented as testable and falsifiable. Repeated unsuccessful attempts to falsify the hypothesis, by testing null hypotheses, build confidence in its acceptability, but never permit statements of truth.

## TESTS OF SIGNIFICANCE IN SIMPLE REGRESSION

The *t* statistic is to Pearson's correlation what chi square is to a contingency table. Whereas chi square indicates the probability that differences in proportions exist in the population (thereby indicating that two variables are statistically related), the *t statistic* indicates the probability that Pearson's correlation coefficient is *not* 0 in the population (thereby indicating that two variables are statistically related). The $t$ statistic behaves in a fashion similar to chi square, may take on any value above 0, and may be referenced for statistical significance in a table of $t$ values.

Suppose, for example, that we have a random sample of 100 citizens over 18 years of age in the United States and discover a Pearson's correlation coefficient of .4 between the age of the individual and the number of times they voted within the last two years. The $t$ statistic permits us to determine the likelihood that had we interviewed everyone over 18 years of age in the U.S. population, older people would in fact have voted more within the last two years (there would have been a positive Pearson's correlation coefficient).

The formula for $t$ is:

$$r\left( \sqrt{\frac{N-2}{1-r^2}} \right)$$

In our example:

$$.4\left( \sqrt{\frac{100-2}{1-.16}} \right)$$

$$= .4 \times \sqrt{(98 / .84)}$$

$$= .4 \times \sqrt{116.6}$$

$$= .4 \times 10.8 = 4.32$$

A $t$ table indicates that the .05 level of significance, with 100 degrees of freedom, requires a $t$ of at least 1.96. Therefore, we are at least 95 percent confident that the correlation between age and frequency of voting is statistically correlated in the population. Degrees of freedom for the $t$ statistic are normally set equal to the number of cases; see if you can figure out why.

Like chi square, the magnitude of $t$ depends on the size of the sample and on the extent of the statistical relationship between the two variables in that sample. Since sample size is in the numerator, larger samples produce larger $t$ values. Since we multiply by the Pearson's correlation of the sample, and subtract that correlation from 1 in the denominator, larger correlations produce larger $t$ values. Moreover, $t$ may be computed for negative correlations. Simply drop the sign when consulting the table.

Again like chi square, a distinction must be made between substantive and statistical significance. A Pearson's correlation of .5 in a sample of 10 would be substantively significant, since we consider .5 a strong relationship; however, it would not produce a statistically significant value for $t$, since 10 is such a small sample. A correlation of .2 in a sample of 5,000 would not be substantively significant, since we consider .2 a very weak relationship; however, it would produce a statistically significant value for $t$, since 5,000 is such a large sample. We would be highly confident that Pearson's correlation was not 0 in the population; however, that does not mean it would be much larger, if at all, than .2.

Of course, in testing hypotheses with Pearson's correlation, we seek relationships that are both substantively *and* statistically significant. Moreover, as with contingency tables, we seek to reject a series of null hypotheses.

## APPLICATION OF BIVARIATE INFERENTIAL STATISTICS

Appendix E reprints a scholarly article by S. Sidney Ulmer, titled "Conflict with Supreme Court Precedent and the Granting of Plenary Review," which appeared in the May 1983 issue of the *Journal of Politics*. Let us move through Ulmer's article, answering each of the questions about research articles identified in Chapter 4.

The general question Ulmer seeks to answer is whether or not the Supreme Court is more likely to agree to hear cases when the lower court ruling being appealed is in conflict with precedents the Supreme Court previously established. He tests two specific hypotheses: The Court is more likely to grant review in conflict cases. The Burger Court differs from the Warren Court in the weight given to precedent when granting review. Ulmer reasons that "the Court itself suggests that conflict with one or more Supreme Court precedents is a significant consideration in shaping the access decision," and he seeks simply to discover the extent to which the Court's assertion is empirically defensible. Ulmer also reasons that there may be differences between the Burger Court and Warren Court since the latter has a greater reputation for activism (less deference to precedent) than the former.

In the first hypothesis, the independent variable is whether or not there was a conflict with precedent and the dependent variable is whether or not the Court granted review. The second hypothesis is a little trickier insofar as it involves three variables. Strictly speaking, the independent variable is time period (Burger Court or Warren Court) and the dependent variable is whether or not there is a relationship between precedent and granting review. In other words, is the statistical relationship between precedent and granting review likely to be stronger or weaker when the Burger Court is compared to the Warren Court? In both hypotheses, the cases are the (lower court) cases!

The data evaluated were derived from all cases during the period 1961–1976 in which review was granted and a 10 percent sample of cases in which review was denied. Conflict was operationally defined as existing in any case in which one or more of the lower court judges alleged a conflict with precedent in a dissent. The dependent variable (grant or deny) is almost certainly valid and reliable since this is a clear, direct measure and a matter of public record. The independent variable (conflict) seems valid as well, although the indicator is not quite as clear and direct. There may be other ways to measure conflict, although most reasonable people would likely judge this to be an acceptable choice. Indeed, Ulmer suggests another indicator in his second footnote, noting possible validity problems with that indicator. Reliability is a bit trickier. Ulmer does not detail with precision the operational definition used to determine whether a dissenter alleged a conflict with precedent. Therefore, different researchers might classify cases differently. For example, does the dissenter have to mention a case and its precedent *explicitly* or may the researcher count a mere *implication*? Different researchers may make different choices, creating inconsistencies.

Table E.1 confirms the first hypothesis. Ulmer presents "total percentages" instead of "column percentages." In other words, for example, 276 is 11.6 percent of all 2,387 cases in the table. This is an unusual practice. However, we may reconstruct the column percentages, noting that 276 of the 830 cases (33 percent) in which there was conflict were granted review while only 270 of the 1,557 cases (15 percent) in which there was not conflict were granted review. The chi square of 76.7 is significant beyond the .001 level, indicating we can be more than 99.9 percent certain that there is a difference in the proportion of conflict cases reviewed when compared to the proportion of nonconflict cases reviewed. The relationship is highly statistically significant.

Table E.2 and Table E.3 confirm the second hypothesis, if we again compute the column percentages. For the Warren Court, 39 percent of conflict cases were reviewed, compared to only 16 percent of nonconflict cases. For the Burger Court, 29 percent of conflict cases were reviewed, compared to only 18 percent of nonconflict cases. Both relationships produce highly statistically significant chi squares. The importance of the pattern, however, lies in the fact that there is a 23 percent difference for the Warren Court, compared to only an 11 percent difference for the Burger Court. That is a big part of the reason the chi square is higher in Table E.2 than in Table E.3. In other words, conflict is a more important factor in determining likelihood of review during the Warren years than during the Burger years. Ulmer suggests these results run counter to what we might expect from an activist court. Also, can you figure out why it is appropriate to compute the gamma statistic even though the variables are dichotomies, with just two values each?

Finally, note Ulmer's statement, "In order to guard against spurious inference, we repeated the analysis, controlling for litigant status, civil liberties issues, and constitutional issues . . . the relationship depicted is not subject to explanation by the variables controlled, and we retain the original inference." This statement is consistent with our discussion of null hypotheses. The null hypothesis is always the opposite of the research hypothesis. There are many possible alternatives to the hypothesis that conflict somehow "causes" review. For example, perhaps civil liberties issues or other constitutional issues are more likely to prompt both conflict and review. Perhaps it only looks like conflict is prompting review because the nature of the issues is prompting both. Maybe conflict really has nothing to do with review, in and of itself. These are among the unlimited possible "counterexplanations." Ulmer "controlled" for some of these possible counterexplanations, thereby gaining additional confidence in his research hypotheses. In other words, he successfully rejected several null hypotheses. "Controlling for third factors" will be discussed in more detail in Chapter 8 and Chapter 9.

## SUMMARY

Bivariate inferential statistics are employed to determine the likelihood that statistical relationships found in a sample exist in the population from which the sample was selected. For contingency tables of nominal or ordinal data computed from random samples of cases, the chi square statistic is used to evaluate whether or not differences of proportions in a random sample indicate similar differences of proportions in the population from which that sample was selected. The computation of chi square is based on comparison of the proportions one would *expect* to find if the variables were unrelated in the population and the proportions one actually *observes* in the contingency table. When expected values are very close to observed values, the chi square statistic is close to 0, indicating little likelihood that any difference of proportions found in the sample also exists in the population. The further away the expected values are from the observed values, the further away from 0 is chi square, indicating an increasing likelihood that any difference of proportions found in the sample also exists in the population.

The standard for evaluating chi square is the .05 level of significance—95 percent certainty that, if the contingency table were constructed for the entire population, there would be differences in proportions. Obtaining results at this level of confidence leads to the conclusion that a relationship between two variables in a sample is "statistically significant"—the observed and expected values are dissimilar enough to indicate at least a 95 percent likelihood that there is a similar relationship in the population. However, since statistical significance depends directly on the size of the sample, large differences in proportions for small samples may not be statistically significant while small differences in proportions for large samples may be. Therefore, we must always take care to distinguish between substantive significance and statistical significance.

Testing for statistical significance is frequently referred to as "testing the null hypothesis" that chi square is *not* significant at the .05 level. Therefore, if chi square *is* significant at the .05 level, we may reject the null hypothesis, gaining confidence in the proposition that the differences in proportions in the contingency table suggest that the independent variable of the research hypothesis exerts a causal influence on the dependent variable.

The *t* statistic is to Pearson's correlation what chi square is to a contingency table. Whereas chi square indicates the probability that differences in proportions exist in the population (thereby indicating that two variables are statistically related), the *t* statistic indicates the probability that Pearson's correlation coefficient is *not* 0 in the population (thereby indicating that two variables are statistically related). The *t* statistic behaves in a fashion similar to chi square, may take on any value above 0, and may be referenced for statistical significance.

We shall see in Chapter 9 and Chapter 10 that the concept of statistical significance has important applications in the public policy process and in litigation. We shall also see that establishing the statistical significance of a relationship is not, by itself, sufficient to reach the conclusion that an independent variable of a research hypothesis causes the dependent variable. As Ulmer observes, it is necessary to control for third factors to avoid spurious inferences. We now turn our attention to a more thorough investigation of the meaning of "spurious relationships" and "controlling for third factors."

# Multivariate Analysis

# Chapter
# 8

# *Introduction to Research Design*

Y ou probably never heard the story about the behavioral scientist who taught a cockroach to run on command. The scientist yelled "run" and the cockroach ran. The scientist then pulled off one of the cockroach's legs, yelled "run," and the cockroach ran, but somewhat slower. The scientist then pulled off all the legs on one side of the cockroach's body, yelled "run," and the cockroach ran in circles. The scientist then pulled off all the cockroach's legs, yelled "run," and the cockroach did not respond. The scientist therefore concluded that cockroaches without legs cannot hear.

The social scientific method employed by political scientists to learn about political reality seeks causal explanations by testing hypotheses logically and rigorously. As we know, the first step in establishing a causal relationship is to determine if two variables are statistically correlated. However, while correlation is a *necessary* condition for causation, it is not a *sufficient* condition. For $X$ to cause $Y$, $X$ and $Y$ must be correlated. However, just because $X$ and $Y$ are correlated does not necessarily mean $X$ *causes* $Y$.

The cockroach's response to the scientist's yell was correlated with whether or not the cockroach had legs. With legs, there was a response; without legs, there was no response. These empirical data are perfectly consistent with the hypothesis that cockroaches without legs are deaf—that removing legs causes loss of hearing. Clearly, however, the cockroach was not deaf and no such causal relationship existed.

If $X$ and $Y$ are correlated, it may be because $X$ is causing $Y$ or it may be because some third variable, which is associated in some way with the existence of $X$, is causing

Y. We know from empirical research that blacks are less likely to vote than whites—that race and likelihood of voting are statistically correlated. Does that mean that there is something about "being black" that causes one not to vote? Probably not. Rather, levels of income and levels of education are presumably the most important agents of causation in voting; blacks vote less not because they are black, but because they tend to have lower income and education levels.

We know from empirical research that military veterans who served in Vietnam are more likely to die of heart disease at an early age than members of the population as a whole. Does that mean that serving in Vietnam causes heart disease (perhaps as a result of exposure to Agent Orange)? Maybe. Maybe not. Conceivably, those who served in Vietnam were of a lower socioeconomic status and those of a lower socioeconomic status are more likely to smoke, and smoking is the primary determinant of heart disease. Although serving in Vietnam and dying of heart disease are statistically correlated, there is not necessarily a causal relationship. Dying of heart disease may have nothing at all to do with serving in Vietnam.

When testing hypotheses, we must always "control for third factors." If testing a hypothesis about the relationship between race and voting, we must control for factors such as income and education. If testing a hypothesis about the relationship between serving in Vietnam and heart disease, we must control for factors such as socioeconomic status and smoking. A variety of methods is appropriate in achieving this purpose. Many choices may be made in designing our research.

# DISTINGUISHING BETWEEN EXPERIMENTAL AND NONEXPERIMENTAL RESEARCH DESIGNS

The classic scientific research design is the experiment. It contains an independent variable and a dependent variable, an experimental group of cases and a control group of cases, a pretest and a posttest, and it may be diagramed as:

$$O_1 \times O_3$$
$$\overline{O_2 \quad O_4}$$

The first line is the experimental group and the second line is the control group. $O_1$ is observation of the value of the dependent variable in the experimental group and $O_2$ is observation of the value of the dependent variable in the control group. $X$ is introduction of the independent variable or the experimental "treatment." $O_3$ is observation of the value of the dependent variable in the experimental group after the treatment, and $O_4$ is observation of the value of the dependent variable in the control group after the treatment in the experimental group. $O_1$ and $O_2$ are pretests; $O_3$ and $O_4$ are posttests.

Experiments entail four comparisons. $O_1$ and $O_2$ are compared to confirm that the value of the dependent variable is the same in both groups of cases. $O_1$ and $O_3$ are compared to determine if the value of the dependent variable changes after introduction of the independent variable. $O_2$ and $O_4$ are compared to confirm that the value of the dependent variable in the control group does not change after introduction of the independent variable in the experimental group. $O_3$ and $O_4$ are compared to determine if the value of the dependent variable in the experimental group changes in relation to the value of the dependent variable in the control group.

Experiments are commonly conducted on animals in health and medical research laboratories. For example, we might wish to determine whether or not a particular substance (such as food dye) causes cancer in rats. We take two groups of rats, determine the incidence of cancer in each group ($O_1$ and $O_2$), inject one group with the treatment ($X$) and, after some set time period, again determine the incidence of cancer in each group. We compare the incidence of cancer in the two groups before treatment to confirm similarity, compare the incidence of cancer in the experimental group before treatment to incidence in the experimental group after treatment to determine if treatment has an impact, compare incidence of cancer in the control group before treatment to incidence in the control group after treatment to confirm similarity, and compare incidence of cancer in the experimental group after treatment to incidence in the control after treatment to determine if treatment has an impact. A variety of statistics are available for such comparisons. Indeed, the chi square statistic may be used in each comparison to establish whether or not a statistically significant difference exists in cancer rate between groups of rats. Can you figure out how, exactly, the contingency tables would be set up?

Experiments may also be conducted with people as the cases. For example, we might select two groups of high school students and administer the Scholastic Aptitude Test ($O_1$ and $O_2$), have one of the groups attend a SAT preparation course ($X$), then administer the SAT to both groups again ($O_3$ and $O_4$). If test scores rise more in the experimental group (which had the preparation session) than in the control group (which did not) we have evidence the session exerts a causal influence on the scores. Again, a variety of statistical techniques is available for such comparisons. One is the "difference of means test," a technique used to determine if statistically significant differences exist between means in two or more sets of cases. This test is discussed in Chapter 10.

Obviously, the purpose of the control group is to "control for third factors"—to establish that changes in the dependent variable occurring in the experimental group result from the independent variable, rather than from third factors. If the value of the dependent variable changes in the experimental group, but not in the control group, we have established causality with some confidence—only, however, if the experimental and control groups contain cases that are alike on all other variables. Therefore, if one of these other variables is causing changes in the experimental group, the changes should show up in the control group as well. Of course, the best way in ensure that all cases are alike on all variables is through random selection of cases and random assignment to the groups. In the SAT example, we would select high school students randomly and then randomly assign them to the experimental and control groups. In practice, random selection from the entire population of rats is not done for laboratory experiments. Rather, rats are bred under controlled conditions for the sole purpose of use in such experiments.

## Quasi-experimental Designs

Experiments are frequently conducted as part of medical research, educational research, and psychological research. However, they are rarely conducted in political science research. Reflect for a moment on the reasons why. Most independent variables of interest in political science research are not "manipulable"—they cannot easily be introduced or withheld at will. Take, for example, the hypothesis that people with college degrees are more likely to vote than people without college degrees. It would be prohibitively expensive, if not impossible, to randomly select two groups of people without college degrees, measure their voting habits, send one group to school for four years, then measure voting habits again. Similarly, take the hypothesis that Jews are more likely to vote Democratic than are Protestants. Obviously, we cannot randomly select two groups of Protestants, measure their voting, then turn one group Jewish before measuring their voting again!

Therefore, research designs in political science are usually quasi-experimental—they are sort of like experiments, but not quite. The most common quasi-experimental design is the *correlational design:*

$$
\begin{array}{c}
X \quad\;\; O \\
\hline
\quad\; O
\end{array}
$$

This is also referred to as the "posttest only" design, or "nonequivalent control group" design. We simply make a single observation for each of two groups, one of which has already been "treated." For example, we randomly select college graduates, randomly select those without college degrees, and compare their incidence of voting; or we randomly select Jews, randomly select Protestants, and compare the proportions voting Democratic. Indeed, we have already seen this method applied in Chapter 4—contingency tables are correlational designs, as are simple regressions.

Yet, this puts us on the horns of a dilemma. The essential difference between a correlational and an experimental design is that the former has no true control group. The term "nonequivalent control group" means that the two groups are not similar to one another on all potential third factors. Distinguishing the two groups of cases on the basis of the value of the independent variable almost always creates a situation in which the two groups differ on other variables as well. Those with college degrees have higher incomes than those without college degrees; perhaps income is the most important factor in determining likelihood of voting, not education. Jews have higher levels of education than Protestants; perhaps education is the most important factor in determining party identification, not religious or ethnic background.

## Spurious Relationships

A spurious relationship exists between two variables when they are correlated with one another, not because a hypothesized independent variable causes a hypothesized dependent variable, but because some third variable is operative. There are two kinds of spurious relationships. First, a third variable may cause both the hypothesized independent variable and the hypothesized dependent variable:

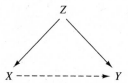

$X$ and $Y$ are correlated, not because $X$ causes $Y$, but because $Z$ causes both. The classic example is the correlation between the number of firefighters at a fire and the amount of fire damage. More firefighters, more damage. Do firefighters cause fire damage? No. What is the third variable causing both $X$ and $Y$?

Second, a third variable may usually be found with, or "go along with," the independent variable. This third variable causes the dependent variable, making it appear that the independent variable causes the dependent variable:

Blacks are less likely to vote than whites. However, blacks have lower income and educational levels than whites. There is nothing about "being black" that leads one to vote less. Rather, income and educational levels are the primary causal determinants. In political science research, the dilemma of spurious relationships cannot usually be solved through experimental control. However, it can be addressed through *statistical control*. It is possible to statistically "hold third factors constant."

## INTRODUCTION TO STATISTICAL CONTROL

Return to the first two hypotheses mentioned in this chapter: Blacks are less likely to vote than whites; military veterans who served in Vietnam are more likely to die of heart disease at an early age. If we find a correlation in a contingency table between race and likelihood of voting, we must statistically "hold education constant" (remove the variation in the education variable) to determine if the correlation between race and voting "holds up." If we find a correlation between serving in Vietnam and dying of heart disease in a contingency table, we must statistically "hold smoking constant" to determine if the correlation between service and heart disease "holds up." The procedure is very simple and may be diagramed as:

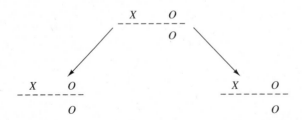

Simply take the set of cases in the original contingency table, separate them into the categories of the suspect third factor, and construct new contingency tables for each category. For example, divide the cases from the race/voting contingency table into those cases with college degrees and those without, then construct two more race/voting contingency tables—one for each group to "hold education constant." All the cases in the first group have a college degree—education does not vary; all the cases in the second group do not have a college degree—education does not vary here either. If the relationship between race and voting still exists after the "control," the relationship between race and voting is not spurious.

Similarly, divide the cases in the Vietnam/heart disease contingency table into those that smoked and those that did not smoke, then construct two more Vietnam/heart disease contingency tables, one for each group, "holding smoking constant." If the relationship between Vietnam service and heart disease continues to exist in these two new tables, then the original relationship is not spurious.

Third factors are referred to as "control variables" or "test factors." By dividing cases into subgroups of these factors, we "statistically hold them constant" or "statistically control" them. Chapter 9 outlines the actual method by which this is done, not only for nominal and ordinal level variables, such as those under discussion here, but also for interval level variables.

## SUMMARY

Correlation is a necessary, but not sufficient, condition for the establishment of causation. If $X$ and $Y$ are correlated, it may be because $X$ is causing $Y$ or it may be because some third variable, which is associated in some way with the existence of $X$, is causing $Y$. Therefore, when testing hypotheses, we must always control for third factors. Experimental research designs automatically control for third factors because they have a control group of cases designed explicitly for that purpose. However, political scientists are usually forced to rely on quasi-experimental correlational designs, posing the dilemma of spurious relationships: a statistical relationship that exists only because some third factor is operative.

In the absence of experimental control, we must rely on statistical control. The various methods available to achieve statistical control are known as "multivariate" statistics. These are the topic of Chapter 9.

# Chapter

# *9*

# Introduction to Multivariate Statistics

$A$s noted in Chapter 8, statistical control entails "holding third factors constant." To achieve this at the nominal and ordinal level, take the set of cases in the original contingency table, divide them into the categories of the third factor, and construct new contingency tables for each category. In this way, the third factor is "held constant." Here, we illustrate the actual method by which this is accomplished.

## STATISTICAL ELABORATION

Table 9.1 contains data contrived for illustrative purposes. Suppose, in a sample of 1,400 cases, those of higher income are more likely to vote than those of lower income: 72 percent of high-income people compared to 50 percent of low-income people. But a critic exclaims, "I think the relationship is spurious. I think education causes both income and voting. Those of higher education make more money; those of higher education are more likely to vote. Income has nothing to do with voting. Education leads to voting."

In response to our critic, we control for the third factor of education through *statistical elaboration*. We elaborate the original contingency table by dividing the 1,400 cases into those with a college degree and those without a college degree. In this way, we hold education constant. These are referred to as "conditional tables" or "partial tables." Note they contain the *same* 1,400 cases as the original table. There are 390 people

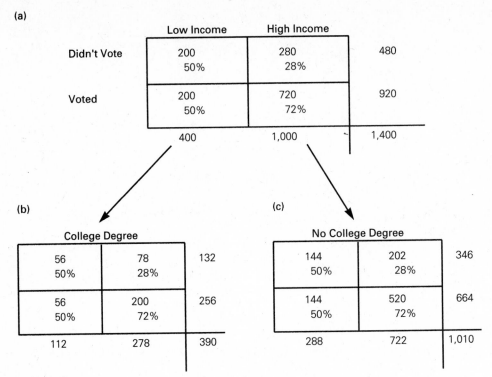

**(a)**

|  | Low Income | High Income |  |
|---|---|---|---|
| Didn't Vote | 200<br>50% | 280<br>28% | 480 |
| Voted | 200<br>50% | 720<br>72% | 920 |
|  | 400 | 1,000 | 1,400 |

**(b)**

College Degree

|  |  |  |
|---|---|---|
| 56<br>50% | 78<br>28% | 132 |
| 56<br>50% | 200<br>72% | 256 |
| 112 | 278 | 390 |

**(c)**

No College Degree

|  |  |  |
|---|---|---|
| 144<br>50% | 202<br>28% | 346 |
| 144<br>50% | 520<br>72% | 664 |
| 288 | 722 | 1,010 |

Table 9.1

with a college degree and 1,010 people without a college degree, for a total of 1,400 people. There are 56 low-income people who did not vote that have a college degree and 144 low-income people who did not vote that do not have a college degree, for a total of 200 low-income people who did not vote.

Among those with a college degree, 72 percent of high-income people voted and only 50 percent of low-income people voted. Among those without a college degree, 72 percent of high-income people voted and only 50 percent of low-income people voted. This pattern is referred to as *replication* since the original contingency table replicates itself when the third factor is held constant. The column percentages remain the same. With replication, we reject the contention that the original relationship is spurious, and gain further confidence in the proposition that income causes voting. Those of high income are more likely to vote, regardless of educational background: In general, higher-income people more likely vote; among those with a college degree, higher-income people still more likely vote; among those without a college degree, higher-income people again still more likely vote.

Table 9.2 is contrived to illustrate that replication is not the only possible result. Suppose in a sample of 420 black people and Jewish people, 27 percent of Jewish people indicate they belong to a community organization (civic club, political club, etc.),

(a)

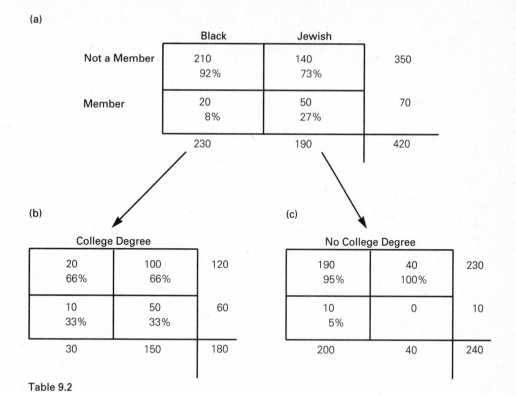

| | Black | Jewish | |
|---|---|---|---|
| **Not a Member** | 210<br>92% | 140<br>73% | 350 |
| **Member** | 20<br>8% | 50<br>27% | 70 |
| | 230 | 190 | 420 |

(b)

**College Degree**

| | | |
|---|---|---|
| 20<br>66% | 100<br>66% | 120 |
| 10<br>33% | 50<br>33% | 60 |
| 30 | 150 | 180 |

(c)

**No College Degree**

| | | |
|---|---|---|
| 190<br>95% | 40<br>100% | 230 |
| 10<br>5% | 0 | 10 |
| 200 | 40 | 240 |

Table 9.2

and only 8 percent of black people indicate such membership. But again our critic complains, "I think the relationship is spurious. I think education leads to involvement in community organizations. Those of higher education are more likely to join community organizations. It so happens that Jews, in general, have higher educational levels than blacks, in general. But ethnic heritage, in and of itself, has nothing to do with joining such organizations. Education is the key."

In response, we again control. But this time our critic is right since the differences between blacks and Jews disappear with education held constant. Among those with a college degree, 33 percent of Jews are joiners and 33 percent of blacks are joiners. Indeed, among those without college degrees the pattern actually reverses itself! None of the Jews are joiners compared to 5 percent of the blacks. With such a pattern, which we refer to as *washout,* because the original relationship disappears, or "washes out," we conclude that this original relationship is spurious. Education, rather than ethnic background, causes joining behavior.

Note the reasons for the pattern. Of 210 black nonjoiners, 190 do not have college degrees and only 20 do. Of 50 Jewish joiners, *all of them* have college degrees. This makes it appear, in the original table, that there was a causal relationship between ethnicity and membership in community groups. But it only *appears* this way.

Of course, pure patterns of replication or washout rarely occur in actual data analysis. Statistical elaboration usually results only in a tendency toward replication or a tendency toward washout. For example, suppose, in Table 9.1, that 65 percent of high-income people with a college degree had voted and 55 percent of low-income people with a college degree had voted. And suppose further that 80 percent of high-income people without a college degree had voted and 40 percent of low-income people without a college degree had voted. This pattern tends toward replication, since differences remain between low- and high-income people after controlling for education. However, the differences are greater for those without a college degree than for those with a college degree. We refer to this pattern as *specification* since the statistical elaboration specifies the conditions under which the original relationship is most likely to hold. There is relationship between income and voting. This relationship is strongest among those without college degrees.

Alternately, suppose that, in Table 9.2, 2 percent of blacks without college degrees had joined community organizations, while 8 percent of Jews without college degrees had. And suppose further that 20 percent of blacks with college degrees were joiners and 30 percent of Jews with college degrees were. This pattern tends toward washout, since the differences between blacks and Jews dissipate when education is held constant. However, some differences still remain. This pattern, too, is referred to as specification, since we may specify the conditions under which there are likely to be the biggest differences between blacks and Jews. Here, it is among the college-educated, although the differences even here are not that great.

In a pattern of specification, both the independent variable in the original contingency table and the third factor exert an influence on the dependent variable. In the voting example, both income and education are important; income is more important. In the joining example, both ethnicity and education are important; education is more important.

## Elaborating Pearson's Correlation Coefficient

Just as we may statistically elaborate a contingency table of nominal or ordinal data by breaking the cases up into the categories of a third nominal or ordinal variable, so too may we statistically elaborate a Pearson's correlation coefficient computed for interval data by breaking the cases up into the categories of a third nominal or ordinal variable. Suppose, for example, a moderate Pearson's correlation of .3 exists between the proportion of land in agricultural production and the proportion of Republicans in the state legislature in the 50 states of the United States. Suppose further the states are divided into those in the South and those not in the South. For Southern states, the correlation is a weak .1 and for non-Southern states a strong .5. This fits the pattern of specification. While the correlation tends toward washout for the Southern states, it strengthens for the non-Southern states. In general, more agricultural states have a higher proportion of Republicans in their state legislatures. This is particularly true of non-Southern states.

Had the correlations gone to 0 for both subgroups of states, a pattern of complete washout would prevail. One might ask, "How can you have a positive correlation for all states and no correlation at all for Southern states, as well as no correlation at all for non-Southern states? This seems impossible, since Southern states and non-Southern states together make up all states!" In fact, it is not impossible. A scatter diagram of the situation, contrived for illustrative purposes, would look something like that displayed in Figure 9.1. Southern states cluster in the lower left, but are spread out so as to produce no correlation for Southern states. Non-Southern states cluster in the upper right, but are spread out so as to produce no correlation for non-Southern states. Yet, there would still be a correlation for *all* states! The situation is analogous to that described for washout in the membership in community organizations example, where nonjoining blacks were most all without college degrees and joining Jews were most all with college degrees. Here, those cases high on agriculture and Republican are all non-Southern; those low on agriculture and Republican are all Southern.

Before proceeding, make certain you can answer the following questions: What would happen to the original correlation of .3 in a situation of perfect replication? What would the scatter diagram look like?

There is one other pattern that may emerge and this pattern, at first glance, seems extremely illogical. An example from actual data, rather than contrived data, illustrates.[1] For all the candidates running for seats in the U.S. House of Representatives in 1978 and 1980, the Pearson's correlation between amount of money spent and percentage of vote received is .09—extremely weak. However, if we elaborate by separating the cases into incumbents and challengers, and compute Pearson's correlations for money and vote in each of these subgroups, we find something very interesting. The correlation for incumbents is −.42 and the correlation for challengers .45. While the correlation for all cases leads to the conclusion that money spent exerts no influence on percentage of vote received, the conclusion is flawed. The elaboration demonstrates that money has a good deal to do with the prospects of a challenger—the more spent, the higher the vote percentage. It also demonstrates that incumbents spending a lot of money get a *lower* percentage of the vote! The explanation is probably that challengers need to spend a lot of money to get votes because they begin at a disadvantage (low name recognition, inability to use the resources of the office for electoral advantage, etc.), while incumbents spend a lot of money only when they perceive themselves to be in electoral jeopardy. Of

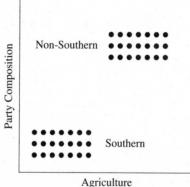

Figure 9.1

course, the original hypothesis assumes that spending leads to votes—spending is the independent variable. However, the analysis suggests that, with incumbents, the amount of money spent might actually be *caused by* perceptions of electoral jeopardy—in other words, maybe spending is really the dependent variable when it comes to incumbents!

In any event, the pattern is referred to as *suppression* because a third factor is suppressing, or "hiding" the relationship between the two original variables. For all cases, spending appeared to be uncorrelated with vote percentage. In fact, however, it is highly correlated with vote percentage—.45 for challengers and −.42 for incumbents. Positive and negative correlations of roughly equal magnitude in subgroups of the cases offset one another, making it appear, among all cases, that no correlation existed.

## Application of Statistical Elaboration

Appendix F reprints pages 306–316 of a book by David C. Baldus, George G. Woodworth, and Charles A. Pulaski, Jr., titled *Equal Justice and the Death Penalty*. Baldus is a professor of law, Woodworth is a professor of statistics, and Pulaski is a practicing attorney. Data from the study on which the book is based were presented to the United States Supreme Court in the 1987 case of *McCleskey* v. *Kemp.* The case was extremely significant because the Court agreed to review *statistical evidence* and hear *statistical arguments.*

The authors are interested in determining whether or not among people eligible to receive the death penalty under state sentencing laws in Georgia during the period 1973–1979, race was a factor in their likelihood of receiving it. In particular, they are interested in determining if race of defendant/race of victim interaction is a factor. Although the authors did more than one study of this likelihood, our emphasis here will be on their "Charging and Sentencing Study (CSS)."

The authors do not explicitly advance any hypotheses; however, one of their main objectives is to determine whether or not blacks are more likely to get the death sentence than whites, whether or not those who kill whites are more likely to get the death sentence than those who kill blacks, and whether blacks who kill whites are more likely to get the death sentence than those in other combinations of the race of defendant/race of victim interaction. The independent variables are race of defendant and race of victim. Whether or not the death sentence was received is the dependent variable. Convicted murderers are the cases. Of course, their study contains a large number of other independent variables as well, and is one of the largest and most systematic of its kind.

The measures for all three variables are valid. Race of defendant, race of victim, and whether or not the death penalty was received may all be determined directly from public records. Of course, as the authors note in another section of their book, inaccuracies may result when the data is recorded from the records. However, as the authors also point out, those who collected the data received extensive training and detailed instructions for dealing with ambiguities and they periodically checked one another's work. All these efforts are designed to ensure the reliability of the measures.

Focus on Table F.1, which "presents the unadjusted race of victim and race of defendant effects in the CSS for all defendants indicted for murder." The authors are reporting percentages as proportions. For example, in white victim cases, 108 of 981 received the death penalty; .11 or 11 percent. In black victim cases, 20 of 1,503 received the death penalty; .0133 or 1.3 percent.

Table 9.3 transforms these data into the cross-tabulation format with which we are familiar, listing race of defendant across the top and whether or not the defendant received the death sentence down the side. Note that while 7 percent of the white defendants received the death penalty, only 4 percent of the black defendants did. But there is a "third factor" operating here—race of victim. When we separate these 2,484 cases into those with white victims on the one hand, and those with black victims on the other, this becomes apparent. For white victims, 21 percent of black defendants were sentenced to death, compared to only 8 percent of white defendants. For black victims, 1 percent of black defendants were sentenced and 3 percent of white defendants. The small overall difference of 7 percent to 4 percent not only washes out in the case of white victims, but it completely reverses itself. The reason is that, of the 60 white defendant cases receiving a death sentence, 58 had white victims; of the 68 black defendant cases receiving the sentence, 50 had white victims. Race of victim is the most important variable here. Those who kill whites are more likely to be sentenced to death. It only appears that whites are more likely to get the sentence than blacks because whites are more likely to kill whites than blacks are.

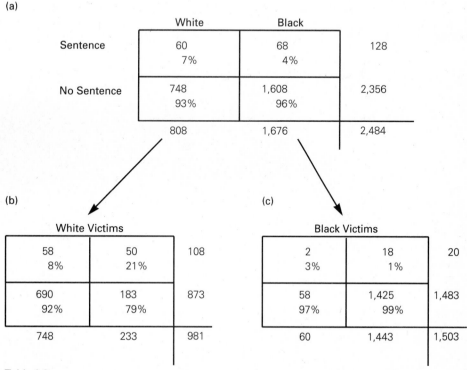

Table 9.3

|  | White to White | White to Black | Black to White | Black to Black |  |
|---|---|---|---|---|---|
| Sentence | 58<br>8% | 2<br>3% | 50<br>21% | 18<br>1% | 128 |
| No Sentence | 690<br>92% | 58<br>97% | 183<br>79% | 1,425<br>99% | 2,356 |
|  | 748 | 60 | 233 | 1,443 | 2,484 |

Table 9.4

Of course, these data may also be presented as in Table 9.4. Here we see clearly that blacks who kill whites are far more likely to get the death sentence than any other defendant/victim combination. Whites who kill whites come in a distant second. Blacks who kill blacks are least likely.

Finally, in Figure F.1, they "control simultaneously for felony circumstances and prior record." As they note, the figure shows "a distinct association between the aggravation level of cases and the magnitude of the race of victim effects." Race of victim effects are modest in the less aggravated cases, while quite pronounced in the more aggravated cases. Here it is a pattern of "specification." Those who kill whites are more likely to get the death sentence. If they killed a white, did so in felony circumstances, and had a prior record, they are even more likely to receive the sentence. The interaction of the variables is of supreme importance. In other portions of their analysis, the authors discovered that some variables had an even more significant impact on race of victim effects.

# INTRODUCTION TO MULTIPLE REGRESSION

Recall from Chapter 4 that simple regression is designed to test hypotheses for which both variables are measured at the interval level. The Pearson's correlation coefficient may be used to determine how much of the variation in $Y$ is explained by $X$, the slope indicates how much $Y$ changes for every 1 unit of change in $X$, and the equation $Y = a + b(x)$ predicts the value of $Y$ for any given case by using its value on $X$ as the predictor.

Multiple regression permits the test of hypotheses that contain more than one independent variable. For example, suppose we hypothesize that median income and median education level in states in the United States influence the level of voter turnout in those states. Median income and median education are the independent variables and voter turnout is the dependent variable. States are the cases. In multiple regression, we may compute partial correlation coefficients, a multiple correlation coefficient, and partial slopes. In addition, we may construct equations such as: $Y = a + b_1(x_1) + b_2(x_2) + \cdots$.

## Partial Correlation Coefficient

The partial correlation coefficient is the correlation between two interval level variables after the effects of a third interval variable have been "partialed out." It is to interval level analysis what statistical elaboration is to nominal and ordinal analysis. For example, suppose the Pearson's correlation coefficient (referred to as the zero-order correlation in multiple regression) between median income and voter turnout is .8, while the zero-order correlation between median education and turnout is .72. It is obvious that "overlap" exists in these two correlations. Some of the variation explained by income in the first correlation is also explained by education in the second correlation. The partial correlation coefficient identifies the extent of this overlap. What is the correlation between education and turnout after the effects of income have been partialed out, or held constant, or statistically controlled? What is the correlation between income and turnout after the effects of education have been partialed out, or held constant, or statistically controlled?

To illustrate, treat income as $X$, turnout as $Y$, and education as $Z$:

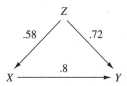

The zero-order correlation between income and turnout is .8, between education and turnout, .72, between education and income, .58. To compute the partial correlation coefficient between income and turnout, controlling for education:

$$r_{xy \cdot z} = \frac{r_{xy} - r_{yz}\,(r_{xz})}{\sqrt{(1 - r_{yz}^2)} \cdot \sqrt{(1 - r_{xz}^2)}}$$

The result:

$$\frac{.8 - .72\,(.58)}{\sqrt{(1 - .52)} \cdot \sqrt{(1 - .34)}}$$

$$= \frac{.38}{(.69)\,(.81)} = .68$$

The correlation between income and turnout, when the effects of education are statistically removed, is .68. Since income and education share some of the variation explained in turnout, the correlation goes down when the shared variation is removed. Basically, the numerator of the equation takes the explained variation that $X$ shares with $Z$ (by multiplying the correlation between $X$ and $Z$ by the correlation between $Y$ and $Z$), and then subtracts this shared variation from the correlation between $X$ and $Y$. As with Pearson's correlation coefficient, discussed in Chapter 4, most of the "action" is in the numerator, while the denominator standardizes the result.

Demonstrate that if $Z$ is uncorrelated both with $X$ and $Y$ (zero-order correlations are both 0), this equation produces a partial correlation coefficient of .8. In other words, if $Z$ is uncorrelated with both $X$ and $Y$, it shares none of the explained variation and the original correlation between $X$ and $Y$ holds. Demonstrate that if the zero-order correlation between Z and X is .9 and the zero-order correlation between Z and Y is .9, this equation produces a partial correlation coefficient close to zero. In other words, Z is explaining almost all the variation in Y and Z is also highly correlated with X; therefore, most of the shared variation gets "taken away from" X.

Take another contrived example, with time points (presidential election years) as the cases, treating inflation as X, level of employment as Z, and percentage vote for the presidential candidate of the party which does not occupy the White House (nonincumbent party) as Y:

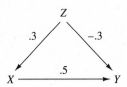

The zero-order correlation between inflation and vote is .5, between employment and vote, −.3, between inflation and employment .3. In other words, high inflation favors the challenging party, high employment hurts the challenging party, and level of inflation and level of employment are positively correlated with one another.

If we compute the partial correlation between X and Y, controlling for Z, the result is .62. In other words, when level of employment is statistically removed, the correlation between inflation and vote becomes stronger. Why? Because level of employment had a depressing effect on the proportion of the vote received by the challenging party and it was also correlated with inflation, which had an opposite effect on proportion of the vote. Therefore, with employment in the equation, part of the positive effect of inflation was eliminated by the depressing effect of employment. With employment statistically removed, the correlation between inflation and vote percentage became stronger. Another way of looking at this would be to say that inflation favors challengers and if employment is not high at the same time, inflation will favor challengers even more.

These partial correlation coefficients may be analyzed with reference to the patterns of statistical elaboration previously discussed. We may do so by treating Z as a "third factor" or "control variable" in each example by asking, "What is the correlation between X and Y?" and then asking, "Does that relationship hold after we control for Z?" In the first example, the correlation between median income and turnout was .8; when median education was controlled, it fell to .7. This is basically "replication"; income has a strong effect, which remains strong after education is controlled. Of course, if the correlation remained at .8 after the control the result would be pure replication. Moreover, if education is highly correlated with both income and turnout, the original correlation of .8 falls to close to 0. This is washout; the correlation disappears after the control. Presumably, education is here causing both income and turnout, only making it appear that income causes turnout. Once education is controlled, this becomes evident.

In the presidential vote example, we have "specification." Inflation is correlated with vote percentage both before and after the control. Inflation is correlated with percentage; it is most strongly correlated with percentage in the absence of high employment.

## Beta

Recall from Chapter 4 that Pearson's correlation coefficient reports the change in the $z$ scores of $Y$ produced by a 1 unit of change in the $z$ scores of $X$. Partial correlation coefficients *may generally be interpreted* in a similar fashion—the slope of the $z$ scores for two variables, while controlling a third variable.

However, another statistic, the *beta weight,* is *actually* the slope of the $z$ scores for two variables, while controlling a third variable. The computation of beta is rather complex and we need not go into it. But bear in mind two important points. First, analysts reporting the results of multiple regression usually report beta weights instead of partial correlation coefficients. Second, although computed somewhat differently, and behaving a little differently, these beta weights may *generally* be interpreted in the same way as partial correlation coefficients.

## Multiple *R*

The multiple correlation coefficient, when squared, indicates the proportion of variation in the dependent variable explained by the simultaneous effects of all the independent variables. In other words, what proportion of the variation in turnout may be explained by the simultaneous operation of income and education; what proportion of variation in presidential vote percentage may be explained by the simultaneous operation of inflation and employment? $R$ varies between 0 and 1 instead of -1 and 1, and, when squared, indicates the total predictive capacity of the equation: $Y = a + b_1 (x_1) + b_2 (x_2) + \cdots$. The computation for multiple $R$ is:

$$R = \sqrt{\frac{r_{xy}^2 + r_{zy}^2 - 2[(r_{xy}) (r_{zy}) (r_{xz})]}{1 - r_{xz}^2}}$$

In the first turnout example, this produces:

$$R = \sqrt{\frac{.64 + .52 - 2 [(.8) (.72) (.58)]}{.66}} = \sqrt{\frac{.49}{.66}}$$

$$= \sqrt{.74}$$

$$= .86$$

The simple correlation between income and turnout was .8. When education is also entered into the equation, the multiple correlation rises to .86. Income explains 64 percent of the variation in turnout ($r^2$). Income and educa tion together explain 74 percent of the variation in turnout ($R^2$). Again, basically, this equation adds together the amount of variation explained by $X$ and the amount of variation explained by $Z$, subtracts the overlap, and standardizes the result.

When education is not correlated with either income or turnout, it makes no additional contribution to the explanation of variation. Using the previous equation would then produce a multiple $R$ of .8. Multiple $R$ may never be smaller in magnitude than any single simple $r$ representing an independent variable in the equation. Adding variables to an equation may increase the total amount of variation explained, but they can never decrease it. Moreover, the less correlated the independent variables are to one another, and the more correlated they are to the dependent variable, the higher multiple $R$ will be. This is because the variation they are each explaining is unique and unshared among them. Indeed, if two independent variables are uncorrelated with one another, $R^2 = r^2 + r^2$. You may demonstrate this for yourself. Assume a situation in which the correlation between $X$ and $Y$ is .3, the correlation between $Z$ and $Y$ is .2, and the correlation between $X$ and $Z$ is 0.

Now use the equation to compute the multiple $R$ for the presidential percentage example. Be careful to handle all the negative signs correctly. You should get a multiple $R$ of .57, indicating that inflation and employment together explain about 33 percent of the variation in vote percentage.

## Partial Slopes

Recall from simple regression that correlation coefficients are standardized scores, used to determine the amount of variation in one variable explained by another variable. Slopes, on the other hand, are unstandardized scores, reported in original units, used to determine how much one variable changes in response to 1 unit of change in another variable. Partial slopes tell us how many units a dependent variable changes, in response to 1 unit of change in an independent variable, when all other independent variables in the regression equation are held constant. In the turnout example, suppose median income had been reported in thousands of dollars and the partial slope for median income was .7. After the effects of median education had been statistically removed, for every thousand dollars of upward change in median income, turnout would go up by .7 percentage points (original units). Similarly, suppose median education had been reported in years and the partial slope for median education was 1.2. That would tell us that, after the effects of median income had been statistically removed, for every year of upward change in median education, turnout would go up by 1.2 percentage points.

The computation of partial slopes (and the constant, $a$) is complex, and almost always done with computer assistance. Indeed, this is true of partial correlation coefficients, beta weights, and multiple correlation coefficients as well. Therefore, we will not demonstrate the computation of partial slopes here. However, keep in mind that these slopes are central to the presentation and interpretation of multiple regression results, which usually take the form: $Y = a + b_1 (x_1) + b_2 (x_2) + b_3 (x_3) + \cdots$.

For a contrived example:

TURNOUT $= 20 + .7$ (INCOME) $+ 1.2$ (EDUCATION)

Therefore, in a state (case) where the median income was \$25 (thousand) and the median education was 12 years the prediction is:

TURNOUT $= 20 + .7 (25) + 1.2 (12) = 51.9\%$

Combined with multiple $R$, partial slopes yield very important information. For example, suppose we have employed multiple regression to determine the impact of undergraduate GPA, LSAT scores, and undergraduate class rank on first-year law school GPA among a sample of first-year law students. We discover that the partial slope for undergraduate GPA is .5, the partial slope for LSAT is .02, the partial slope for class rank is −.2 (class rank is negatively correlated with performance; lower class rank, better performance), and the multiple $R$ is .4. This tells us that undergraduate GPA, LSAT scores, and undergraduate class rank together explain 16 percent of the variation in law school performance the first year. On average, 1 grade point in undergraduate GPA is worth .5 grade points in law school, 1 point on the LSAT is worth .02 grade points in law school, and 1 point lower on class rank is worth .2 grade points.[2]

## Tests of Significance for Multiple Regression

The $f$ statistic determines the statistical significance of partial correlation coefficients, just as the $t$ statistic determines the statistical significance of zero-order correlations. While the $t$ statistic indicates the probability that Pearson's correlation coefficient is not 0 in the population, the "$f$ statistic" indicates the probability that the partial correlation coefficient is not 0 in the population. It indicates the likelihood that two interval level variables are correlated in the population, after the effects of third interval level variables have been removed. It behaves in a manner similar to chi square and $t$, may take on any value above 0, and may be referenced for statistical significance in a table of $f$ values.

As noted previously, analysts reporting the results of multiple regression usually report the beta weight instead of the partial correlation coefficient. In so doing, they usually report a $t$ statistic similar to that reported for zero-order Pearson's correlation coefficients. However, the $f$ statistic for the partial correlation coefficient may generally be interpreted in the same manner as the $t$ statistic for the beta weight.

Suppose, in the law school example that the partial correlation between undergraduate GPA ($X$) and first-year law school GPA ($Y$), controlling for LSAT ($Z$), was .2 for a random sample of 20 law school students. The $f$ statistic permits us to determine the likelihood that had we analyzed data for *all* law school students, there would have in fact been a positive partial correlation.

The formula for $f$ is:

$$\left( \frac{r^2_{xy \cdot z}}{1 - r^2_{xy \cdot z}} \right) (N - 3)$$

In our example:

$$\left( \frac{.04}{.96} \right) (17) = .708$$

An $f$ table indicates that the .05 level of significance, with 17 degrees of freedom, requires an $f$ of at least 4.45. (Degrees of freedom are set to $N - 3$ when there is one control variable.) Therefore, we are *not* at least 95 percent confident that the partial correlation between undergraduate GPA and first-year law school GPA, controlling for LSAT, is not 0 in the population. A partial correlation of only .2 with a sample of only 20 is insufficient to conclude a statistical relationship in the population.

Alternately, in the inflation, employment, vote example presented earlier, suppose we had data for 40 presidential elections:

$$\left(\frac{(.62^2)}{1 - .62^2}\right)(37) = 23.1$$

An $f$ table indicates that the .05 level of significance, with 37 degrees of freedom, requires an $f$ of at least 4.08. Therefore, we are *at least* 95 percent confident that the partial correlation between inflation and vote, controlling for employment, is not 0 in the population "of all presidential elections." We may conclude a statistically significant relationship.

The $f$ statistic may also be computed for multiple $R$ to determine the likelihood that multiple $R$ is not 0 in the population—the likelihood that the independent variables explain some of the variation in the dependent variable. The equation is:

$$\left(\frac{R^2}{1 - R^2}\right)\left(\frac{N - k - 1}{k}\right)$$

where $k$ is the number of independent variables. Degrees of freedom are set equal to $N - k - 1$. In the law school example, with a multiple $R$ of .4 and 30 cases:

$$\left(\frac{.16}{.84}\right)\left(\frac{27}{3}\right)$$

$$= .19 \times 9 = 1.71$$

With 27 degrees of freedom and three independent variables, an $f$ statistic of 2.98 is required at the .05 level. Therefore, we *cannot* be 95 percent certain that the combined effects of undergraduate GPA, LSAT score, and class rank explain any of the variation in first-year law school GPA. (Be reminded that this is a contrived example. With real data, these three variables would surely be powerful explanatory factors.)

In the inflation, employment, vote example with a multiple $R$ of .68 and 40 cases:

$$\left(\frac{.46}{.54}\right)\left(\frac{37}{2}\right)$$

$$= .85 \times 18.5 = 15.73$$

With 37 degrees of freedom and two independent variables, an $f$ statistic of 3.23 is required at the .05 level. Therefore, we are *at least* 95 percent certain that the combined effects of inflation and employment explain a portion of the variation in vote.

## Application of Multiple Regression

Appendix G reprints a scholarly article by John Hibbing and Sara Brandes, "State Population and the Electoral Success of U.S. Senators," which appeared in the November 1983 issue of the *American Journal of Political Science.* The general question Hibbing and Brandes seek to answer is why senators are less "safe" than members of the U.S. House of Representatives—in other words, why do senators seeking reelection lose more frequently than representatives seeking reelection? They speculate that one possible explanatory factor may be size of constituency. Senators represent larger and more heterogeneous constituencies (entire states), while representatives represent smaller (about one-half-million people) and more homogenous constituencies. For example, a senator from New York must represent blacks, whites, city dwellers, farmers, and suburbanites, while a representative from Harlem must represent mostly black city dwellers. Therefore, it will be more difficult for the senator to always please all constituents, and easier for the representative to do so.

However, Hibbing and Brandes do not do a comparative analysis of senators and representatives; rather, they test a hypothesis for senators only: Incumbent senators from larger states do less well in elections than incumbent senators from smaller states. Of course, this hypothesis is consistent with the reasoning used to explain the differences between senators and representatives; in other words, if that reasoning is correct, there should be differences between incumbent senators from larger states and incumbent senators from smaller states. The independent variable is size of states, the dependent variable is electoral success, and the cases are states (although Hibbing and Brandes are interested in seeing how well senators do, they are actually "taking the measures" on states, as we shall see).

They operationally define size of state as the number of congressional districts in the state (about one for every half-million people). For example, California has 45 congressional districts, whereas South Dakota and other small or sparsely populated states have only one. They operationally define electoral success as the mean share of the two-party vote that all incumbent senators received in a state between 1946 and 1980. If their hypothesis is correct, we would expect the mean share of the vote going to incumbents to be smaller in larger states and larger in smaller states (a negative correlation). These are both interval level variables.

In addition, they operationally define an interval level third factor they want to control statistically—level of statewide party competition. They use the "folded" statewide Democratic vote for congressional candidates from 1946 to 1980. If statewide Democratic vote was 50 percent, there is very high competition. If it is 100 percent, there is no competition. "Folding" means that Democratic percentages falling below 50 percent are assigned the corresponding percent (above 50 percent) for Republicans. In other words, if the Democratic vote was 10 percent, that would show up as 90 percent (little competition). Obviously, if the Democrats are getting 10 percent of the two-party vote, the Republicans are getting 90 percent. All they are interested in is measuring *level of competition*. A 40 percent vote for Democrats is the same level of competition as a 60 percent vote for Democrats. So this scale just runs from 50 to 100. If Democrats or Republicans get 60 percent, it is 60; if Democrats or Republicans get 70 percent, it is 70, and so on.

Hibbing and Brandes report the results of a multiple regression as:

$$Y = 52.48 + .8 \text{ (competition)} - .17 \text{ (size)}$$

$$R = .87$$

Competition and size together explain 76 percent of the variation in incumbent share of two-party vote. For every 1 unit of upward change in the competition scale of 50 to 100, the share of incumbent two-party vote goes up .8 percent, after the effects of size have been statistically removed. Since 100 represents no competition, movement toward 100 benefits incumbents. This makes sense, insofar as we would expect incumbents to do better in noncompetitive states. For every 1 unit of upward change in the population indicator (about one-half-million people) incumbent vote percent declines .17 percent, after the effects of competition have been statistically removed.

Hibbing and Brandes do not report partial correlation coefficients nor beta weights. If they had, we would know whether competition or size were the more important variable in explaining turnout. We know they together explain 76 percent of the variation, but we do not know which explains more. Remember that correlation coefficients and betas are standard scores, while slopes use original units. Just because one slope has a value that is greater in magnitude than another does not mean that particular independent variable necessarily has more impact. For example, an independent variable measured in dollars and going up to thousands of dollars might have a very small slope compared to an independent variable measured in percents and going up only to 100, since slope measures change in the dependent variable for 1 unit of change in the independent variable. This could be true even though the dollar variable was more highly correlated with the dependent variable and explained more of the variation. In fact, however, in the Hibbing and Brandes equation, competition probably *does* explain more of the variation in incumbent vote. This is because competition and size are measured on similar scales (50 to 100 and 1 to 45).

Hibbing and Brandes also divide their cases (states) into Southern and non-Southern and do the analysis for each subset. Among Southern states, the multiple $R$ rises to .9 and 82 percent of the variation is explained. Among non-Southern states, the multiple $R$ falls to .41 and 17 percent of the variation is explained. This fits the pattern of specification. The overall multiple correlation is .87. The correlation is stronger for Southern states, weaker for non-Southern States. Competition and size are strong predictors of incumbent success. This is particularly true in Southern states.

Finally, note that Hibbing and Brandes report levels of significance for their equations. They note that, in each equation, competition and size are both statistically significant in their relationship with vote percent. In addition, they report the $f$ statistic for the multiple $R$ for each equation. In the first equation, $R$ is .87 and $f$ is 71.66, highly statistically significant. For Southern states, $R$ is .9 and $f$ is 22.85, again highly statistically significant. For the non-Southern states, $R$ is .41 and $f$ is 3.89, which is also statistically significant at the .05 level.

## SUMMARY

With cross-tabulations displaying a relationship between nominal or ordinal variables, we control for third factors through statistical elaboration. We elaborate the original contingency table by dividing the cases into the categories of the third factor, thereby holding this third factor constant, and reconstruct the original contingency table in each category. If the "conditional" tables show a pattern similar to the original table, replication prevails, indicating that the original relationship holds up and is not spurious. If the relationship in the original table disappears, we refer to it as washout, and conclude the original relationship is spurious. Pure patterns of replication or washout rarely occur in actual data analysis. Statistical elaboration usually results only in a tendency toward replication or a tendency toward washout. This is referred to as specification, since the statistical elaboration specifies the conditions under which the original relationship is most likely to hold. In a pattern of specification, both the independent variable in the original contingency table and the third factor exert an influence on the dependent variable.

Multiple regression permits us to control for third factors when the independent variable is interval, the dependent variable is interval, and the third factor is interval. It also permits us to test hypotheses that contain more than one independent variable. In multiple regression, we compute partial correlation coefficients or beta weights, a multiple correlation coefficient, and partial slopes. The partial correlation coefficient is the correlation between two variables after the effects of a third variable have been held constant, or statistically controlled. If the original correlation coefficient (zero-order correlation) goes down, that means the third factor is exerting an influence on the relationship; if it completely disappears, that means the original relationship was spurious. If the original correlation remains the same, that means the third factor was exerting no impact. In rare instances when the original correlation goes up, that means a negatively correlated third factor was exerting an impact on the relationship.

The multiple correlation coefficient, when squared, indicates the proportion of variation in the dependent variable explained by the simultaneous effects of all the independent variables and control variables. It varies between 0 and 1 and, when squared, indicates total variation explained. Partial slopes tell us how many units a dependent variable changes, in response to 1 unit of change in an independent variable, when all other independent and control variables in the regression equation are held constant. Combined with the multiple $R$, partial slopes give us very important information—we can discover how much variation in a dependent variable is explained and how much, on average, that dependent variable changes for 1 unit of change in each of the independent variables.

Political practitioners and political scientists must always be very careful to grasp the "multivariate" nature of political reality. For example, legal arguments about the impact of race on likelihood of receiving the death sentence would be vacuous in the absence of an appreciation of the multivariate nature of the phenomenon. An attorney attempting to demonstrate that blacks were more likely to get the death penalty than whites would be stymied by the Georgia evidence that whites are more likely to get the death penalty than blacks! Only a legal advocate with an appreciation for the interaction of defendant race, victim race, and death penalty would be effective in their advocacy.

Similarly, in the face of the argument that blacks who kill whites are more likely to get the death penalty, a skilled prosecutor in a death penalty case, attempting to rebut the argument, would raise a plethora of possible "confounding factors." For example, perhaps murders committed during robberies are more likely to elicit the death penalty than family violence murders (blacks are more likely to kill whites in the former than the latter). She would generate multivariate statistical evidence bearing on whether such confounding factors were at work (if, that is, the evidence supported the prosecution's argument!).

Similarly, political scientists seeking to identify the factors contributing to incumbent reelection rates cannot just "think bivariate." They must be prepared to confront the variety of causal factors likely operating in a complex political world. Certainly, size of constituency is a factor; just as certainly, level of party competitiveness plays a role.

Obviously, in attempting to uncover the complex statistical interrelationships among all the variables operating in a complex political world, a variety of measurement and data collection techniques is available. In addition, quantitative research designs may be constructed in a variety of ways. Chapter 10 introduces the two most common data-generation techniques and discusses research design in more detail.

# NOTES

1. The author analyzed actual data for candidates for the House of Representatives for 1978 and 1980. See also Gary C. Jacobson, *Money in Congressional Elections,* New Haven: Yale University Press, 1980.
2. It is becoming increasingly common for analysts reporting the results of multiple regression to simply report the multiple $R$ and the partial slopes. See Gary King, "How Not to Lie with Statistics: Avoiding Common Mistakes in Quantitative Political Science," *American Journal of Political Science*, 30:3, August 1986.

# *10*

# *Data-Generation Techniques and Alternate Research Designs*

$P$olitical scientists and political practitioners, in relying on numbers to conduct their research, discharge their responsibilities, and advance their political objectives, employ two basic varieties of data-collection techniques. Choice of technique frequently depends on the cases under scrutiny, and choice of technique often dictates the statistical tools most appropriate for analyzing the data and testing the research hypotheses. The two basic varieties are survey data and aggregate data.° Generally, although there will al-

---

°These two research techniques are those commonly employed in *quantitative research.* Of course, there are many research techniques that do not involve extensive quantification and statistical analysis. Traditional historical research, in which primary documents are analyzed, is one example. Field research, where behavior is observed firsthand, is another example. In addition, some varieties of quantitative research are not, strictly speaking, either survey or aggregate. *Content analysis,* when the researcher codes the content of written documents for the purpose of "measuring" themes in the documents and proceeds to conduct statistical analysis of the themes, is an example.

ways be exceptions, *survey data* are employed when people are the cases and the appropriate statistical tools are those employed at the nominal and ordinal levels of measurement. *Aggregate data* are employed when the cases are aggregates of people (such as cities, states, countries) and the appropriate statistical tools are those employed at the interval level of measurement.

# SURVEY RESEARCH

When conducting survey research, or public opinion polls, the quality of the data hinges on two questions: *Who* was interviewed? *How* were they interviewed? For both questions, the research should be conducted to ensure *representativeness* and avoid *bias*. In other words, in any single survey research endeavor, it is necessary that enough of the right kinds of people are asked enough of the right kinds of questions.

## Who

Chapter 5 showed us that purely random samples are seldom possible; therefore, purely representative samples are seldom possible. However, the techniques currently employed in survey research are close enough to being purely random that the effect will be representativeness. The most common technique is the *multistage cluster sample*. In this approach, geographic clusters of people are selected randomly in several stages. For example, in an election survey, we might select 500 counties randomly across the United States, then select 2 voting precincts randomly from each county, then select 2 voters randomly from each precinct. This would yield 2,000 respondents. While the respondents themselves would not have been selected randomly from a list of all voters in the nation, the effect would be very similar.

A fairly common current practice is to treat telephone exchanges as geographic clusters of people. Suppose, for example, we wished to select a representative sample of 1,200 Pennsylvanians. We might first select 200 telephone exchanges (the first six digits of a phone number, including the area code) randomly from the four area codes—215, 412, 717, and 814. Second, we might generate 6 random phone numbers for each exchange, yielding a total of 1,200 telephone numbers. The difficulty here, however, is that different telephone exchanges cover different sized clusters of people. For example, in the 717 area, perhaps there are twice as many people with 342 exchanges as with 347 exchanges, and three times as many people with 347 exchanges as 969 exchanges.

This difficulty is resolved by weighting the exchanges, in the first step of selection, in such a way that those covering more phone numbers have a proportionally greater chance of being selected. We'll give an overly simplified example of the effects of this strategy. The example only covers four hypothetical exchange areas in Pennsylvania, but the principles may be extended statewide or nationwide, to any large population.

| Exchange | Population | Weighting | Probability |
|----------|-----------|-----------|-------------|
| 215-691 | 16,000 | 12 | .545 |
| 717-342 | 8,000 | 6 | .273 |
| 717-347 | 4,000 | 3 | .136 |
| 717-969 | 1,330 | 1 | .045 |

Suppose we have four exchanges covering the population sizes (total number of phone numbers) indicated. We want to select one exchange randomly and then select one telephone number randomly from that exchange area. We construct a list with the first exchange listed 12 times, the second exchange listed 6 times, the third exchange listed 3 times, and the fourth exchange listed once—in other words, the list is weighted to reflect population. We select an exchange randomly from the list. Since 215-691 is listed 12 out of 22 times, to reflect its population proportion, there is a 54.5 percent chance that it will be the exchange selected. Similarly, there is a 4.5 percent chance that 717-969 will be the exchange selected.

Suppose it is 215-691. We now select a telephone number randomly from that exchange. The probability that any single phone number in that area will be selected is $1 / 16{,}000 = .0000625$. Now suppose it was 717-969 that was selected, and a phone number is selected from that exchange. The probability that any single phone number in that area will be selected is $1 / 1{,}330 = .00075$. Therefore, this multistage process has the effect of giving each phone number in the population an equal chance of being selected. The 215-691 exchange has a .545 probability of selection. If selected, a single number in that area has a .0000625 probability of selection. Therefore, the probability of that number being selected after the two-stage selection process is $.545 \times .0000625 = .000034$. The 717-969 exchange has a .045 probability of first-stage selection. If selected, a single number in that area has a .00075 probability of selection. Therefore, the probability of that number being selected is $.045 \times .00075 = .000034$. It works the same for each of the areas of differing population size, so each number in the population has an equal chance.

Of course, there are some special circumstances in which truly random selection of individual people takes place. In particular, this is possible if we have a list of everyone in the population. We selected a pure random sample in the student survey discussed in earlier chapters. We had a list of the approximately 3,500 full-time day students and randomly selected 600 of these by taking every sixth name on the list after a "random start." We rolled a die and started at that name on the list. The die roll was three, so we took the third, ninth, fifteenth, . . . people on the list. This created the conditions under which everyone on the list had an equal chance of selection. The first person and every sixth thereafter had one chance in six; the second person and every sixth thereafter had one chance in six, and so on.

## How

If our sample is not effectively random, and therefore not representative, and therefore biased, the opinions of those selected will not reflect the opinions of everyone in the population. Similarly, if the questions we ask of the respondents selected are not worded in such a way that the true opinions of these respondents are elicited, those opinions will not be reflective of the population, even if the sample were selected randomly. In other words, questions can be biased just as samples can be biased. The bias may be blatant, or it may be subtle.

For example, suppose we were interested in surveying a population for their views on abortion, to determine if the pro-choice or pro-life position enjoyed more support. We might ask, "Are you anti-abortion—or do you support the murder of innocent babies in their mothers' wombs?" Or we could ask, "Are you pro-choice—or do you believe the government should be able to strip women of their constitutional right to privacy?" Obviously, both these questions are blatantly biased. An overwhelming proportion of the respondents would surely answer that they were anti-abortion to the first question, and an overwhelming proportion of respondents would surely answer that they were pro-choice to the second question. Regardless of the survey researcher's personal opinion on the issue, if the survey researcher wants to get a true reading of opinions, he must strive to structure a question that is biased in neither direction. Nonbiased questions on sensitive issues such as this often take the following form:

> As you know, many people consider themselves to be pro-life and many others consider themselves to be pro-choice. Those who are pro-life believe that abortion is morally wrong. Some believe it is murder. Those who are pro-choice believe the decision to have an abortion should be left to the choice of the woman. They believe government regulation is a violation of women's rights. Would you say you are pro-life or would you say you are pro-choice?

Of course, any reasonable person would agree that the first two questions used as examples are biased. But question bias is most pernicious when it is least obvious. For example, in 1992, Congress passed, over President Bush's veto, a bill designed to regulate the cable television industry. One provision of the bill was that the Federal Communications Commission would set rates for cable television companies operating as monopolies in certain communities. Suppose we wanted to determine, through a survey, whether or not the general public thought such regulation was a good idea, and asked, "Congress recently passed, and President Bush vetoed, a bill requiring the Federal Communications Commission to decide how much cable television companies, in communities where only one company operates, may charge for their services. Do you generally support or generally oppose such regulation?" The difficulty with this question is that it may bias responses into the "oppose" direction since the question contains a statement that President Bush vetoed the legislation. Respondents who like Bush, or respect the office of the presidency, may oppose the regulation for that reason. Reference to the president should be left out of the question. The popularity of, or respect for, the president is a separate issue that could be dealt with in separate questions.

Often questions on current public issues are asked in phases. For example, the survey might first ask, "Congress has passed legislation regulating the cable television industry, are you by any chance familiar with that legislation?" Those who are familiar with the legislation can then be asked whether they support it or oppose it. Those who are unfamiliar with the legislation can be given a brief description of its content, then asked if they support or oppose it. In this way, when the data are analyzed, a distinction may be made between the opinions of those who were familiar with the issue and the opinions of those who were not.

In addition, good survey questions should be as short, as clear, as concise, and as unambiguous as possible. Obviously, this is not a good question:

> Congress is considering cutting the capital gains tax because they believe that such a cut would permit people who have made profits on their investments to take more of those profits and reinvest them and they also believe that if taxes on the profits are lower that people will have more incentive to invest in the first place and that investment creates jobs

and a cut in capital gains taxes will therefore lower the unemployment rate. Do you agree or disagree that the capital gains should be cut?

Clearly, this is a poor question because it attempts to deal simultaneously with too many different issues: taxes, investment, unemployment, and so forth. The question is "run on" and confusing. Therefore, the responses may reflect the confusion of the respondent rather than his or her position on the capital gains tax.

Of course, the need to provide the respondent with sufficient information to form a reasoned judgement (as in the cable television example) and the need to avoid confusion and ambiguity is often a difficult balancing act. Trial-and-error experience in actually conducting survey research is necessary in striking the appropriate balance.

Moreover, care must always be taken not to intimidate the respondent. For example, many surveys are designed to elicit the opinions of those who are likely to vote. Therefore, the surveyor wants only to speak to those respondents who are registered to vote. Yet, being asked by a stranger, over the telephone, whether or not you are registered to vote may be intimidating. In the minds of most, being registered is "good" and socially acceptable, while not being registered is "bad" and socially undesirable. Therefore, the number of people reporting that they are registered may be higher than the number actually registered.

Steps may be taken to minimize these effects. For example, before asking the registration question, the surveyor might ask one or two simple nonintimidating questions, such as the respondent's city and state of residence. Then the surveyor might ask, "As you know, some people are registered to vote, while other people, perhaps because they have been busy with other things, have not had a chance to register for the upcoming election. Are you, by any chance, registered to vote, or have you not had a chance to register?" Asking this as the third question, and stating it in a nonintimidating way, is likely to yield more accurate responses.

Finally, the order in which questions are asked on a survey may bias the responses. Most surveys ask what are referred to as "demographic" questions—race, religion, age, income, level of education, and the like. These questions usually appear at the end of the questionnaire since they are "personal" questions. Obviously, if a stranger phones your home, and the first question asked is how much money you make, you are unlikely to be too cooperative. However, if a number of other questions are asked first, and a "rapport" has developed between the respondent and the interviewer, such personal questions will be less threatening.

There is another concern relevant to order that must be kept in mind when asking questions. Surveyors are frequently interested in establishing the degree of "name recognition" among candidates, particularly in state and local races and in presidential primaries. For example, during the 1992 Democratic presidential primary, a surveyor might have asked:

Can you tell me which of the following names you are familiar with?

|  |  | Yes | No |
|---|---|---|---|
| (1) | Paul Tsongas | ____ | ____ |
| (2) | Douglas Wilder | ____ | ____ |
| (3) | John Kerrey | ____ | ____ |
| (4) | Bill Clinton | ____ | ____ |

| (5) | Jerry Brown | ___ | ___ |
| (6) | Tom Harkin | ___ | ___ |
| (7) | Cliff Zukin | ___ | ___ |

However, during the interviewing, the order of the names would have been shuffled. One-seventh of the respondents would have been given Tsongas's name first, one-seventh Wilder's name first, and so on. This is because there is a tendency for respondents to be more likely to answer yes at the beginning of a list, and less likely to answer yes at the end of a list. The reasons for this are not entirely clear, but the shuffling prevents the person at the top of list from getting more yes responses than justified. There is also a tendency for respondents to answer yes even if they have not heard of the candidate. Therefore, some surveyors "make up" a name and include it on the list. So, for example, if 5 percent of the respondents say they have heard of Cliff Zukin, we can be fairly certain that the numbers for the real candidates are inflated by about 5 percent.

Appendix H contains part of a questionnaire from a 1989 Eagleton survey, part of a questionnaire from a 1983 Louis Harris poll, and part of an analysis by Raymond J. Adamek titled "Abortion and Public Opinion in the United States." Note the introductory section of the Eagleton questionnaire. It is designed to convince the respondent to agree to be interviewed. This is very important, because each individual phone number called has been selected randomly and for the sample to be representative, the surveyor must make sure that someone available at that phone number is actually interviewed. Mentioning Rutgers University lends credibility (presumably) to the survey, and there are three "probes" the interviewer may use if the respondent balks.

Note also that Eagleton is "screening" for registered voters. If the respondent is not registered, Eagleton does not want that person in the sample—in other words, they want a *random sample of registered voters*. However, Eagleton may be overestimating the number of registered voters by asking this question first, for the reasons already mentioned—they may be getting respondents in the sample who are not registered to vote. Note also what is called a "skip pattern" on all the included pages, represented by arrows. If the respondent is not registered, or says he or she probably or definitely won't vote, the interview is terminated. Eagleton asks if the respondent has heard of Courter—if yes, they ask for an evaluation; if no, they skip to the next questions. Skip patterns are very common in public opinion questionnaires.

Turning our attention to the Harris questionnaire, note that, on page 248, Harris is recording the number of *callbacks*, or the number of times it took to get an answer at the randomly selected telephone number. Callbacks are very common and are designed to ensure that someone at the randomly selected number will be interviewed. In addition, by recording the number of callbacks, it is possible to analyze the data later to determine what kinds of respondents are likely to be home a lot and what kind are not likely to be home a lot. Such analysis can aid in determining the sorts of biases likely to result from never being able to get in touch with certain kinds of people.

Note later in the poll (on page 249), in the list of things that will or will not happen, the instruction ROTATE—START AT "X". This is an instruction to the interviewer to start at the statement with an X next to it. One-eleventh of the interviews will start at the first statement, one-eleventh will start at the second statement, and so forth. This is done for the reasons noted in the candidate example. Finally, do you see any problems with Question 5e on the page 250?

Study the Adamek analysis closely. Make sure you understand why the percentage results differ in each instance. Compare the first question to the second question in A, B, and C.

## Administration

Questionnaires may be administered to a sample of respondents in at least three different ways: face-to-face, over the telephone, or by mail. Telephone interviews are now much more common than face-to-face interviews for at least two reasons. First, they are much less expensive. Sending interviewers out across the country in national surveys is obviously very expensive. Second, telephone interviews minimize what is known as the "interaction effect." In face-to-face interviews, the interaction between the characteristics of the interviewer and the characteristics of the respondent may bias responses. For example, if a black were interviewing a white, or vice versa, this could bias responses for questions on civil rights policy.

Of course, cost and "interaction" are concerns nonetheless in telephone interviewing. Let us suppose we interview 1,000 randomly selected people for 20 minutes each; one interviewer can complete about two 20-minute interviews in an hour, after callbacks and other delays are taken into account. Therefore, interviewing costs would be about 500 people-hours. In other words, 50 interviewers interviewing for 10 hours could complete the 1,000 interviews, or 100 people interviewing for 5 hours, or some other combination. Interviewers must also be trained for any single survey to make certain they understand the skip patterns, to make certain they do not bias the responses by the their tone of voice, and so forth. Suppose this adds another 100 people-hours. Suppose further that we are paying our interviewers $7 per hour—interviewing costs would then be over $4,000. If taking a statewide poll, we would expect, in most states, a minimum telephone bill of about $4,000 or $5,000 as well, so we are already up to close to $10,000. And we have not even considered the costs of selecting the sample, entering the data into a computer, or analyzing the data.

Currently, *the direct costs* of conducting a 20-minute interview of 1,000 people usually run about $30,000–$40,000. Indeed, well-known survey research firms such as the Harris organization or the Gallup organization may, depending on the complexity of the information to be collected, charge upward of $100,000 for such a survey. There is a lesson here. If someone tells you they can conduct a survey for you for a few hundred dollars, do not sign up with them. They may be able to conduct such a survey, but they will not be able to conduct it correctly, and the results will be valueless.

Interaction effects may also present difficulties in telephone interviewing. For example, considerable evidence suggests that men and women will respond differently to certain kinds of questions, depending on whether they are interviewed by a male or a female.[1] When polled on the abortion issue, women are more likely to give stronger pro-choice responses when interviewed by a woman than when interviewed by a man. Clearly, such effects are most likely to show up with questions relevant to women's issues. Of course, the key to managing interaction effects is to understand their role in interviewing and take reasonable steps to minimize them.

So why not just do mail surveys? They are less expensive and there are no interaction effects. The obvious reason mail surveys are frowned upon is that they suffer from the most serious form of bias—"self-selection bias." The quickest way to make sure you *do not* get a random sample is to let people decide whether or not they want to be in the sample! Obviously, those who choose to return mail questionnaires will be very different than those who choose not to—they will be more interested in the issues, they will have stronger opinions on the issues, and so forth. Suffering even greater self-selection bias are the "900 call-in polls" conducted by the media. At the risk of sounding overly critical, we must conclude that the results of these polls, as an indication of public opinion, are simply worthless.

Of course, under certain circumstances, if care is taken, mail surveys can yield useful results. If the population is relatively small, and if several "waves" are sent out, the effects of self-selection bias are minimized. For example, in the University of Scranton survey of 400 students we randomly selected 600 students from among a population of 3,500, and mailed out two "waves." The first time we sent out the questionnaire to 600 people, 300 people returned it. We then sent it out again, to the 300 who had not returned it, and got 100 more replies. Our sample of 400 had self-selection bias; it did not have as much self-selection bias, however, as it would have if we had stopped after the first wave. Indeed, had we conducted a third wave, we probably could have pushed the sample size up to 450, having even less bias. In addition, it would be possible to compare the characteristics of the first 300 to those of the second 100 and then the third 50, to determine the sorts of people likely underrepresented by the bias.

The information needed to compile the Nielson television ratings is gathered by mail. The organization will first telephone and request participation, then send a postcard thanking the respondent for agreeing to participate, then send a booklet in which to record one week of television viewing, then send a postcard reminding the respondent to mail back the booklet. By taking these simple, relatively inexpensive steps, self-selection bias is substantially reduced.

## AGGREGATE DATA

Aggregate data are collected when the cases are aggregates of people instead of individual people. The data may be *longitudinal* or *time series*. Longitudinal data are collected from different locations at one point in time. For example, if cities are the cases, or states are the cases, or countries are the cases, we collect longitudinal aggregate data. Time series data are collected over time in one location—the time points are the cases. For example, the Fenton article, reprinted in Appendix D and discussed in Chapter 4, is a time-series analysis. The cases, or the points at which the measurements are taken, are election years. These measurements are taken for aggregates of people in one location—the eligible electorate in the United States.

With aggregate data, we "count things" to take our measures. If measuring the population of states, we count people to assign a value to each state. If measuring the proportion of states' budgets devoted to education, we count dollars to assign a value to each state. But the things that are being counted are *not* the cases. To appreciate the importance of this distinction, consider the difference between measuring income for individual people, as in survey data, and measuring income for aggregates of people, say states. The distributions would differ:

|  | *Income of Individuals* | *Median Income of States* |
|---|---|---|
| $30,000 or under | 600 | 10 |
| Over $30,000 | 1,400 | 40 |
|  | 2,000 cases | 50 cases |

With aggregate data, a very important distinction must be made between *units of analysis* and *units of observation*. The units of analysis are the cases. The units of observation are the things we are counting. To illustrate the importance of this distinction, we briefly review the work the famous French sociologist, Emile Durkheim. In 1897, he published *Le Suicide,* one of the first quantitative analyses done by a social scientist.[2] Durkheim measured suicide rates in different regions of Austria and Germany, as well as measuring other aggregate characteristics of the regions, such as religion. His units of analysis were regions, and his units of observation were people. He counted people to assign measures to regions.

He found that suicide rates were higher in regions with a higher proportion of Protestants. Does this mean that Protestants were more likely to commit suicide? No! Reaching such a conclusion is referred to as the *ecological fallacy,* imputing the characteristics of the aggregate to the characteristics of the individual by confusing units of analysis and units of observation. The only permissible conclusion is that people who live in regions with a high proportion of Protestants are more likely to commit suicide than people who live in other regions. Of course, *one possible* explanation for the pattern is that Protestants as individuals are more likely to commit suicide. But there are other possible explanations.

Durkheim's explanation addressed the norms of religious communities. He theorized that Protestant communities are more individualistically oriented, while Catholic communities are more collectively oriented. He theorized that, as a result, there is likely more anomie among members of Protestant communities—more disconnectedness from society. This is a *contextual* explanation, not an explanation that relies on the characteristics of individual people.

Take another example. Suppose we discover, by consulting public opinion poll data for individual states and aggregate medical data for those states, that states in which there is a high rate of abortion also have a higher proportion of citizens who consider themselves pro-life. Obviously, such a finding would *not* suggest that the pro-life citizens were the ones having the abortions! Rather, it would suggest a contextual explanation. Within the context of high abortion rates, people are more likely to oppose abortion.

Before the development of survey research, political scientists studying voting behavior often correlated the characteristics of aggregates at the precinct level. For example, they correlated the proportion of blacks to the proportion of the Democratic vote. This research suffered from the ecological fallacy. Of course, in this instance, it was probably correct that the aggregate correlations existed because blacks were voting Democratic. However, there was no empirical evidence for that. Such evidence can only be sought at the individual level, where people are the cases.

## INTRODUCTION TO TIME-SERIES ANALYSIS

There are at least three varieties of time-series analysis: univariate forecasting, bivariate forecasting, and interrupted time series. In univariate forecasting, time points are the cases, but time may also be treated as one of the variables. Generally, univariate forecasting displays a *trend line*, such as that presented in Figure 10.1. The figure displays government expenditures in the United States as a percent of GNP every ten years from 1950 to 1990. Suppose we wanted to "project the trend" and forecast what the percentage is likely to be in the year 2000. How would we do that? One strategy is to treat time, on the horizontal axis, as the $X$ variable, percent GNP, on the vertical axis, as the $Y$ variable, and compute a simple regression using $Y = a + b (X)$ to predict the value of percent GNP in the year 2000. The slope of the regression equation would be equal to the average change per year in the $Y$ variable, which would be used to predict $Y$'s value in the year 2000. Here, the slope would be a little over .2, or a little over 2 percent per decade.

### Bivariate Forecasting

In bivariate forecasting, we correlate two variables across time, in a fashion similar to that employed by Fenton in Appendix D. For example, in Figure 10.2, we graph unemployment rate along with percent of GNP accounted for by government spending, to test the hypothesis that government spending influences unemployment. Here, we would compute a simple regression with government spending as $X$, unemployment as $Y$, and the time points as cases.

However, this presents a problem. It is absolutely impossible to control for all the other things that happen with the passage of time. Long-term trends may result from a plethora of historical patterns. As Stephen Jay Gould puts it, there will be strong positive correlations between "my age, the population of Mexico, the price of swiss cheese, my pet turtle's weight, the average distance between galaxies. . . ."[3] Obviously, none of these things causes any of the other things; yet, the passage of time, in a sense, "causes" them all. In other words, unemployment may be highly correlated with government ex-

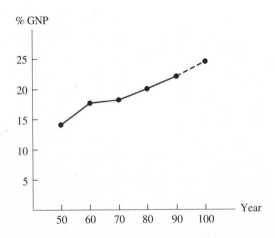

**Figure 10.1**

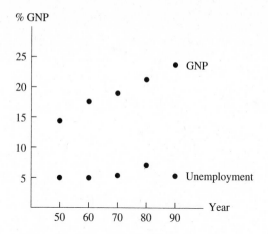

**Figure 10.2**

penditures even though the latter has no causal impact on the former. Therefore, in bivariate forecasting, we must control for the passage of time, or "de-trend" the data. This is done through multiple regression, using both time and government expenditures as independent variables, and computing the partial correlation between expenditures and employment, controlling for years. In this example, we would discover that although government expenditures and unemployment are positively correlated initially (about .5), they are negatively correlated (about −.5) after the data are de-trended. In other words, after we statistically remove the passage of time, government expenditures appear to bring down unemployment.

## Interrupted Time Series

Those responsible for analyzing the impact of public policy frequently establish an indicator for the social or economic problem the policy is designed to solve, take measures at time points before the policy is launched, take measures at time points after the policy is launched, and compare the latter to the former in an attempt to determine the impact of the policy. This is referred to as *impact analysis* and employs interrupted time series—in other words, the public policy is the interruption. The public policy is the independent variable and the social or economic indicator is the dependent variable.

The method may be employed with either survey or aggregate data. For example, we might survey people in a community about their level of satisfaction with the public transportation system both before and after a policy rerouting or expanding that system, to determine if the level of satisfaction rose as a result of the "impact" of the policy.

Appendix I reprints a study by political scientist Francis W. Hoole, titled "Evaluating the Impact of International Organizations," which appeared in the Summer 1977 issue of *International Organization*. The article is interesting not only because it uses interrupted time series, but also because it has a very useful presentation of alternate research design. Hoole writes about correlational and experimental designs, and he also shows us what an interrupted time series design looks like:

$$O_1 \, O_2 \, O_3 \, O_4 \, O_5 \, O_6 \times O_7 \, O_8 \, O_9 \, O_{10} \, O_{11} \, O_{12}$$

In other words, we take observations at a series of time points, introduce the independent variable, and take additional observations for a similar series of time points.

Let us focus on pages 264–267, paying particular attention to the diagram (Figure I.1) on p. 267. Hoole's research question is whether or not the World Health Organization's (WHO) smallpox eradication program had an impact on the number of countries reporting cases of smallpox, and his hypothesis grows directly from this research question. The independent variable is the program, the dependent variable is the number of countries reporting cases of smallpox, and the cases are the years 1950–1976. He discovers that the number of countries reporting smallpox decreased at an average annual rate of 2.1 per year before program implementation and an average annual rate of 4.6 per year after im plementation.

These trends may be specified more precisely, employing what is known as "dummy variable regression." We enter year, number of countries reporting, and a "dummy variable" for "before and after program" into a regression equation. All years before the program are assigned the value of 0 and all years after the program are assigned the value of 1. The partial slope between year and number of countries reporting shows the average decrease in number of countries reporting per year, after the effects of the program are statistically removed. The partial slope between the dummy variable and number of countries reporting shows the decrease in average number of countries reporting each year from the period before implementation to the period after implementation, once the yearly downward trend in the data is statistically removed (detrended). Performing this analysis with the Hoole data leads to an equation looking something like this:

$$\text{countries reporting} = a - 16\,(\text{dummy}) - 2.1\,(\text{year})$$

In other words, the average number of countries reporting per year dropped by 16 after the program was implemented, while the yearly downward trend was 2.1.

Dummy variable regression may be used any time we have a dichotomous predictor variable. For example, if we take the data on campaign expenditures by candidates for the House of Representatives discussed in Chapter 9, score challengers 0 and incumbents 1, and do a regression to determine the impact of the dummy variable and the amount of money spent on the percentage of the vote, we get something like:

$$\% \text{ of vote} = a + 20\,(\text{dummy}) + .2\,(\text{money spent})$$

In other words, being an incumbent is worth 20 points, even after the effects of expenditures are statistically removed. After the effects of incumbency are removed, money is not worth much of anything.

## INTRODUCTION TO ANALYSIS OF VARIANCE

Dummy variable regression permits us to determine the impact of an independent variable measured at the nominal level on a dependent variable measured at the interval level. In the interrupted time series example, "before versus after" is the nominal independent variable and number of countries reporting smallpox is the dependent interval level variable. In the campaign finance example, "incumbent versus challenger" is the nominal independent variable and percentage of vote is the interval dependent variable.

Dummy variable regression is very similar to a more common strategy for determining the impact of a nominal independent variable on an interval dependent variable—*analysis of variance.* Analysis of variance groups cases into the categories of the independent variable and proceeds to determine if the mean values on the dependent variable within each category are significantly different from one another. Is the mean value of number of countries reporting smallpox in the "before" group significantly different from the mean value of the number of countries in the "after" group? Is the mean vote percent in the "incumbent" group significantly different from the mean vote percent in the "challenger" group?

Analysis of variance compares the *within group variance* to the *between group variance.* If the means of the dependent variable are different from category to category, and if the dependent variable varies very little within the categories but varies a lot between the categories, analysis of variance produces statistically significant differences in the means. If the means are similar to one another, and the dependent variable varies a lot within the categories, analysis of variance does not produce statistically significant differences. Therefore, analysis of variance requires consideration not only of the means within the categories, but also of the standard deviations around the means within the categories.

## Difference of Means Test

In the simplest form of analysis of variance, the independent variable has only two categories and a *t* statistic is computed to determine if the mean of the dependent variable in the first category is significantly different from the mean of the dependent variable in the second category. This is simply referred to as the *difference of means test,* where the formula for *t* is:

$$\frac{X_1 - X_2}{\sqrt{\dfrac{N_1 s_1^2 + N_2 s_2^2}{N_1 + N_2 - 2}} \cdot \sqrt{\dfrac{N_1 + N_2}{N_1 N_2}}}$$

$X_1$ and $X_2$ are the means in each group, $N_1$ and $N_2$ are the number of cases in each group, and $S_1$ and $S_2$ are the standard deviations around the mean in each group.

Suppose we have a random sample of 20 males and 20 females who took the SAT on a particular day. We want to determine whether or not there is a statistically significant difference between the mean male math score and the mean female math score. In other words, can we be confident, at the .05 level, that the mean math score for the entire population of males who took the exam on that day is different from the mean math score for the entire population of females who took the exam that day? Suppose that, in our sample, the mean for males is 475 and the standard deviation is 25; suppose the mean for females is 470 and the standard deviation is 20:

$$\frac{475 - 470}{\sqrt{\dfrac{(20)(625) + (20)(400)}{20 + 20 - 2}} \cdot \sqrt{\dfrac{20 + 20}{(20)(20)}}}$$

$$= \frac{5}{\sqrt{\dfrac{12,500 + 8,000}{38}} \ \sqrt{\dfrac{40}{400}}}$$

$$= \frac{5}{\sqrt{540} \ \cdot \ \sqrt{.1}}$$

$$= \frac{5}{(23)(.3)} = \frac{5}{7} = .7$$

Degrees of freedom are set equal to the total number of cases (40) minus 2. At the .05 level, a $t$ statistic of at least 2.02 is required. Therefore, we fall short. With only a 5-point difference in the means, and only 40 cases in the sample, we cannot be 95 percent confident that the mean male math score is different from the mean female math score in the population.

Analysis of variance may also be applied to Hoole's data by estimating means and standard deviations from the graph on page 267: There are 17 "before" years with a mean of approximately 61 and a standard deviation of approximately 11. There are 10 "after" years with a mean of approximately 15 and a standard deviation of approximately 8:

$$\frac{61 - 15}{\sqrt{\dfrac{(17)(121) + (10)(64)}{17 + 10 - 2}} \ \cdot \ \sqrt{\dfrac{17 + 10}{(17)(10)}}}$$

$$= \frac{46}{\sqrt{\dfrac{2,057 + 640}{25}} \ \cdot \ \sqrt{\dfrac{27}{170}}}$$

$$= \frac{46}{\sqrt{108} \ \cdot \ \sqrt{.16}}$$

$$= \frac{46}{(10.4)(.4)} = \frac{46}{4.16} = 11$$

Obviously, the difference between 61 and 15 is so large that, even with only 27 cases (years), the analysis of variance produces a statistically significant result. We have confidence that the smallpox eradication program resulted in a decline in the number of reported cases that would not have occurred by chance had the trend not been interrupted by the program.

## Extension of the Basic Principle

Analysis of variance may be extended to situations in which the independent variable has more than one category. For example, in a random sample of students, we may wish to determine whether or not white students, black students, and Asian students have significantly different mean SAT scores. Similarly, we may take a random sample of congressional candidates, divide them into incumbents, those challenging incumbents, and those running for "open seats," and use analysis of variance to determine if statistically significant differences exist in their mean vote percentages. Computation of analysis of variance would use the means, the standard deviations and the number of cases to compare the variation within groups to the variation between groups. The result would be an *f* statistic interpreted in a fashion similar to the *t* statistic used for two categories. Recall from our discussion of simple and multiple regression that *f* and *t* behave in a similar fashion.

Finally, *multiple analysis of variance* may be used to determine the simultaneous impact of two or more nominal level independent variables on an interval level dependent variable; for example, the simultaneous impact of male/female and white/black/Asian on SAT scores. The analysis would actually entail the computation of an *f* statistic in a comparison of six group means: male/white, male/black, male/Asian, female/white, female/black, female/Asian. If both variables were dichotomous, as with male/female and white/black, the result would be the same as a multiple regression with two independent dummy variables (0 and 1 for males and females; 0 and 1 for whites and blacks) and an interval level dependent variable.[*]

## Application of Analysis of Variance

Appendix J reprints an article by Judith Trent, Paul A. Mongeau, Jimmie D. Trent, Kathleen E. Kendall, and Ronald B. Cushing titled "The Ideal Candidate," which appeared in the November 1993 issue of the *American Behavioral Scientist*. The article demonstrates the application of the simplest form of analysis of variance, the difference of means test, in scholarly research on the role of the media in presidential campaigns.

The authors are interested in discovering whether the views of reporters regarding desirable candidate qualities differ from the views of voters, whether such views are likely to vary from election to election, and whether such views are likely to be different for Republicans and Democrats. Although they test a number of hypotheses designed to answer these research questions, we will focus on the question of whether the views of reporters differ from the views of voters, and the analysis of the differences in means reported in Table J.2.

The analysis is designed to determine whether significant differences exist in the importance assigned to candidate characteristics such as experience, moral character, honesty, and so forth. The authors interviewed 236 reporters and 444 voting citizens attending presidential campaign rallies in New Hampshire during the 1988 and 1992 primaries. They asked respondents to rate, from 1 (strong disagreement) to 5 (strong agreement), the desirability of nine candidate characteristics. The independent variable

---

[*]Dummy variable regression and analysis of variance are based on the same statistical principles. The *t* statistic for a Pearson's correlation coefficient in a dummy variable regression of gender and SAT scores, with male coded 0 and female coded 1, would achieve the same level of statistical significance as a *t* statistic in a difference of means test between the scores of males and females. Similarly, an *f* statistic for a multiple *R* in a dummy variable regression of gender, race, and SAT scores, with male coded 0 and female coded 1 and white coded 0 and black coded 1, would achieve the same level of statistical significance as an *f* statistic in a multiple analysis of variance using the same three variables.

is whether or not the respondent is a reporter or a citizen, the dependent variables are the nine candidate characteristics, and the cases are all 680 respondents.

The independent variable is certainly valid and reliable. Subjects are either reporters or citizens and such a distinction is easily made and recorded. Some may question the validity of the 5-point scale for measuring attitudes. The criticism is particularly compelling insofar as means will be computed from the scale. A statistical purist would argue that the Likert scale is an ordinal level variable, while means may only be computed at the interval level. Yet, application of interval level statistics to Likert scales is common practice among social scientists. The scale probably poses no reliability problems, unless respondents are telling interviewers what they "think they want to hear" for some reason, for some of the characteristics.

For 1988, the authors found statistically significant differences in means for 6 of the 9 characteristics; in each instance, the public felt the characteristic was more important than the reporters thought it was. For 1992, the public and the media differed for only 4 of the 11 characteristics; again, in each instance, the public felt the characteristic was more important than the reporters. These results are reported on pages 277–278. One conclusion the authors derive from this analysis is that the media may not be the "opinion leaders" they are often assumed to be. Perhaps it is the reverse—the media follow the more strongly held views of the electorate.

Note, on pages 277–278, that for each characteristic, the authors report the number of cases in the sample, the $t$ statistic, and the level of significance. Note also that in Trent et al.'s footnote 1, they state "Given the sample sizes in both the 1988 and 1992 samples, small mean differences would be statistically significant at the .05 level of significance even though these differences would be substantively unimportant. Therefore, the .01 level of significance is used for almost all analysis." The authors are here making a distinction between substantive and statistical significance, as we discussed in Chapter 7. Recall that if there are large number of cases in the sample, the results may be statistically significant even if they are substantively uninteresting.

Two final notes. In Table J.1, and the accompanying commentary, the authors look at the differences between reporters and citizens on a number of demographic characteristics, such as party identification. Here, they are dealing with contingency tables instead of means, and report chi square instead of $t$. In Table J.3, and the accompanying commentary, the authors look at mean differences across more than one category of an independent variable: Republican, Democrat, and Independent. Therefore, they use an $f$ statistic rather than a $t$ statistic.

## SUMMARY

The two basic varieties of data employed by political scientists and political practitioners are survey data and aggregate data. When conducting survey research or public opinion polls, the quality of the data hinges on two questions: Who was interviewed? How were they interviewed? For both questions, the research should be conducted to ensure representativeness and avoid bias. In other words, in any single survey research endeavor, it is necessary that enough of the right kinds of people are asked enough of the right kinds of questions.

Most survey research is now done by selecting telephone exchanges randomly, weighing them in accordance with the population covered by the exchanges, and generating phone numbers randomly. When constructing the questionnaire to be administered, the questions themselves must be clear, concise, avoid biased wording, and avoid biased question order. Questionnaire construction is a skill developed through experience. When costs and other factors are taken into account, telephone interviews are generally preferred to face-to-face interviews and mail questionnaires.

Aggregate data are collected when the cases are aggregates of people instead of individual people. It may be longitudinal or time series. Longitudinal data are collected from different locations at one point in time. Time-series data are collected over time in one location. With aggregate data, we "count things" to take our measures. The cases are the units of analysis, but the things being counted are the units of observation. The distinction between units of analysis and units of observation must always be kept clear in the analysis of aggregate data to avoid the ecological fallacy—imputing the characteristics of the aggregate to the individual.

There are at least three varieties of time-series analysis: univariate forecasting, bivariate forecasting, and interrupted time series. In univariate forecasting, time points are the cases, but may also be treated as one of the variables. Generally, univariate forecasting displays a trend line. In bivariate forecasting, we correlate two variables across time. When doing so, however, we must de-trend the data by entering time into the regression analysis. Interrupted time series determines the impact of a particular event on a trend.

Dummy variable regression or difference of means tests may be used to compare the "before" scores to the "after" scores. This is a particularly useful method for determining the impact of a public policy on a particular social or economic problem. Moreover, dummy variable regression and difference of means tests are appropriate in any situation where we have an independent variable with two categories and an interval level dependent variable. Both methods are based on the principles of analysis of variance, which permit tests of hypotheses with nominal level independent variables and interval level dependent variables.

# NOTES

1. See Richard Marin, "Woman Asking Women About Men Asking Women," *The Washington Post Weekly Edition*, January 15–21, 1990.
2. Emile Durkheim, *Le Suicide,* New York: The Free Press, 1951.
3. Stephen Jay Gould, *The Mismeasure of Man,* New York: Norton, 1981, p. 250.

# Appendix
# A

# An Equity Analysis
# of Pennsylvania's Basic
# Instruction Subsidy Program,
# 1977–80

CYNTHIA A. CRONK
*Indiana University of Pennsylvania*

GARY P. JOHNSON
*St. John's University*

A major ongoing issue in school finance and its reform is the equity of state school finance systems. In recent years no other single issue has so dominated the school finance reform movement and its literature. The considerable research and writing since 1970 on the equity of state school finance systems has produced a well defined and generally accepted methodology for the measurement of equity.[1] The methodology embodies the conceptual principles of equal treatment of equals (horizontal equity) and equal opportunity (fiscal neutrality) and employs statistical measures of each principle.

This paper reports the results of a study that examines the equity of Pennsylvania's public school finance system. The study was undertaken after the passage of a major legislative school finance reform bill (Act 59), allowing for the examination of the equity consequences of a legislated and politically determined reform effort. The measures of equity were computed and analyzed over a three-year period, providing an opportunity to observe the equity of the state system following the reform. While most studies use total expenditures, current operating expenditures, or total state and local tax revenues

---

1. For a comprehensive description and discussion of this emerging methodology, its use, and several related issues, see Allan Odden, Robert Berne, and Leanna Stiefel, *Equity in School Finance* (Denver, Colorado: Education Finance Center, Education Commission of the States, October, 1979).

per pupil in measuring equity, this study used an alternative statistic in the analysis called actual instructional expense (AIE).[2]

# BACKGROUND: ACT 59, THE BASIC INSTRUCTION SUBSIDY PROGRAM AND AIE

The state of Pennsylvania passed a fundamental school finance reform measure in 1977. Act 59 was designed to change significantly the way public schools in the Commonwealth were financed. As Pennsylvania entered the national arena of school finance reform, its goals were not unlike those of other reform states: more adequate levels of funding and greater equity. The school finance system that emerged from the 1977 legislative action is essentially a percentage equalizing aid program where the state shares the financial responsibility for financing public education with local school districts. This study assesses the equity consequences of Act 59 for the years 1977–80 and focuses on the basic instruction subsidy, the vehicle through which approximately 70 percent of state funds are allocated to local districts.[3]

The present finance system differs in several important respects from the prereform system. Under the old system, reimbursement to the local school district was determined by multiplying school district weighted average daily membership (WADM) by the local school district aid ratio (comparing district and statewide market value per pupil) which, in turn, was multiplied by the school district's actual instructional expense per pupil, or $750, whichever was less. As Fier and Fowler have noted, one of the major motivating factors for changing the school subsidy system in 1977 was that all 504 school districts expended more that $750 per pupil in actual instructional expense. This resulted in the formula being driven solely by WADM—which in most districts was declining."[4] Under Act 59, the new school finance system removed the $750 maximum reimbursement figure based on WADM and replaced it with a base earned for reimbursement (BER).

---

2. Actual instructional expense (AIE) is an actual dollar amount per pupil and is called the per pupil net cost of instruction in a school district. This includes all general fund expenses (total expenditures) except the following: (a) health service, transportation, debt service, capital outlay, homebound instruction, and outgoing transfers; (b) tuition payments received; (c) monies received from the state for driver education, special education, vocational curriculum and area vocational curriculum, and area vocational technical schools; (d) funds received from the state or federal government under the Elementary and Secondary Education Act, Economic Opportunity Act, Manpower Training and Development Act, including projects under section 2508.3 of the Public School Code. Source: William B. Castetter, Norman B. C. Ferguson, and Richard S. Heisler, *Guide to Pennsylvania School Finance* (Philadelphia, Penn.: Center for Field Studies, Graduate School of Education, 1980), p. 161.

3. The basic instruction subsidy allocation for 1979–80 was reported to be $1,451,845,176 or 72.7 percent of the total appropriation of $1,997,782,730. *Pennsylvania Public School Finance Program, 1979–80* (Harrisburg, Penn.: Pennsylvania Department of Education, 1980).

4. Robert Fier and William Fowler, "The Effect of School Finance Reform in Pennsylvania: 1979–1980," a paper presented at the annual meeting of the American Educational Research Association (1981), p. 5.

The maximum BER for a given year is equal to the median statewide AIE per pupil, with a particular school district BER determined by local school district tax effort. Because of the upward drift in median statewide AIE, the BER increases each year, as does a local school district's potential for reimbursement. Districts that tax at a higher rate to provide an education expenditure equal to the statewide median AIE receive a higher reimbursement than those that tax at a lower rate.[5] Thus, the basic instruction subsidy is determined by the number of reimbursable pupils (WADM), the percentage of state aid (aid ratio), and the base earned for reimbursement (BER) resulting from tax effort.[6]

Act 59 also changed the measure of local school district fiscal capacity. School district wealth was measured previously by market value per pupil, but is now a combined measure of personal income per pupil (10 percent) and market value per pupil (60 percent). Lastly, the reform bill included certain financial provisions and modifications for sparsity, density, and poverty conditions as part of the calculations determining a school district's basic instruction subsidy.

As noted earlier, the measure chosen for this analysis is actual instruction expense (AIE). When the equity of a school finance system is considered, an implicit assumption is that dollars per pupil equate proportionally to education per pupil. The variable AIE reflects most closely per pupil classroom expense after certain noninstructional expenses have been factored out. It is, therefore, a better measure of both financial and educational equity than most other expenditure or revenue figures traditionally used in equity studies.

## EQUITY: THE CONCEPTUAL FRAMEWORK

Equity standards establish a basis on which to assess the equity of a state's school finance system. The two equity standards used in this research are equalization and fiscal neutrality. Strictly interpreted, the equalization standard requires that each pupil in the state receive equal or near equal amounts of expenditures, revenues, or some other allocated resource, while fiscal neutrality requires that no relationship exist between local school district wealth and local school district spending. Table A.1 sets out the conceptual framework and shows the linkage between the standards and the four questions used to define these standards.[7]

It should be noted that these two standards of equity are not necessarily consistent with one another. The equalization standard requires little or no variation in resources among the state's pupils, while fiscal neutrality allows local choice to determine significantly the per pupil resource level as long as choice is not dependent upon the wealth of the local district. In short, the equity standards of equalization and fiscal neutrality may

---

5. Pennsylvania State Educational Association, "VOICE" (December, 1980):12.

6. Ibid., p. 12.

7. The questions are drawn from Odden et al., p. 7.

TABLE A.1   SCHEME OF CONCEPTUAL FRAMEWORK USED IN THE EQUITY ANALYSIS

| *Conception:* Per pupil expenditures should be equal. | *Conception:* There should be no relationship between local wealth and local spending. |
|---|---|
| A standard establishes a basis on which to make comparisons in measuring a given equity concept. | |
| A standard that characterizes expenditure per pupil equality is referred to as *equalization.* The standard of equalization is defined in terms of four questions: | A standard that characterizes no relationship between local wealth and local spending is referred to as *fiscal neutrality.* The standard of fiscal neutrality is defined in terms of four questions: |
| Equity for whom? (group of concern) Equity of what? (treatment) What are the different equity principles that can be used to determine whether the distribution is fair? (principles) How should the degree of equity be measured? (statistics) | |
| The choices made in addressing the above questions define the standard of equalization and include: | The choices made in addressing the above questions define the standard of fiscal neutrality and include: |
| 1. *Group*—Children 2. *Treatment*—Expenditures 3. *Principle*—Equal treatment of equals 4. *Statistics*—Dispersion measures that describe the variation in per pupil expenditures | 1. *Group*—Children 2. *Treatment*—Expenditures and local school district wealth 3. *Principle*—Equal opportunity 4. *Statistics*—Measures that describe the relationship between local wealth and local spending |

produce conflicting school finance goals. Even with this inconsistency, equity analysis of a state's school finance system can proceed by accounting for both standards in separate and distinct ways. Each standard, taken separately, reveals important information about the equity characteristics of a state's school finance system.

# METHOD OF ANALYSIS

The equity of the basic instruction subsidy program was examined against the standards of equalization and fiscal neutrality for each of three years subsequent to the passage of Act 59. Six measures of dispersion were used in assessing the equalization standard and included the range, restricted range, federal range ratio, coefficient of variation, McLoone Index, and Gini coefficient. The standard of fiscal neutrality was assessed using Pearson product moment correlation coefficients and elasticity coefficients from a simple linear regression analysis. Also, certain other issues related to the wealth measure and school district spending were explored utilizing correlation and regression techniques.

Data were obtained from three primary sources: (1) the annual Department of Education Controller's Office (DECO) 505 reports, (2) the State Tax Equalization Board, and (3) The Division of Child Accounting and Subsidies. Data were collected on all school districts in Pennsylvania for the years 1977–78 through 1979–80.

# FINDINGS

The equity analyses reveal that Pennsylvania has not met the requirements of either equity standard. More precisely, the basic instruction subsidy program is characterized by an unequal distribution of AIE and a strong, positive relationship between school district spending and wealth.

Table A.2 sets out the results of the dispersion analysis and includes the three-year averages for the six dispersion measures. Several specific findings emerge. The mean difference in AIE between the highest spending district and the lowest spending district for the three years was $1,316. Looking at the restricted range, the mean difference between the AIE of the district at the 95th percentile and the AIE of the district at the 5th percentile for the three years was $618. The mean federal range ratio indicates that the district at the 95th percentile spent, on an average, 1.66 times the AIE of the district at the 5th percentile over the three years.

Two-thirds of the state's school districts have continued to move further from the annual mean AIE over the three years, from 16.76 to 17.02 to 17.62 percent, while the cost to bring districts below the median AIE up to the median AIE was slightly over $80 million for the 1979–80 school year (as determined by the McLoone Index). Perhaps even more revealing, five of the six dispersion measures indicate a drift toward a less equitable school finance system in the three years since the passage of Act 59.

Three major findings emerge from the analysis of fiscal neutrality. First, the relationship between district wealth and district spending was consistently strong, with a .77 correlation in 1979–80, and a range from .76 to .78 over the three years. Second, in 1979–80, 59 percent of the variation in AIE could be accounted for solely by variations in school district wealth. A similar finding emerged for each of the previous two years. Finally, the elasticity coefficients, which estimate the percent change in AIE associated with a 1 percent change in district wealth, ranged in value from .28 in 1977 to .33 in 1979, evidencing a tendency to increase slightly over the previous year for each of the three years. The elasticity coefficient of .33 in 1979–80 indicates that as district wealth increases by 1 percent, district spending increases one-third of 1 percent, everything else remaining the same. It can be concluded, on the basis of these findings, that the school finance system in Pennsylvania does not meet the fiscal neutrality standard, since a strong positive relationship exists between school district spending and school district wealth.

TABLE A.2   RESULTS OF THE AIE DISPERSION ANALYSIS AND THREE YEAR MEAN VALUES FOR THE YEARS 1977–78, 1978–79, AND 1979–80

| Dispersion-type Measures | 1977–78 | 1978–79 | 1979–80 | Mean $\overline{X}$ |
|---|---|---|---|---|
| Range | 1133 | 1273 | 1541 | 1316 |
| Restricted Range | 537 | 598 | 719 | 618 |
| Federal Range Ratio | .63 | .64 | .70 | .66 |
| Coefficient of Variation | 16.76 | 17.02 | 17.62 | 17.15 |
| McLoone Index | .920 | .910 | .919 | .916 |
| Gini Coefficient | .1301 | .1299 | .1287 | .1296 |

The relationship between district market value per weighted average daily membership (WADM) and district personal income per weighted average daily membership (WADM) also was examined with correlation analysis for the years 1978 and 1979. In both years, the correlation value exceeded .70. These findings suggest that the combined measure of fiscal capacity used to calculate school district aid ratios may offer no real advantage. Specifically, the inclusion of personal income in the wealth measures has little or no distributional consequences statewide in terms of dissolving the relationship between district wealth and district spending.

A further analysis was undertaken based on wealth stratas. The 504 school districts were stratified into three tiers based on wealth per WADM and a regression analysis was performed on each tier. The coefficients of determination ($r^2$) indicate that spending in high wealth districts (top one-third of districts in the state) is associated more closely with wealth than in middle and low wealth districts. Another possible interpretation of these findings is that less variation in wealth and AIE exists in middle and low wealth districts than high wealth districts. Generally, the elasticity coefficients indicate that spending is more responsive to changes in wealth in middle wealth districts than low and high wealth districts. The 1979–80 elasticity coefficients show that as wealth increases by 1 percent in middle wealth districts, spending increases by over four-tenths of 1 percent. The elasticity coefficients for the low wealth districts indicate that a 1 percent change in wealth is associated with only a one-tenth of 1 percent change in spending.

## DISCUSSION AND CONCLUSION

Pennsylvania's school finance system fails by established and widely accepted criteria to be an equitable school finance arrangement. More precisely, the Pennsylvania school finance system is characterized by a substantially unequal distribution of AIE across the 504 school districts, and a strong, positive linear relationship between school district wealth and school district spending.

The inclusion of personal income in the fiscal capacity measure has left the relationship between local wealth and spending unchanged. The correlation analysis between market value and personal income indicates that many people with high, middle, and low incomes tend to live in school districts with correspondingly similar property-value patterns. Thus, while the architects of Act 59 chose to include personal income along with property value to measure wealth, that decision has proved inconsequential in its effect on either equity standard.

The dispersion measures indicate that the reformed school finance system has preserved wide differences in spending across local school districts. If, for example, the three-year mean restricted range of $618 is multiplied by twenty-five (an average sized classroom), the result is $15,450. This implies that the district at the 95th percentile spends, on average $15,450 more per classroom than the district at the 5th percentile. It is easy to imagine the qualitative variations in instructional outcomes that such a difference might produce. While some difference in spending is legitimate, a spending variation of this magnitude is suspect. Unless and until dispersion in spending can be accounted for by legitimate variations in educational need, the school finance system will continue to violate the standard of equalization and vex the principle of equal treatment of equals. Further, the findings indicate a three year post-reform drift toward greater inequity in the basic instruction subsidy program.

Act 59 has been ineffective in producing a more equitable school finance system. Instead, this legislation has preserved a dual system of finance in which wealthy school districts are able to spend more for education at lower tax rates, while less wealthy school districts spend less for education and make higher tax efforts. Act 59 applied fiscal redistribution remedies that were marginal at best, and left intact the basic structure of educational funding in Pennsylvania.

# EPILOGUE

Since the completion of this study, the Pennsylvania legislature has revised the way that the basic instruction subsidy payment to school districts is calculated.[8] During 1982, Pennsylvania ended the subsidy distribution formula specified in Act 59. Since it was not politically feasible to draft a new funding formula, the Pennsylvania lawmakers chose instead to freeze Act 59's distribution formula and return to a formula similar to the one used prior to Act 59. Currently, subsidy allocations to school districts are calculated on the basis of school district weighted average daily membership (WADM) multiplied by the school district aid ratio (which still incorporates both personal income and market value). These district figures are then calculated on a proportionate basis with statewide WADM and a statewide aid ratio. However, the actual level of subsidy is not to exceed the legislative appropriation, regardless of the amount indicated by the formula calculations.

There were several reasons for the new legislative action that reversed Act 59. First and foremost, Act 59 could not be fully funded given the escalating costs resulting from the annual upward drift in the base earned for reimbursement. That is, state allocations for the basic instruction subsidy continued to fall behind the amount to which school districts were entitled under the Act 59 formula. Second, Act 59 did not alter, in any substantial way, the basic allocation of resources. Certain geographic locations within the state maintained their wealth-determined advantage while other locations continued to struggle under an eroding financial base. Some have asserted that Act 59 was nothing more than a poor disguise designed to preserve the status quo.[9]

Finally, wealthy school districts continued to enjoy a fiscal advantage over less wealthy school districts. Act 59 had established a local tax effort incentive among school districts whereby districts competed against each other by taxing themselves at higher rates in an effort to acquire more state aid. This incentive, coupled with the use of market value assessment to generate local tax dollars, favors school districts with high property value. Conversely, those school districts with low property value were further weakened and held hostage by a state finance system based on local wealth.

8. Pennsylvania Laws, Act 115, 1982.

9. Telephone interview comment from spokesperson for the Pennsylvania School Boards Association (Harrisburg, Penn.: November 11, 1982).

In conclusion, Pennsylvania does not have an equitable distribution formula. The school finance system, having failed to meet either equity standard under Act 59, has replaced one unacceptable school finance formula with another.

# Appendix
# B

The Star-Ledger/*Eagleton Poll*

*Embargoed—Not for Release Until:*
*Sunday, November 1, 1992*

Release: SL/EP 41-1 (EP 91-1)

Contact: Janice Ballou
or Ken Dautrich

---

## Release Information

A story based on the survey findings presented in this release and background memo will appear in Sunday's *Star-Ledger*. Other newspapers may also use this information in their Sunday editions. Electronic media may release after 5:00 P.M. Saturday, October 31, 1992. We ask users to properly attribute this copyrighted information to "*The Star-Ledger*/Eagleton Poll."

---

All of the percentages in this release are based on "likely voters"—New Jersey residents who report they are currently registered to vote and say that they are probably or definitely going to vote. In addition, some results that will be specifically noted are reported for "probable voters"—likely voters who have the greatest probability of actually voting on Election Day and who have had undecided voters assigned to a vote choice.

---

## CLINTON LEADS IN NEW JERSEY

In the closing days of the election, it appears that Democrat challenger Bill Clinton will receive more votes from New Jersey voters than the incumbent President George Bush. However, the size of Clinton's margin of victory will depend on who actually votes on November 3. Likely New Jersey voters give Democrat Bill Clinton a 12 point lead over Republican incumbent George Bush—42 to 30 percent—while Ross Perot has support

*ATTENTION RADIO STATIONS:* Audio is available after 5:00 P.M. on Saturday, October 31, 1992, from (908)932-3605 (Rutgers Feature Phone).

from 18 percent and 9 percent remain undecided. However, the margin between the candidates declines to 8 points among those voters who have the highest probability of voting—Clinton 45 percent, Bush 37 percent and Perot 17 percent. In addition, at this time, the campaign momentum favors George Bush.

The latest *Star-Ledger*/Eagleton Poll was conducted by telephone with a random sample of 801 likely voters in two waves between October 23 and 29. The poll also shows that even at this late date there are still many voters who are indecisive about their choice for President.

## VOTE CHOICE

Among likely voters, Governor Bill Clinton currently gets 42 percent of the votes compared to 30 percent who prefer President George Bush, and 18 percent who pick Perot. Nine percent report that they have not yet decided who they would vote for. These results are about the same as a mid-October poll that gave Clinton 44 percent, Bush 31 percent, Perot 17 percent, and showed 8 percent undecided.

The poll also shows changes between the two waves of interviewing. George Bush gains 10 percentage points from 25 percent to 35 percent and Ross Perot declines 8 points from 22 to 14 percent, while the support for Clinton stays about the same— (Wave 1—42%; Wave 2—43%).

Poll Director Janice Ballou noted, "The increase in the Bush support during the past week is at the expense of Ross Perot. George Bush has been more aggressive as a campaigner, and Perot's discussion of additional reasons for withdrawing from the race earlier this year may also have contributed to the changes. This may be an indicator of increased momentum for Bush in the closing days of the campaign."

Clinton receives much stronger partisan support than George Bush. While 87 percent of the Democrats support Clinton, 67 percent of the Republicans choose Bush. Clinton leads among independent voters with 35 percent compared to 29 percent who pick Perot and 25 percent Bush.

At this time, males are more likely to vote for Clinton (39%) than Bush (31%) or Perot (22%). Women are also more likely to say they will vote for Clinton (45%) than Bush (29%), but fewer women than men support Perot (14%). At this time women are also more likely to be undecided by a margin of 12 to 8 percent.

The margin between Clinton and Bush is about 12 percentage points for all age groups. However, younger voters (25%) are more likely to say they will vote for Perot than those who are middle age (17%) or those 50 years old and older (15%).

## PROBABLE VOTERS

The poll also estimated the vote choice based on those who have the highest probability of voting in the election and assigned undecided voters to a candidate. These probable voters also select Clinton, however the margin between the candidates narrows to 8 percentage points. Clinton receives 45 percent, Bush 37 percent and Perot has 17 percent.

## THE POTENTIAL FOR CHANGE

Even at this point in the election 9 percent of the voters say they have not decided on a candidate. In addition, about 1-in-5 voters who select a candidate say they might change their mind before election day. Current Perot supporters are the most likely to say they will change—38 percent compared to 17 percent of the Clinton supporters and 17 percent of those who now pick Bush. Also, 11 percent who do not currently support Clinton say they might vote for him; 12 percent who do not currently pick Bush say they might select the President; and 18 percent who do not currently support him say they might vote for Perot.

## IMPRESSIONS OF THE CANDIDATES

More voters have a favorable impression of the Democratic contender Bill Clinton (51%) and Ross Perot (50%) than they do of incumbent George Bush (40%). Comparing the three Vice-Presidential candidates, Clinton's running mate Al Gore receives favorable ratings from 56 percent of the state's registered voters while Dan Quayle gets 34 percent and James Stockdale is at 18 percent. Overall, these ratings are similar to those in the mid-October survey.

## THE CONGRESSIONAL ELECTION

On an overall statewide basis, more likely voters say they will vote for Democrats (41%) than Republicans (35%) in Tuesday's congressional races. Twenty-three percent have not yet decided who they will vote for. In September, 44 percent said they would vote for Democrats and 31 percent selected Republicans. Clinton supporters (71%) are more likely to say they will vote for Democrats, and by about the same percentage, Bush voters (73%) select Republican congressional candidates. Those who pick Perot are more likely to select Republicans (42%) than Democrats (28%).

# Background Memo—Release SL/EP41-1 (EP91-1), Sunday, November 1, 1992

The latest *Star-Ledger*/Eagleton Poll was conducted in two waves. Wave 1 was conducted with 401 likely voters between October 23 and 25, 1992; Wave 2 was conducted with 400 likely voters between October 25 and 29, 1992. New Jerseyans, 18 years and older, who reported being registered and say they would "definitely" or "probably" vote in November's election were interviewed by telephone. The figures in this release are based on the sample size of 801 likely voters and are subject to a sampling error of about ±3.5 percent, results from the individual samples of 400 have a sampling error of about ±5 percentage points. In addition, some results are presented for 580 "probable voters." These are likely voters who have the greatest probability of actually voting on election day. The sampling error for this group is about ±4 percentage points. Sampling error is the probable difference in results between interviewing everyone in the population versus a scientific sample taken from that population. Sampling error does not take into account other possible sources of error inherent in any study of public opinion. The questions and figures referred to in this release are presented below. The location of each question on the actual questionnaire is in brackets.

"How much interest do you have in this election—a lot, some, a little or none at all?" [Q.3].

|  | A Lot | Some | Little/None | Don't Know | Total | (n) |
|---|---|---|---|---|---|---|
| **Late October, 1992—Likely Voters** | **79%** | **15%** | **6%** | **1%** | **101%** | **(801)** |
| **Past Surveys** | | | | | | |
| Mid-October, 1992—Likely Voters | 77 | 17 | 6 | — | 100 | (801) |
| September, 1992—Likely Voters | 67 | 23 | 8 | 2 | 100 | (650) |
| November, 1988—Likely Voters | 65 | 27 | 7 | 1 | 100 | (963) |
| September, 1988 | 48 | 33 | 18 | 1 | 100 | (505) |
| October, 1984*—Likely Voters | 76 | 20 | 3 | 1 | 100 | (850) |

"I'd like to get your general impression of the presidential candidates. For each name I read, please tell me if your general impression of him is favorable or unfavorable. If you don't have an opinion on a candidate, just say so.

First, is your general impression of (START AT DESIGNATED POINT) favorable or unfavorable? [PROBE: Would that be very or somewhat (favorable/unfavorable)?]" [Q.4]

---

*In October, 1984 the following question was asked: "How much interest do you have in this Presidential election—a lot, some, a little, or none at all?"

| | Very Favorable | Somewhat Favorable | Somewhat Unfavorable | Very Unfavorable | Don't Know | Total | (n) |
|---|---|---|---|---|---|---|---|
| **Bush** | | | | | | | |
| **Late October, 1992** | | | | | | | |
| **—Likely Voters** | **18%** | **22%** | **21%** | **34%** | **6%** | **101%** | **(801)** |
| **Past Surveys** | | | | | | | |
| Mid-October, 1992—Likely Voters | 17 | 25 | 19 | 32 | 7 | 100 | (801) |
| September, 1992—Likely Voters | 18 | 28 | 20 | 30 | 4 | 100 | (650) |
| November, 1988—Likely Voters | 27 | 30 | 14 | 21 | 8 | 100 | (963) |
| **Clinton** | | | | | | | |
| **Late October, 1992** | | | | | | | |
| **—Likely Voters** | **25** | **26** | **15** | **28** | **6** | **100** | **(801)** |
| **Past Surveys** | | | | | | | |
| Mid-October, 1992—Likely Voters | 24 | 30 | 17 | 24 | 6 | 101 | (801) |
| September, 1992—Likely Voters | 21 | 34 | 20 | 17 | 8 | 100 | (650) |
| November, 1988—Likely Voters (Dukakis) | 16 | 25 | 23 | 27 | 9 | 100 | (963) |
| **Perot** | | | | | | | |
| **Late October, 1992** | | | | | | | |
| **—Likely Voters** | **16** | **34** | **19** | **17** | **14** | **100** | **(800)** |
| **Past Surveys** | | | | | | | |
| Mid-October, 1992—Likely Voters | 16 | 33 | 19 | 17 | 15 | 100 | (800) |
| **Gore** | | | | | | | |
| **Late October, 1992** | | | | | | | |
| **—Likely Voters** | **26** | **30** | **15** | **16** | **12** | **99** | **(801)** |
| **Past Surveys** | | | | | | | |
| Mid-October, 1992—Likely Voters | 27 | 30 | 13 | 16 | 15 | 101 | (801) |
| September, 1992—Likely Voters | 25 | 32 | 13 | 8 | 22 | 100 | (650) |
| **Quayle** | | | | | | | |
| **Late October, 1992** | | | | | | | |
| **—Likely Voters** | **13%** | **21%** | **21%** | **36%** | **9%** | **100%** | **(801)** |
| **Past Surveys** | | | | | | | |
| Mid-October, 1992—Likely Voters | 10 | 24 | 22 | 35 | 11 | 102 | (801) |
| September, 1992—Likely Voters | 10 | 26 | 23 | 32 | 9 | 100 | (650) |
| **Stockdale** | | | | | | | |
| **Late October, 1992** | | | | | | | |
| **—Likely Voters** | **4%** | **14%** | **23%** | **26%** | **33%** | **100%** | **(801)** |
| **Past Surveys** | | | | | | | |
| Mid-October, 1992—Likely Voters | 4 | 14 | 20 | 24 | 38 | 100 | (801) |

"If the election for President were held today and you had to choose between Bill Clinton, the Democrat; George Bush, the Republican; and Ross Perot, the independent, who would you vote for? (IF RESPONDENT SAYS "OTHER," PROBE: 'But, if you had to choose only between Clinton, Bush, and Perot who would you vote for?')" [Q.5]

| | Clinton | Bush | Perot | Undecided | Total | (n) |
|---|---|---|---|---|---|---|
| **Late October, 1992** | | | | | | |
| **—Likely Voters-Total** | **42%** | **30%** | **18%** | **9%** | **99%** | **(801)** |
| **WAVE 1** | **42** | **25** | **22** | **11** | **100** | **(400)** |
| **WAVE 2** | **43** | **35** | **14** | **9** | **101** | **(401)** |
| **Probable Voters** | **45** | **37** | **17** | **—** | **99** | **(580)** |
| *Party ID* | | | | | | |
| —Democrat | 87 | 4 | 4 | 5 | 100 | (229) |
| —Independent | 35 | 25 | 29 | 10 | 99 | (329) |
| —Republican | 10 | 67 | 14 | 10 | 101 | (215) |
| *Age* | | | | | | |
| —18–29 | 38 | 27 | 25 | 9 | 99 | (121) |
| —30–49 | 43 | 31 | 17 | 9 | 100 | (335) |
| —50 and older | 43 | 31 | 15 | 10 | 99 | (326) |
| *Race* | | | | | | |
| —White | 38 | 32 | 20 | 9 | 99 | (654) |
| —Non-white | 64 | 18 | 8 | 9 | 99 | (127) |
| *Gender* | | | | | | |
| —Male | 39 | 31 | 22 | 8 | 100 | (401) |
| —Female | 45 | 29 | 14 | 12 | 100 | (400) |
| *Male* | | | | | | |
| —Democrat | 86 | 6 | 5 | 3 | 100 | (98) |
| —Independent | 34 | 23 | 35 | 8 | 100 | (177) |
| —Republican | 9 | 67 | 15 | 9 | 100 | (117) |
| *Female* | | | | | | |
| —Democrat | 88% | 3% | 3% | 6% | 100% | (131) |
| —Independent | 36 | 28 | 23 | 13 | 100 | (152) |
| —Republican | 11 | 66 | 13 | 10 | 100 | (98) |
| *Income* | | | | | | |
| —Under $20,000 | 51 | 30 | 10 | 9 | 100 | (106) |
| —$20,001—$30,000 | 53 | 28 | 15 | 5 | 101 | (86) |
| —$30,001—$50,000 | 42 | 30 | 22 | 7 | 101 | (219) |
| —Over $50,000 | 40 | 31 | 18 | 11 | 100 | (287) |
| *1988 Vote* | | | | | | |
| Bush | 24 | 47 | 19 | 11 | 101 | (412) |
| Dukakis | 78 | 5 | 10 | 7 | 99 | (236) |
| *1984 Vote* | | | | | | |
| Reagan | 25 | 46 | 19 | 10 | 100 | (380) |
| Mondale | 79 | 3 | 10 | 7 | 99 | (199) |
| **Past Surveys** | | | | | | |
| Mid-October, 1992 | | | | | | |
| —Likely Voters-Total | 44 | 31 | 17 | 8 | 100 | (801) |
| WAVE 1 | 45 | 31 | 15 | 9 | 100 | (401) |
| WAVE 2 | 42 | 31 | 19 | 6 | 98 | (400) |
| September, 1992* | | | | | | |
| —Likely Voters | 46 | 38 | 11 | 6 | 101 | (650) |
| April, 1992 | 34 | 55 | 8 | 4 | 101 | (623) |
| November, 1988 | | | | | | |
| —Likely Voters | 35** | 54 | 1*** | 10 | 100 | (963) |

If undecided: "Do you lean more towards Clinton, more towards Bush, or more towards Perot?" [Q.7]

| | Leans Clinton | Leans Bush | Leans Perot | Neither | Total | (n) |
|---|---|---|---|---|---|---|
| **Late October, 1992**<br>**—Likely Voters** | 17% | 27% | 14% | 42% | 100% | (79) |
| **Past Surveys**<br>Mid-October, 1992<br>—Likely Voters | 31 | 25 | 12 | 32 | 100 | (62) |

"Are you very sure about your choice or do you think you might change your mind before election day?" [Q.6A]

| | Sure<br>About Choice | Might<br>Change Mind/<br>Don't Know | Total | (n) |
|---|---|---|---|---|
| **Late October, 1992**<br>**—Likely Voters** | 79% | 21% | 100% | (722) |
| *Vote Choice* | | | | |
| —Clinton | 83 | 17 | 100 | (346) |
| —Bush | 83 | 17 | 100 | (248) |
| —Perot | 62 | 38 | 100 | (128) |
| *Party ID* | | | | |
| —Democrat | 88 | 12 | 100 | (219) |
| —Independent | 70 | 30 | 100 | (293) |
| —Republican | 82 | 18 | 100 | (194) |
| **Past Surveys**<br>Mid-October, 1992<br>—Likely Voters | 72 | 28 | 100 | (736) |

Combined Q.5, Q.6a, Q.7

| | Firm<br>Clinton | Soft<br>Clinton | Lean<br>Clinton | Firm<br>Bush | Soft<br>Bush | Lean<br>Bush | Firm<br>Perot | Soft<br>Perot | Lean<br>Perot | Undecided | Total | (n) |
|---|---|---|---|---|---|---|---|---|---|---|---|---|
| **Late October, 1992**<br>**—Likely Voters** | 35% | 7% | 2% | 25% | 5% | 3% | 11% | 7% | 1% | 4% | 100% | (798) |
| **Past Surveys**<br>Mid-October, 1992<br>—Likely Voters | 33 | 11 | 2 | 24 | 7 | 2 | 9 | 8 | 1 | 4 | 99 | (798) |

*In September the question was introduced with the following wording: "Even though Ross Perot stopped campaigning for president, his name will be on the ballot and you can vote for him."

**Percentage who say they would vote for Dukakis.

***Percentage who say they would vote for "other" candidate.

Combined Q.5, Q.6a, Q.7, Q.8b–d

| | Clinton | | | | Bush | | | | Perot | | | | | | |
|---|---|---|---|---|---|---|---|---|---|---|---|---|---|---|---|
| | Not Others | Firm | Soft | Lean | Not Others | Firm | Soft | Lean | Not Others | Firm | Soft | Lean | Unde-cided | Total | (n) |
| **Late October, 1992** | | | | | | | | | | | | | | | |
| **—Likely Voters** | 29% | 7% | 7% | 1% | 21% | 5% | 4% | 2% | 7% | 4% | 7% | 1% | 4% | 99% | (798) |

"When did you decide who you would vote for—in the last few days, in the last couple weeks, in the last month or two, or did you know all along?" [Q.6b]

| | Last Few Days | Last Couple Weeks | Last Month or Two | Knew All Along | Don't Know | Total | (n) |
|---|---|---|---|---|---|---|---|
| **Late October, 1992** | | | | | | | |
| **—Likely Voters** | 10% | 23% | 29% | 36% | 2% | 100% | (720) |
| *Vote Choice* | | | | | | | |
| —Clinton | 8 | 21 | 37 | 32 | 2 | 100 | (345) |
| —Bush | 9 | 12 | 24 | 54 | 2 | 101 | (248) |
| —Perot | 19 | 46 | 21 | 13 | 1 | 100 | (127) |
| **Past Surveys** | | | | | | | |
| Mid-October, 1992 | | | | | | | |
| —Likely Voters | 13 | 19 | 28 | 37 | 2 | 99 | (735) |

"Would you say you are voting more for (CANDIDATE NAMED IN Q.5 OR Q.7) or more against the other candidates?" [Q.8A]

| | More For | More Against | Don't Know | Total | (n) |
|---|---|---|---|---|---|
| **Late October, 1992** | | | | | |
| **—Likely Voters** | 57% | 38% | 6% | 101% | (762) |
| *Vote Choice* | | | | | |
| —Clinton | 52 | 41 | 7 | 100 | (344) |
| —Bush | 61 | 36 | 3 | 100 | (248) |
| —Perot | 65 | 32 | 3 | 100 | (128) |
| *Party ID* | | | | | |
| —Democrat | 59 | 35 | 6 | 100 | (223) |
| —Independent | 49 | 45 | 6 | 100 | (310) |
| —Republican | 68 | 30 | 2 | 100 | (207) |
| **Past Surveys** | | | | | |
| Mid-October, 1992 | | | | | |
| —Likely Voters | 50 | 44 | 5 | 99 | (772) |

"Is there any chance you might vote for (NAME OF EACH CANDIDATE NOT SE-LECTED AS VOTE CHOICE), or have you decided that you will definitely not vote for him no matter what else happens in the campaign?" [Q.8B–Q.8D]

| | Is A Chance I Might Vote For Him | Definitely Will Not Vote For Him | Don't Know | Total | (n) |
|---|---|---|---|---|---|
| **Bush** | | | | | |
| **—Late October, 1992** | **18%** | **79%** | **3%** | **100%** | **(497)** |
| —Mid-October, 1992 | 23 | 74 | 3 | 100 | (509) |
| **Clinton** | | | | | |
| **—Late October, 1992** | **21** | **77** | **2** | **100** | **(407)** |
| —Mid-October, 1992 | 25 | 71 | 4 | 100 | (406) |
| **Perot** | | | | | |
| **—Late October, 1992** | **23** | **76** | **1** | **100** | **(625)** |
| —Mid-October, 1992 | 26 | 71 | 3 | 100 | (638) |

<u>Combination of Q.5, Q.7, and Q.8B–Q.8D.</u>

| | Bush Firm | Bush Might Change | Bush Lean | Bush Might Vote | Bush Definitely Not Vote | Don't Know | Total | (n) |
|---|---|---|---|---|---|---|---|---|
| **Late October, 1992** | | | | | | | | |
| **—Likely Voters** | **25%** | **5%** | **3%** | **12%** | **50%** | **6%** | **101%** | **(801)** |
| *Vote Choice* | | | | | | | | |
| —Clinton | — | — | — | 10 | 88 | 2 | 100 | (346) |
| —Bush | 83 | 17 | — | — | — | — | 100 | (248) |
| —Perot | — | — | — | 33 | 65 | 2 | 100 | (128) |
| —Undecided | — | — | 27 | 16 | 10 | 47 | 99 | (76) |
| **Past Surveys** | | | | | | | | |
| Mid-October, 1992 | | | | | | | | |
| —Likely Voters | 24 | 7 | 2 | 15 | 48 | 5 | 101 | (801) |

| | Clinton Firm | Clinton Might Change | Clinton Lean | Clinton Might Vote | Clinton Definitely Not Vote | Don't Know | Total | (n) |
|---|---|---|---|---|---|---|---|---|
| **Late October, 1992** | | | | | | | | |
| **—Likely Voters** | **35%** | **7%** | **2%** | **11%** | **40%** | **6%** | **101%** | **(801)** |
| *Vote Choice* | | | | | | | | |
| —Clinton | 82 | 17 | — | — | — | — | 99 | (346) |
| —Bush | — | — | — | 11 | 88 | 1 | 100 | (248) |
| —Perot | — | — | — | 31 | 66 | 3 | 100 | (128) |
| —Undecided | — | — | 17 | 21 | 16 | 46 | 100 | (76) |
| **Past Surveys** | | | | | | | | |
| Mid-October, 1992 | | | | | | | | |
| —Likely Voters | 33 | 11 | 2 | 13 | 36 | 5 | 100 | (801) |

(Combination of Q.5, Q.7, and Q.8B–Q.8D continued)

| | Perot Firm | Perot Might Change | Perot Lean | Perot Might Vote | Perot Definitely Not Vote | Don't Know | Total | (n) |
|---|---|---|---|---|---|---|---|---|
| **Late October, 1992** | | | | | | | | |
| **—Likely Voters** | **11%** | **7%** | **1%** | **18%** | **58%** | **6%** | **101%** | **(801)** |
| *Vote Choice* | | | | | | | | |
| —Clinton | — | — | — | 21 | 77 | 2 | 100 | (346) |
| —Bush | — | — | — | 22 | 78 | 1 | 101 | (248) |
| —Perot | 62 | 38 | — | — | — | — | 100 | (128) |
| —Undecided | — | — | 14 | 25 | 18 | 44 | 101 | (76) |
| **Past Surveys** | | | | | | | | |
| Mid-October, 1992 | | | | | | | | |
| —Likely Voters | 9 | 8 | 1 | 21 | 56 | 5 | 100 | (801) |

"There will be an election for the U.S. House of Representatives in your district in November. If you were voting today, would you vote for the Democratic candidate or the Republican candidate?" [Q.9]

| | Democrat | Republican | Other | Undecided | Total | (n) |
|---|---|---|---|---|---|---|
| **Late October, 1992** | | | | | | |
| **—Likely Voters** | **41%** | **35%** | **1%** | **23%** | **100%** | **(801)** |
| *Party ID* | | | | | | |
| —Democrat | 82 | 4 | 1 | 13 | 100 | (229) |
| —Independent | 34 | 31 | — | 35 | 100 | (329) |
| —Republican | 9 | 78 | — | 12 | 99 | (215) |
| *Presidential Vote Choice* | | | | | | |
| —Clinton | 71 | 6 | — | 22 | 99 | (346) |
| —Bush | 11 | 73 | — | 15 | 99 | (248) |
| —Perot | 28 | 42 | 1 | 29 | 100 | (128) |
| **Past Surveys** | | | | | | |
| September, 1992 | | | | | | |
| —Likely Voters | 44 | 31 | 1 | 24 | 100 | (663) |
| November, 1988 | | | | | | |
| —Likely Voters | 37 | 39 | — | 24 | 100 | (963) |

# Appendix C

## Home Style: Allocation of Resources

RICHARD F. FENNO, JR.

## HOME STYLE

What do the House member perceptions have to do with House member actions? The question of behavior naturally follows the question of perception. But what kind of behavior? Where? And with respect to what? The conventional political science answer would be: Behavior in Congress. How, we would ask, do member constituency perceptions affect their committee work, their voting record, their influence, their allegiances, their accomplishments—on Capitol Hill? These are legitimate, fascinating, time-honored questions. But they focus on a context removed from the one in which members puzzle out their several constituencies. The concern that generates and disciplines the perceptions we have just described is neither first nor foremost a Washington-centered concern. It is a concern for political support at home. Representatives and prospective representatives think about their constituencies because they seek support in their constituencies. They want to be nominated and elected, then renominated and reelected. For most members of Congress most of the time, this electoral goal is primary. It is the prerequisite for a congressional career and, hence, for the pursuit of other member goals. And the electoral goal is achieved—first and last—not in Washington but at home.

Of course, House members do many things in Washington that affect their electoral support at home. Political scientists interpret much of their behavior in Washington, particularly their voting records, as a bid for the support of their constituents.[1] Equipped with the more complex view of "their constituents" elaborated [earlier] . . . we could, if we wished, reexplore the electoral rationale behind voting patterns in Congress. It is hoped that some political scientists will do exactly that. But the experience of traveling with members in their districts turns one's attention in a different direction. For one sees House members working to maintain and enlarge their political support at home by going to the district and doing things *there*. What they do at home to win support is not, of course, unrelated to what they do in Washington to win support. And we shall have some thoughts on the linkages later. But the starting point of this research—*behavior at home*—is a departure from the more conventional starting point, behavior in Washington.

Those who do political science research on Congress have, because of their Washington focus, systematically underestimated the proportion of their working time that representatives spend in their districts. As a result, we have also underestimated its perceived importance to them. In all existing studies of congressional time allocation, for example, time spent outside of Washington is simply not counted. So, political scientists talk about "the average work week of a congressman" as if he never left Washington. We have tallied and compared the amount of time members spend in committee, on the House floor, doing research, helping constituents with their problems—but all of it in Washington.[2] Yet thirteen of my representatives—those whose appointment and travel records I have been able to check carefully for 1973, a nonelection year—averaged twenty-four trips to the district and spent an average of eighty-three days in their districts that year. That is, on the average, they went home every other week for about three and a half days. A survey conducted in 419 House offices indicated that the average number of trips home during 1973 (not counting recesses) was 35, and the average number of days spent in the district (counting recesses) was 138 days.[3] No fewer than 131, nearly one-third, of the 419 members went home to their districts every single weekend. Obviously, the direct personal cultivation of the House members' four constituencies take a great deal of their time. They must think it helps them win and hold political support. If they think it is worthwhile to go home so much, it should be worthwhile for political scientists to take a commensurate degree of interest in what they do there and why.

As they cultivate their constituencies, members of Congress display what I shall call their *home style*. When they discuss the importance of what they are doing, they are discussing the importance of an individual's home style to the achievement of his electoral goal. The remainder of this book will be mostly about home style—its elements, its antecedents, its varieties, its transformations, its consequences, and its relation to each member's perceived constituencies. Succeeding chapters will be organized around three basic ingredients of home style. The first is the congressman's *allocation* of his personal resources and those of his office. The second is the congressman's *presentation* of self to others. The third is the congressman's *explanation* of his Washington activity to others. Every congressman allocates, presents, and explains. And a large part of this activity takes place in the district. Each member's amalgam of these three activities—as manifested in the district—constitutes his or her home style.

## ALLOCATION OF RESOURCES: TIME AND STAFF

Every member of Congress makes a basic decision with regard to his or her home style: How much and what kinds of attention shall I pay to home? Or, to put it another way: Of all the resources available to me, which kinds and how much of each shall I allocate to activity at home? For now, "home" means the geographical constituency, "the district." And the allocative decisions we study are those concerning distribution of resources between the district and Washington. The job of a congressman requires that some things be done in Washington and others be done in the district. At the least, legislation is passed in one place and elections occur in the other. The allocative problem, therefore, comes with the job. And this built-in strain between the need to attend to Washington business and the need to attend to district business affects the work of each individual and the work product of the institution. The strain is both omnipresent and severe. Members give up the job because of it. Congressional reforms are advocated to alleviate it. The allocative decisions we shall examine represent, individually and collectively, House members' efforts to cope with it.

There are, of course, different resources to allocate between Washington and the district, and alternative ways to allocate those resources. Our concern is with resources allocated directly to the district. And the resources we shall examine are the House member's *time* and the House member's *staff.* How much time to spend physically in the district and how much staff to place physically in the district are among the most basic of a member's allocative decisions. Separately and together they help shape each member's home style.

Time is a House member's scarcest and most precious political resource. If there is an exemplary congressional complaint, surely "there isn't enough time" must be it. In deciding how to spend his time, in Washington, in the district and, for our purposes, between Washington and the district, a member confronts his most difficult allocative dilemma. When he is doing something at home, he must give up doing some things in Washington and vice versa. He must choose and trade off. Different representatives make different allocative choices and different allocative trades.

We shall focus, first, on the frequency with which various representatives returned to their districts in 1973. "This is a business, and like any business you have to make time and motion studies," said one member. "All we have is time and ourselves, so we have to calculate carefully to use our time productively." It is not true, of course, that "all" the congressman has is time and himself. The office carries with it a large number of ancillary resources—a staff, office space, office expense allowances, free mailing privileges, personal expense accounts—all of which occupy our attention when we detail the advantages of incumbency. Each congressman chooses how he will use these resources. The most significant of these choices involve the use of staff. If "Whom shall I appoint to my staff?" ranks first in importance, "How shall I distribute my staff between Washington and the district?" ranks next. Therefore, our second focus will be on this distributive decision. We shall examine one indicator of it—the percentage of a member's total expenditure on staff salaries he allocates to the salaries of his district staff.[4]

The information on trips home and staff allocation was collected on Capitol Hill in June 1974. Six students, each of whom had just finished working for four months, full time, in a House member's office, conducted a survey by visiting every member's office and talking to his or her administrative assistant or personal secretary. The question about the frequency of member trips home usually produced an educated estimate (e.g., "every week," "once a month," "every other week"). The question about staff allocation yielded more precise answers. Each student presented the *Report of the Clerk of the House* for 1973, with its list of each representative's staff members and their salaries; and the person answering simply designated which staff members were located in the district. A briefer, follow-up survey was conducted by four students with similar "Hill experience" in May 1975. This survey added to the store of information on those 1973 members who were still in Congress. It produced a little information, too, on the first-termers of that year.[6] In 1973, it should be noted, each representative was reimbursed for thirty-six round trips to his or her district. Members were not, of course, required to use any of these allowances to the maximum.

## Personal Attentiveness: Trips Home

In 1973, members of Congress showed a good deal of personal attentiveness to their districts; but they also showed a lot of variation in the degree of their attentiveness. Members averaged thirty-five trips home that year; and the median number was thirty. But the least attentive of them went home four times, whereas the most attentive went home 365 times.[5] Because some members are home so seldom and others so much, there is considerable variation in home styles. So the question arises: Which members go home most often and which less so—and why? In this book we can only begin to answer the question. We can group House members according to the frequency with which they visit their districts. And we can then cross-tabulate these groupings with a number of factors that we might reasonably expect to be related. For this purpose we have grouped House members into three categories by frequency of 1973 trips home: *low* (less than twenty-four trips), *medium* (twenty-four to forty-two trips), *high* (more than forty-two trips).[6]

One reasonable supposition would be that representatives in electoral jeopardy will decide to spend more of their time at home than will representatives whose seats are well protected. As a generalization, however, this supposition receives no confirmation—not when political science's conventional measures of electoral safeness are used. As Table C.1 shows, the frequency of trips home does not increase as electoral margins decrease, or vice versa. There is just not much of a relationship at all.[7] But there is so much inherent plausibility to the original supposition that it probably should not be cast aside permanently. It may just be that our conventional indicators of electoral marginality are inadequate. Despite their extensive use, they have not helped to produce stable generalizations anywhere in the congressional literature.[8] Perhaps objective measures that captured more electoral history, included primary election information, and took into account the member's career stage would prove superior. But my experience . . . inclines me to believe that subjective assessments of electoral safety are more valid. Electoral statistics cannot capture the uncertainty members feel about their renomination and reelection. (Nor can they capture any existing sense of security among members in objectively marginal districts.) Certainly, we cannot understand that

Table C.1    TRIPS HOME AND ELECTORAL MARGIN

| | Frequency of Trips Home (1973) | | | |
| *Election Margin (1972)* | *Low (0–23)* | *Medium (24–42)* | *High (43+)* | *Total* |
|---|---|---|---|---|
| Less than 55% | 21 (29%) | 28 (38%) | 24 (33%) | 73 (100%) |
| 55–60% | 18 (32%) | 18 (32%) | 20 (36%) | 56 (100%) |
| 61–65% | 22 (27%) | 17 (20%) | 44 (53%) | 83 (100%) |
| More than 65% | 68 (33%) | 66 (32%) | 73 (35%) | 207 (100%) |
| Total | 129 | 129 | 161 | 419 |

*Note:* Gamma = −.03

uncertainty until we first figure out the logic underlying a member's assessment of his electoral situation. For now we can only guess that subjective assessments of electoral safeness (however arrived at) might be more strongly correlated with the frequency of trips to the district. But we cannot know. After all, members of Congress have other reasons for going home or staying in Washington.

A related hunch would lead us to expect that members who have been in office longer will spend less time at home. Part of the argument here overlaps with our previous one: the longer in office, the more secure the seat, the less the felt need to return to the district. But the more important, distinctive part of the reasoning would be that with increased seniority comes increased influence and responsibility in the House and, hence, the need to spend more time in Washington. The newcomer feels no such Washington pull. As one first-termer noted, "A congressman lives in two worlds, the one back home and the one in Washington. A freshman congressman can do more good at home than he can in Washington." A third leg of the argument might be that length of service correlates with age and that older members would return home less often than younger members because it would be more burdensome physically to do so. Our basic hunch is supported by the data—but not as strongly or as consistently as we had imagined. A simple correlation between terms of service and number of trips home shows that as seniority increases, home visits decrease—as we would expect. But the correlation is exceedingly weak.[9] And age appears to have little effect independent of seniority.[10] When the seniority data are grouped, however, the nature and the strength of the relationship become clearer.

Table C.2 illustrates the relationship between the three categories of personal attentiveness and three levels of seniority. The summary statistics continue to be unimpressive. But the reason is that for the middle levels of seniority, no allocative pattern is evident. If we look only at the low and high seniority levels, it is clear that the frequency of trips home is much greater for the low seniority groups than it is for the high seniority group. The relationship between length of service and trips home, we conclude, is not a consistent, linear relationship. But for those at the beginning of their House careers and for those farthest along in their House careers, congressional longevity is likely to be one determinant of their time allocation decisions. The most senior member of my group, a man with important legislative responsibilities, spent twenty-one working days at home in 1973. "I come home when I have something to do. If Paul [his district representative] says it's absolutely necessary, I'll come. . . . I may be at a stage in my career

Table C.2    TRIPS HOME AND SENIORITY

| Seniority | Frequency of Trips Home | | | |
| | Low (0–23) | Medium (24–42) | High (43+) | Total |
|---|---|---|---|---|
| Low (1–3 terms) | 34 (22%) | 44 (28%) | 78 (50%) | 156 (100%) |
| Medium (4–7 terms) | 43 (28%) | 59 (38%) | 52 (34%) | 154 (100%) |
| High (8+ terms) | 52 (48%) | 26 (24%) | 31 (28%) | 189 (100%) |
| Total | 129 | 129 | 161 | 419 |
| | (Mean seniority =7.0 terms) | (Mean seniority = 5.0 terms) | (Mean seniority = 4.7 terms) | |

Note: Gamma = −.30

where I'll have to call in all my chips at home so that I can devote full time to legislation." By contrast, the least senior member of the group spent sixty-one working days at home in 1975. He said, "Our class works their districts much harder than the older congressmen. We're back here all the time." Congressional newcomers appear to be more singleminded in pursuing the electoral goal than are the veterans of the institution.

A third reasonable hunch would be that the more time-consuming and expensive it is to get to his district, the less frequently a congressman will make the trip. Leaving money aside, because we have no information on the private wealth of House members,[11] but recalling that for 1973 to 1974, each member was provided with a "floor" of thirty-six trips, we would expect to find that as distance from Washington increases the number of trips home decreases. It is not easy to get a measure of distance that captures each representative's actual door-to-door travel time. We shall use region as a surrogate for distance, on the theory that if any relationship is present, it will show up in a regional breakdown. And it does. Table C.3 indicates that the members nearest Washington, D.C. (East) spend a good deal more time at home than do the members who live farthest away from the Capitol (Far West). The less Washington time members have to sacrifice to get home, the more likely they are to go. At least this proposition holds at the extremes of distance. If distance is a factor for the other three regional groups, it does not show up here. Our guess is that distance is a more problematical factor in those intermediate ranges.

Every member of Congress divides his or her time between work and family. If a member's family remains at home in the district, we would expect that member to return to the district more often than if the family moves to Washington. Table C.4

#### Table C.3    TRIPS HOME AND REGION

| | Frequency of Trips Home | | | |
|---|---|---|---|---|
| Region | Low (0–23) | Medium (24–42) | High (43+) | Total |
| East[a] | 5 (5%) | 20 (20%) | 76 (75%) | 101 (100%) |
| South[b] | 36 (35%) | 32 (30%) | 36 (35%) | 104 (100%) |
| Border[c] | 9 (26%) | 10 (29%) | 16 (45%) | 35 (100%) |
| Midwest[d] | 29 (28%) | 47 (44%) | 30 (28%) | 106 (100%) |
| Far West[e] | 50 (69%) | 20 (27%) | 3 ( 4%) | 73 (100%) |
| Total | 129 | 129 | 161 | 419 |

[a]Conn., Maine, Mass., N.H., N.J., N.Y., Pa., R.I., Vt.
[b]Ala., Ark., Fla., Ga., La., Miss., N.C., S.C., Tenn., Tex., Va.
[c]Del., Ky., Md., Mo., Okla., W.Va.
[d]Ill., Ind., Iowa, Kans., Mich., Minn., Nebr., N.Dak., Ohio, S.Dak., Wis.
[e]Alaska, Ariz., Calif., Colo., Hawaii, Idaho, Mont., Nev., N.Mex., Oreg., Utah, Wash., Wyo.

#### Table C.4    TRIPS HOME AND FAMILY RESIDENCE

| | Frequency of Trips | | | |
|---|---|---|---|---|
| Family Residence | Low (0–23) | Medium (24–42) | High (43+) | Total |
| Washington area | 87 (41%) | 89 (42%) | 37 (17%) | 213 (100%) |
| District | 3 (4%) | 6 (8%) | 69 (88%) | 78 (100%) |
| Unmarried | 5 (14%) | 12 (32%) | 20 (54%) | 37 (100%) |
| Total | 95 | 107 | 126 | 328 |

strongly supports this supposition.[14] Almost nine out of ten (88 percent) representatives whose families remain at home fall into the high trips home category. Less than two in ten (17 percent) representatives whose families move to Washington fall in the high trips home category. To put the finding somewhat differently, the average number of trips home for House members with families in Washington was twenty-seven, for House members with families in the district, it was fifty-two, and for unmarried members the average was forty-four trips.

We have no basis for deciding whether the family decision produces the home style or whether the home style produces the family decision. That is, do members come home because their families decided to stay there, or do their families decide to remain at home because the member has decided to come home a lot? Both processes seem plausible; and both are supported by interview data. Two midwestern members, each of whom considers his district marginal, explained:

> The family decided to split the school year—the first semester in Pikestown, the second semester in Virginia. So at first I was a weekend warrior. I was home every week up through January, to the end of the first semester. After January it dropped off to an average of twice a month. That lasted for the first two years. Then, when we sold our house in Pikestown and bought a home in Virginia, I stayed on the two trips a month routine.

> I came home every weekend for two years. That's how I got reelected. The two previous congressmen moved their families to Washington and became congressmen. They got to like Washington real fine; but they didn't come back home often enough. Both were defeated after one term. My family stayed in Hopeswell. . . . If my family had moved to Washington, I would have been home less and I would not have been reelected.

Whatever the logic, it is clear that some decisions about home style are family related.

To sum up thus far, the decision to allocate time between home and Washington is affected by seniority—whether his seniority is very high or very low. The decision is affected by the distance from Washington to home—if the distance is very long or very short. It is affected by the location of one's family—whether the family moves to Washington or stays in the district. The electoral margin, objectively measured, has little effect on time allocations. Other factors affecting these allocations, which are suggested by our interviews but for which we cannot collect across-the-board information, will be discussed later.

## Staff Attentiveness: District Staff Strength

Members of Congress also decide what kind of staff presence they wish to establish in the district. Here, too, we find great variation. Our measure of district staff strength—the percentage of total staff expenditure allocated to district staff—yields percentages for 1973 as low as 0 percent and as high as 81 percent. A question arises as to whether members' decisions about staff vary systematically according to decisions about trips home. Intuitively, it seems plausible that a member whose decision to cultivate "home" is reflected in lots of trips there would display a consistent attentiveness to home by placing a large staff there. A congressman in office one month described his allocative decisions as complementary:

> I'll go home every weekend. . . . Yesterday morning at 6:00 I was at the Bluffton mill. Were people ever pleased and surprised. "We didn't think you'd be back." People get very

impressed with themselves around here. I can't wait to get home every weekend. . . . We have eight staff in the district and six here [in Washington]. That's a first; at least we're saying it's a first. And we have three district offices. . . . My predecessor had one person in one office. People are going bananas. They've never seen anything like it.

Yet it is also plausible that a member may view personal and staff allocations as alternative rather than complementary ways of cultivating the district. If he cannot be there, he will allocate a large staff there; if he goes home a lot, he may feel no need to establish a sizable staff presence. "I was so available out there, traveling so much, that I didn't feel the need to beef up the district office. Since I've been in Washington more, I've strengthened the district office." When we correlate staff strength with trips home, however, neither relationship shows up very strongly. Such support as there is tends to favor—but very weakly—the complementary rather than the alternative mode.[13]

In Table C.5 this relationship is investigated further. The table clusters and cross-tabulates the two allocative decisions. For our measure of district staff strength, we have divided the percentage of expenditures on district staff into thirds. The lowest third ranges from 0 to 22.7 percent; the middle third ranges from 22.8 to 33.5 percent; the highest third ranges from 33.6 to 81 percent. The cross-tabulation of Table C.5 also shows a weak overall relationship between the decisions on time and staff. Again, the evidence points more toward the complementary than the alternative notion of the relationship. But it is the weakness of the finding that remains striking. If we had information on all 419 districts, on their homogeneity or heterogeneity for example, we might find patterns linking personal and staff attentiveness patterns to perceptions of the district. For now, however, we shall treat the two decisions as if they were made independently of one another and, hence, deserve separate examination.

What kinds of House members, then, emphasize the value of large district staff operations? Once again, it turns out, they are not members in special electoral trouble. Table C.6 displays the total lack of any discernible effect of electoral situation (objectively measured) on district staff strength. And, as indicated in Table C.7, seniority also makes no difference in allocative decisions affecting staff. That it does not adds strength to our notion that the relationship between seniority and home visits discovered earlier is accounted for by career and goal factors rather than electoral factors. If seniority showed equal importance in home trips and staff allocation, an electoral explanation would seem most plausible. But because seniority seems only to affect home visits, an explanation more closely related to home visits (i.e., the partial displacement over time of the reelection goal by the goal of influence in the House) seems most plausible. We shall return to this idea later. . . .

Table C.5    TRIPS HOME AND DISTRICT STAFF EXPENDITURES

| | Frequency of Trips Home | | | |
|---|---|---|---|---|
| *District Staff Expenditures* | *Low (0–23)* | *Medium (24–42)* | *High (43+)* | *Total* |
| Lowest third | 53 (39%) | 42 (31%) | 40 (30%) | 135 (100%) |
| Middle third | 42 (30%) | 55 (40%) | 41 (30%) | 138 (100%) |
| Highest third | 31 (23%) | 32 (23%) | 75 (54%) | 138 (100%) |
| Total | 126 | 129 | 156 | 411 |

*Note:* Gamma = .28

Table C.6   DISTRICT STAFF EXPENDITURES AND ELECTORAL MARGIN

| Electoral Margin, 1972 | District Staff Expenditures (1973) | | | |
|---|---|---|---|---|
| | Lowest Third | Middle Third | Highest Third | Total |
| Less than 55% | 20 (27%) | 28 (38%) | 26 (35%) | 74 (100%) |
| 55–60% | 20 (36%) | 20 (36%) | 16 (28%) | 56 (100%) |
| 61–65% | 24 (29%) | 29 (35%) | 29 (35%) | 82 (100%) |
| More than 65% | 72 (36%) | 61 (30%) | 68 (34%) | 201 (100%) |
| Total | 136 | 138 | 139 | 413 |

Note: Gamma = –.04

Table C.7   DISTRICT STAFF EXPENDITURES AND SENIORITY

| Seniority | District Staff Expenditures | | | |
|---|---|---|---|---|
| | Lowest Third | Middle Third | Highest Third | Total |
| Low (1–3 terms) | 45 (29%) | 54 (35%) | 56 (36%) | 155 (100%) |
| Medium (4–7 terms) | 44 (29%) | 56 (37%) | 51 (34%) | 151 (100%) |
| High (8+ terms) | 47 (44%) | 28 (26%) | 32 (30%) | 107 (100%) |
| Total | 136 | 138 | 139 | 413 |

Note: Gamma = –.13

Table C.8   DISTRICT STAFF EXPENDITURES AND REGION

| Region | District Staff Expenditures | | | |
|---|---|---|---|---|
| | Lowest Third | Middle Third | Highest Third | Total |
| East[a] | 16 (16%) | 31 (31%) | 52 (53%) | 99 (100%) |
| South[b] | 47 (46%) | 36 (35%) | 19 (19%) | 102 (100%) |
| Border[c] | 18 (55%) | 8 (24%) | 7 (21%) | 33 (100%) |
| Midwest[d] | 39 (37%) | 34 (32%) | 33 (31%) | 106 (100%) |
| Far West[e] | 16 (22%) | 29 (40%) | 28 (38%) | 73 (100%) |
| Total | 136 | 138 | 139 | 413 |

[a]Conn., Maine, Mass., N.H., N.J., N.Y., Pa., R.I., Vt.
[b]Ala., Ark., Fla., Ga., La., Miss., N.C., S.C., Tenn., Tex., Va.
[c]Del., Ky., Md., Mo., Okla., W.Va.
[d]Ill., Ind., Iowa, Kans., Mich., Minn., Nebr., N.Dak., Ohio, S.Dak., Wis.
[e]Alaska, Ariz., Calif., Colo., Hawaii, Idaho, Mont., Nev., N.M., Ore., Utah, Wash., Wyo.

The other variables discussed earlier (family residence and distance from Washington) have no obvious implications for staff allocation. But the variable we used as a surrogate for distance—region—is revealing in its own right. Table C.8 displays staff allocation patterns by region. It is a twin to Table C.3, which related region to home visits. Table C.8 reveals distinctively regional allocation patterns—some similar, some different from those in Table C.3. Easterners, again, rank highest in the allocation of resources to the district. Far westerners no longer rank lowest; but neither do they appear to compensate strongly for their paucity of home visits with heavy staff allocations. Table C.8 reveals other regional patterns that did not show up at all in Table C.3. The southern and border regions emerge with distinctive patterns of staff allocation. To a marked degree, representatives from these two areas eschew large staff operations. If we combine tables C.3 and C.8, every region except the Midwest reveals a noteworthy pattern of resource allocation. In the East we find a high frequency of home visits and large district staffs. In the Far West, we find a low frequency of home visits. In the southern and border regions, we find small district staffs. Region, we conclude, has a substantial effect on home style.

## Personal and Staff Attentiveness: Some Patterns

Regions, however, are composites of several states. Although regional regularities often reflect state regularities, they can also hide them. Both situations are present in this instance. Table C.9 displays state-by-state allocation patterns of personal and district staff attentiveness. For each state delegation we have computed the mean number of trips

Table C.9    ALLOCATION PATTERNS: BY STATE

| District Staff Attentiveness | Personal Attentiveness | |
|---|---|---|
| | Above the Median in Trips Home | Below the Median in Trips Home |
| Above the median in district staff expenditures | Connecticut (E)[a] | |
| | Massachusetts (E) | California (FW) |
| | New York (E) | Colorado (FW) |
| | Tennessee (S) | Hawaii (FW) |
| | Illinois (MW) | Idaho (FW) |
| | Maine (E) | Iowa (MW) |
| | New Hampshire (E) | Kansas (MW) |
| | Pennsylvania (E) | New Mexico (FW) |
| | Rhode Island (E) | Wyoming (FW) |
| | South Carolina (S) | |
| | Vermont (E) | |
| Below the median in district staff expenditures | Kentucky (B) | Alabama (S) |
| | Maryland (B) | Arizona (FW) |
| | North Carolina (S) | Florida (S) |
| | Virginia (S) | Louisiana (S) |
| | West Virginia (B) | Minnesota (MW) |
| | Delaware (B) | Oklahoma (B) |
| | Indiana (MW) | Oregon (FW) |
| | Montana (FW) | Washington (FW) |
| | Ohio (MW) | Wisconsin (MW) |
| | | Arkansas (S) |
| | | Michigan (MW) |
| | | Nebraska (MW) |
| | | South Dakota (MW) |
| | | Texas (S) |
| | | Utah (FW) |

[a]States that fall five trips or more above or below the median *and* whose district staff expenditures fall 5 percent or more above or below the median are underlined. States not listed fall on the median in one or both instances. Regional classifications are in parentheses.

home made by its members in 1973. We have then divided the state delegations into those whose averages fell above and below the median number of trips for all House members (thirty trips). Also, for each state delegation, we computed an average of the percentage of staff expenditures allocated to the district staff by its members. We then divided the state delegations into those whose averages fell above and below the median percentage for all House members (29 percent). The result is a crude fourfold classification of states according to their combined personal and staff resource allocations to "home." The underlined states fall strongly into their particular patterns; the others display weaker tendencies. Each state is further identified by its regional classification.

There are, as Table C.9 shows, distinctive state allocative patterns. Some were foreshadowed in the regional patterns. For example, the eastern states cluster in the high trips home category; and the far western states cluster in the low trips home category. Southern and border states cluster in the weak district staff category. Other state patterns, however, appear here for the first time. The large number of states clustering in both low trips home and small district staff categories, for example, were totally obscured in our regional data.

The relevance of state delegations to patterns of resource allocation at home will come as no surprise to students of Congress. There is virtually no aspect, formal or informal, of the legislative process on Capitol Hill that has not already revealed the importance of the state delegation.[14] How much that importance is the product of extensive communication among delegation members and how much the product of similar expectations emanating from similar districts has never been definitively answered. Nor can it be here. Most likely both processes are involved. State delegation members probably talk to one another about their allocative practices and follow one another's example and advice. Also, certain expectations and traditions probably develop within states, or within sections of states, so that members feel constrained to make resource allocations that are not too far out of line with those expectations. Perhaps they follow a successful predecessor in these matters.

Explaining distinctive regional and state allocation patterns is a good deal more difficult than discovering them. And only a few speculations will be attempted. The sharp separation between eastern and far western states in trips home is doubtless a function of distance. And, it now appears more strongly, some far western state delegations, particularly California's, do compensate for the infrequency of their home visits by maintaining a relatively large staff presence in the district. But, if California representatives invest heavily in this compensatory allocative strategy, why don't the representatives from Washington and Oregon do likewise? The research of John Macartney into the activity of congressional district staffs in California provides a clue. Macartney finds that the California district staffs are heavily populated by party activists and perform many partylike functions:

> The incumbent's staff, in short, allows him to attract and retain the nucleus of his personal political organization. . . . The incumbent fields a publicly paid team of experienced veterans to do a task they have succeeded in before, perhaps many times before, and which differs very little from their everyday jobs.[15]

The suggestion is, then, that in states with weak party organizations (e.g., California) district staffs may be large because they are surrogate electoral organizations. Yet Washington and Oregon are not known as strong party organization states.[16] Why are district staffs in those states smaller than California's? Perhaps Macartney's hunch should be broadened: The more a district staff is called on to perform electoral activity at home (for whatever reason), the larger it will be. Lacking any other studies like Macartney's to tell us what district staffs in particular areas actually do, we shall resist the temptation to roam about in Table C.9 with this speculative proposition. Students of state politics are, however, invited to do so if they wish.

The decision of most southern and border-state representatives to spend relatively little on their district staff operations provides an interesting puzzle. Maryland and Virginia present special cases, because proximity to Washington allows the Washington staff to be, in effect, the district staff. For the other states we might offer a couple of explanations. One is simply that the demand for district staff services is greater, say, in the northeastern states than in the southern and border areas. The welfare-social services case load may be larger in the older, urbanized areas. And, although there is no absolute reason why heavy case loads must be handled by district staffs, writing to Washington is more difficult and less immediately satisfying than going personally to the district office for help. In a similar vein, district offices may be more likely to become ombudsmen on local matters (i.e., city problems) in older, urban areas, where party organizations traditionally handle all levels of problems and where the representative remains more tied to a local party organization than in the southern and border areas. Local political involvements, that is, will increase the case load of the district office.

A second, not inconsistent, explanation may be the tradition of highly personalized, nonbureaucratized politics in the southern and border areas. People there expect to deal directly with well-known, highly visible public officials rather than with faceless bureaucrats. For the congressman, the problem is not just that tradition runs counter to a big district staff. It is that a large district staff might give the necessary reputation and visibility to an ambitious district staffer, thereby turning him into a political competitor. Where personal relationships are traditional, the congressman must make sure that he monopolizes those relationships. Thus, fear of competition may keep district staffs small and clerical in areas where an entrepreneurial politics is strongest.

If, however, personal attentiveness is a tradition and a necessity in southern and border states, we would expect all states in these regions to rank equally high in this respect. Instead, we find considerable variety. At first glance, the variety seems to be related to distance, with states in the Near South receiving more attention than states in the Far South. But the marked difference among Kentucky, Tennessee, and Alabama would seem to require a more complex explanation, perhaps on a district-by-district basis. That, we cannot do. Finally, speaking of complexity, the similar disposition of resources by the conglomeration of states with low trips home and small district staffs in Table C.9 defies even an explanatory guess. We shall have to know more about state and local politics and about the actual employment of resources at home before we can develop satisfying explanations.

The variation of allocative practices across regions and states indicates that home style is affected by the congressman's geographical constituency. That constituency, the district, is, after all, the closest thing to a "given" in his nest of perceptions. And we know from our studies of internal House politics that the geographical constituency has an important effect on individual allocative decisions there—on the choice of committee assignments, for example.[17] So we should not be surprised to find that home style is related to place. That raises a larger question about the allocation of resources and, more generally, about home style. Is a congressman's home style imposed on him, by the district he represents, or is a congressman's home style something he chooses and then imposes on his district? We shall consider that question and work our way toward an answer. . . . For now, we would only say that despite the evident effect of geographical constituency on home style, there is enough absence of regularity in Table C.9 to indicate that the allocative aspects of home style are also a matter of individual choice.

Interviews help uncover other dimensions of individual choice. One, in particular, seems noteworthy. House members sometimes choose to allocate their resources to home in ways that deliberately sharpen the contrast between themselves and other members, past or present, with whom they will be compared. That is, instead of acquiescing in a regional or local allocative pattern they deliberately adopt a contrasting pattern in order to gain a stylistic identity for themselves as individuals.

A congressman who shares a metropolitan area with two other House members and has a one-person district staff answered the question, Why don't you have a highly paid district staff like your two colleagues? in this way:

> I wanted to submerge the district function. If you have a big staff, you create expectations, you encourage people to come to you and you get a huge case load. Secondly, I wanted to have the image that "Guy does it himself." If people know that Lola [the staff] is just a conduit, they will feel that the decision is made in Washington and is made by me. . . . I don't want anyone speaking for me. Thirdly, I wanted the casework done in the Washington office, so I would be better informed on who we are helping and how. . . . Finally, a little contrapuntal contrast with my two neighbors doesn't hurt me in my opinion. They play up district services and they have much better identification as the local congressmen than I could have. No matter what I did, I could never achieve the magnificent local identification they have. I would always stand in their shadow. They have created expectations that people don't have of me. . . . I'm trying to gain my identification in another way. So, there are several reasons. Put them all together, they spell Lola.

Another House member described his decision to come home a lot as a self-conscious effort to create an identity different from that of the powerful, recently retired member he had replaced:

> My predecessor paid no attention to his constituents and did not tend the district. His life was back there [in Washington] where he was a powerful figure because of his position and his native ability. He was terribly important to the major interests here. He was powerful and feared here. But he couldn't abide coming back here. He hated to fly. When he did come, he did everyone a favor, so to speak. And he touched the elites—the Chamber of Commerce, the local establishment. He would attend ceremonies and cut ribbons. But he didn't care about mingling with ordinary citizens. Everything I do is in contrast. He came home twice a year. I come home every month for a week, hold open houses all over the district, and talk to ordinary people. Out here, that makes news. It's nothing that lots of others don't do back East. But people see me as different because of the contrast with my predecessor.

Both these House members made allocative decisions at variance with accepted local practice. And, the point is, they did so as a matter of individual choice.

Even here geographical constraints still apply. The standard by which these two representatives judge their degree of contrast is a local, not a national, standard. The first member's two colleagues have 30 percent of their staff allocation in the district—no better than the median figure nationally. And the second member's once-a-month home visits are far below the national average. They remind us that there is no one national allocative standard against which all House members can be compared. The overall picture is, then, one in which allocative practices result from an interaction between individual choice and geographically related constraints.

## CONCLUSION

. . .We discovered that House members have a fairly complicated set of perceptions of "the constituency." In this chapter, we began to understand how they might come by such perceptions. In brief, they go home to their districts often and spend a lot of time there. Because the members apparently devote a considerable amount of their resources to home activity, political scientists need to devote more of their resources to studying that activity. We have categorized member activity at home as allocating resources, presenting themselves, and explaining their Washington behavior. And we have labeled the combination of these three activities as home style.

Our examination of the allocation of personal and staff resources to the district indicates that we can expect a wide variety of home styles among House members. Among the factors that appear to influence the allocation of a representative's time and money to his or her district are personal goals, family residence, distance, established local expectations, and the desire to create new local expectations. From our aggregate analysis, therefore, we know that the allocative aspects of home style are the product of both personal and constituency factors. There is a lot left unanswered, particularly questions about the effect of electoral uncertainty and of local political patterns on allocative styles. Answers here must await new or different data. But if we take with us our conclusion about the importance of individual choice and contextual constraints in accounting for varieties of style, we shall have a useful perspective with which to study some individual cases. . . .

## NOTES

1. On constituency and voting, see John Kingdon, *Congressmen's Voting Decisions* (New York: Harper & Row, 1973). On the more general point, see David Mayhew, *Congress: The Electoral Connection* (New Haven: Yale University Press, 1974).
2. The basic research was done by John Saloma, and is reported in his *Congress and the New Politics* (Boston: Little, Brown, 1969, Chap. 6; in Donald Tacheron and Morris Udall, *The Job of the Congressman* (Indianapolis: Bobbs Merrill, 1966), pp. 280–88; and in *Guide to the Congress of the United States,* Congressional Quarterly (Washington, D.C., 1971), pp. 532–549. But no one has expanded Saloma's work beyond the Washington context. An intriguing analysis of Washington time budgets, based on an audit of incoming communications to a congressional subcommittee is David Kovenock, "Influence in the U.S. House of Representatives: A Statistical Analysis of Communications," *American Politics Quarterly* 4 (October 1973): 430–33, 440–44. A pioneer work, which would have given us a wider perspective, but

which seems to have been neglected is Dorothy H. Cronheim, "Congressmen and Their Communication Practices," unpublished manuscript, Ann Arbor, Michigan, 1957.

3. The "total days home" figure (138) was based on 401 answers. The disparity in figures between my 13 members and the 419 members is probably the result of two factors. First, whereas one-third of the larger group went home every weekend, none of my thirteen members did. The greatest number of trips for them was forty-five. Second, a comparison between records I checked and the replies to the survey question in the same offices (twelve) indicates a consistent tendency for the verbal replies to inflate the actual figures. Number of trips was exaggerated in nine cases, was the same in two cases, and was lower in one case. Total number of days at home was exaggerated in ten cases and was lower in two cases. Because the disparities were much greater with regard to total days spent at home and because, in any case, total days at home is a more difficult figure to pin down, we shall not use this figure further in our aggregate analysis. We shall, instead, use the more reliable figure for number of trips. In some respects the total number of days home is the more informative figure. Any complete analysis ought to take both trips and days into account. In most cases we have not done so. For example, one member made 25 trips home and spent 51 days there, whereas another member made 21 trips home and spent 106 days there.

4. Other kinds of data were collected that might also be useful as an indication of district staff strength. Three of them correlated very highly with the indicator we are using, so we do not seem to be missing much by relying on one indicator. Our measure—percentage of staff expenditures allocated to district staff—correlated at .861 with number of people on the district staff, at .907 with the percentage of total staff members allocated to the district, and at .974 with the dollar amounts spent on district staff. We also have recorded the rank, in the total staff hierarchy, of the highest-paid person on the district staff, as another indicator of district staff allocation practices. We have not utilized that indicator, but we might note that the range is from first (i.e., the highest-paid district staffer is the highest-paid of all the congressman's staffers) to more than ninth (we stopped counting after nine).

5. There were eleven members who went home every night: eight from Maryland, two from Virginia, and one from Pennsylvania. In computing averages, they were coded at 98 trips (more than anyone else) rather than at 365, to minimize distortion. Also to minimize distortion caused by these cases, I have used the median number of trips in this chapter analysis, rather than the average number of trips.

6. The most common replies were "every week," "once a month," "twice a month," "every other week," "between once and twice a month," "three or four times a month," etc. Representatives placed in the "low" category were those whose staffers were unwilling to go as high as "twice a month." Those whose trips were reported as "once a week" or more fell into the "high" category. But some respondents said, "every week except for a few" or "every week, but maybe he missed one or two here or there." So, we decided to try to capture that sense by including in the "high" category people who were reported to have made somewhat less than 52 trips. (Doubtless those who said they went home every week missed a few too.) Because a sizable group had 40 trips and none had 41 or 42, we cut at that point and made 43 + the "high" category. The middle category were those who remained—people who went home at least twice a month (24 trips) but not as often as 43 times in 1973.

7. Neither does the frequency of 1973 home visits bear any relationship to whether the member's electoral margin declined, increased, or remained the same between 1972 and 1974. The measure of association we have employed for our cross-tabulations is the *gamma;* and we have listed its value beneath the tables where appropriate to give the reader some feeling for the strength of the relationship. Roger Davidson finds, relatedly, that marginality does not affect the budgeting of times between legislative and constituency activities in Washington. Davidson, *The Role of the Congressman* (New York: Pegasus, 1973), pp. 102–03.

8. See Morris Fiorina, *Representatives, Roll Calls and Constituencies* (Boston: Lexington, 1974). The piece of research that dovetails best with my research is Warren Miller, "Majority Rule and the Representative System of Government" in Erik Allandt and Yrjo Littunen, *Cleavages, Ideologies and Party Systems* (Helsinki, 1964), chap. 10. Miller uses subjective marginality as the measure of competitiveness and relates it to the policy attitudes of representatives and their reelection constituencies.

9. The correlation coefficient (Pearson's *r*) is −.23.

10. Lacking essential data on the physical debilities (real or imagined) of House members, we cannot proceed with our hunches about age. But the correlation between seniority and age is .69, which suggests that the age factor is pretty well accounted for in our seniority calculations. This is most true for the younger members; most of the members under forty-five years of age are also in the one-to-three-term seniority group. Comparing those between forty-five and sixty with those over sixty, we find that the tendency of trips home to decline with seniority is a little bit greater among the older age group. This suggests a slight independent influence of age, but not enough to make it worth pursuing here.

11. As a reminder, however, that money does count, and in nonobvious ways, consider this comment by a member in the high seniority category:

> In the early years, I didn't make many trips home. It was simply a matter of money. . . . I come home more now. I get a bigger travel allowance and I get asked to speak more. I never pay any of my own money to come home. I can't. But when you speak, your way is paid. . . . I go home much more now than when I first went to Congress. But I don't work as hard as I used to when I'm home.

12. The number of cases is lower here than in the other parts of the analysis because the data were collected in 1975, after a number of the 1973 members were no longer available for questioning.

13. The correlation coefficient is .20.

14. For example, Aage Clausen, *How Congressmen Decide: A Policy Focus* (New York: St. Martins, 1973); Barbara Deckard, "State Party Delegations in the U.S. House of Representatives: A Study in Group Cohesion," *Journal of of Politics* 34 (February 1972): 199–222; John Ferejohn, *Pork Barrel Politics* (Stanford: Stanford University Press, 1974); Donald Matthews and James Stimson, *Yeas and Nays: Normal Decision Making in the U.S. House of Representatives* (New York: Wiley, 1975).

15. John D. Macartney, "Political Staffing: A View From the District," Ph.D. dissertation, University of California, Los Angeles, 1975, p. 195.

16. Indeed, Washington's congressional delegation is very much against strong party organization. See John H. Kessel, "The Washington Congressional Delegation," *Midwest Journal of Political Science* 8 (February 1964): 2.

17. Kenneth Shepsle demonstrates that in applying for committee assignments, a freshman member is very likely to apply for the same committee as his predecessor when there is an identifiable relationship between the predecessor's committee jurisdiction and the geographical constituency—that is, in cases where expectations in the geographical constituency would be well formed. Kenneth Shepsle, *The Giant Jig Saw Puzzle* (Chicago: University of Chicago Press, 1978).

# Appendix
# *D*

## *Turnout and the Two-Party Vote*

JOHN H. FENTON
*University of Massachusetts*

The conventional wisdom tells us that Democratic candidates for national office usually win elections when there are large turnouts and Republicans are likely to win if the turnout is small. In the 1976 presidential election it was widely assumed that a small turnout would be a harbinger of good electoral fortunes for President Ford and the Republicans. Typical was a *Time* magazine observation on November 1, 1976, that "more than 70 million Americans may stay at home next week. That would surely boost Gerald Ford's election chances. . . ."[1] The source of this wisdom is findings such as the following reported by V. O. Key in *Politics, Parties, and Pressure Groups:* "Those elements with the lowest voting rates consist in larger measure of persons with Democratic rather than Republican predispositions. . . . Democratic candidates would have been strengthened, at least in recent decades, by compulsory voting or by some other means of bringing out substantially the entire electorate. Analysis after analysis has shown a higher preference for the Democratic cause among those who stayed away from the polls than among those who voted."[2]

---

1. *Time Magazine*, November 1, 1976, 32.

2. V. O. Key, Jr., *Politics, Parties and Pressure Groups* (5th ed.; New York: Thomas Y. Crowell Company, 1964), 589–590.

More recently, the *Congressional Quarterly Almanac* contained the following estimate of the political effect of increased turnout in elections: "Democrats would gain the most from increased voter participation. According to Democratic Party surveys, 70 percent of the 54 million nonregistered Americans would register as Democrats. Increased voter registration also could result in heavier voting by minority groups, who traditionally vote Democratic. Another Democratic gain could come from labor unions who would be able to run extensive voter registration drives with registration forms printed at government expense."[3]

Of course, V. O. Key never said that a high level of turnout would inevitably and invariably help Democrats and hurt Republicans. However, findings such as Key's and the *Congressional Quarterly's* have left little doubt in most minds that, "all other things being approximately equal," high turnout is good for Democrats and bad for Republicans. Certainly, this assumption has permeated the debate over postcard registration.

This paper tests the hypothesis that Democrats benefit from high turnouts and Republicans from low turnouts by, first, examining the relationship between Democratic and Republican victory margins and turnout. If the hypothesis is correct, then there should be a negative relationship between victory margin and turnout for the Republicans and a positive relationship between the two variables for Democrats.

Figure D.1 is a scattergram showing the relationship between the size of Republican presidential election victories, 1828–1976, and the size of turnout.[4] Inspection of the figure provides reassurance to the purveyors and consumers of conventional wisdom. As expected, TURNOUT is highly related to the size of Republican election victo-

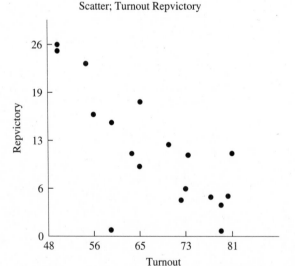

Scatter; Turnout Repvictory

**Figure D.1** Republican Victory Margins and Turnout in the Presidential Elections from 1828–1976*

*Before 1865, the major alternative to Democratic is classified as Republican.

---

3. *Congressional Quarterly Alamac*, Vol. XXXII, 1976, Washington, D.C., 518.

4. Before 1856, the major alternative to Democratic is classified as Republican.

ries and the relationship is negative since the slope is equal to −.584. The Pearson correlation coefficient between the variables is $r = -.78$, and $r^2 = 0.61$ which means that 61 percent of the variation in the size of Republican victories is related to the size of turnout.

Figure D.2 is a scattergram picturing the relationship between the size of Democratic victories and size of turnout. Inspection of Figure D.2 shows little relationship between size of turnout and Democratic victory margins. However, the relationship that does exist is also negative since the slope is −.363. The Pearson correlation coefficient between the variables is −.45, which means 20 percent of the variance in the size of Democratic victories is related to the size of turnout.

Somewhat surprisingly then, we find that the relationship between size of victory and turnout is negative for both Democrats and Republicans, but with the relationship much stronger for Republican victories than for Democratic victories. Does this provide support then for the original hypothesis that Democrats profit from high turnouts? On the contrary, inspection of Figure D.1 leads us to believe that the strong negative Republican relationship with turnout is as much a product of big turnouts in narrow victories as smaller turnouts in landslide victories. Comparison of the two figures reveals a pronounced clustering of narrow Republican victories accompanied by very high turnouts. This induced us to obtain the average turnout in narrow Republican victories, narrow Democratic victories and one-sided Republican and Democratic victories for comparative purposes. Table D.1 contains the result of this inquiry. According to the table, over the course of American two-party history, 1828–1976, average turnout has been greatest in closely contended contests, and least by far in the years of landslide victories by either party. There is little difference in the size of the turnout when party is taken into account. However, the little difference that exists favors the Republicans.

It occurred to us that the failure to find a relationship between turnout and Democratic victories might be due to differences in the party's relationship to the electorate during different time frames. Therefore, we obtained the average turnout figures

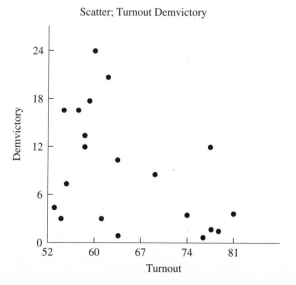

**Figure D.2**

Table D.1    AVERAGE AND STANDARD DEVIATION OF TURNOUT BY PARTY
VICTORIES, 1828–1976

| Party Victory | N | Mean Turnout | St Dev |
|---|---|---|---|
| DEM LANDSLIDE (By more than 10 percentage points) | 8 | 60.98 | 7.51 |
| REP LANDSLIDE (By more than 10 percentage points) | 10 | 62.52 | 10.62 |
| NARROW DEM (10 percentage points or less) | 12 | 67.74 | 10.54 |
| NARROW REP (10 percentage points or less) | 8 | 73.56 | 7.34 |

Table D.2    AVERAGE AND STANDARD DEVIATION TURNOUT BY PARTY VICTORIES AND
TIME PERIODS

| | N | Av Turnout for Rep Victories | St Dev | N | Av Turnout for Dem Victories | St Dev |
|---|---|---|---|---|---|---|
| 1828–1856 | 2 | 76.5* | 5.30 | 6 | 66.4 | 10.91 |
| 1860–1892 | 5 | 76.8 | 4.09 | 4 | 78.3 | 2.99 |
| 1896–1928 | 7 | 62.6 | 11.59 | 2 | 60.2 | 1.98 |
| 1932–1976 | 4 | 59.73 | 3.45 | 8 | 58.6 | 4.08 |

*Before 1856, the major alternative to Democratic is classified as Republican.

by Republican and Democratic victories for the periods 1828–1856, 1860–1892, 1896–1928, 1932–1976. Table D.2 contains the results of this analysis. The table reveals that the average turnout has been about the same in good and bad Democratic years in every time frame. The small difference generally favors the Republicans.

More importantly, however, Tables D.1 and D.2 would seem to undermine if not demolish the hypothesis that Democrats benefit from high turnout and Republicans from low turnouts. Rather, it would seem that the size of turnout is related almost exclusively to the margin of victory, with little if any party advantage attached to the size of turnouts.

The explanation for the paradox of non-voters being dominantly Democratic and yet little or no relationship existing between turnout and Democratic electoral fortunes would seem to reside, first, in the fact that interest in elections is related to the margin of victory and, secondly, to the electoral circumstances that have made the Democratic party the majority party over most of the nation's political history.

For example, in 1977 there are twice as many committed Democrats as Republicans in the electorate (44.7 percent Democratic compared to 22.3 percent Republican).[5] The remainder of the electorate is either Independent, committed to a third party, or totally uninterested. Therefore, in any "normal" American election with a "normal" turnout and "normal" voting behavior, i.e., Democrats by and large voting Democratic,

---

5. *The Gallup Opinion Index*, Report #140, March 1977, 31.

Republicans voting Republican and Independents dividing their votes somewhat more evenly between the candidates, the Democrats are certain to win. On the other hand, Republican victory would seem to require a somewhat abnormal electoral situation, such as an unusually attractive Republican candidate or an unusually unattractive Democratic candidate or intense dissatisfaction of a portion of the electorate with Democratic performance in office. Any one of these circumstances in an election would almost certainly evoke great interest in the election and abnormally high turnout. This has been true over most of American electoral history, ranging from the election of "Tippecanoe and Tyler too" in 1840 to "Ike and Dick" in 1952.

It should not be generalized from these findings that increased turnout will have little or no effect on party fortunes. Rather, it is a fact that abnormal interest in an election due to the nature of the candidates or the nature of the issues tends to accompany Republican victory and we would maintain that it is a necessary condition of Republican victory. On the other hand, postcard registration may generally increase "normal" turnout to the disadvantage of Republican candidates by making the "normal" electorate even more Democratically-inclined than at present, and thereby requiring an increasingly abnormal interest in the election to produce a Republican victory.

# Appendix
# *E*

## Conflict with Supreme Court Precedent and the Granting of Plenary Review

S. SIDNEY ULMER
*The University of Kentucky*

This paper presents preliminary findings from a study designed to fill a gap in political scientists' knowledge about the extent to which the Supreme Court grants or denies plenary review when conflict with one or more of its precedents is claimed. The findings are that the presence of conflict promoted the granting of review between 1961 and 1976, including the Warren Court terms (1961–68), even in the face of controls for litigant status, civil liberty issues, and constitutional issues, but that it was a poorer predictor during the Burger Court terms (1969–76).

I

In granting and denying plenary review of cases coming from lower courts the Supreme Court exercises what is almost totally a discretionary power. The use of this discretion appears to be responsive to a number of "cues" (Teger and Kosinski, 1980; Songer, 1979; Brenner, 1979; Ulmer, 1981; Baum, 1977; Tanenhaus, 1963; cf. Provine, 1980, pp. 77–78). Although the Court itself suggests that conflict with one or more Supreme Court precedents is a significant consideration in shaping the access decision,[1] political scientists have made no attempt to validate or disconfirm the proposition. We do know that the Court denies review to some cases in which there is a direct conflict with Supreme Court precedent (Feeney, 1975). What we do not know is the extent to which the Court grants or denies review when conflict is claimed and when its presence is not

The research on which this paper is based has been supported by The National Science Foundation (Grant #SES-77-26066-01).

1. The Court also suggests in its procedural Rule #17 that conflict in the circuits is a factor influencing the decision to grant or deny review. We do not examine that factor in this note.

alleged. The author is currently engaged in a longitudinal study of the Supreme Court's jurisdictional decisions. In this note we report some preliminary findings bearing on the role of conflict in determining the jurisdictional decision.

Specifically, we address two questions: (1) Is the Supreme Court more likely to grant plenary review in cases in which the rulings are in conflict with one or more Supreme Court precedents? (2) Has the Burger Court, in deciding whether to grant or deny review, given greater or lesser weight to conflict with Supreme Court precedent than has the Warren Court?

The data to be used in evaluating these hypotheses were derived as follows. For the 1961–76 terms (i.e., 8 terms of the Warren Court and 8 years of the Burger Court) all *paid* cases in which plenary review was granted were identified—whether the case came on appeal or on certiorari. For paid cases denied review a 10 percent sample was drawn and then weighted to reflect the ratio of grants and denials in each appropriate time period. The data then were analyzed (a) for the entire period, (b) for the Warren period, and (c) for the Burger terms. To identify "conflict cases," we isolated all cases in which one or more judges below dissented. In such cases we determined whether a dissenter alleged a conflict between the decision of his majority and a previous ruling of the Supreme Court. A conflict case is defined as one in which such an allegation was made.[2] A concomitant effect is to control for dissent below.

## II

We first examined the 1961–76 terms to determine if the Court's decisions to grant or deny review were associated with the presence or absence of conflict. Table E.1 arrays the relevant data. As the table shows, there is a significant relationship. The presence of conflict promotes the granting of review. The gamma (Kirkpatrick, 1974) of .407 shows that in using conflict to predict decision, predictive error can be reduced 40.7 percent. We infer that the Court does pay *some* attention to conflict in deciding whether to grant plenary review.

Table E.1   CONFLICT WITH SUPREME COURT PRECEDENTS, 1961–76

|  | Conflict Present |  | Conflict Absent |
|---|---|---|---|
| Review Granted | 276 (11.6%) |  | 270 (11.3) |
| Review Denied | 554 (23.2) |  | 1287 (53.9) |
|  | $x^2$ = 76.7 | $p \leq .001$ | gamma = .407 |

2. Another possible indicator to "conflict" is the claim of a petitioning party in his jurisdictional brief. That indicator has not been employed with the data set used in this paper. Preliminary investigations in other contexts suggest that the padding of such claims may undermine their use as an indicator to conflict. However, given certain refinements now being pursued by the author, such claims may eventually prove to be an index to conflict.

In order to guard against spurious inference, we repeated the analysis controlling for litigant status,[3] civil liberty issues,[4] and constitutional issues.[5] As previously noted, the selection of cases effectively controlled for dissension below.[6] Under controls the gamma declined slightly to .360. Thus, the relationship depicted is not subject to explanation by the variables controlled, and we retain the original inference.

## III

We next examined the same relationships for the Warren Court terms. Table E.2 reveals a significant relationship once again. The presence of conflict is associated with the decision to grant plenary review and its absence with decisions to deny review. The gamma of .533 shows an even stronger relation between the two variables than that revealed for the 1961–76 terms. When we controlled for dissension below, constitutional issues, civil liberty issues, and litigant status the gamma increased to .592. We infer that the Warren Court was substantially influenced by conflict in exercising its jurisdictional discretion.

The analysis is applied to the Burger Court in Table E.3. As in tables E.1 and E.2, the relationship is positive and $p \leq .001$. The gamma of .287 shows a relatively weak ability of conflict to predict decision. Moreover, when controls were introduced the

Table E.2   CONFLICT WITH SUPREME COURT PRECEDENTS, 1961–68

|  | Conflict Present | | Conflict Absent |
|---|---|---|---|
| Review Granted | 119 (11.4%) | | 121 (11.6) |
| Review Denied | 185 (17.8) | | 616 (59.2) |
| | $x^2 = 61.5$ | $p \leq .001$ | gamma = .533 |

Note: The cell entries for the Warren and Burger courts do not sum, in every case, to the cell entries for the 1961–76 period. This is due to the fact that the weights necessary to equate the ratio of grants to denials in the samples with appropriate population ratios varied slightly.

Table E.3   CONFLICT WITH SUPREME COURT PRECEDENTS, 1969–76

|  | Conflict Present | | Conflict Absent |
|---|---|---|---|
| Review Granted | 157 (11.7%) | | 149 (11.1) |
| Review Denied | 381 (28.4) | | 654 (48.8) |
| | $x^2 = 20.6$ | $p \leq .001$ | gamma = .287 |

Note: The cell entries for the Warren and Burger courts do not sum, in every case, to the cell entries for the 1961–76 period. This is due to the fact that the weights necessary to equate the ratio of grants to denials in the samples with appropriate population ratios varied slightly.

3. Scored as Upperdog or Underdog. For an explanation of these terms see Ulmer (1981).

4. Scored as present or absent.

5. Scored as present or absent..

6. I.e., whether the Court immediately below was unanimous or nonunanimous.

gamma dipped to .169. We infer that conflict was a poor predictor of jurisdictional decision in the 1969–76 terms, and that the Warren Court gave substantially greater weight than did the Burger Court to conflict in granting or denying review.


## IV

The results of these preliminary analyses do not contradict the findings of Feeney (1975) that the Court denies review in a significant number of conflict cases each term. Indeed, in the 1961–76 terms the Court denied review in two-thirds of the cases involving conflict with one or more Supreme Court precedents. For the Warren Court the comparable figure was 61 percent; for the Burger Court, 71 percent. At the same time, we must conclude that conflict with precedent is significantly related to the Court's jurisdictional decisions. The strength of that relationship, although not overwhelming, is sufficient to suggest that those who construct cue models of access decision making should seriously consider including conflict as a possible explanatory variable.

The Warren Court, by giving about four times the weight to conflict as did the Burger Court, forces one to consider that the Warren Court was influenced by traditional "legal" variables as well as by the kind of behavioral and/or attitudinal factors so frequently alleged to have motivated it.


## REFERENCES

Baum, Lawrence (1977). "Policy Goals in Judicial Gatekeeping: A Proximity Model for Discretionary Jurisdiction." *American Journal of Political Science* 21: 13–35.

Brenner, Saul (1979). "The New Certiorari Game." *The Journal of Politics* 41: 649–55.

Feeney, Floyd (1975). *Report to the Commission on Revision of the Federal Court Appellate System.* Reprinted in *Structure and Internal Procedures: Recommendations for Change.* Washington, D.C., pp. 93–133.

Kirkpatrick, Samuel A. (1974). *Quantitative Analysis of Political Data.* Columbus: Charles E. Merrill Publishing Co.

Provine, Doris M. (1980). *Case Selection in the United States Supreme Court.* Chicago: University of Chicago Press.

Songer, Donald R. (1979). "Concern for Policy Outputs as a Cue for Supreme Court Decisions on Certiorari." *The Journal of Politics* 41: 1185–94.

Tanenhaus, Joseph, Marvin Schick, Matthew Muraskin, and Daniel Rosen (1963). "The Supreme Court's Certiorari Jurisdiction: Cue Theory." In S. Sidney Ulmer (ed.), *Courts, Law, and Judicial Processes.* New York: The Free Press, pp. 273–83.

Teger, Stuart, and Douglas Kosinski (1980). "The Cue Theory of Supreme Court Certiorari Jurisdiction: A Reconsideration." *The Journal of Politics* 42: 834–46.

Ulmer, S. Sidney (1981). "Selecting Cases for Supreme Court Review: Litigant Status in the Warren and Burger Courts." In S. Sidney Ulmer (ed.), *Courts, Law, and Judicial Processes.* New York: The Free Press, pp. 284–97.

# Appendix
# *F*

## McCleskey v. Kemp:
## *Background, Record, and Adjudications*

DAVID C. BALDUS, GEORGE G. WOODWORTH,
AND CHARLES A. PULASKI

In this chapter we first describe the legal background against which the McCleskey case developed in the state and federal courts and the circumstances of our involvement in the case. We then describe the data from our Georgia studies that we presented in the McCleskey case, with special reference to the Charging and Sentencing Study (CSS). We also report some results that we developed for the McCleskey hearing but did not offer in evidence and some analyses of the CSS data that we conducted subsequent to the hearing. Finally, we describe in detail the rulings and analyses of the trial court, the Eleventh Circuit Court of Appeals, and the Supreme Court, with special reference to our Georgia studies and to issues of proof in discrimination cases. . . .

## THE BACKGROUND TO *McCLESKEY V. KEMP*

### The Legal Context in Which *McCleskey* Arose

By the early 1980s, the decisions of the United States Supreme Court suggested three possible constitutional grounds for challenging the manner in which post-*Furman* capital-sentencing systems were being applied. The first possible "as applied" claim was that a death-sentencing system violated the cruel and unusual punishments provision of the Eighth Amendment because it routinely imposed comparatively excessive death sentences. The basis for this claim was language in *Furman v. Georgia* and the Court's decision in *Godfrey v. Georgia* (1980).[1] *Furman* characterized as arbitrary death sentences that could not be meaningfully distinguished from cases that generally received lesser sentences. *Godfrey* involved a death sentence imposed upon an estranged husband for the shotgun slaying of his wife and mother-in-law at a time in which he was distraught over a separation from his wife and child. The *Godfrey* majority vacated the death sentence on the ground that it had been imposed under circumstances that, on the basis of the Georgia Supreme Court's own prior decisions, did not establish the relevant, statutorily designated aggravating circumstance—vile and wanton slaying—upon which it was based. The majority opinion also quoted with approval the language of *Furman* requiring that a death-sentencing system must "in short, provide a 'meaningful basis for distinguishing the few cases in which [the penalty] is imposed from the many cases in which it is not.'"[2] Suggesting that most domestic homicides in Georgia did not result in a death sentence, the court stated that there was "no principled way to distinguish [Godfrey's] case, in which the death penalty was imposed, from the many cases in which it was not."[3]

There were two compelling reasons why a systemwide constitutional challenge on the theory of arbitrariness and comparative excessiveness did not appear promising. First, in spite of the outcome of *Godfrey,* the degree of support in the Supreme Court for any broader attack on comparative excessiveness was unclear. Indeed, of the original five supporters of the concept in *Furman v. Georgia,* only Justices Brennan, Marshall, and White remained on the Court. And no recent decision of the Supreme Court or any federal Court of Appeals had invalidated a death sentence on the ground of comparative excessiveness.[4]

The second problem with a challenge to a death-sentencing system on this theory of arbitrariness was the lack of an accepted standard for measuring excessiveness in an individual case and for challenging the constitutionality of an entire system on this basis. Both the *Furman* and *Godfrey* discussions of arbitrariness and excessiveness were based on quite general concepts, and there was no lower-court jurisprudence either defining the concept with particularity or identifying methods of proof that would be sufficient to support a successful claim.

The second possible basis for an as-applied challenge would focus on the lack of comparative-proportionality review in the supreme courts of those states whose statutes did not require such a review. The opinions of certain justices in *Gregg* implied that the Eighth Amendment might require an effective system of comparative-proportionality review, particularly in jurisdictions that gave sentencing juries extremely broad discretion.[5] Also, the *Godfrey* opinion had emphasized the importance of the appellate-review function in ensuring rational and consistent death sentencing.[6] On the basis of these decisions, a 1981 California federal habeas corpus case, *Pulley v. Harris,* challenged a death sentence on the grounds that the California statute did require a proportionality review in the case. Harris's claim was successful in the United States Court of Appeals but was ultimately rejected in the United States Supreme Court. By a 7–2 vote, *Pulley v.*

*Harris* (1984) held that comparative proportionality was not constitutionally required, regardless of the degree of jury discretion involved.[7]

The third possible constitutional challenge suggested by the case law was a claim of racial discrimination. The Supreme Court's decisions in the 1960s and 1970s had previously applied the equal-protection clause of the Fourteenth Amendment to condemn state discrimination on racial grounds in such contexts as jury selection and public school administration. It seemed probable that these decisions would extend to discrimination in the application of a facially neutral death-sentencing statute if the required burden of proof could be met. Since *Washington v. Davis* (1976), it has been plain that in order to prevail under an equal-protection claim a claimant must establish purposeful or intentional discrimination.[8] It was unclear, however, whether an equal protection claimant had to establish a "conscious" purpose or intent to discriminate, or whether evidence of a nonconscious but identifiable response to the racial characteristics of the cases would be sufficient. Finally, it was not clear whether proof of purposeful discrimination in the system as a whole would be a sufficient basis for granting a defendant relief if he were a member of a disadvantaged minority. For example, in Fourteenth Amendment jury-discrimination cases, a black defendant's conviction will be vacated if he can show purposeful discrimination against blacks in the selection of jury pools from which venires are drawn. Following this model, a black defendant's death sentence would be vacated if he can show classwide, purposeful race-of-defendant discrimination in his death-sentencing system. Alternatively, compelling evidence of classwide, purposeful discrimination might serve only to create a presumption of discrimination in individual cases, which the state could rebut with evidence of the particulars of the defendant's case. Whatever the uncertainties were on these issues, it was clearly perceived that evidence of classwide discrimination was relevant to a Fourteenth Amendment equal-protection claim.

The Supreme Court's decision in *Furman v. Georgia* also established the relevance of racial discrimination under the Eighth Amendment. Although the majority of the *Furman* justices considered the claims of racial discrimination to be unproven, their opinions clearly indicated that proof of purposeful discrimination would create a sufficient risk of arbitrariness and caprice to sustain a finding of arbitrariness under the Eighth Amendment's cruel and unusual punishments provision. The Court's post-*Furman* decisions, particularly *Zant v. Stephens*, strengthened this belief. In *Zant*, the Court stated that the defective statutory aggravating circumstance under attack in the case was not equivalent to attaching "the 'aggravating' label to factors that are constitutionally impermissible or totally irrelevant to the sentencing process, such as for example the race, religion, or political affiliation of the defendant."[9] This language clearly implied that race-of-defendant or race-of-victim discrimination, whether overt or covert, would be constitutionally impermissible.[10] What was unclear, however, was whether a discrimination-based Eighth Amendment claim required proof of purposeful discrimination in the same manner as the equal-protection clause. It was also unclear what the appropriate remedy would be for a defendant who successfully established an Eighth Amendment violation on the basis of racial discrimination.

In the post-*Furman* period the most detailed analysis of the proof that might be required of a claimant alleging arbitrariness and discrimination in the application of a death-sentencing system came in the 1982 Fifth Circuit case *Smith v. Balkcom.* Smith's allegation of race-of-victim discrimination was supported by a statewide statistical analysis that showed a race-of-victim disparity in death-sentencing rates among Georgia cases reported to the FBI. The court rejected the claim on several methodological grounds, the principal one being that the study controlled for only a single statutory aggravating circumstance—whether the case involved a serious contemporaneous offense. The court's criticisms of Smith's study suggested, however, the type of proof that might support a claim of arbitrariness and discrimination in capital sentencing.

> In some instances, circumstantial or statistical evidence of racially disproportionate impact may be so strong that the results permit no other inference but that they are the product of a racially discriminatory intent or purpose. . . . Smith's evidence, however, does not present such a case. The raw data selected for the statistical study bear no more than a highly attenuated relationship to capital cases actually presented for trial in the state. The leap from that data to the conclusion of discriminatory intent or purpose leaves untouched countless racially neutral variables. The statistics are not inconsistent with the proper application of the structured capital punishment law of the state found constitutional in *Gregg v. Georgia* . . . . Here, the proffered evidence would not have been of sufficient probative value to have required response and no hearing was required. . . .
>
> No data is offered as to whether or not charges or indictments grew out of reported incidents or as to whether charges were for murder under aggravating circumstances, murder in which no aggravating circumstances were alleged, voluntary manslaughter, involuntary manslaughter, or other offenses. The data are not refined to select incidents in which mitigating circumstances were advanced or found or those cases in which evidence of aggravating circumstances was sufficient to warrant submission of the death penalty vel non to a jury. No incidents resulting in not guilty verdicts were removed from the data. The unsupported assumption is that all such variables were equally distributed, racially, sexually, offender and victim, throughout the SHRS [Supplemental Homicide Reports to the FBI from the local police]. No conclusions of evidentiary value can be predicated upon such unsupported assumptions.[11]

The clear implication of the *Smith* opinion was that proof that met these requirements, as well as those of *Washington v. Davis,* would compel the court to consider classwide claims of discrimination under the Fourteenth and Eighth Amendments.

## Our Involvement in *McCleskey*

In 1980, while we were completing the data-collection stage of the Procedural Reform Study (PRS), lawyers at the NAACP Legal Defense and Educational Fund, Inc. (LDF) requested us to undertake an empirical research study that might prove useful in their efforts to challenge the post-*Furman* application of the death penalty. We accepted their offer, but advised the LDF representatives that our results might prove to be of limited usefulness or even damaging to their cause. We agreed, however, that, if requested, we would testify concerning our findings in litigation on behalf of death-row inmates represented by the LDF. In exchange for this commitment, the LDF agreed to finance the study through a grant from the Edna McConnell Clark Foundation and to give us complete discretion as to the publication and dissemination of our findings.

In the summer and fall of 1980, we explored with the LDF's attorneys the focus and location of the contemplated study. It was agreed from the outset that the study should focus on racial discrimination. The most suitable state for the study was unclear, however, and we tentatively explored several possibilities. Georgia was finally selected because of its prominence as a death-sentencing jurisdiction, because a pilot study from the Procedural Reform Study gave us some idea of what a more extensive study might produce, and because of the high quality of the data on homicide cases that were available in that state.

In the winter of 1980 and the spring of 1981, we developed an expanded questionnaire for the new Charging and Sentencing Study (CSS), and we collected data over the summer and early fall of 1981. At the same time, we also began an analysis of the PRS data. By the spring of 1982 we had produced a set of preliminary findings from the PRS. In the summer and fall of 1982, the LDF cited these findings in several Georgia cases to support its request for a post-conviction hearing on the issue of arbitrariness and discrimination in the application of Georgia's post-*Furman* death-sentencing system. Only one of these requests was granted. On October 8, 1982, J. Owen Forrester, a federal district judge in Atlanta, ordered an evidentiary hearing on the issue. The petitioner in that case was Warren McCleskey.

## McCleskey's Claims

McCleskey, a black man, had been convicted on October 12, 1978, in the Superior Court of Fulton County, Georgia, of the murder of police officer Frank Schlatt, who was white. The circumstances of McCleskey's crime, arrest, and trial were described by the United States Supreme Court as follows:

> The evidence at trial indicated that McCleskey and three accomplices planned and carried out the robbery. All four were armed. McCleskey entered the front of the store while the other three entered the rear. McCleskey secured the front of the store by rounding up the customers and forcing them to lie face down on the floor. The other three rounded up the employees in the rear and tied them up with tape. The manager was forced at gunpoint to turn over the store receipts, his watch, and $6.00. During the course of the robbery, a police officer, answering a silent alarm, entered the store through the front door. As he was walking down the center aisle of the store, two shots were fired. Both struck the officer. One hit him in the face and killed him.
>
> Several weeks later, McCleskey was arrested in connection with an unrelated offense. He confessed that he had participated in the furniture store robbery, but denied that he had shot the police officer. At trial, the State introduced evidence that at least one of the bullets that struck the officer was fired from a .38 caliber Rossi revolver. This description matched the description of the gun that McCleskey had carried during the robbery. The State also introduced the testimony of two witnesses who had heard McCleskey admit to the shooting.[12]

McCleskey's postconviction petition asserted a number of constitutional claims. Most relevant to the subject of this book was his assertion that his death sentence was unconstitutional because it had been imposed discriminatorily on the basis of his race and the race of his victim. In support of his request for a hearing on this issue, McCleskey's petition argued that the evidence he planned to present would support a finding that Georgia had applied its death-sentencing statute in a manner that violated the Fourteenth Amendment's equal-protection clause because it purposefully discriminated against defendants who were black and defendants whose victims were white. He also argued that such a discriminatory application of the death penalty constituted an arbitrary, capricious, and irrational application of the death sentence and violated the Eight Amendment of the United States Constitution.

# THE *McCLESKEY V. KEMP* RECORD

The hearing that Judge Forrester ordered in *McCleskey* took place over two weeks in August 1983. It began with several days of testimony describing the background of our empirical studies and the data-collection process we employed. Next, we presented our empirical findings and our interpretation of their meaning and validity.[13] The State then presented two expert witnesses who challenged the validity both of our data base and of our statistical procedures, and who explained how, in their opinion, these imperfections might have affected the validity of our empirical findings.[14] The State's experts also argued that the more aggravated nature of the white-victim cases explained the racial disparities in our findings; these experts did not, however, offer their own multivariate analyses of our data or of any other data that estimated a race-of-defendant or race-of-victim effect. The State's experts also pointed out that, even in the life-sentence cases included in our study, white-victim cases were generally more aggravated than black-victim cases. This, they argued, undercut McCleskey's claim of race-of-victim discrimination because if, as McCleskey asserted, such discrimination did occur, those white-victim cases that resulted in life sentences should be less aggravated than the pool of life-sentence cases involving black victims. In rebuttal to the State's arguments, McCleskey's lawyers offered additional testimony, including that of Richard Berk, a sociologist and expert on criminal justice.[15]

## Findings from the Procedural Reform Study (PRS)

The findings of the Procedural Reform Study constitute only a small part of the statistical evidence presented in the *McCleskey* hearing. . . . We will describe those findings that were presented in the *McCleskey* hearing only briefly.[16]

The first set of PRS findings addressed in the hearing were a series of multiple-regression analyses that estimated race-of-victim disparities in the rates at which defendants convicted of murder at trial were sentenced to death. We estimated the race-of-victim coefficients in these analyses after simultaneously adjusting variously for 5 to 150-plus nonracial aggravating and mitigating factors. . . . We selected these factors on either *a priori* grounds or on the basis of both *a priori* considerations and the statistical significance of their relationship to the sentencing outcome. These analyses showed average race-of-victim disparities among defendants convicted of murder at trial ranging between 8 and 9 percentage points, all of which were statistically significant beyond the .05 level. We also presented the results of small-scale logistic-regression analyses that controlled for from 5 to 10 legitimate background factors such as the defendant's prior record or the number of victims. These results produced odds multipliers of 2.8 and 3.0, significant at the .01 level.[17] These results were quite comparable to the race-of-victim findings reported . . . , which were produced after the *McCleskey* hearing.

The second set of PRS findings presented were race-of-victim disparities in prosecutorial and jury decision making, estimated with partial-regression coefficients. The largest prosecutorial linear model, which included simultaneous controls for more than 150 legitimate background variables, showed a statistically significant race-of-victim effect of 13 percentage points, while a smaller model, which limited background factors to 21 variables showing a statistically significant nonperverse relationship to the prosecutorial decision to seek a death sentence, produced a race-of-victim odds multiplier of 3.4, significant at the .0001 level.[18] The linear jury analyses, which controlled for all statutory aggravating factors and forty-three mitigating factors, showed race-of-victim disparities ranging from 16 ($p = .05$) to 23 ($p = .04$) percentage points.[19]

The results of the logistic-regression analyses of the prosecutorial and jury decisions that we presented showed mixed results. The prosecutorial results consisted of race-of-victim disparities estimated in four separate procedures that controlled for from five to twenty-one background variables; the estimated death-odds multipliers for the race-of-victim variables were from 2.8 to 3.4, all significant beyond the .01 level.[20] In contrast, comparable jury analyses produced only small death-odds multipliers (from 1.2 to 1.4), none of which was statistically significant beyond the .10 level.[21]

The PRS regression results on jury decision making presented in the *McCleskey* hearing provided weaker evidence of race-of-victim discrimination than the results presented . . . , which were produced after the hearing. Although the race-of-victim disparities in both sets of findings have a sign consistent with the discrimination hypothesis, the magnitude and level of statistical significance of the disparities in the *McCleskey* PRS evidence is considerably lower. We note, however, that the jury race-of-victim findings reported . . . were also mixed in terms of the observed level of statistical significance. On balance, we place the most confidence in the . . . jury results estimated in cross-tabular analyses, which show a race-of-victim effect of approximately 14 percentage points (statistically significant at approximately the .10 level).[22]

## Findings Presented from the Charging and Sentencing Study (CSS)

As noted above, our findings from the Procedural Reform Study constituted only a small part of the evidence that we presented in the *McCleskey* hearing. Our second investigation, the Charging and Sentencing Study, is the principal source of evidence in the *McCleskey* record.

### The Statewide Evidence from the Charging and Sentencing Study (CSS)

The findings from the Charging and Sentencing Study that we presented in the *McCleskey* case parallel to a striking degree the statewide results from the Procedural Reform Study reported earlier in this book. By and large, the results of the two studies differ only with respect to the race-of-defendant effects estimated within the white-victim cases.

The primary objective of the CSS discrimination analyses presented to the court was to estimate racial disparities in death-sentencing rates among defendants indicted for murder. Such disparities would reflect the combined effects of all decisions made from the point of indictment through the jury's sentencing decision.

To place in perspective the racial disparities estimated within this population of cases, we note that the death-sentencing rate for all defendants indicted for murder was 5 percent (128/2,484). This average rate is substantially lower than the 18 percent

Table F.1   UNADJUSTED RACE-OF-VICTIM AND RACE-OF-DEFENDANT DISPARITIES IN DEATH-SENTENCING RATES, AMONG ALL MURDER AND VOLUNTARY MANSLAUGHTER CASES (POST-*FURMAN* GEORGIA)[1]

|  | Rates and Disparities |
|---|---|
| I.   Race-of-victim disparity | |
| White-victim cases (WV) | .11 (108/981) |
| Black-victim cases (BV) | .0133 (20/1,503) |
| Difference (WV – BV) | .10 pts. |
| Ratio (WV/BV) | 8.3 |
| II.   Race-of-defendant disparity | |
| Black-defendant cases (BD) | .04 (68/1,676) |
| White-defendant cases (WD) | .07 (60/808) |
| Difference (BD-WD) | –3 pts. |
| Ratio (BD/WD) | .57 |
| III.   Defendant/victim racial composition | |
| 1. Black defendant/white victim (B/W) | .21 (50/233) |
| 2. White defendant/white victim (W/W) | .08 (58/748) |
| 3. Black defendant/black victim (B/B) | .01 (18/1443) |
| 4. White defendant/black victim (W/B) | .03 (2/60) |
| All cases | .05 (128/2484) |

[1]The disparities are estimated for the universe of all cases that resulted in a murder or voluntary manslaughter conviction. When the analysis is limited to death-eligible cases, the race-of-victim disparity is 12 percentage points (.14 for white-victim cases versus .02 for black-victim cases), while the race-of-defendant disparity is –3 points (.07 for black defendants versus .10 for white defendants). The rates by defendant/victim racial combination in the death-eligible cases are B/W .23, W/W .11, B/B .02, and W/B .04. . . .

death-sentencing rate reported in the Procedural Reform Study for defendants convicted of murder at trial. The reason, of course, is that it is based on the very much larger pool of defendants indicted for murder, most of whom never reach trial because they plead guilty to murder or to a lesser offense.[23]

Table F.1 presents the unadjusted race-of-victim and race-of-defendant effects in the CSS for all defendants indicted for murder. Part I shows a 10-percentage-point difference in the rates at which white- and black-victim cases result in death sentences. And when characterized with a ratio measure, the death-sentencing rate for the white-victim cases is 8.3 times (.11/.0133) higher than the rate for the black-victim cases.[24]

Although the unadjusted −3 point race-of-defendant disparity in part II of Table F.1 suggests that, overall, black defendants enjoy a slight advantage in the system, the breakdown of rates by the defendant-victim racial combinations shown in part III of the table suggests that, within the white-victim cases, black defendants may be treated more punitively than white defendants—that is, the death-sentencing rate is .21 (50/233) for the black defendants with white victims, versus .08 (58/748) for the white defendants with white victims.

Starting with these unadjusted racial disparities, we developed a series of multivariate analyses to estimate statewide race-of-defendant and race-of-victim effects after adjustment for a variety of legitimate nonracial background factors.

**Statewide Adjusted Race-of-Victim Disparities: Overall Effects**   We commenced the analysis using cross-tabular techniques that controlled for variables our

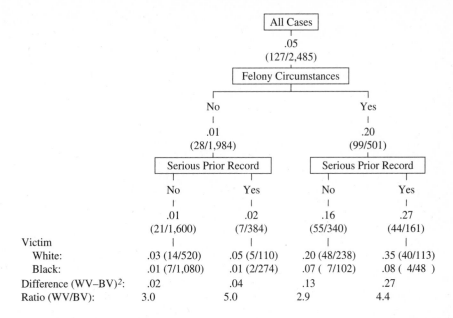

**Figure F.1** Race-of-Victim Disparities in Overall Death-Sentencing Rates, Controlling Simultaneously for Felony Circumstances and Prior Record (Charging and Sentencing Study)[1]

[1]Entries in this table are estimated death-sentencing rates for the indicated case categories. The rates are computed as numbers of death sentences divided by estimated numbers of cases in each category. The estimated numbers of cases are weighted counts of sampled cases. The totals of 2,485 and 127 (rather than 2,484 and 128) reflect roundoff error.

[2]The average difference is .055, which is significant at the .0001 level (Mantel-Haenszel Z = 5.39).

prior research indicated were important in terms of explaining which Georgia homicide defendants received a death sentence. Figure F.1 presents the results of one such analysis offered in the *McCleskey* hearing.[25] It estimates, among defendants indicted for murder, race-of-victim effects after adjustment for the contemporaneous "felony circumstances" and "serious prior record" variables. The "All cases" row of figures indicates the death-sentencing rates among the four subgroups of cases produced with these two control variables. It shows sharply rising death-sentencing rates as the cases become more aggravated.

The next-to-bottom row of figures in Figure F.1 measures the race-of-victim disparities within each of the four subgroups of cases. It shows a distinct association between the aggravation level of cases and the magnitude of the race-of-victim effects. Among the less aggravated cases, in which the death-sentencing rates are quite low, the race-of-victim effects are also quite modest. But among the more aggravated cases, which show .16 and .27 death-sentencing rates, the race-of-victim disparities are 13 and 25 percentage points, respectively.

While cross-tabular analyses have the virtue of simplicity and clarity, they are dependent on large sample sizes to develop stable estimates. Even with a universe of over 2,400 cases, Figure F.1 makes plain that the death-sentencing activity in the system is substantially confined to the 501 cases involving a contemporaneous felony. With this many cases, the limits of a fine-grained cross-tabular analysis are quickly reached. Thus, we relied primarily on multiple-regression analyses to produce the principal multivariate support for McCleskey's claims.

## NOTES

1. 446 U.S. 420 (1980).
2. *Id.* at 427.
3. *Id.* at 433.
4. Zant v. Stephens, 462 U.S. 862 (1983), provided further evidence that the Supreme Court's commitment to evenhanded death sentencing might be slipping. First, the Court reconceptualized the role of statutory aggravating circumstances under the Georgia statute in a manner that increased the risk of inconsistent death sentencing. The question in *Zant* was whether a defendant could be condemned to die based on a jury finding of three statutory aggravating circumstances, one of which was later found to have been constitutionally invalid. The defendant argued that the statutorily designated aggravating circumstances in the Georgia statute were intended not only to determine if the defendant was death-eligible, but also to guide the jury when it decided the actual sentence. In support of this argument the defendant cited various passages from *Gregg* that praised Georgia's statutory aggravating circumstances for guiding and channeling the jury's sentencing discretion in capital cases, thereby minimizing the risk of arbitrary or inconsistent sentences. *See, e.g.,* Gregg v. Georgia, 428 U.S. 153, 192, 197–98 (1976). The defendant also noted that the trial judge's instructions in his particular case had suggested that the jury should consider the relevant statutory aggravating circumstances when deciding the defendant's fate. Zant v. Stephens, 462 U.S. at 865–66. The trial judge's instructions are quoted in full in Zant v. Stephens, 456 U.S. 410, 411n.1 (1982).

   In contrast to the defendant's *Gregg*-based concept of the function of the statutory aggravating circumstances, the Georgia Supreme Court offered a substantially different construction. Responding to a certificate of inquiry from the United States Supreme Court, the Georgia court described its system for classifying capital defendants as a three-stage process with the following criteria governing each stage:

   Stage One: Includes all defendants convicted of murder, that is, an unlawful killing with malice aforethought.

   Stage Two: Includes those defendants convicted of murder who are death-eligible in that, beyond a reasonable doubt, a statutorily designated aggravating circumstance is present in their case.

   Stage Three: Includes those death-eligible defendants who, based on all aggravating and mitigating factors in the case, actually receive a death sentence. See Zant v. Stephens, 462U.S. at 870–72 (citing Zant v. Stephens, 250 Ga. 97, 99–100; 297 S.E. 2d 1, 3–4 (1982)).

   The significant difference between the defendant's *Gregg*-based model of the Georgia statute and that proposed in *Stephens* by the Georgia Supreme Court lies in the criteria determining inclusion in the third category. The defendant's *Gregg*-based model presumed that statutory aggravating criteria would play an influential role in guiding the jury's deliberations concerning what sentence to impose. Thus, the trial judge's instructions, which gave emphasis to a constitutionally defective criterion, might well have distorted the jury's decision.

On the other hand, the model suggested in *Stephens* by the Georgia Supreme Court downplayed the importance of the statutory aggravating circumstances with respect to the third-stage determination. According to the Georgia court, the statutory aggravating circumstances only served to determine whether the defendant was death-eligible. Once the jury made that determination, the statutory aggravating circumstances were of no further importance. When selecting those death-eligible defendants who would actually receive death sentences, according to the Georgia Supreme Court, the jury was entitled to consider any factors or circumstances that it deemed important; the legislative criteria were of no significance at this stage. Zant v. Stephens, 462 U.S. at 871–72 (quoting 250 Ga. at 99–100, 297 S.E.2d at 3). The Georgia court's description of the process appears to be an accurate portrayal of Georgia jury-charging practices before and after *Zant.*

In *Stephens,* the United States Supreme Court adopted the Georgia Supreme Court's construction of the statute as authoritative and ruled it was constitutional for two reasons. First, a majority of the justices rejected the defendant's argument that *Gregg* had attributed to the Georgia statutory aggravating circumstances the function of guiding the jury's sentencing discretion. *Id.* at 875. Second, the Court also rejected the contention that such guidance was constitutionally required. No such restriction on the jury's sentencing discretion was necessary, concluded the *Stephens* majority, because the Georgia statute requires a bifurcated sentencing procedure and "mandates meaningful appellate review of every death sentence," which would prevent the imposition of arbitrary or inconsistent death sentences. *Id.* at 875.

The second indication in *Stephens* of a possible retreat from the Court's earlier commitment to evenhanded death sentencing was Justice Stevens's suggestion that the two valid aggravating circumstances in the case "adequately differentiate this case in an objective, evenhanded and substantively rational way from the many Georgia murder cases in which the death penalty *may not be imposed*" (emphasis added). *Id.* at 879. The key shift was from the Court's earlier empirical test of whether a death-sentenced defendant's case could be distinguished from the many cases in which lesser sentences *are not imposed* to a nonempirical test of whether the death-sentenced defendant's case could be distinguished from cases in which death sentences are not authorized by law, regardless of the frequency with which death sentences are actually imposed in similar cases. In effect, the new test of excessiveness merely asks whether the death sentence imposed is authorized under the state law.

5. To be sure, the death-sentencing system approved in Jurek v. Texas, 428 U.S. 262 (1976) provided no provision for comparative-proportionality review. Yet in its decision approving the Texas system in *Jurek,* the United States Supreme Court characterized its system of appellate review as one capable of ensuring evenhanded death sentencing. *Id.* at 276. The expectation as to the importance of comparative-proportionality review was particularly strong with respect to jurisdictions that included a system of proportionality review as part of their post-*Furman* death-sentencing system.

6. 446 U.S. 420, 429 (1980).

7. 465 U.S. 37 (1984). Justice White's majority opinion did acknowledge that prior opinions (most recently in Zant v. Stephens) had emphasized the importance of proportionality review, but denied that such a review process was constitutionally required. *Id.* at 45–46. In *Gregg,* he explained, the Court had regarded comparative-sentence review as no more than "an additional safeguard against arbitrary or capricious sentencing." *Id.* at 45. Furthermore, in *Stephens,* it was "the jury's finding of aggravating circumstances, not the State Supreme Court's finding of proportionality" that made the death sentence rational. *Id.* at 50. In other words, suggested Justice White, so long as the jury had found at least one valid statutory aggravating circumstance to exist, that finding would adequately differentiate the defendant's death sentence from other life sentence cases "in an objective, evenhanded, and substantively

rational way," thereby satisfying the relevant constitutional requirements. *Id.* at 50n.12 (quoting Zant v. Stephens, 462 U.S. at 879).

There are at least two possible explanations for the Court's apparently revisionistic treatment of comparative-sentence review in *Harris.* One possibility is that, implicitly, the Court was endorsing the model of the Georgia death-sentencing system, which assumed that prosecutors and juries would regularly seek and impose the death penalty in death-eligible cases, thereby making comparative-sentence review constitutionally unnecessary. Justice White's majority opinion makes no reference to this presumption, but it does provide a logical explanation for the result.

The second possibility is that the Court had altered its earlier views of the constitutional importance of consistency in death sentencing. One can read *Harris* to suggest that sentencing juries may pick and choose among death-eligible defendants, exercising the sort of "untrammeled discretion" that *McGautha* endorsed and that *Furman* condemned, so long as at least one statutorily designated aggravating circumstance exists in the case of each defendant condemned to death. *Compare* McGautha v. California, 402 U.S. 183, 207–8 (1971), with Furman v. Georgia, 408 U.S. 238, 248 (1972) (Douglas, J., concurring). *See also* Zant v. Stephens, 462 U.S. at 906–12 (Marshall, J., dissenting). Although such a primitive model of a constitutionally satisfactory capital-sentencing procedure seems to run counter to the Court's opinions in *Gregg* and *Stephens,* it is, however, technically consistent with *Godfrey* and, of course, Pulley v. Harris itself. More to the point, such a minimally restrictive statutory procedure can avoid inconsistent, capricious sentencing results—which *Furman* specifically rejected—only if juries exercise their discretion when sentencing death-eligible defendants in a regular, consistent manner. In other words, whether or not the *Harris* majority intended to invoke the factual presumption that prosecutors and juries would regularly seek and impose death sentences in death-eligible cases, the accuracy of such a presumption was essential to the *Harris* ruling, if *Furman* was still good law. *Harris* also foreclosed constitutional claims that state courts that did conduct statutorily mandated proportionality reviews applied ineffective review procedures.

8.  426 U.S. 229 (1976).
9.  462 U.S. at 885.
10. More recently, in Turner v. Murray, a majority of the justices appeared to recognize the risk of discrimination in capital sentencing when they agreed that a defendant's Sixth Amendment right to an impartial jury in a capital case involving an interracial murder authorized him to voir dire prospective jury members concerning possible racial prejudice on their part. 476 U.S. 28 (1986). However, only a minority of the justices believed that the denial of this Sixth Amendment right to voir dire the jury invalidated the underlying conviction. Consequently, the Court vacated the death sentence, but declined to order a new trial. Justice White's opinion explained that the capital-sentencing proceeding merited this special protection because of the broad discretion jurors exercise under state law and the concomitant opportunity to discriminate on racial grounds. Although technically a Sixth Amendment case, therefore, *Turner* really applies only in the capital-sentencing context.
11. Smith v. Balkcom, 671 F.2d 858, 859–60 & n. 33 (5th Cir. Unit B 1982) (citations omitted).
12. McCleskey v. Kemp, 107 S. Ct. 1756, 1762 (1987). The trial judge had also imposed two consecutive life sentences on McCleskey for his role in the armed robbery. McCleskey v. Zant, 580 F.Supp. 338, 344 (N.D.Ga. 1984).
13. McCleskey was represented by John C. Boger, NAACP Legal Defense and Educational Fund, Inc.; Tim Ford, Seattle; and Robert Stroup, Atlanta. Professor Baldus described the background of the study. Edward Gates then explained the data-collection efforts in which he participated in both the Procedural Reform and Charging and Sentencing Studies. Next Professor Baldus presented the substantive findings. Professor Woodworth then gave his opinion

about the validity of the statistical procedures used, described the diagnostic and "worst-case" analyses he conducted, and presented his interpretation of our principal findings.

14. The state's experts were Dr. Joseph Katz, Assistant Professor, Department of Quantitative Methods, Georgia State University, and Dr. Roger Burford, Professor of Quantitative Business Analysis, Louisiana State University.

15. Richard Berk was then Professor of Sociology at the University of California at Santa Barbara and a member of the National Research Council sentencing panel. *Research on Sentencing: The Search for Reform* (A. Blumstein, J. Cohen, S. Martin, & M. Tonry eds. 1983).

16. On the issue of race-of-defendant discrimination, in both the jury and prosecutorial statewide multiple-regression analyses from the PRS presented in the *McCleskey* hearing (whether conducted with linear or logistic-regression procedures), the coefficients estimated for the "black defendant" variable were generally negative, suggesting that black defendants had a lower chance of both advancing to a penalty trial and receiving a death sentence, although none of the estimates was statistically significant beyond the .10 level. . . .

17. The results were presented in DB 98, on which note table 2 is based. The exhibits presented in the *McCleskey* hearing were largely developed during the period March–June 1983. During that time and up until the hearing in August 1983 and beyond, we corrected any errors in the PRS and CSS data sets that we discovered in our cleaning of the data or that were brought to our attention by the State's experts in *McCleskey*. As a result, it is not possible to replicate exactly some of the exhibits that we submitted in *McCleskey* with the data in the archives at the University of Michigan. . . .

All references in the text to the record (R.) refer to the transcript of the evidentiary hearing held in the United States District Court for the Northern District of Georgia, August

**Table F.2   RACE-OF-VICTIM DISPARITIES IN DEATH SENTENCING: AMONG DEFENDANTS CONVICTED OF MURDER AT TRIAL, ESTIMATED WITH ORDINARY LEAST-SQUARES AND LOGISTIC-REGRESSION COEFFICIENTS, CONTROLLING FOR ALTERNATIVE SETS OF NONRACIAL BACKGROUND FACTORS AND THE RACE OF DEFENDANT (PROCEDURAL REFORM STUDY)**

| Nonracial Background Variables Controlled For | Ordinary-Least-Squares Regression Coefficient (with Level of Statistical Significance) | Death-Odds Multiplier | Logistic-Regression Coefficient (with Level of Statistical Significance) |
|---|---|---|---|
| 1. Five legitimate factors | .09 (.03) | 2.8 | 1.03 (.002) |
| 2. Nine legitimate factors | .09 (.02) | 2.8 | 1.02 (.005) |
| 3. All statutory aggravating factors | .09 (.01) | 3.0 | 1.1 (.01) |
| 4. All statutory aggravating factors and 43 mitigating factors | .09 (.02) | 4.6 | 1.53 (.01)[a] |
| 5. 150 + nonracial aggravating and mitigating factors and 4 suspect factors | .09 (.01) | — | —[b] |
| 6. 32 statistically significant variables from the file showing a statistically significant relationship ($p \leq .10$) with the death-sentencing result | .08 (.02) | 5.1 | 1.63 (.004)[a] |

[a]These logistic results were not presented in *McCleskey*.

[b]The analysis involves too many variables for simultaneous adjustment in a logistic analysis.

Table F.3 REGRESSION COEFFICIENTS (WITH THE LEVEL OF STATISTICAL SIGNIFICANCE) FOR RACIAL VARIABLES IN ANALYSES OF PROSECUTORIAL DECISIONS TO SEEK AND JURY DECISIONS TO IMPOSE CAPITAL PUNISHMENT, CHARGING AND SENTENCING STUDY (CSS) AND PROCEDURAL REFORM STUDY (PRS)

| A | B | C | | D | E |
|---|---|---|---|---|---|
| | | Controlling for | | | |
| | | Full File of Statutory Aggravating Factors and Mitigating Factors | | All Factors in File | |
| | All Statutory Aggravating Factors | All Factors Simultaneously | Factors with Statistical Significance at the .10 Level | Regardless of Statistical Significance | If Statistically Significant at the .10 Level |
| I. Prosecutor decision to seek a death sentence | | | | | |
| A. Race of victim | | | | | |
| 1. CCS | .24 (.001) | .28 (.0001) | .28 (.0001) | .24 (.01) | .15 (.001) |
| 2. PRS | .14 (.01) | .15 (.001) | .15 (.001) | .13 (.005) | .14 (.001) |
| B. Race of defendant | | | | | |
| 1. CSS | .14 (.01) | .18 (.01) | .17 (.001) | .17 (.03) | .12 (.01) |
| 2. PRS | .04 (.41) | .005 (.91) | −.001 (.98) | .00 (.99) | .01 (.73) |
| II. Jury sentencing decision | | | | | |
| A. Race of victim | | | | | |
| 1. CSS | .11 (.19) | .26 (.01) | .13 (.08) | —[a] | .02 (.75) |
| 2. PRS | .08 (.40) | .23 (.04) | .16 (.05) | — | .23 (.001) |
| B. Race of defendant | | | | | |
| 1. CSS | −.02 (.76) | −.02 (.82) | .05 (.46) | — | −.00 (.91) |
| 2. PRS | −.08 (.30) | −.06 (.46) | −.05 (.47) | — | −.03 (.61) |

[a]Valid simultaneous adjustment for all factors in the files was not possible because of the limited number of penalty-trial decisions.

8–22, 1983. "DB" and "GW" references indicate exhibits that were submitted by, respectively, Professors Baldus and Woodworth. Table F.3 and Table F.4.

18. These results were presented through DB 95 & 96, on which Tables F.3 and F.4 are based.

19. The PRS jury results reported in column E of Table F.3 were based on 19 variables screened with a linear stepwise procedure from the variables listed in app. L, sched. 15, minus the interaction terms. The procedure estimated a race-of-defendant coefficient of −.03 ($p = .61$).

20. These results were presented through DB 96, on which Table F.4 is based. The background variables referred to in note 6 of Table F.4 were nonperverse variables screened from the variables in app. L, sched. 15, minus the interaction terms with linear procedures. The logistic race-of-victim regression coefficient estimated in a model with 18 nonperverse legitimate background variables screened with logistic procedures was $b = 1.2$ ($p = .001$).

Because the outcome variable in all of these analyses is binary (yes/no), we have greater confidence in estimates produced with logistic procedures than in estimates produced with linear procedures.

21. These results were presented through $DB_{97}$, on which Table F.5 (p. 232) is based.

22. The regression analyses . . . which suggest stronger race-of-victim effects, are based on more variables (many interaction terms) than those presented in the McCleskey case.

Table F.4   RACE-OF-VICTIM AND RACE-OF-DEFENDANT DISPARITIES IN PROSECUTORIAL DECISION MAKING ESTIMATED WITH LOGISTIC-REGRESSION PROCEDURES, CONTROLLING FOR ALTERNATIVE SETS OF NONRACIAL BACKGROUND VARIABLES

| | | Race of Victim | | Race of Defendant |
| --- | --- | --- | --- | --- |
| A. Background Variables Controlled For | B. Death-Odds Multiplier | C. Regression Coefficient (w/level of statistical significance) | D. Death-Odds Multiplier | E. Regression Coefficient (w/level of statistical significance) |
| I. Changing and Sentencing Study | | | | |
| A. Five legitimate factors[1] | 4.8 | 1.56 (.0001) | 2.0 | .68 (.005) |
| B. Nine legitimate factors[2] | 5.1 | 1.63 (.0001) | 2.3 | .82 (.02) |
| C. Ten statistically significant ($p \leq .10$) nonarbitrary factors | 3.3 | 1.21 (.02) | 2.4 | .86 (.10) |
| II. Procedural Reform Study | | | | |
| A. Five legitimate factors | 2.8 | 1.03 (.002) | .73 | −.32 (.23) |
| B. Nine legitimate factors | 2.8 | 1.02 (.005) | .81 | −.21 (.47) |
| C. All statutory aggravating variables | 3.2 | 1.15 (.0001) | 1.1 | .11 (.68) |
| D. 21 statistically significant nonarbitrary factors | 3.4 | 1.22 (.0001) | 1.1 | .12 (.71) |

[1]The five variables are (a) felony circumstances, (b) serious prior record, (c) family, lover, liquor, or barroom quarrel, (d) multiple victims, and (e) stranger-victim.

[2]The nine variables are those listed in note 1 plus (a) defendant not the triggerman, (b) physical torture, (c) mental torture, and (d) rape or helpless victim or motive to silence a witness.

23. When the death-sentencing rates in the two studies are based on murder-trial convictions, the figures are virtually identical, .17 (128/762) for the Charging and Sentencing Study versus .18 (112/606) for the Procedural Reform Study.

24. The ratio measure used here is one of several commonly used "multiplier" methods for comparing two numbers. Other such measures would be the ratio of the death-sentencing rates in black- and white-victim cases, .12 (.0133/.11), and the ratio of the arithmetic difference between the two rates, .91 (.10/.11).

25. The overall race-of-victim effect in Figure F.1, calculated since the *McCleskey* hearing, is 6 percentage points, significant at the .0002 level (Mantel-Haenszel Z = 6.1).

Table F.5 RACE-OF-VICTIM AND RACE-OF-DEFENDANT DISPARITIES IN JURY DECISION MAKING ESTIMATED WITH LOGISTIC-REGRESSION PROCEDURES, CONTROLLING FOR ALTERNATIVE SETS OF NONRACIAL BACKGROUND VARIABLES

| A. Background Variables Controlled For | Race of Victim | | Race of Defendant | |
|---|---|---|---|---|
| | B. Death-Odds Multiplier | C. Regression Coefficient (w/level of statistical significance) | D. Death-Odds Multiplier | E. Regression Coefficient (w/level of statistical significance) |
| I. Changing and Sentencing Study | | | | |
| A. Five legitimate factors[1] | 1.2 | .18 (.63) | .76 | −.28 (.34) |
| B. Nine legitimate factors[2] | 1.4 | 1.63 (.0001) | 2.3 | .82 (.02) |
| C. Thirteen statistically significant nonarbitrary factors | 3.4 | 1.23 (.02) | 1.3 | .28 (.50) |
| II. Procedural Reform Study | | | | |
| A. Five legitimate variables | 1.3 | .24 (.57) | .67 | −.41 (.21) |
| B. Nine legitimate variables | 1.4 | .32 (.46) | .73 | −.31 (.37) |
| C. All statutory aggravating factors | 1.4 | .36 (.43) | .67 | −.41 (.27) |
| D. Eleven statistically significant nonarbitrary factors | 1.36 | .31 (.57) | .57 | −.57 (.21) |

[1]The five variables are (a) felony circumstances, (b) serious prior record, (c) family, lover, liquor, or barroom quarrel, (d) multiple victims, and (e) stranger-victim.

[2]The nine variables are those listed in note 1 plus (a) defendant not the triggerman, (b) physical torture, (c) mental torture, and (d) rape or helpless victim or motive to silence a witness.

# Appendix
# G

---

## State Population and the Electoral Success of U.S. Senators

JOHN R. HIBBING
*University of Nebraska–Lincoln*

SARA L. BRANDES
*University of Iowa*

In this study, we tested the hypothesis that the number of people in a constituency is inversely related to the success of incumbent legislators. To conduct this test, we focused on the U.S. Senate, an ideal laboratory for an analysis of the effects of constituency size. The results indicate that senators from heavily populated states do indeed enjoy less of an incumbency advantage than senators from lightly populated states. We close by discussing why constituency size matters and by noting the contribution this finding makes to understanding the widely cited disparity between the electoral success of incumbent senators and representatives.

Of the countless differences between the House and the Senate there is one that has only recently begun to draw scholarly attention: the quite distinctive levels of electoral success achieved by incumbents in the two bodies.[1] Despite the relatively good performance of incumbent senators in 1982, post–World War II senators on the whole have not been nearly as successful at the polls as incumbent representatives during the same time period. To be specific, from 1946 to 1980 incumbent senators seeking reelection received on average only 57.4 percent of the two-party vote. Members of the House, on the other hand, averaged 62.8 percent in their reelection attempts.[2] This contrast in levels of success is evident even if other measures of electoral performance, such as the

---

1. See Richard Fenno (1982) for a good recent treatment of the numerous differences between the House and the Senate.

2. A difference of 5.4 points may not seem like much, but in the world of congressional elections it is quite a lot. Consider that the change in the level of competition for House elections that occurred in the mid-1960s and that has evoked so much interest among political scientists—the so-called vanishing marginals (see Mayhew, 1974)—amounts to a change of only about 5 points, on average.

percentage victorious or the percentage in some arbitrarily defined "marginal" range, are employed. Finally, we should note that the gap between the electoral success of incumbents in the House and the Senate seems to be expanding rather than contracting (see Alford and Hibbing, 1983).

Thus it seems quite clear that for at least the last 35 years incumbent senators have been much more electorally vulnerable than incumbent representatives. This being established, the key question becomes why representatives are safer than senators. The primary purpose of our research was to answer that question.

Several explanations for the puzzle of safe representatives and vulnerable senators have been offered. Some of these explanations point to the *institutional* differences between the Senate and the House. For example, one former member of Congress—Otis Pike—believes the nature of the Senate may make it more difficult for senators to distance themselves from controversial national issues. He argues that senators "are not known as people, but by the policies they set forth," while representatives, probably because of the larger membership of the House, may be better equipped to downplay any role they may have had in national policy decisions (Pike, 1980). If this is the case, it is likely that fewer constituents will be alienated by the benign service activities of the representative than by the tough policy votes cast by the senator. Representatives may also benefit from the very two-year term about which so many of them complain. It could be that constituents are less suspicious of someone who was (re)elected only 24 months earlier than of someone who has not faced the electorate for six years. The lengthy hiatus from voter judgment may make reelection more difficult for senators. Finally, there may be something about the Senate as an institution that attracts high-quality challengers, and, of course, the better the challenger the worse the electoral performance of the incumbent, ceteris paribus. This is in contrast to House races in which many challenges are not of a serious nature (see Jewell, 1981). The quality of challenger explanation has been given wide play in the wake of the 1978 Center for Political Studies (CPS) election survey. This survey indicated that although respondents were able to identify and rate Senate incumbents, they could not identify and rate House challengers nearly as well as they could House incumbents (Mann and Wolfinger, 1980; Abramowitz, 1980; Hinckley, 1980a, 1980b, and 1981).[3]

---

3. The finding that generated so much interest in the "quality-of-challenger" argument is not resting on solid ground. The 1978 CPS election survey does not include a representative sample of voters in Senate races The most thorough account of the resultant problems is in Westlye (1983). For now, suffice it to say that three states with extremely competitive Senate races in 1978 (Texas, Illinois, and Michigan) were overrepresented in the 1978 survey (see Mann and Wolfinger, 1980, p. 618). Consequently, the conclusion that Senate races typically involve surprisingly visible challengers may be owed in part to the quirks of the sample. A more important problem for the "quality-of-challenger" argument is that it is not really much of an explanation at all but instead a description of what happens when incumbents are vulnerable, as many in the Senate are. Challengers respond to the perceived odds of defeating the incumbent. This is so obvious as to be trivial, but it is borne out in research by Kazee (1982) and Jacobson and Kernell (1981). Thus the quality of challenge is caused by something else—it is a dependent variable that has frequently been used as an independent variable. Why are there better challenges in the Senate? Because there is a better chance of winning. Knowing this tells us little about the reason incumbents are so safe in the House and so vulnerable in the Senate. Quality of challenge is more a symptom than a cause of incumbency advantage. Recognition of this fact is occasionally made (see, for example, Hinckley, 1980a, p. 648, and 1980b, p. 460), but at some point recognition alone becomes insufficient.

Although there is clearly some merit to these institutional explanations, we believe the most important reason senators are vulnerable and representatives are safe has more to do with the nature of senatorial constituencies than the nature of the Senate as an institution. Senatorial constituencies (i.e., states) generally have much larger populations than the constituencies served by members of the House. In other words, senators usually must attempt to please many more people than representatives, and their quite understandable difficulties in doing so may be the reason for their relatively poor showing at the polls. It is on this variable based on constituency size that we concentrated our efforts.

There are several reasons to expect constituency population to have an important effect on the electoral success of incumbent politicians. For example, it could be argued that representatives, because of their smaller constituencies, are able to meet personally virtually every politically significant person in the district, while senators usually have no similar opportunity. Senators' faces may be familiar, but it is probably because of television rather than personal appearances. Senators "are not expected to get to the local Lion's Club meeting but get to address the state convention. They are introduced as 'Senator,' not by their first names" (Pike, 1980). Relatedly, representatives are usually able to do more constituency service work than senators (see Uslaner, 1981), and it is commonly believed that this type of work is electorally rewarding. Another important reason constituency size is expected to matter is that large constituencies like states tend to be quite heterogeneous, but the population of an individual congressional district is more likely to be fairly homogenous. The relative heterogeneity of states makes it less likely one party will have a large advantage in number of identifiers and, therefore, makes it less likely that incumbents will enjoy a sizable electoral advantage over challengers. In other words, House seats may be more secure because districts, unlike most states, tend to identify with one party (Abramowitz, 1980, p. 633; Dodd, 1981, p. 407). Finally, size of constituency may act as a rough surrogate for the fit of a political unit with a media market. Lightly populated states may tend to have poorer fits with media markets (e.g., Nevada, Alaska, Connecticut) than heavily populated states, thus making it more difficult for challengers to mount a viable campaign (for some impressive evidence on the importance of media market congruence with political units, see Campbell, Alford, and Henry, 1982).

As can be seen, all of these explanations are based in one way or another upon the difference in constituency size between the House and the Senate. Unlike most representatives, senators must represent entire states, making it all but impossible for them (1) to get to be known by most constituents on a personal basis, (2) to perform meticulous constituent service work in all corners of the state, and (3) to see and act on the basis of an overall consensus in the state on most issues and on party preference (because the diversity of interests across the state means there probably is not overall consensus). Thus, implicit in these explanations is the notion that the underlying reason for the different levels of incumbency advantage in the two houses of Congress is the difference in the number of constituents per member. Consequently, we feel there is a more than sufficient theoretical basis for expecting to find an inverse relationship between constituency size and the mean electoral performance of incumbent legislators.

# STUDY DESIGN

There was a readily available way to test our hypothesis that large constituencies mean difficult times for incumbent officeholders. This test is obvious once one makes the simple observation that the difference in constituency size between the Senate and House is a variable and not a constant—that is, in some states substantial difference exists between the constituencies of senators and representatives; yet in others, there is none. In Alaska, Delaware, Nevada, North Dakota, Vermont, and Wyoming, the size of the senators' constituency matches perfectly with the size of the representative's constituency. These six states all have only one congressional district; therefore, district lines are contiguous with state lines, and senators and representatives share exactly the same constituency. On the other extreme we find some states in which there is a world of difference between House and Senate constituency size. While the 45 members of the California delegation in the U.S. House each serve constituencies of slightly more than 500,000 people (as do nearly all members of the House of Representatives), the two senators from California must attempt to satisfy well over 23 million residents of the state.

The diverse populations of Senate constituencies (it would take 59 Alaskas to equal the population of California) provided an ideal opportunity to test our hypothesis that the number of people in a constituency was negatively related to incumbent electoral success. If the size of the constituency affected the success of incumbent legislators in the ways we anticipated, senators from heavily populated states would do substantially worse on election day than senators from lightly populated states. The framers of the Constitution, when they disregarded population in apportioning the Senate, laid the groundwork for such a test, and by being able to look at the role of constituency size without moving to a different body the effects of many confounding factors were controlled.

The results of this test would put us in a better position to judge the true explanation for the Senate-House differences in the level of incumbent electoral performances. If we found the size of the constituency *did* make a difference, doubt would be cast on explanations relying solely on the institutional factors mentioned earlier, since there is no way these explanations would lead us to predict systematic variation in electoral success according to constituency size (the six-year term, for example, applies to all senators and not just to those from large states). If, on the other hand, we found constituency size was *not* related to the level of electoral success of incumbent senators, our preferred explanation—different average constituency populations in the Senate and House—would become considerably less promising.

Though there have been occasional glances at the constituency size hypothesis (see Westlye, 1983; and Hinckley, 1970, p. 839) it is somewhat odd that there has never been a thorough analysis of its veracity, especially in light of the degree to which some of the common explanations of senatorial vulnerability depend on the "size-of-constituency" argument. Our intent was to supply the needed look at the role of constituency size in causing the vulnerability of senators.

The measure of incumbent safety we chose was the mean share of the two-party vote of all Senate incumbents who ran for reelection in the particular state between

1946 and 1980.[4] This measure was preferred over those such as the percentage in some marginal range or the percentage victorious because it did not rely on a single cutoff point—that is, it did not dichotomize a naturally continuous variable. The key independent variable is the population of the state. To operationalize this concept, we used the number of congressional districts in each state. Since the apportioning of districts is based on state population, this measure provides an extremely accurate and easily interpretable estimation of the size of the Senate constituency.[5]

In order to specify the equation properly we included other variables we knew were related to the success rates of incumbent senators in various states. The most obvious control variable is the level of statewide party competition.[6] The fifty states have widely disparate political cultures (see Patterson, 1968), varying from highly competitive two-party states to states that are perenially dominated by one of the two major parties (see Ranney, 1965). The level of party competition is certainly likely to have a strong influence on the average level of success of incumbent senators. Senators serving highly competitive two-party states will usually do much worse on election day than incumbent senators from one-party dominant states.

Given the importance of this variable, we included a measure of statewide competition in our equation. The measure used was the folded statewide vote for all Democratic candidates in races for the U.S. House of Representatives. What this means is that we took the average share of the two-party vote garnered by all the state's Democratic candidates who ran for a House seat between 1946 and 1980. This figure was then folded at 50 percent so that a 75 percent mean Democratic vote was the same as a 25 percent Democratic vote. This folding procedure is appropriate because we were not concerned with whether the state leaned toward the Democratic or Republican party

---

4. The time period needed to be fairly lengthy because each state has only two senatorial elections every six years. By including 18 congressional election years in the data set, we were able to base our state averages on 12 elections to the U.S. Senate. On the other hand, by not extending the study back any further we avoided some of the complications arising from the years of depression and World War II.

5. In cases in which the number of districts in a state was altered by the reapportionment process we have averaged the number of districts across this time period.

6. Another potentially important control variable is tenure, since it is possible that electoral performance improves with tenure. (See Kostroski, 1978, for evidence that this is not the case in the Senate.) However, we have not included a measure of this variable for several reasons. First, tenure becomes less important in our study because the state is the unit of analysis. The operationalization would have to be the mean tenure level in a state, and the law of averages would tend to decrease variation from state to state. Nonetheless, some differences in mean tenure level from state to state do exist. Some southern states, for example, had only four or five senators during the 36-year period we have studied. The key problem is that mean tenure level, not surprisingly, is very closely related to the level of statewide competition. Since mean tenure level is not much more than a proxy for the level of competition in the state and since its inclusion would create severe multicollinearity problems, we have not included it as a separate variable.

but with how competitive the state has been in the postwar period.[7] With this operationalization we expected a positive relationship between the electoral success of incumbent senators and the level of party competition (high figures on our scale of competition equated with greater dominance by one party or the other and led us to predict
higher levels of electoral success for incumbent senators).

To determine the effect of constituency population on the level of senatorial incumbency advantage in the states, we regressed the mean share of the two-party vote on
the population of the state (as measured by the number of congressional districts in the
state) and also on the level of party competition in the state.

## THE FINDINGS

The results of our regression analysis are presented in Equation (G.1), which follows:

$$Y = 52.48 + .80^{\circ}(\text{comp.}) - .17^{\circ}(\text{size}) + e \qquad \text{(G.1)}$$

$$(11.42) \qquad (-2.01)$$

where $N = 48$; $R^2 = .76$; $F = 71.66$; $Y$ = average vote for all Senate incumbents between 1946 and 1980 (by state); comp. = folded statewide Democratic House vote between 1946 and 1980 (by state); size = mean number of congressional districts in a state
between 1946 and 1980; ( ) = $t$ ratio; "$^{\circ}$" indicates variables significant at .05, and
$e$ = error term.

The interpretation of the findings is made easier if one does not lose sight of the
fact that the state, not individual senators and not individual election years, is the unit of
analysis in the study. Though we obtained mean figures for each state by averaging our
variables across several different elections, these averages were then analyzed cross-
sectionally and not in a time-series fashion. In other words, the comparison is between
New York and North Dakota during the postwar years and not between the election of
1960 and the election of 1970.

The results of the regression squared quite nicely with our expectations.[8] The $R^2$
is a very respectable .76, indicating that we are accounting for about three-fourths of the
variance in the performance of incumbent senators with the two independent variables
in Equation (G.1). The two regression coefficients are in the directions we predicted. As
expected, the greater the level of competition in a state, the worse the electoral performance of incumbent senators in that state. The size of the coefficient for competition is

---

7. Several other operationalizations of the level of statewide competition were attempted, including the folded
mean vote for Democratic gubernatorial candidates in the state from 1946 to 1980 and a modification of the
Ranney index of statewide party competition. However, since some of the states had as few as eight gubernatorial races during the time period and since the Ranney index includes items that, for our purposes, are ex-
traneous, we have settled on the statewide vote in House races as the best and most stable indicator of party
competition in the states.

8. Alaska and Hawaii have not been included because for nearly half of the period under study they were not
states and, thus, did not have Senate elections.

quite large and easily meets the traditional tests of statistical significance.[9] But the strong and direct relationship between the level of competition in a state and the average margin of victory for incumbent senators in that state is hardly surprising. All this means is that competitive states usually have competitive Senate elections. It would have been startling if this were not the case.

The real relationship of interest is between the size of the state and the success of incumbent senators from that state. We expected this coefficient to be negative because highly populous states like New York and California should also be the states in which incumbent senators do not do particularly well in their bids for reelection. The results presented in Equation (G.1) indicate that such is the case. The coefficient for state population is in the expected direction and is significant at the .05 level.

The coefficient for the size variable means that for each increment of 500,000 people within a state (the rough equivalent of a congressional district's population), incumbent senators' average share of the two-party vote goes down about one-sixth of a percentage point. To illustrate what this can mean, we have only to compare the average incumbent senator from a state like Delaware with the average incumbent senator from New York. Other things being equal, and assuming that both states have the mean level of competition for the 48 states (i.e., comp. = 12), we expect an incumbent senator from Delaware who is seeking reelection to receive 61.91 percent of the two-party vote—52.48 + (.80 × 12) − (.17 × 1)—since Delaware has only one congressional district. Our comparable senator from equally competitive New York would do markedly worse given the parameters of Equation (G.1). The mean number of congressional districts apportioned to New York since World War II was 41.7, so the typical incumbent senator from the Empire state is predicted to garner only 54.97 percent of the vote in a reelection bid (52.48 + (.80 × 12) − (.17 × 41.7) = 54.97). Thus a range of nearly 7 percentage points in electoral performance is expected solely because of differences in the populations of the states. Obviously, our equation is predicting that the electoral life of a senator from a heavily populated state will be anything but relaxing. Such a senator starts out at a 6- or 7-percentage point disadvantage compared with a senator from the most lightly populated of states, other things being equal. Equation (G.1) offers strong support for our hypothesis that the population of a constituency is inversely related to the electoral success of incumbent officeholders.

## REFINEMENTS

As is always the case, there could be alternative explanations for the relationship we claim to have uncovered. Though we cannot address all the possibilities, we can consider a couple of the most plausible alternatives. One reason Equation (G.1) may be a misspecification of the relationship is multicollinearity. There is reason to believe the size of the state and the level of competition in the state (the two independent variables

---

9. Some believe significance tests in these circumstances are not needed because there is no probability sample being used. We have included the tests for those who like to have some indication of the stability of a coefficient even when probability samples are not employed.

in Equation (G.1)) may be related;[10] however, the data do not support this contention. Somewhat surprisingly, size of state and level of party competition are almost completely unrelated ($r = .02$). Thus multicollinearity is not a problem in Equation (G.1).

A second potentially misleading element of Equation (G.1) has to do with the different plane of competition present in southern states during much of the time period we have used. The South traditionally has not been very competitive, and its senators have usually had little difficulty in general elections. Further, most of the states in the South have relatively small populations. (This situation has changed rapidly in recent years, especially in Florida and Texas, but in general most southern states during our 36-year period were not heavily populated.) Given these facts, it is possible the relationship detected in Equation (G.1) that we attributed to the population of the state may in fact be due to the relative safety of most southern senators.

This possibility can be simply tested by repeating the Equation (G.1) regression separately for southern states and for nonsouthern states. If the coefficient for size of the state is negative within each region, the explanation for the finding in Equation (G.1) could not be the different plane of competition between the regions. Equations (G.2) and (G.3) present the results of these separate regression analyses.[11]

Equation (G.2): southern states only:

$$Y = 55.19 + .99°(\text{comp.}) - .98°(\text{size}) + e$$

$$(6.60) \qquad (-2.89)$$

where $N = 13$, $R^2 = .82$, $F = 22.85$. (See Equation (G.1) for an explanation of the variables.)

Equation (G.3): nonsouthern states only:

$$Y = 54.97 + .29°(\text{comp.}) - .12°(\text{size}) + e$$

$$(2.06) \qquad (-1.71)$$

where $N = 35$, $R^2 = .17$, and $F = 3.89$. (See Equation (G.1) for an explanation of the variables.)

---

10. Past research has revealed a relationship between the percentage of a state's population living in urban areas and the level of competition (see Eulau, 1957; Gold and Schmidhauser, 1960; Ranney, 1965, p. 68), and it seems quite likely that states with large populations tend to be those with high proportions of urban dwellers (New York and California, for instance). In fact, the law of averages leads us to expect constituencies to become decreasingly monolithic as individuals are added to them. Therefore, it would be quite reasonable to anticipate a relationship between state population and party competition.

11. For our purposes the South has been defined as including the following states: Alabama, Arkansas, Florida, Georgia, Kentucky, Louisiana, Mississippi, North Carolina, South Carolina, Tennessee, Texas, Virginia, and West Virginia.

The results of this test reveal important regional differences. In the South, state population has a more powerful effect on the electoral returns of incumbent senators than it does in the rest of the country. The small N for the South suggests the possibility that this finding may simply be an indication that Texas and Florida have fairly competitive senatorial elections while the rest of the South does not. But the more important point is that even with the South excluded, the coefficient for constituency size remains in the predicted direction and slips only marginally in magnitude (from −.17 to −.12) and significance level (from −2.01 to −1.71—the latter barely achieving the .05 level). Interregional differences do not explain the findings in Equation (G.1).[12] State population matters in both regions and in both instances the effect, as expected, is a negative one. Regardless of region, Senators in highly populous states do not do as well electorally as senators from lightly populated states.

## IMPLICATIONS

The population of a state has an important impact on the electoral success of incumbent senators in that state. Other things being equal, senators from populous states like New York and California can expect to average about 6 to 7 percentage points fewer than senators from lightly populated states like Delaware, North Dakota, and Vermont. A regional breakdown revealed that although the relationship existed in all parts of the country, it was particularly strong in the South. Apparently, we are safe in concluding that for incumbent legislators the more constituents there are, the more difficult they are to please.

We believe the results of this research are helpful in understanding the differences in electoral success not only among senators but also between representatives and senators. Representatives are safer partly because of the simple reason their constituencies are usually smaller. When constituencies in the House and Senate are the same size, representatives are not much safer than senators. In Delaware, for example, the average incumbent senator received 52.8 percent ($N = 12$) of the vote, and incumbent representatives averaged 53.3 percent ($N = 18$). In North Dakota and Vermont incumbent representatives actually did worse electorally than incumbent senators. Conversely, in New York, Senate incumbents ran 17 percentage points behind candidates for reelection to the House, while in California the gap was nearly 20 points.

---

12. This conclusion is supported by the results of an alternative procedure designed to test for the effect of regional variations. When a dummy variable for South/non-South is added to Equation (G.1), the following results are obtained:

$$Y = 52.64 + .74°(comp.) - .17°(size) + 2.01(region) + e,$$

$$(4.93) \qquad (-1.79) \qquad (.65)$$

where the variables are the same as those in Equation (G.1) except the region is coded "1" if South and "0" if non-South.

The key findings are that (1) the coefficient for region is not statistically significant and (2) the addition of region to the equation does not reduce the size of the coefficient for state population.

Explanations of the different rates of electoral success of incumbents in the House and the Senate that rely solely on what we have called "institutional" factors, while not disproven by our results, must be regarded as sadly incomplete. Since the population of a senator's state does make a difference, it seems likely that the success of House incumbents is due in part to their relatively small constituencies and not just to differences in issues considered, challengers offered, or length of terms served.[13]

For now we leave unanswered the important question of exactly why constituency size matters to such a degree. In the future researchers may want to sort out the varying contributions made by population heterogeneity (see Sullivan, 1973), constituency service opportunities, and media market congruence with political boundaries.

We hope the basic findings described here will assist scholars in the important task of comparing legislative elections both within the United States and across national borders.[14] In a broader sense, we also hope variables based on the population size of various political units will be better utilized in the future. Though many political changes obviously cannot be traced to population growth,[15] it is hard to believe that population size is not somehow connected to the feelings of alienation and mistrust toward the government that are prevalent in many countries today (see Dahl and Tufte, 1973). As societies become more heavily populated is it only natural for people to have feelings of inefficacy in the face of an increasingly distant and depersonalized political system. Our findings are certainly consistent with these notions, and future studies may be able to move us closer to coming to grips with the role of population size in explaining our displeasure with political systems in general, and not just with incumbent senators in the United States.

# REFERENCES

Abramowitz, Alan I. 1980. A comparison of voting for U.S. senator and representative in 1978. *American Political Science Review*, 74 (September): 633–640.

Alford, John R., and John R. Hibbing. 1983. Incumbency advantage in the Senate. Paper presented at the annual meeting of the Midwest Political Science Association, Chicago, April.

---

13. Modifications of some of the institutional explanations could make them more compatible with our findings. For instance, if a rationale could be constructed and verified about why high-quality challenges for Senate seats are staged in large states but not in small states (perhaps something to do with their ability to make better use of television and other modern campaign techniques), the quality of challenger argument would certainly be consistent with our findings.

14. For a good recent summary of what is known about legislative elections in a comparative framework see Ragsdale (1982). Also see Hinckley, Hofstetter, and Kessel (1976) for an excellent example of the kinds of questions comparative election research should ask.

15. For example, changes in the population size of constituencies obviously cannot explain the decline in the competitiveness of House seats that occured in the mid-1960s. The population of House constituencies has grown steadily since about 1920 (when the number of representatives stabilized at 435), yet in recent decades representatives have become, in the main, safer rather than more vulnerable.

Campbell, James E., John R. Alford, and Keith Henry. 1982. Television markets and congressional elections: The impact of market/district congruence. Paper presented at the annual meeting of the Southern Political Science Association, Atlanta, Ga., October 28–30.

Dahl, Robert A., and Edward R. Tufte. 1973. *Size and democracy*. Stanford, Calif.: Stanford University Press.

Dodd, Lawrence C. 1981. Congress, the Constitution, and the crisis of legitimation. In Lawrence C. Dodd and Bruce I. Oppenheimer, eds., *Congress reconsidered*. Washington, D.C.: Congressional Quarterly.

Eulau, Heinz. 1957. The ecological basis of party systems: The case of Ohio. *Midwest Journal of Political Science*, 1 (August): 125–135.

Fenno, Richard F., Jr. 1981. The U.S. Senate: A bicameral perspective. Paper presented at the annual meeting of the American Political Science Association, New York, September.

Gold, David, and John R. Schmidhauser. 1960. Urbanization and party competition: The case of Iowa. *Midwest Journal of Political Science*, 4 (February): 62–75.

Hinckley, Barbara. 1970. Incumbency and the presidential vote in Senate elections. *American Political Science Review*, 64 (September): 836–842.

———. 1980a. The American voter in congressional elections. *American Political Science Review*, 74 (September): 641–650.

———. 1980b. House reelections and Senate defeats: The role of the challenger. *British Journal of Political Science*, 10 (October): 441–460.

———. 1981. *Congressional elections*. Washington, D.C.: Congressional Quarterly.

Hinckley, Barbara, Richard Hofstetter, and John Kessel. 1976. Information and the vote: A comparative election study. *American Politics Quarterly*, 2 (April): 131–158.

Jacobson, Gary C., and Samuel Kernell. 1981. *Strategy and choice in congressional elections*. New Haven, Conn.: Yale University Press.

Jewell, Malcolm E. 1981. The political environment of congressional elections. Paper presented at the annual meeting of the Southern Political Science Association, November, Memphis, Tenn.

Kazee, Thomas. 1982. Recruiting congressional challengers: The deterrent effect of incumbency. Paper presented at the annual meeting of the Midwest Political Science Association, April, Milwaukee, Wis.

Kostroski, Warren L. 1978. The effect of number of terms on the reelection of senators, 1920–1970. *Journal of Politics*, 40 (May): 488–497.

Mann, Thomas E., and Raymond E. Wolfinger. 1980. Candidates and parties in congressional elections. *American Political Science Review*, 74 (September): 617–632.

Mayhew, David R. 1974. Congressional elections: The case of the vanishing marginals. *Polity*, 6 (Spring): 295–317.

Patterson, Samuel C. 1968. The political cultures of the American states. *Journal of Politics*, 30 (February): 187–209.

Pike, Otis. 1980. Why weren't representatives ousted? In *Detroit Free Press*, 15 November.

Ragsdale, Lyn. 1982. Responsiveness and legislative elections: Toward a comparative study. Paper prepared for presentation at the Legislative Research Conference, Iowa City, Iowa, October.

Ranney, Austin. 1965. Parties in state politics. In Herbert Jacob and Kenneth Vines, eds., *Politics in the American states.* Boston: Little, Brown.

Sullivan, John. 1973. Partial correlates of social, economic, and religious diversity in the American states. *Journal of Politics,* 35 (February): 70–84.

Uslaner, Eric M. 1981. The case of the vanishing liberal senators: The House did it. *British Journal of Political Science,* 11 (January): 105–113.

Westlye, Mark C. 1983. Competitiveness of Senate seats and Senate voting behavior. *American Journal of Political Science,* 27 (May)

# Appendix
# H

Eagleton Poll 77 (SL/EP27)
Form A
October – November, 1989

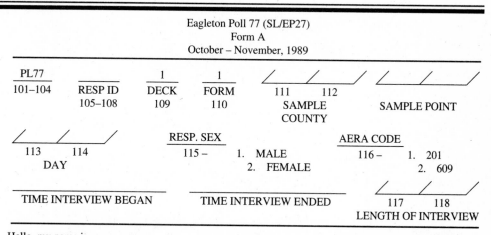

PL77
101–104    RESP ID    DECK    FORM    111    112
           105–108    109     110     SAMPLE    SAMPLE POINT
                                      COUNTY

113    114    RESP. SEX              AERA CODE
DAY           115 –    1. MALE       116 –    1. 201
                       2. FEMALE              2. 609

TIME INTERVIEW BEGAN    TIME INTERVIEW ENDED    117    118
                                                LENGTH OF INTERVIEW

Hello, my name is _____ (first and last name).
I'm on the staff of the Eagleton Poll, and I'm taking a public opinion survey of New Jersey adults for
Rutgers University. I'd like your views on what New Jersey is like as a place to live and on some topics
currently in the news.

IF RESPONDENT DECLINES TO PARTICIPATE, POSSIBLE PROBES:
—Your participating is very important because only 1000 people have been
   randomly selected for this survey and your views will represent many
   people throughtout the state.
—IF "DON'T KNOW ENOUGH": There are no right or wrong answers. We
   are only interested in your opinions. They are just as important as anybody
   else's.
—IF "NOT INTERESTED," "DON'T WANT TO": I just need one more
   interview to complete my quota. Won't you please help me?

1. To begin with, are you currently registered to vote here in New Jersey? (IF YES, PROBE: As a
   Democrat, Republican, Independent or something else?)

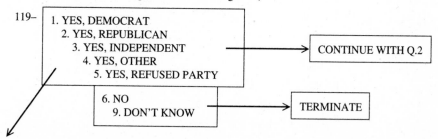

119–
1. YES, DEMOCRAT
2. YES, REPUBLICAN
3. YES, INDEPENDENT    →    CONTINUE WITH Q.2
4. YES, OTHER
5. YES, REFUSED PARTY

6. NO    →    TERMINATE
9. DON'T KNOW

2. As of now, how likely are you to vote in the election for governor this November—will you definitely
   vote, probably vote, probably not vote, or definitely not vote?

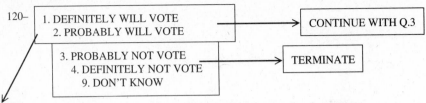

120–
1. DEFINITELY WILL VOTE
2. PROBABLY WILL VOTE → CONTINUE WITH Q.3

3. PROBABLY NOT VOTE
4. DEFINITELY NOT VOTE
9. DON'T KNOW → TERMINATE

3. How interested are you in the outcome of this election—very, somewhat, not very, or not at all interested?

121– 1. VERY INTERESTED
2. SOMEWHAT INTERESTED
3. NOT VERY INTERESTED
4. NOT AT ALL INTERESTED
9. DON'T KNOW

4. The Republican candidate is Jim Courter—have you ever heard of him before?

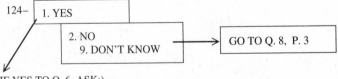

122–
1. YES

2. NO
9. DON'T KNOW → GO TO Q. 6

(IF "YES" TO Q. 4, ASK:)

5. Is your general impression of Courter favorable or unfavorable?
(IF FAVORABLE OR UNFAVORABLE, PROBE: Is that very (favorable/unfavorable) or somewhat (favorable/unfavorable) ?

123– 1. VERY FAVORABLE
2. SOMEWHAT FAVORABLE
3. SOMEWHAT UNFAVORABLE
4. VERY UNFAVORABLE
9. NO OPINION/DON'T KNOW

6. The Democratic candidate is Jim Florio—have you ever heard of him before?

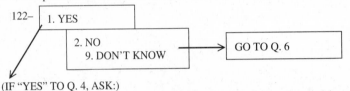

124–
1. YES

2. NO
9. DON'T KNOW → GO TO Q. 8, P. 3

(IF YES TO Q. 6, ASK:)

7. Is your general impression of Florio favorable or unfavorable?
(IF FAVORABLE OR UNFAVORABLE, PROBE: Is that very (favorable/unfavorable) or somewhat (favorable/unfavorable) ?

125– 1. VERY FAVORABLE
2. SOMEWHAT FAVORABLE
3. SOMEWHAT UNFAVORABLE
4. VERY UNFAVORABLE
9. NO OPINION/DON'T KNOW

8.  If the election was today, would you vote for Jim Courter the Republican; or Jim Florio, the Democrat? (IF "WOULDN'T VOTE," PROBE: Would you not vote because you're undecided now, or don't you plan to vote in the election?)

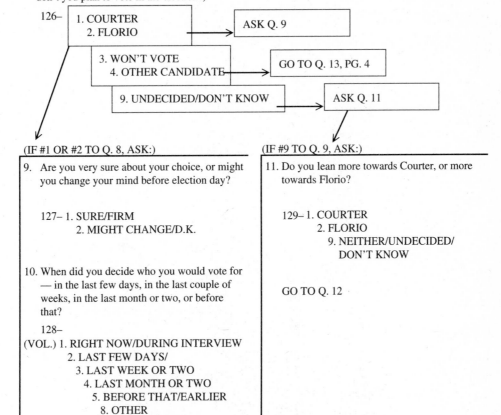

126–   1. COURTER
       2. FLORIO        →  ASK Q. 9

       3. WON'T VOTE
       4. OTHER CANDIDATE  →  GO TO Q. 13, PG. 4

       9. UNDECIDED/DON'T KNOW  →  ASK Q. 11

---

**(IF #1 OR #2 TO Q. 8, ASK:)**

9.  Are you very sure about your choice, or might you change your mind before election day?

    127– 1. SURE/FIRM
          2. MIGHT CHANGE/D.K.

10. When did you decide who you would vote for — in the last few days, in the last couple of weeks, in the last month or two, or before that?

    128–
(VOL.) 1. RIGHT NOW/DURING INTERVIEW
       2. LAST FEW DAYS/
        3. LAST WEEK OR TWO
         4. LAST MONTH OR TWO
          5. BEFORE THAT/EARLIER
           8. OTHER
            9. DON'T KNOW

GO TO Q. 12

**(IF #9 TO Q. 9, ASK:)**

11. Do you lean more towards Courter, or more towards Florio?

    129– 1. COURTER
          2. FLORIO
           9. NEITHER/UNDECIDED/
            DON'T KNOW

GO TO Q. 12

---

12. Regardless of who you plan to vote for, who do you think will win the election for Governor?

    130– 1. FLORIO
          2. COURTER
          9. DON'T KNOW/NO OPINION

LOUIS HARRIS AND ASSOCIATES, INC.
630 Fifth Avenue
New York, New York 10111

Study No. 832112

November 1983

Sample Point No |__|__|__|__|__|__|__|
10-11-12-13-14-15-16

Interviewer's Name (PLEASE PRINT): _____

Telephone No. _____ (17–26)

------------------------------------------------------------------------

Hello, I'm _____ from Louis Harris and Associates, the national research firm in New York. We are conducting the Harris Survey and would like to ask you some questions, if you don't mind.

------------------------------------------------------------------------

Are you 18 years of age or older? (IF NO, ASK IF ANYONE IN HOUSEHOLD IS 18 YEARS OLD OR OLDER AND ASK TO SPEAK WITH THAT PERSON. IF NO ONE IN HOUSEHOLD IS 18 OR OLDER, NOT ELIGIBLE.)

Yes . . . . . _____ (CONTINUE WITH QUESTIONNAIRE)
No . . . . . _____ (NONELIGIBLE)
Refused. . . _____ (REFUSAL)

FROM OBSERVATION:   Sex

Male . . . . . . (27(_____ –1
Female. . . . . . . ._____ –2

RECORD — DO NOT ASK

This interview was completed on the:

1st  dialing. . . (28(_____ –1
2nd  dialing. . . . . ._____ –2
3rd  dialing. . . . . ._____ –3
4th  dialing. . . . . ._____ –4
5th  dialing. . . . . ._____ –5

1a. A year from now, as a result of economic conditions, do you feel (READ EACH ITEM), or not?

| ROTATE — START AT "X" | | | Will<br>Happen | Will Not<br>Happen | Not<br>Sure |
|---|---|---|---|---|---|
| ( ) | 1. | The rate of inflation will remain relatively low, as it has for the past year | (29(____–1 | ____–2 | ____–3 |
| ( ) | 2. | Interest rates on borrowing will have come down sharply | (30(____–1 | ____–2 | ____–3 |
| ( ) | 3. | Unemployment will be reduced to below where it is now | (31(____–1 | ____–2 | ____–3 |
| ( ) | 4. | More people will be losing homes and farms because they can't meet mortgage payments | (32(____–1 | ____–2 | ____–3 |
| ( ) | 5. | The economy will be expanding at a healthy rate | (33(____–1 | ____–2 | ____–3 |
| ( ) | 6. | More factories will be shutting down | (34(____–1 | ____–2 | ____–3 |
| ( ) | 7. | Your own spending as a consumer will be going up sharply | (35(____–1 | ____–2 | ____–3 |
| ( ) | 8. | The elderly, the poor, and the handicapped will be especially hard hit | (36(____–1 | ____–2 | ____–3 |
| ( ) | 9. | The rich and big business will be much better off | (37(____–1 | ____–2 | ____–3 |
| ( ) | 10. | More people will be going hungry | (38(____–1 | ____–2 | ____–3 |
| ( ) | 11. | Mortgage rates will be lower so that more new housing will be available | (39(____–1 | ____–2 | ____–3 |

1b. Do you think the country is in a <u>depression</u>, or not?

        In a depression ......................(40(_____–1
        Not in a depression ......................._____–2
        Not sure........................................._____–3

1c. Do you think the country is in a <u>recession</u>, or not?

        In a recession..........................(41(_____–1
        Not in a recession......................._____–2
        Not sure........................................._____–3

1d. A year from now, do you feel the country will be in a recession, or not?

        Will be in a recession.............(42(_____–1
        Will not be in a recession..............._____–2
        Not sure........................................._____–3

5e. For some time now, the Russains have had their latest intermediate-range nuclear missiles in place, where they are aimed at major population centers in Western Europe. The U.S. plan for countering the Soviet missiles is to install in the next month our latest Pershing II and Cruise missiles in Great Britain, West Germany, and Italy, where these missiles will be aimed at major population centers in the Soviet Union. Let me read you some statements that have been made about this nuclear missile situation in Western Europe. For each, tell me if you agree or disagree with that statement.

| READ EACH STATEMENT |
|---|

| ROTATE — START AT "X" | | Agree | Disagree | Not Sure |
|---|---|---|---|---|
| (  ) 1. | If we install our latest missiles in Western Europe, the Russians say they will break off the Geneva nuclear arms negotiations and will put new nuclear missiles in Eastern Europe, so our putting these nuclear missiles in place next month will bring us close to a dangerous nuclear confrontation with the Russians ....................................(73(____ –1 | _____–2 | _____–3 |
| (  ) 2. | The only hope for getting the Russians to agree to control nuclear arms in Europe is for the U.S. to install enough of our latest missiles, so the Russians know their population centers would be destroyed if they used <u>their</u> missiles ..............(74(____ –1 | _____–2 | _____–3 |
| (  ) 3. | It is unnecessary for us to put our latest nuclear missiles in Europe, since we already have sea-based, air-based, and land-based long-range missiles which can destroy Russian population centers many times over..........................................(75(____ –1 | _____–2 | _____–3 |
| (  ) 4. | Even though it's a high risk, if we want to protect ourselves and our allies in Western Europe, then we have to match the Russians missile for missile....................................(76(____ –1 | _____–2 | _____–3 |

5f. Many people in Western Europe are worried that if the U.S. puts new nuclear missiles into Western Europe, there will be a nuclear confrontation there between the U.S. and Russia, which could lead to a nuclear war. Do you share this worry of people in Western Europe, or not?

Share this worry ....................(77(_____ –1
Don't share it................................ _____–2
Not sure........................................ _____–3

5g. All in all, do you favor or oppose (READ EACH ITEM)?

| DO NOT ROTATE | | Favor | Oppose | Not Sure |
|---|---|---|---|---|
| 1. | The U.S. <u>delaying</u> installation of Pershing II and Cruise missiles in Western Europe to see if an agreement can be reached on controlling intermediate-range nuclear missiles in Western Europe ........................................................................(78(____ –1 | _____–2 | _____–3 |
| 2. | The U.S.<u>going ahead</u> with plans to install our latest intermediate-range nuclear missiles in Western Europe .............(79(____ –1 | _____–2 | _____–3 |

## The Effect of Question Wording on Response: Three Examples

| A. **Questions Regarding a Human Life Amendment (HLA)** | Responses* Should Be | Shouldn't Be |
|---|---|---|
| 1. "Do you think there should be an amendment to the Constitution prohibiting abortions, or shouldn't there be such an amendment?" | 29 | 67 |
| 2. "Do you believe there should be an amendment to the Constitution protecting the life of the unborn child, or shouldn't there be such an amendment?" | 50 | 39 |

Referring to the HLA in a positive sense (protecting) rather than in a negative sense (prohibiting), and mentioning the unborn child causes over one fifth of the respondents to change their response.

Source: New York Times/CBS News Poll. *The New York Times*, August 18, 1980, p. 1. Both questions were asked of the same respondents.

| B. **Questions Regarding the Abortion Decision** | | |
|---|---|---|
| 1. "As you may have heard, in the last few years a number of states have liberalized their abortion laws. To what extent do you agree or disagree with the following statement regarding abortion: The decision to have an abortion should be made solely by a woman and her physician?" | Agree 64 | Disagree 31 |
| 2. "Do you think it should be lawful for a woman to be able to get an abortion without her husband's consent?" | Yes 24 | No 67 |

When the circumstances surrounding an abortion are specified (the woman is married), apparent support for woman's unlimited "right to choose" diminishes sharply.

Source: Question 1 was commissioned by Planed Parenthood and asked in a Gallup poll. *The Gallup Opinion Index*, Report 87, Sept. 1972. Question 2 was commissioned by Blake and asked in a Gallup poll two months after Question 1. Blake (1973)

| C. **Questions Regarding the Supreme Court Decisions of 1973** | | |
|---|---|---|
| 1. "The U.S. Supreme Court has ruled that a woman may go to a doctor to end a pregnancy at any time during the first three months of pregnancy. Do you favor or oppose this ruling?" | Favor 47 | Oppose 44 |
| 2. "The U.S. Supreme Court has ruled that a woman may go to a doctor for an abortion at any time during the first three months of pregnancy. Do you favor or oppose this ruling?" | 43 | 54 |

Changing the way abortion itself is referred to affects the outcome of the poll.

Source: Question 1: Gallup poll conducted March, 1974. *The Gallup Opinion Index*, Report 106, April 1974. Question 2: Sindlinger, "Special Hitchhicker on Abortion," for *National Review*, May 1974.

*All responses in this and subsequent tables will be given in percentages. Figures may not add to 100 percent because of rounding, or because the "Other," "Don't Know" and "No Answer" responses have been omitted.

From Table 1
Do you believe there should be an amendment to the Constitution protecting the life of the unborn child, or shouldn't there be such an amendment?

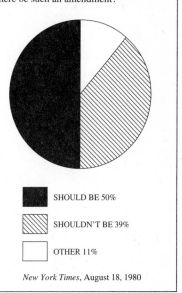

SHOULD BE 50%

SHOULDN'T BE 39%

OTHER 11%

*New York Times*, August 18, 1980

What do you think about abortion? Should it be legal as it is now, legal only in such cases as saving the life of the mother, rape or incest, or should it not be legal at all?

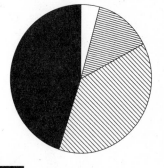

LEGAL AS PRESENT 38%

 LEGAL ONLY IN EXTREME CIRCUMSTANCES 45%

 SHOULD BE TOTALLY ILLEGAL 13%

 NO RECORDED OPINION 4%

CBS News/New York Times Poll, 1985

# Appendix
# I

# Evaluating the Impact of International Organizations

FRANCIS W. HOOLE
*Indiana University*

Evaluation research involves the use of the scientific method to evaluate the impact of public programs. The cross-disciplinary evaluation research literature provides a useful orientation for the examination of activities of international organizations. The primary advantage of this approach is that more dependable cause and effect statements are possible. The major limitations relate to its applicability, vary from case to case, and should not be underestimated. Yet they do not preclude its beneficial use by international organization scholars and policy makers. The smallpox eradication program of the World Health Organization serves as the basis for an illustration of the evaluation research methodology.

## INTRODUCTION

What difference do international organizations make? When the Carnegie Endowment for International Peace announced in this journal in 1970 that it had decided to give funding priority to research on this question it seemed that the answer would be of interest primarily from an academic standpoint.[1] The question appears to have significant practical importance today as various international organizations are undergoing crises concerning their abilities to accomplish objectives. Unfortunately, little more of a systematic nature is known about the answer today than was known seven years ago.

The primary concern of this article is with the method of evaluating the impact of international organizations. In my opinion the evaluation research approach contains a useful orientation and should serve as the basis for new studies on the impact of activities of international organizations.

### The Evaluation Research Approach

The past few years have witnessed numerous systematic evaluation studies (e.g., the negative income tax experiments in the United States) and the development of a cross-disciplinary body of literature on the methodology of evaluation research. One observer

---

1. *International Organization* 24 (Winter 1970): 160–61.

has identified over one hundred and fifty systematic social experiments that have been undertaken recently.[2] A basic bibliography of evaluation research would include well over two hundred and fifty items (excluding citations to the aforementioned experiments).[3] There are already several good overviews of this literature and there is no need to review it here in detail.[4] Some introductory comments are in order so that its potential relevance for the international organization field will be clarified.

There is no commonly accepted definition of the concept of evaluation. However, most evaluation researchers would not disagree too much with Edward Suchman's view of evaluation as "the determination (whether based on opinions, records, subjective or objective data) of the results (whether desirable or undesirable; transient or permanent; immediate or delayed) attained by some activity (whether a program, or part of a program, a drug or a therapy, an ongoing or one shot approach) designed to accomplish some valued goal or objective (whether ultimate, intermediate, or immediate, effort or performance, long- or short-range)."[5] There also would be considerable agreement with Joseph Wholey and his associates when they contend that "evaluation is research, the application of the scientific method to experience with public programs to learn what happens as a result of program activities."[6]

The evaluation research orientation toward evaluation can be distinguished from that of optimization techniques (e.g., linear programming) which focus primarily on

2. Robert F. Boruch, "Bibliography: Illustrative Randomized Field Experiments For Planning and Evaluation," mimeo, Evanston, Illinois, Northwestern University, 1974.

3. Cf. Carol H. Weiss, *Evaluation Research, Methods of Assessing Effectiveness* (Englewood Cliffs, N.J.: Prentice-Hall, 1972): 129–54.

4. Henry Riecken, Robert F. Boruch, Donald T. Campbell, Nathan Caplan, Thomas K. Glennan, Jr., John W. Pratt, Albert Rees and Walter Williams, *Social Experimentation: A Method for Planning Social Intervention* (New York: Academic Press, 1974); Weiss, *Evaluation Research;* Joseph S. Wholey, John W. Scanlon, Hugh G. Duffy, James S. Fukumoto and Leona M. Vogt, *Federal Evaluation Policy, Analyzing The Effects of Public Programs* (Washington, D.C.: The Urban Institute, 1973); Alice M. Rivlin, *Systematic Thinking for Social Action* (Washington, D.C.: The Brookings Institution, 1971); Samuel P. Hayes, Jr., *Evaluating Development Projects,* 2nd Edition (Paris: United Nations Educational, Scientific and Cultural Organization, 1966); Howard E. Freeman and Clarence C. Sherwood, *Social Research and Social Policy* (Englewood Cliffs, New Jersey: Prentice-Hall, 1970); Ilene N. Bernstein and Howard E. Freeman, *Academic and Entrepreneurial Research, The Consequences of Diversity in Federal Evaluation Studies* (New York: Russell Sage Foundation, 1975); Agency for International Development, *Evaluation Handbook,* Second Edication (Washington, D.C.: Agency for International Development, 1974); Francis G. Caro, ed., *Readings in Evaluation Research* (New York: Russell Sage Foundation, 1971); Gene M. Lyons, ed., *Social Research and Public Policies, The Dartmouth/OECD Conference* (Hanover, New Hampshire: University Press of New England, 1975); Peter H. Rossi and Walter Williams, eds., *Evaluating Social Programs: Theory, Practice, and Politics* (New York: Seminar Press, 1972); Carol H. Weiss, ed., *Evaluating Action Programs, Readings in Social Action and Education* (Boston: Allyn and Bacon, 1972); Elmer L. Struening and Marcia Guttentag, eds., *Handbook of Evaluation Research,* Volume 1 (Beverly Hills, California: Sage Publications, Inc., 1975); Marcia Guttentag and Elmer L. Struening, eds., *Handbook of Evaluation Research,* Volume 2 (Beverly Hills, California: Sage Publications, Inc., 1975); William R. Leonard, Beat Alexander Jenny and Offia Nwali, *UN Development Aid, Criteria and Methods of Evaluation* (New York: Arno Press, 1971); and, Edward A. Suchman, *Evaluation Research, Principles and Practice in Public Service and Social Action Programs* (New York: Russell Sage Foundation, 1967).

5. Suchman, *Evaluation Research:* 31–2.

6. Wholey et al., *Federal Evaluation Policy:* 19.

evaluating possible alternatives and determining the optimal allocation of resources (given a certain set of constraints). It also can be distinguished from the orientation toward evaluation of systematic monitoring methods such as network analysis (as well as traditional audit reports and financial statements) which focus primarily on the process by which a program is implemented. The main concern of evaluation research is the impact of a program. It is devoted to obtaining sound empirical evidence regarding the effectiveness of social action programs (the evidence can be used as the basis for optimization, cost benefit and other analyses or simply as general information for policy makers). The evaluation research approach utilizes a hypothesis testing orientation where the hypothesis involves conjecture regarding the impact of a program. The key ingredient is the use of the scientific method to test the impact hypothesis.

There are two important uses for the evaluation research approach: "first, to supply information that allows policy makers, planners, and professionals to make rational decisions about social development and human resource problems. . . ; and second, to add to knowledge available about social and interpersonal behavior and the social environment, and to explicate and refine the practice principles that underlie programming efforts."[7] The former use is most relevant for policy makers in international organizations while the latter pertains most to international organization scholars.

## The Methodology of Evaluation Research

The evaluation research methodology is concerned with the operational procedures involved in the systematic empirical examination of hypotheses regarding the impact of social action programs.[8] The impact hypothesis suggests that there is a relationship between the social action program, or some aspect of it, and a measure or indicator of some behavior or condition. An example of an impact hypothesis will be found in the smallpox eradication program case study which appears later in this article. It sets up the reported empirical examination and is stated in the following manner: the intensified worldwide smallpox eradication program of the World Health Organization resulted in a reduction in the number of countries in the world reporting cases of smallpox.

---

7. Bernstein and Freeman, *Academic and Entrepreneurial Research:* 1.

8. The work of Donald T. Campbell and associates provides the methodological orientation for the evaluation research literature. The basic works are Donald T. Campbell and Julian C. Stanley, *Experimental and Quasi-Experimental Designs for Research* (Chicago: Rand McNally, 1963); Donald T. Campbell, "Reforms as Experiments," *American Psychologist* 24 (April 1969): 409–29; Donald T. Campbell and H. Laurence Ross, "The Connecticut Crackdown on Speeding, Time Series Data in Quasi-Experimental Analysis," *Law and Society Review* 3 (August 1968): 33–53; H. Laurence Ross, Donald T. Campbell and Gene V. Glass, "Determining the Social Effects of a Legal Reform, The British 'Breathalyser' Crackdown of 1967," *American Behavioral Scientist* 13 (March–April 1970): 493–509; Riecken et al., *Social Experimentation;* Donald T. Campbell, "Assessing the Impact of Planned Social Change," in Lyons, ed., *Social Research and Public Policies:* 3–45; and Thomas D. Cook and Donald T. Campbell, "The Design and Conduct of Quasi-Experiments and True Experiments in Field Settings," in M. D. Dunnette, ed., *Handbook of Industrial and Organizational Psychology* (Chicago: Rand McNally, 1975): 223–326.

Several things should be noted about the impact hypothesis. The independent variable can be the entire social action program or any aspect of it, such as a program strategy or an alternative means of implementing a project. Thus the focus can be on the project, program, or any other meaningful unit for analysis. The dependent (impact) variable can be an indicator of a stated goal or an unanticipated side effect. In many instances an investigator will examine several independent and dependent variables. The evaluation research methodology offers no help in the important task of identifying the appropriate variables and the form of the relationship between them. In some situations the impact hypothesis may be formally derived from an axiomatic theory. Yet in most instances the impact hypothesis will be of an ad hoc nature and will be based on the circumstances surrounding a specific activity and the insights of those specifying the hypothesis. The same methodological approach is used to test derived and ad hoc hypotheses. A comprehensive evaluation of an activity will undoubtedly involve numerous impact hypotheses.

For each test of an impact hypothesis there are alternative explanations for the observed results. Many of these explanations form the basis for rival hypotheses that utilize the same dependent variable as the impact hypothesis but alternative independent variables. Other explanations suggest why no impact was observed. Examples of rival explanations will be found in the smallpox eradication program case study. One of these can be stated in the following manner: specific events occurring at the same time as the intensified worldwide smallpox eradication program of the World Health Organization resulted in a reduction in the number of countries in the world reporting cases of smallpox. In this statement a new independent variable has been introduced into the impact hypothesis.

Thomas D. Cook and Donald T. Campbell have identified thirty-five possible rival explanations.[9] They have classified them into four categories: (1) internal validity; (2) statistical conclusion validity; (3) external validity; and (4) construct validity.[10] Internal validity is most important and "the priority-ordering of the other . . . [types of validity] varies with the kind of research being conducted."[11] The strongest causal interpretation for an impact hypothesis is possible when there is strong empirical support for it and a refutation of each potential rival explanation.[12]

---

9. The types of validity, rival explanations, and research designs discussed here were originally presented in Cook and Campbell, "The Design and Conduct of Quasi-Experiments and True Experiments in Field Settings." The terminology is that of Cook and Campbell.

10. For elaboration on the types of validity and the rival explanations see Cook and Campbell, "The Design and Conduct of Quasi-Experiments and True Experiments in Field Settings": 224–46.

11. Cook and Campbell, "The Design and Conduct of Quasi-Experiments and True Experiments in Field Settings": 245.

12. Basic to the evaluation research approach is the idea that it is impossible to establish that a social action program actually caused an observed impact. A causal explanation is retained if three conditions are present: (1) the cause precedes the effect in time; (2) treatments covary with effects (if the cause and effect are not related then one could not cause the other); and (3) there are no alternative explanations that are more plausible. The impact hypothesis deals with the first and second points while the rival explanations deal with all three points.

The threat to internal validity casts doubt on whether the hypothesized causal relationship between operational versions of the variables specified in the impact hypothesis actually exists in the specific circumstances that are examined. There are fourteen challenges to internal validity.

*History.* Specific events occuring at the same time as the activity being evaluated might account for the observed impact.

*Maturation.* The maturation explanation suggests that "processes within the respondents or observed social units producing changes in the impact variable as a function of the passage of time per se, such as growth, fatigue, [or] secular trends"[13] might have caused the observed impact.

*Testing.* The effect of earlier tests upon the scores obtained on later tests of the impact variable might have produced the observed impact.

*Instrumentation.* The observed impact may be due to a change in the means of measuring the impact variable.

*Statistical Regression.* This explanation is concerned with a possible statistical artifact: "If the group was selected because it was extreme on some measure [of the impact variable], statistical reasoning indicates that it will appear less extreme on subsequent tests [of the impact variable], even though the intervening treatment may be completely ineffectual."[14]

*Selection.* The differential selection of cases for treatment and control groups may have produced the observed difference between groups.

*Mortality.* The differential loss of cases for treatment and control groups may have produced the observed difference between groups.

*Interactions with Selection.* One or several of the aforementioned explanations could have interacted with selection to produce the observed impact.

*Ambiguity About the Direction of Causal Inference.* It may not be possible to tell which variable is actually the cause and which is the effect. This explanation is a threat especially when a cross-sectional correlational study is undertaken.

*Diffusion or Imitation of the Treatment.* The cases in the control group may have learned the information given to the experimental group, thereby receiving the treatment and eliminating it as a possible cause of the difference in impact observed for the groups.

*Compensatory Equalization of Treatment.* Those administering the treatment may have given it to both the treatment and control groups, thereby eliminating the treatment as a possible cause of the difference in impact observed for the groups.

*Compensatory Rivalry.* A competitive spirit may have developed in the control group and motivated an effort which clouds the real difference between it and the treatment group on the impact variable.

*Resentful Demoralization of Respondents Receiving Less Desirable Treatments.* The respondents in the control group may have become resentful and demoralized because they did not receive the treatment. They may have acted in such a way that created a bias in the observed results.

---

13. Campbell, "Reforms as Experiments": 411.

14. Ross, Campbell and Glass, "Determining the Social Effects of a Legal Reform": 495.

*Local History.* The "different treatments . . . [may] be associated with all the unique historical experiences that each group has"[15] and the treatment may not be responsible for the observed difference between groups.

The rival explanations in the internal validity category are the most important because they raise questions about whether the obtained results can be causally interpreted.

Statistical conclusion validity is concerned with whether the conclusion regarding the impact was a statistical artifact resulting from inappropriate uses of statistical techniques. There are six explanations in this category.

*Statistical Power.* The statistical techniques that were used may have led to an incorrect conclusion because of small sample size, an inappropriate setting of the level of significance, or the selection of a one-sided hypothesis.

*Fishing and the Error Rate Problem.* Chance could have produced the statistical conclusion regarding impact. This explanation is a threat especially when a search involving a large number of differences is undertaken.

*The Reliability of Measures.* Measures of low reliability may have produced the statistical conclusion regarding impact.

*The Reliability of Treatment Implementation.* Lack of standardization of the implementation of the social action program may have produced the statistical conclusion regarding impact.

*Random Irrelevancies in the Experimental Setting.* Features of the experimental setting other than the treatment may have produced the statistical conclusion regarding impact.

*Random Heterogeneity of Respondents.* Heterogeneity of respondents with respect to variables that affect the impact variable may have produced the statistical conclusion regarding impact.

These explanations cast doubt on the test of the null hypothesis regarding impact and, therefore, on the conclusions arrived at through the use of statistical tests of significance. They are of interest only when tests of significance are used.

External validity focuses on whether the observed results of an impact study can be expected to be the same at a later time (e.g., next year), in a different setting (e.g., another country), or when other persons are involved. This category contains six explanations.

*Interaction of Treatment and Treatments.* It may not be valid to generalize to a situation where only one treatment is given if the cases in the experimental group received more than one treatment.

*Interaction of Testing and Treatment.* It may not be valid to generalize to situations where the testing is not identical.

*Interaction of Selection and Treatment.* It may not be valid to generalize to situations where the categories of respondents (e.g., persons, cities, countries) are not identical.

*Interaction of Setting and Treatment.* It may not be valid to generalize to situations where the setting (e.g., university campus) is not identical.

*Interaction of History and Treatment.* It may not be valid to generalize to situations in the past and future because they are not identical.

---

15. Cook and Campbell, "The Design and Conduct of Quasi-Experiments and True Experiments in Field Settings": 229.

*Generalizing Across Effect Constructs.* The observed impact might not hold for other impact variables and constructs.

These confounding explanations are relevant only when an attempt is made to generalize to other times, settings, and persons.

Those rival explanations that focus on problems of generalization from operational measures to theoretical constructs are in the construct validity category. There are nine explanations of this type.

*Inadequate Pre-Operational Explication of Constructs.* Inadequate initial clarification of the theoretical construct may have led to the development of operational measures which do not adequately represent the construct.

*Mono-Operation Bias.* Single operational measures may underrepresent a construct and/or contain irrelevancies.

*Mono-Method Bias.* The use of the same method for giving treatments and/or collecting data on responses may result in a bias in regard to the construct.

*Hypothesis-Guessing within Experimental Conditions.* The subjects may have tried to guess the hypothesis being tested and the observed impact may have been generated as a reaction to that guess.

*Evaluation Apprehension.* The subjects may be apprehensive about being evaluated and may therefore have biased their reported attitudes or behavior.

*Experimenter Expectancies.* The observed impact may have been the result of a data collection bias resulting from the hopes and expectations of the experimenter.

*Confounding Levels of Constructs and Constructs.* The operational procedures may not have covered the full range of possible values for the variables and thus may have missed part of the relationship between variables.

*Generalizing Across Time.* It may not be valid to generalize from the impact observed using the operational measures to the conclusion that the impact would hold across time for the theoretical construct because the observed impact may be of a short duration.

*Interaction of Procedure and Treatment.* The operational procedures may have allowed the respondents to gain information which created a bias in the observed results.

These confounding explanations are of interest only when an attempt is made to generalize across treatments and measures to theoretical constructs.

The evaluation research approach follows a falsification strategy in testing impact hypotheses. Correlation is not confused with causation and a systematic effort to disconfirm observed impact results is required through the examination of rival explanations. The listing of challenges to the validity of impact studies may seem so overwhelming that some might want to forgo undertaking such a study. This is not a satisfactory alternative because rival explanations do exist and they present challenges to the causal explanation contained in any study. The evaluation research approach attempts to make explicit the rival explanations and to control their effect.

There are numerous ways of doing this. Among the most powerful methods for controlling explanations in the construct validity category are (1) multiple operationalization; (2) placebo treatments; and (3) double blind experiments.[16] There are several

---

16. Cook and Campbell, ibid: 238–45.

techniques for increasing external validity: (1) random sampling; (2) use of heterogeneous groups of persons, settings, and times; (3) generalization to modal instances; and (4) generalization to target instances.[17] The explanations in the statistical conclusion category are controlled through the creative and correct use of statistical techniques. Campbell and his associates have presented over twenty different research designs that are useful in various circumstances for controlling explanations in the internal validity category.[18] These designs are of three types: (1) experimental; (2) quasi-experimental; and (3) pre-experimental.[19] They serve as the basis for evaluation research studies. The methods of controlling explanations in the statistical conclusion validity, external validity, and construct validity categories are added as refinements to them as circumstances dictate. For the sake of brevity a discussion of only seven designs will be presented here (most of the others are variations or elaborations of designs which are discussed). The designs were selected because of their potential relevance for international organization scholars and policy makers. The focus here is on the control of explanations in the internal validity category. The most simple versions of the designs are presented.

*One Group Posttest-Only Design.* The basis of this design is a single post-treatment observation for a single case which received the treatment. It can be diagramed in the following manner:

XO

where O is the observation or measure of the impact variable and X is the treatment (international organization activity). The problems with this frequently used pre-experimental design are: (1) it does not allow the detection of a pretest-posttest change or a treatment-nontreatment comparison; and (2) it does not control any of the plausible rival explanations in the internal validity category. It is the weakest of all designs.

*One Group Pretest-Posttest Design.* This design utilizes pretest data (collected for the period before the treatment) and posttest data (collected for the period after the treatment):

$$O_1 \, X \, O_2$$

where O is the observation or measure of the impact variable and X is the treatment. This frequently used pre-experimental design is stronger than the last design because it makes possible the detection of a pretest-posttest change in the value of the impact vari-

17. Cook and Campbell, ibid: 234–48.

18. Campbell and Stanley, *Experimental and Quasi-Experimental Designs for Research;* and Cook and Campbell, "The Design and Conduct of Quasi-Experiments and True Experiments in Field Settings": 245–98.

19. These design types differ primarily in regard to their control of explanations in the internal validity category. Experimental designs equate treatment and control groups by randomization, thereby isolating the effect of the treatment and helping to rule out numerous rival explanations in the internal validity category. When quasi-experimental designs are used the rival explanations must be considered one at a time. The use of time-series data and non-equivalent control groups is frequent in the quasi-experimental designs. These designs are suggested for use when the more powerful experimental designs are not feasible. Pre-experimental designs do not use randomization and make insufficient use of the quasi-experimental controls. They are designs of last resort.

able. It is still very inadequate. The history, maturation, testing, and statistical regression explanations usually present serious problems when this design is used.

*Posttest-Only Design with Non-Equivalent Groups.* This design utilizes a single post-treatment observation for the impact variable for both the treatment group and a nonrandomly selected control group:

$$\begin{array}{c} XO \\ \hline O \end{array}$$

where O is the observation or measure of the impact variable and X is the treatment. This design makes possible the comparison of a group of cases where a certain activity has been undertaken and a group of cases where a different activity or no activity has occurred. The selection and interactions with selection explanations make this pre-experimental design weak. It is used frequently in social science research (many correlational studies are of this type) but it usually does not allow strong causal inferences.

*Untreated Control Group Design with Pretest and Posttest.* This design utilizes pretest and posttest data for both a group which received the treatment and one which did not:

$$\begin{array}{c} O_1 \, XO_2 \\ \hline O_1 \, O_2 \end{array}$$

where O is the observation or measure of the impact variable and X is the treatment. The treatment and control groups have not been equated through the use of randomization. This quasi-experimental design can be seen as a combination of the pre-experimental posttest-only design with non-equivalent groups and the pre-experimental one group pretest-posttest design. It is a stronger design than either of them. If the treatment had any impact there should be a difference in the change observed for the groups. The statistical regression, interactions with selection, and local history explanations are difficult to control when this design is used.

*Interrupted Time-Series Design.* The basis of the interrupted time-series design is the existence of periodic observations for the impact variable and the introduction of a treatment at some point:

$$O_1 \, O_2 \, O_3 \, O_4 \, X \, O_5 \, O_6 \, O_7 \, O_8$$

where O is the observation or measure of the impact variable (the number of data points can vary) and X is the treatment. This quasi-experimental design can be seen as the extension over time of the one-group pretest-posttest design. It has the advantage of facilitating identification of an interruption in the data pattern and the comparison of trends before and after the intervention. The history explanation is especially difficult to control when this design is used.

*Interrupted Time-Series Design with a Non-Equivalent No-Treatment Control Group Time-Series.* The basis of this design is the existence of periodic observations for the impact variable for two groups and the introduction of a treatment at some point for one of the groups:

$$\frac{O_1\,O_2\,O_3\,O_4\,X\,O_5\,O_6\,O_7\,O_8}{O_1\,O_2\,O_3\,O_4 \qquad O_5\,O_6\,O_7\,O_8}$$

where O is the observation or measure of the impact variable (the number of data points can vary) and X is the treatment. The treatment and control groups have not been equated through the use of randomization. This quasi-experimental design has the virtues of the interrupted time-series design and adds controls available through an untreated control group design with pretest and posttest. It facilitates the control of all rival explanations presenting challenges to the internal validity of a study.[20]

*Pretest-Posttest Control Group Design.* This is the classical experimental design. It employs pretest and posttest data for a group which received the treatment and one which did not:

$$O_1 \;\; X \;\; O_2$$

$$O_1 \qquad O_2$$

where O is the observation or measure of the impact variable and X is the treatment. If the treatment had any impact there should be a difference in the change observed for the groups. This design differs from the untreated control group design with pretest and posttest in that here the groups have been equated through the use of randomization. Many of the rival explanations in the internal validity category are unambiguously ruled out by the process of randomization. This design facilitates the control of all rival explanations presenting challenges to the internal validity of a study. It should be used whenever feasible.

The normal social science measurement, data collection, and data analysis techniques are available for use in evaluation research studies. The details of these techniques and issues regarding their proper use are of the greatest importance. However, I will not consider these details here.[21] I prefer to devote the limited available space to an illustrative examination of the impact of the smallpox eradication program of the World Health Organization (WHO).

## The WHO Smallpox Eradication Program

A smallpox attack begins with a fever and general aching. A rash then develops on various parts of the body. There is no cure for smallpox and approximately thirty percent of

20. Both this design and the interrupted time-series design are most powerful when the impact is abrupt and can be noted as a pretest-posttest ($O_4 - O_5$) change because plausible rival hypotheses are more easily controlled for a short period. Both designs require that data be available for an extended period prior to the initiation of the program. This means that the data probably were collected for some purpose other than to evaluate the program. These designs would be most useful for evaluating macro programs that cover environments where a social indicator system has been in existence for some time.

21. For an introduction to these matters and a discussion of their relevance for the study of international organizations see Francis W. Hoole, "The Behavioral Science Orientation to the Study of International Administration," in Robert S. Jordan, ed., *Multinational Cooperation, Economic, Social, and Scientific Development* (New York: Oxford University Press, 1972): 327–64.

those who catch the disease die from it. Survivors are essentially immune against further attack. Fortunately smallpox is passed only from person to person and most patients can transmit it only during a two week period. There is a vaccine, developed in 1796, which is quite successful in protecting persons from catching smallpox. Because of these factors smallpox is the most susceptible to eradication of the infectious diseases. It is easily identified and there is a feasible means of breaking the chain of transmission.

Smallpox was once endemic throughout the world. During the first half of the twentieth century both Europe and North America became essentially free from it. The 1950s saw the same result achieved in several African, Asian, and Latin American countries. The threat of reintroduction of smallpox into these countries and the relative ease with which it can be contained led the Assembly of the World Health Organization, in 1958, to call for the global eradication of the disease. Unfortunately there was no increase in the resources available for this task in the WHO regular budget. Voluntary contributions were invited but the response was limited. There was little apparent impact as a result of the 1958 action by the WHO Assembly.

The member states of WHO decided in 1966 to conduct an intensified worldwide smallpox eradication program with significantly increased financial resources to be made available through the regular budget of WHO.[22] It was felt that a coordinated global effort of increased technical assistance could eradicate the disease from the world in ten years. No insurmountable technical problems were foreseen and the failure of countries to eliminate smallpox on their own was viewed as resulting principally from a lack of funds and organization failures in establishing surveillance and vaccination activities. The goal of the WHO intensified worldwide smallpox eradication program was a "zero incidence of smallpox."[23]

When the intensified program was begun, in January of 1967, smallpox was endemic in thirty African, Asian, and Latin American countries. Fourteen additional countries had imported cases during 1967. Most projects in the endemic countries were begun during the first two years of the intensified effort. The last was started in 1971. Since January of 1967 WHO projects have been conducted in fifty different countries and the incidence of smallpox has steadily declined. Forty-four countries reported smallpox cases in 1967. Only two countries did so in 1976. It now appears that smallpox was eradicated from the world during 1976, exactly ten years after the beginning of the

---

22. For background on the WHO smallpox eradication program see *WHO Expert Committee on Smallpox, First Report*, World Health Organization Technical Report Series No. 283 (Geneva: World Health Organization, 1964); *Smallpox Eradication*, Report of a WHO Scientific Group, World Health Organization Technical Report Series No. 393 (Geneva: World Health Organization, 1968); *WHO Expert Committee on Smallpox Eradication*, Second Report, World Health Organization Technical Report No. 493 (Geneva: World Health Organization, 1972); Special issue entitled "Smallpox, Point of No Return," *World Health* (February–March 1975); "Smallpox Eradication," in *The Second Ten Years of the World Health Organization*, 1958–67 (Geneva: World Health Organization, 1968): 105–11; "Smallpox Eradication Programme," Annex 15, *Nineteenth World Health Assembly*, Part I, World Health Organization Official Records No. 151 (Geneva: World Health Organization, 1966): 106–21; "Smallpox," *Handbook of Resolutions and Decisions of the World Health Assembly and Executive Board*, Volume I, 1948–72 (Geneva: World Health Organization, 1973): 89–97.

23. *WHO Expert Committee on Smallpox Eradication*, Second Report: 9.

intensified worldwide smallpox eradication program of the World Health Organization.[24] A disease may have been eliminated for the first time in the history of mankind.

## Evaluating the Impact of the WHO Smallpox Eradication Program

There are various aspects of the worldwide smallpox eradication program that deserve systematic evaluation. For example, it would be interesting to compare systematically the relative effectiveness of mass and containment vaccination campaigns or jet injector guns and bifurcated needles. For this illustration the overall intensified program is evaluated. The independent variable is the smallpox eradication program of the World Health Organization. Among the meaningful indicators for assessing the impact of the smallpox program would be the number of deaths from smallpox in the world and number of countries reporting smallpox cases. For this illustration a single indicator is used. The primary goal of the smallpox eradication program is the zero incidence of smallpox. This study utilizes as the dependent variable the number of countries in the world reporting smallpox cases. The impact hypothesis is: the intensified worldwide smallpox eradication program of the World Health Organization resulted in a reduction in the number of countries in the world reporting cases of smallpox.

The operational procedures that are used are straightforward. The intensified WHO smallpox program began on January 1, 1967. The period prior to 1967 is considered to be the no treatment era. The 1967–76 period is considered to be the treatment era. Annual data for the impact variable, the number of countries in the world reporting cases of smallpox, were obtained from the office of the chief of the WHO smallpox eradication unit.[25] There may be some error in these data. However, they appear to be quite reliable. They do have the virtue of being the best data available and were used by policy makers in the World Health Organization.

The evaluation research design should allow for an empirical examination of the impact hypothesis while ruling out as many rival explanations as possible. The choice of the design is limited by the nature of the data that can be utilized. An experimental de-

24. WHO will declare the disease eradicated only after a two year period during which no cases are located. What has the WHO program cost so far? It has been estimated that the countries with smallpox eradication programs have spent approximately two-hundred million dollars and that international aid has amounted to another fifty million dollars. Of the latter amount roughly twenty-two million dollars came from the WHO regular budget, fourteen million dollars came from the US, eight million dollars came from the USSR, and the remainder (six million dollars) was contributed by other countries. The most impressive program in the history of public health has cost approximately two-hundred and fifty million dollars. Surely the smallpox eradication program of the World Health Organization has been a bargain. It has been estimated that one hundred and fifty-one million dollars were spent in 1968 in protecting individuals from smallpox in the United States, even though there had not been a smallpox case in the US for several years. In 1971 the WHO smallpox eradication program succeeded in eliminating smallpox from the Western hemisphere and compulsory smallpox vaccination was abolished in the United States. Most of the money being spent on the disease was saved. Because of the WHO smallpox eradication program the savings in the US between 1971 and 1975 amounted to more than all of the contributions made by the United States government to the World Health Organization since the creation of the agency in 1948. These cost estimates were taken from F.J. Tomiche, "Fruits of Victory," *World Health* (February–March 1975): 26–28.

25. I am especially grateful to Mr. Jacques Copland for his assistance.

sign cannot be employed here because randomization was not used in the choice of countries to receive the treatment in the WHO smallpox eradication program. The use of a quasi-experimental design employing a non-equivalent control group is not feasible because the program was made worldwide when it was initiated. The interrupted time-series design is the most powerful feasible design. It will be utilized.

Annual data on the number of smallpox cases for 1950–76 are presented in Figure I.1. The number of countries reporting smallpox cases fluctuated downward prior to 1967. The number of countries decreased from a high of eighty-two in 1950 to a low of forty-four in 1966. After the intensified program was begun the number of countries reporting cases decreased from forty-four in 1967 to two in 1976.

The years were regressed on the number of countries to determine the trends. The dummy variable strategy of Gujarti[26] was used:

$$Y_t = a + b_1 X_t + b_2 D_t + b_3 (X_t \cdot D_t) + e_t \tag{I.1}$$

where $Y_t$ equals the number of countries reporting smallpox cases, $X_t$ equals the years, $D_t$ is a dummy variable with O used for the 1950–66 time period and 1 for the 1967–76 era, a is the intercept, the b's are fixed coefficients, and e is an error term that takes into

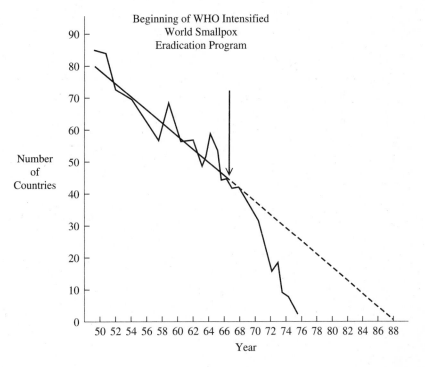

Figure I.1

26. Damodar Gujarti, "Use of Dummy Variables in Testing Equality Between Sets of Coefficients in Two Linear Regressions: A Note," *The American Statistician* 24, 1 (1970): 50–52; and Damodar Gujarti, "Use of Dummy Variables in Testing for Equality Between Sets of Coefficients in Linear Regressions: A Generalization," *The American Statistician* 24, 5 (1970): 18–22.

account factors not otherwise included in the equation. A number of assumptions concerning the form of the model (linear), disturbances (zero mean, homoskedastic variance, nonautoregressive), and independent variable (stationary and independent of the disturbance term) must be satisfied for the parameters to be estimated using the general linear regression model and for the resulting estimates to be optimal (unbiased, efficient, and consistent).[27] All required assumptions, with the exception of the one concerning stationarity, are reasonable in this case.[28] Because of the importance of the assumption of non-autocorrelated error terms the Durbin-Watson d statistic[29] and the Theil-Nagar[30] .01 level for it were used to examine the first order independence of the disturbances. While the statistical techniques used do not offer optimal solutions to all problems, on balance they appear to be adequate for their purpose.[31]

The ordinary least squares technique provided satisfactory estimates (Durbin-Watson d = 1.62) for equation I.1.[32] (The relevant information has been plotted in Figure I.1.) The trend for the 1950–66 era indicates that the number of countries reporting smallpox cases decreased at the average annual rate of 2.1 per year. An extrapolation of the trend for the 1950–66 era indicates that smallpox would have been eradicated in twenty-one years, in 1987, had that trend continued.[33] The trend for 1967–76, the pe-

---

27. For a general treatment of regression analysis see J. Johnston, *Econometric Methods,* 2nd Edition (Tokyo: McGraw-Hill Kogakusha, Ltd., 1972).

28. Unfortunately the effect of the violation of the stationarity assumption is not well understood.

29. J. Durbin and G. S. Watson, "Testing for Serial Correlation in Least Squares Regression," Part I, *Biometrika* 37 (1950): 409–28; and J. Durbin and G. S. Watson, "Testing for Serial Correlation in Least Squares Regression," Part II, *Biometrika* 38 (1951): 159–78.

30. H. Theil and A. G. Nagar, "Testing the Independence of Regression Disturbances," *Journal of the American Statistical Association* 56 (1961): 793–806.

31. In future analyses consideration will be given to trying to adapt Box-Jenkins ARIMA models, which have the advantage of handling nonlinearities and higher order autoregressive schemes for the disturbances, for analysis of the smallpox data. For information on autoregressive integrated moving average models see G.E.P. Box and G.M. Jenkins, *Time Series Analysis: Forecasting and Control* (San Francisco: Holden-Day, 1970); Thomas H. Naylor, Terry G. Seaks and D. W. Wichern, "Box-Jenkins Methods: An Alternative to Econometric Models," *International Statistics Review* 40 (1972): 123–37; G.E.P. Box, and G.C. Tiao, "A Change in level of nonstationary time series," *Biometrika* 52 (1965): 181–92; and G.V. Glass, G.C. Tiao and T.O. Maguire, "The 1900 revision of German divorce laws: Analysis of data as a time-series quasi-experiment," *Law and Society Review* 6 (1971): 539–62.

32. All statistical analysis reported in this paper was done on the CDC 6600 computer at Indiana University. A revised version of the BMDO2R program was prepared for this analysis by David H. Handley. I am most grateful to him.

33. What would have happened had the WHO intensified program not been initiated? It is unlikely that the trend would have gone downward any faster without the WHO program. That circumstance would mean that the smallpox eradication program actually slowed down progress and did more harm than good. It is more likely that the number of countries reporting cases would have leveled off at around forty-four and stayed near that level for a period. This scenario would reflect the situation where all countries that were going to bring smallpox under control for a period had done so. Another likely alternative is that the trend would have continued to move downward at approximately the same rate. Under this assumption smallpox would have been eliminated in countries as public health infrastructures were developed, in the course of normal events, and the general level of health improved. It is, of course, impossible to say definitely what would have happened had the WHO intensified program not been undertaken.

riod after the start of the WHO program, indicates that the number of countries reporting cases decreased at an average of 4.6 per year. The average decrease in countries reporting cases is greater after the initiation of the intensified program. Is the change statistically significant? To answer that question, the hypothesis that the coefficients describing the 1950–66 era belong to the same regression as the coefficients describing the 1967–76 era was examined. The proper test of this hypothesis involves the use of Chow's F test.[34] The value for the $F$ ratio was 19.25, which is significant well beyond the .0001 level. The post-intervention trend is significantly different than the pre-intervention trend. There is strong empirical support for the impact hypothesis.

Can the observed results be accounted for by other explanations? The rival explanations in the external and construct validity categories will not be examined because there is no immediate concern with generalizing the observed results across times, settings, and persons or across treatments and measures. Some explanations in the internal validity category are not plausible because they concern differences in treatment and control groups. There is no control group utilized here. The remaining explanations in the internal validity category and those in the statistical conclusion group are examined for plausibility of explanation of the reduction in the number of countries reporting smallpox cases.

*History.* Specific events occurring at the same time as the program might account for the observed impact. There was no other worldwide smallpox program which occurred during the 1967–76 era and which might have produced the observed change in the trend in the number of countries reporting smallpox cases. It would have been possible to have more faith in ruling out this explanation if a control group design had been feasible because the specific events occurring at the same time as the program could be expected to have affected both treatment and control group cases, and thus to have been controlled. If the program had been abruptly introduced and the impact had been immediate then only other events during 1967, rather than the entire 1967–76 era, could have had an effect. More faith in the ruling out of this explanation would have been possible in that circumstance.

*Maturation.* The maturation explanation suggests that "processes within the respondents or observed social units producing changes in the impact variable as a function of the passage of time per se, such as growth, fatigue, [or] secular trends,"[35] might have caused the observed impact. There may have been a maturation process operating in the public health field. As the delivery of medical care became more effective and basic health infrastructures in countries became better established the incidence of smallpox might have decreased naturally. However, it would appear to be unlikely that the maturation process would cause the observed sudden change in the impact variable. Furthermore, we would expect to find other diseases being eradicated if this explanation were highly plausible.

*Testing.* The effect of earlier tests upon the scores obtained on later tests of the impact variable might have produced the observed impact. In the smallpox case the

34. G.C. Chow, "Tests of Equality Between Sets of Coefficients in Two Linear Regressions," *Econometrica* (1960): 591–605.

35. Campbell, "Reforms as Experiments": 411.

concern is with the effect of publicity regarding a social indicator on later values of that indicator. It seems defensible to assign a very low plausibility to the challenge presented by this explanation because of the nature of the indicator and the unlikely possibility that a testing effect would suddenly develop at the same time as the program.

*Instrumentation.* The observed impact may be due to a change in the means of measuring the impact variable. Because a major part of the WHO program involved setting up better surveillance systems there was a change in the calibration of the measuring instrument. However, this instrumentation change would tend to work against the observed success of the program. After the WHO intensified program was initiated it was less likely that cases of smallpox would go unreported. The increase in the number of countries during the 1950–76 period also presents a potential instrumentation problem, but again the bias is against the observed success of the program. The decrease in the number of countries reporting smallpox cases is even more impressive because of changes in instrumentation.

*Statistical Regression.* This explanation is concerned with a possible statistical artifact: "If the group was selected because it was extreme on some measure, statistical reasoning indicates that it will appear less extreme on subsequent tests, even though the intervening treatment may be completely ineffectual."[36] Had the WHO intensified program been initiated as a reaction to a crisis, rather than to a chronic situation, the prospect of the observed impact being an artifact would have been greater. This explanation seems unlikely because the trend in the number of countries reporting smallpox cases started down long before the intervention.

*Ambiguity About the Direction of Causal Inference.* It may not be possible to tell which variable is actually the cause and which variable is the effect. This explanation is a threat especially when a cross-sectional correlational study is undertaken. In this study it is not a plausible explanation.

*Statistical Power.* The statistical techniques that were used may lead to an incorrect conclusion because of small sample size, an inappropriate setting of the level of significance, or the selection of a one-sided hypothesis. There is no opportunity for checking on this explanation by increasing the sample size because all of the available data were used. Had the sample been larger it might have been possible to adapt more sensitive statistical techniques (such as the Box-Jenkins ARIMA methods)[37] for use in this study. The results observed appear to be so clear that it is doubtful that a change in the sample size or level of significance would have produced a different conclusion. Furthermore, it is hard to see how the hypothesis is one-sided. This rival explanation seems unlikely in this situation, although it is not ruled out.

*Fishing and the Error Rate Problem.* Chance could have produced the statistical conclusion regarding impact. This explanation is a threat especially when a search in-

---

36. Ross, Campbell and Glass, "Determining the Social Effects of a Legal Reform": 495.

37. See the citations in footnote 31. Cook and Campbell note that a sample of fifty cases should be available for use of these techniques. See Cook and Campbell, "The Design and Conduct of Quasi-Experiments in Field Settings": 275.

volving a large number of differences is undertaken. This rival explanation seems unlikely because no searching was done for statistically significant cutting points.

*The Reliability of Measures.* Measures of low reliability may have produced the statistical conclusion regarding impact. This explanation would have been quite plausible had an indicator such as number of cases of smallpox or number of deaths from smallpox been used because the reliability of those measures is quite low. It is likely that the public health service in a country knows whether the country had any cases of smallpox. There is a high degree of reliability in the measure utilized.

*The Reliability of Treatment Implementation.* Lack of standardization of the implementation of the social action program may have produced the statistical conclusion regarding impact. The lack of standardization of the implementation of the smallpox eradication program would tend to work against the observed impact. This would appear to be a plausible explanation had no impact been observed.

*Random Irrelevancies in the Experimental Setting.* Features of the experimental setting other than the treatment may have produced the statistical conclusion regarding impact. In this situation these features would tend to work against the observed impact. This would appear to be a plausible explanation had no impact been observed. It is difficult to see how it is a plausible explanation in this study.

*Random Heterogeneity of Respondents.* Heterogeneity of respondents with respect to variables that affect the impact variable may have produced the statistical conclusion regarding impact. In this situation the heterogeneity would tend to work against the observed impact. It would appear to be a plausible explanation had no impact been observed. It is difficult to see how it is a plausible explanation in this study.

Thus after consideration of the relevant rival explanations there appears to be no highly plausible rival explanation for the observed impact. The impact hypothesis has not been convincingly falsified.

It is hoped that this study has presented a meaningful illustration of the use of the evaluation research approach and that it has motivated international organization scholars and policy makers to obtain further details from the relevant literature. The smallpox case was presented because of its clarity in conveying the essence of the evaluation research approach. Most impact studies of international organization activities will be more complex and the impact will be less clear. The evaluation research approach will be of greater assistance in helping to sort out the cause and effect relationship in those cases.

## Evaluation Research and International Organization Scholars

The evaluation research approach can be of help to scholars in setting up research designs when cause and effect statements of the impact of international organization activities are being examined. There are two prerequisites for an evaluation research study: (1) there is a clearly stated impact hypothesis; and (2) it is possible to obtain meaningful data for the specified variables. The evaluation research approach can be of assistance in designing tests for specific hypotheses when these conditions exist. Different designs will be appropriate for different studies.

The approach is relevant for a wide range of international organization issues (e.g., social and economic development, peacekeeping, ocean resources, human rights, integration).[38] It should be helpful in studying the impact of treaties, resolutions, court decisions, changes in institutional arrangements, funding levels, leadership styles, programs, program strategies, and other problems when it is difficult to sort out facts. Because of complexity and cost the evaluation research approach should not be used to examine questions where the answer is already well known (and accepted without controversy) or to examine trivial questions.

In many studies the essential concern will be whether a specific international organization activity has been effective. The evaluation research approach handles this type of concern (the smallpox eradication program case study is of this type). For many international organization scholars, however, the crucial question will be: how effective is an international organization in relation to other possible ways of handling a problem? The evaluation research approach facilitates this type of inquiry by allowing for the expansion of the basic research design to include more than one type of social action program or by treating the cases without the international organization activity as control group cases.

For some international organization scholars the research foci that are most significant, and at the same time most interesting, concern what might be labeled indirect impact. The effect might take place in a complex system of interaction in which important consequences are latent rather than manifest. The initial problem here is to define the nature of the impact (including possible latent as well as manifest consequences). The evaluation research approach offers no dogmatic or magic solution to these measurement and specification problems. It encourages initiative and creativity in identifying and measuring impact variables (whether latent or manifest, goal derived or unanticipated).

The most serious difficulties in utilizing the evaluation research approach are of an applied nature. There is a shortage of meaningful and reliable data in many countries. There is little agreement on how to measure many concepts. The approach is relatively expensive. Ethical problems may arise concerning issues such as (1) withholding treatment from control group cases, (2) confidentiality of information, and (3) termination of treatment without disruption of subjects' lives.[39] The level of methodological expertise needed to handle many research foci is high. The seriousness of these and other applied problems will vary from study to study. These difficulties are not peculiar to the evaluation research approach, although they may be highlighted by it. Evaluation researchers need to do the best that they can in any given circumstance, handling problems in a flexible and creative manner. The applied problems should not be underestimated. Yet the difficulties in the application of the evaluation research approach are not sufficient to limit seriously its utility by international organization scholars. The applied problems are no more serious than in other areas of the social sciences.

---

38. I know of only one published study in the international organization field that has used evaluation research methodology. It was focused on international integration. See James A. Caporaso and Alan L. Pelowski, "Economic and Political Integration in Europe: A Time-Series Quasi-Experimental Analysis," *American Political Science Review* 65 (1971): 418–33.

39. For an excellent general discussion of the potential ethical problems involved in evaluation research see Riecken et al., *Social Experimentation*: 245–69.

# Evaluation Research and International Organization Policy Makers

The potential uses and advantages for the policy maker are generally the same as for the scholar. The potential problems for the policy maker are more numerous. The same difficulties in applying the methodology exist for both the scholar and policy maker.[40] Several organization problems also must be solved if the evaluation research approach is to be helpful to policy makers.[41]

Decisions on international organization activities are the result of political processes which tend to emphasize factors other than effectiveness evidence regarding ongoing activities. Impact information will be used only if it is made meaningful for policy makers. International organizations must work on (1) narrowing the gap between evaluation findings and action alternatives, (2) identifying meaningful ways of disseminating results, and (3) reducing delays in obtaining answers. These efforts can be facilitated by careful selection of evaluation studies after a critical examination of political conditions, ethical considerations, methodological factors, and policy making requirements.

A serious potential problem lies in the resistance of bureaucracies to systematic evaluation and its implied change. At the heart of this resistance is the identification of the bureaucrats and agency with the program. This means that the evaluation becomes an assessment of the bureaucrats and agency, a very threatening prospect. As Campbell notes: "If the political and administrative system has committed itself in advance to the correctness and efficacy of its reforms, it cannot tolerate learning of failure."[42] He suggests two remedies that have great relevance here: (1) evaluation research should not be used in ad hominem research; and (2) "advocates . . . [should] justify new programs on the basis of the seriousness of the program rather than the certainty of any one answer and combine this with an emphasis on the need to go on to other attempts at solution should the first one fail."[43]

There are several difficulties that can develop in the relationship between evaluators (whether inside or outside) and program personnel. Personality, role, values, frame of reference, and institutional differences can lead to friction over data collection, record keeping, selection of program participants, and the timing and ability to hold

---

40. There is an additional methodological problem which may be of special salience for some policy makers: how can the impact of a particular agency activity be evaluated when a program is a joint one? The activity by the agency must be isolated and an experimental or quasi-experimental design should be set up within the general program research design if it is imperative to know the separate impact.

41. The cost of evaluation research will not be discussed in this section but may be seen as an organization problem by some readers. Not all programs require evaluation and all programs being evaluated do not require the same level of funding. Based upon the experience in evaluating domestic programs in the United States it is suggested that between one and two percent of the budget for program activities be allocated for systematic evaluation research. This percentage can be adjusted as experience is gained. For additional information on the US experience see Wholey et al., *Federal Evaluation Policy*: 77–82, and Bernstein and Freeman, *Academic and Entrepreneurial Research*: 140.

42. Campbell, "Reforms as Experiments": 410.

43. Campbell, "Assessing the Impact": 35.

constant the evaluation research design. Among the suggestions for lessening these tensions are: (1) support for evaluation research studies from high level administrators; (2) involvement of practitioners in the evaluation; and (3) clear role definition and authority structure.[44]

The difficulties are not sufficient to limit seriously the use of the evaluation research approach by policy makers. Carol Weiss has noted that: "The [evaluation] research process takes more time and costs more money than offhand evaluations that rely on intuition, opinion, or trained sensibility, but it provides a rigor that is particularly important when (1) the outcomes to be evaluated are complex, hard to observe, made up of many elements reacting in diverse ways; (2) the decisions that will follow are important and expensive; and, (3) evidence is needed to convince other people about the validity of the conclusions."[45] These conditions frequently confront policy makers in international organizations. They should use the evaluation research approach when this happens.

## CONCLUSIONS AND SUGGESTIONS FOR FURTHER RESEARCH

The evaluation research approach is not a panacea that will eliminate the inherent difficulty in evaluating the impact of international organization activities. These activities involve complex tasks which are attempted in difficult environments. Evaluating their effectiveness will always be problematical. The evaluation research approach can be of assistance in this undertaking. The primary advantage is that more dependable cause and effect statements are possible. There are also side benefits. The evaluation research approach forces clarification of what the treatment or program consists of and a clear statement in operational terms of the objectives of the activities. Its potential for providing valuable impact information is great, provided that it is used in a sensible manner with its limitations as well as its advantages being understood.

Researchers in the international organization field should begin to document the limitations inherent in the evaluation research approach in addition to using it to study substantive questions. A significant amount has been written regarding the problems in using the evaluation research approach for the examination of the impact of social action programs in the United States. A contribution could be made by the clarification of applied problems in the international organization field.

---

44. Cf. Weiss, *Evaluation Research:* 104–7.

45. Weiss, *Evaluation Research:* 2.

# Appendix J

# The Ideal Candidate

## A Study of the Desired Attributes of the Public and the Media Across Two Presidential Campaigns

JUDITH S. TRENT
*University of Cincinnati*

PAUL A. MONGEAU
JIMMIE D. TRENT
*Miami University*

KATHLEEN E. KENDALL
*University at Albany, SUNY*

RONALD B. CUSHING
*University of Cincinnati*

The view of image as a transaction between what a candidate does and the evaluative response that voters have to it creates at least three critical questions as yet unanswered in the literature of political communication. First, although the power of the media to affect the success or failure of political campaigns and candidates has been demonstrated by researchers and is popularly believed, do the views of individual media members regarding the qualities necessary for presidential candidates differ significantly from those of the electorate? Second, although voters share many beliefs about the personal qualities that presidential candidates ought to possess, do these attributes vary from presidential election to election? Finally, although voter assessment of a candidate's image is a major determinant of voter behavior and voters have a mental picture of an ideal candidate that they use to evaluate actual candidates, do the evaluative dimensions differ by party affiliation? The answers to these questions were determined from the results of a survey of 236 professional journalists covering and 444 voting citizens attending presidential rallies in New Hampshire in 1988 and 1992.

Syndicated columnist Jeff Greenfield (1993) noted that "ever since the Nixon-Agnew days of the late 1960s, conservatives have insisted that the press is shot through with bias, [and] that it has become part of the 'adversary culture' at war with traditional values, sound economics and a vigorous foreign policy" (p. A7; all quotations from the *Cincinnati Enquirer* are copyrighted by the *Cincinnati Enquirer* and are used here by permission).

Greenfield's statement implies that members of the media have different, more liberal values than the general population and that these values are used to affect public opinion. If such is the case, if the media do have political values that are more liberal than those of the general population, these differences would exist between media covering the political rallies of presidential candidates during the New Hampshire primary and individual citizens attending such political events.

## FOCUS OF THE STUDY

This study was designed to compare media and voter criteria for determination of presidential political image attributes across campaigns. The focus was on seeking answers to three research questions: First, although the probability that the media has the power to affect the success or failure of political campaigns and candidates has been demonstrated by researchers and is popularly believed, do the views of individual media members regarding the qualities required of presidential candidates differ significantly from those of the electorate? Second, do the characteristics required by the media and/or the electorate vary from presidential election to election? Finally, do the evaluative dimensions differ by party affiliation of the electorate?

Without question, the role played by the media in American presidential campaigns has been the subject of countless research studies. Although areas of investigation have covered a wide spectrum, probably the one that has received the most attention is the influence of media coverage of the campaign (Johnston, 1990). Within media effects research, the area directly concerned with this study is media or content bias.

The early research on content bias sought to measure overt political leaning in news content, particularly the coverage of elections. Originally an outgrowth of propaganda research (Davis, 1990), studies conducted in the 1960s found that news content was balanced in its treatment of major party candidates (Stempel, 1961, 1965, 1969) in that most journalists avoided ideological language, attributed ideological positions to specific sources, and presented all sides on an issue (Graber, 1971). The results of more recent studies, however, have not always agreed. For example, in investigations of the visual components of election coverage, some researchers have concluded that not only is the visual image of a candidate as important as the verbal content about the candidate (Kepplinger, 1982; Masters, Sullivan, Feola, & McHugo, 1987; Moriarty & Garramone, 1986) but that there have been differences in the way candidates in the same race have been visually presented (Moriarty & Garramone, 1986).

Despite suggestions that coverage might not be balanced, the direction of bias as favoring liberals, as suggested by Greenfield (1992, 1993) earlier in this article has popular support but relatively little documentation from research. (One study by Lichter & Rothman, 1981, however, did find that on social issues journalists are more liberal than business leaders.) Political communication scholars have been more interested in the effects that media might have on the images of political candidates. Even though questions regarding whether the opinions of the media differ from those of the voting public would seem to precede questions regarding whether media is changing voter opinions, research has centered on the effect of media on candidate image perception. The findings of Hofstetter, Zukin, and Buss (1978) suggest that network news reinforces or intensifies preexisting candidate image perceptions and issue positions. Atwood and Jarvis (1976) found that television presentation of images was generally not an accountable factor in voting behavior, and Sanders and Pace (1977) claimed limited effects of media on candidate image perception. Czepiec (1976) found that network news exposure had less impact on image adoption than did party identification in the 1972 presidential campaign. Pike (1985) demonstrated that television dependency and candidate images held by voters were only weakly associated in the 1980 presidential election campaign.

There is some evidence that criteria for assessing candidates remains relatively stable across campaigns. For example, Miller, Wattenberg, and Malanchuk (1985) found that people have in mind a certain "picture" of what a president should be and evaluate candidates accordingly. In a second study, Miller, Wattenberg, and Malanchuk (1986) examined open-ended survey responses gathered in the national election studies conducted by the University of Michigan's Center for Political Studies in each presidential election between 1952 and 1984. The frequencies of references to characteristics were counted and grouped into five umbrella categories: competence, integrity, reliability, charisma, and personal dimension. They found that respondents who used the competence, integrity, or reliability dimension for evaluating a presidential candidate in one election were significantly more likely to employ the same dimension four years later. Competency, defined as involving the candidate's past political experience, ability as a statesman, comprehension of political issues, and intelligence, was the most prevalent characteristic in terms of frequencies of responses.

Hellweg, Dionisopoulos, and Kluger (1986) concluded from other research by Hellweg and King (1983) that voters use candidate-specific criteria in making evaluations and suggested further research in the area. The use of candidate specificity in the criteria used for judging candidates suggests that inconsistency in the selection of characteristics judged across elections would be the norm when some or all of the candidates are different. If the criteria used are specifically adopted for judging a particular candidate, when different candidates are being evaluated, different criteria should be used. If the criteria are not selected for the specific candidate, the ratings of specific criteria should remain constant across elections.

Harrison, Stephen, Husson, and Fehr (1991) examined sex differences in the criteria used by college students in determining their preferences in the 1984 presidential campaign. Although their review of relational literature led the researchers to hypothesize that women would use interpersonal criteria whereas men would select issue-oriented evaluative factors, they found that their expectations of men were verified, but women used both issue and interpersonal determinants.

Husson, Stephen, Harrison, and Fehr (1988) examined the extent to which communication behavior (e.g., talks fast, speaks loudly) affects audience members' images of political candidates. Reagan partisans and Mondale partisans agreed that two of the behavioral actions were influenced but supported their own candidate in judgments of performance on those items. Of the seven other favorably rated communication behaviors that were considered important, Reagan's partisans judged him favorably on six and Mondale's partisans considered him superior on one.

Both the Husson et al. (1988) and Harrison et al. (1991) results are of interest to the current study because they found that the criteria used in selecting a presidential choice varied significantly with the sex and political party preference of the subjects. The subject pools of both studies were limited to university students, but they might forecast factors that affect voter and media criteria.

## METHOD AND PROCEDURE

The answers to the focus questions were sought through surveying 236 professional journalists and 444 voting citizens attending presidential campaign rallies and candidate appearances in New Hampshire during the last 10 days before the 1988 and 1992 primary elections. Questionnaires were collected at 10 different locations during each primary election.

The 1988 survey instrument requested subjects to mark a 5-point scale, with 5 indicating *strong agreement* and 1 indicating *strong disagreement* with each of nine statements that asserted the desirability of a presidential candidate possessing specific image characteristics: "have experience in office," "energetic and aggressive leader," "faithful to the spouse," "forceful public speaker," "moral character," "talk about nation's problems," "honest," "younger than 60," and "male."

The 1992 survey instrument duplicated that of 1988 with the exception that the item "younger than 60" was changed to "65" and two characteristics, "remain calm and cautious" and "have solutions to problems," were added. The changes were made to allow examination of the effect of context on criteria application. The age was changed to reflect the fact that the older candidate, George Bush, had passed 65 in 1992. The items added in 1992 were to reflect the rhetorical posture of the primary Republican candidate George Bush (the experience that could allow him to remain calm and cautious even in a crisis) and the Democratic front-runner Bill Clinton (the candidate with a substantive plan for solving the country's problem).

## RESULTS[1]

### Description of Sample Demographics

A demographic description of the 1988 and 1992 samples is presented in Table J.1. Several differences appear when the media sample is compared to the public sample. The media and public samples differed in party affiliation in both 1988 ($\chi^2[2] = 42.32, p < .001$) and in 1992 ($\chi^2[2] = 19.90, p < .001$). In both campaigns, the media sample was more likely than the public sample to be Independent and less likely to be Republican. In addition, the public sample's party affiliation changed between the 1988 and 1992 campaigns: Whereas the proportion of Democrats remained relatively stable, the proportion of Independents increased, and the proportion of Republicans decreased.

The media and public samples also differed by age. In 1992, the media sample was significantly younger than the public sample ($\chi^2 = 38.62, p < .001$). The same pattern appears in the 1988 sample; however, age differences do not reach the chosen level of statistical significance ($\chi^2[5] = 13.55, p < .02$).

Table J.1    DEMOGRAPHICS OF 1988 AND 1992 SAMPLES

| Demographic Item | Media | | Public | |
|---|---|---|---|---|
| | 1988 | 1992 | 1988 | 1992 |
| Total sample | 111 | 125 | 268 | 176 |
| Party affiliation | | | | |
| Republican | 9 | 13 | 106 | 42 |
| Democrat | 43 | 41 | 101 | 73 |
| Independent | 45 | 70 | 49 | 54 |
| Age (in years) | | | | |
| 18–30 | 36 | 36 | 79 | 42 |
| 31–40 | 48 | 42 | 80 | 29 |
| 41–50 | 15 | 35 | 58 | 35 |
| 51–60 | 6 | 8 | 25 | 25 |
| 61–70 | 1 | 1 | 15 | 31 |
| 71+ | 0 | 1 | 2 | 8 |
| Sex | | | | |
| Male | 72 | 101 | 132 | 76 |
| Female | 27 | 22 | 95 | 95 |

Note: Subgroup samples that do not sum to the total sample are due to missing data.

Finally, the media and public samples differed by sex. The proportion of males in the media sample significantly exceeded that in the public sample in both the 1988 ($\chi^2[1] = 9.90, p < .01$) and 1992 samples ($\chi^2[2] = 42.32, p < .001$).

## Most/Least Important Characteristics

Mean values for the importance of all candidate characteristics across the 1988 and 1992 samples for both the media and public are presented in Table J.2.

Those characteristics deemed most or least important remained relatively stable across campaigns and samples. Two characteristics, that the candidate should talk about the problems facing the country and that the candidate be honest, were consistently rated as most important by both samples in both 1988 and 1992. That the candidate be male and be younger than 60/65 years of age were consistently rated as the least important characteristics.

## Ratings of Candidate Characteristics: Media Versus Public

**The 1988 Campaign**    The media and public samples differed in their ratings of six of the nine characteristics included in the 1988 survey. In all six cases, the public sample felt that the characteristic was more important than did the media sample. These characteristics were that the candidate should be an energetic and aggressive leader ($t[375] = 3.79, p < .001$), faithful to one's spouse ($t[374] = 7.39, p < .001$), a forceful public speaker ($t[374] = 4.09, p < .001$), not be accused of violating the law ($t[368] = 2.89, p < .01$), talk about the problems facing the nation ($t[373] = 4.80, p < .001$), and be a male ($t[376] = 5.24, p < .001$).

Table J.2   MEAN IMPORTANCE RATINGS OF PRESIDENTIAL CANDIDATE CHARACTERISTICS, BY SAMPLE AND SURVEY

| Candidate Characteristic | Media | | Public | |
|---|---|---|---|---|
| | 1988 | 1992 | 1988 | 1992 |
| Have experience in office | 4.15 | 4.11 | 3.93 | 4.13 |
| Energetic and aggressive leader | 3.87 | 3.60 | 4.22 | 4.18 |
| Faithful to the spouse | 3.23 | 3.28 | 4.08 | 3.61 |
| Forceful public speaker | 3.78 | 3.90 | 4.21 | 4.17 |
| Moral character | 3.76 | 4.08 | 4.13 | 4.35 |
| Talk about nation's problems | 4.67 | 4.84 | 4.86 | 4.85 |
| Honest | 4.65 | 4.75 | 4.79 | 4.85 |
| Younger than 60/65 years of age | 2.59 | 2.80 | 2.76 | 2.97 |
| Male | 1.66 | 1.83 | 2.36 | 2.01 |
| Remain calm and cautious | —— | 4.06 | —— | 4.26 |
| Have solutions to problems | —— | 4.11 | —— | 4.48 |

**The 1992 Campaign**   The public and media samples differed in their evaluation of the importance of 4 of the 11 characteristics included in the 1992 survey. As was true with the 1988 survey, for all significant differences, the public sample found the characteristic to be more important than the media sample. These characteristics were that the candidate should be an energetic and aggressive leader ($t[297] = 5.91, p < .001$), faithful to one's spouse ($t[298] = 2.80, p < .01$), talk about the problems facing the country ($t[297] = 2.62, p < .01$), and be a person of the highest personal integrity ($t[298] = 2.87, p < .01$).

## Ratings of the Candidate Characteristics: 1988 Versus 1992 Campaigns

Ratings of those characteristics common to both the 1988 and 1992 surveys were analyzed to determine if media and public ratings of candidate characteristics changed between the two campaigns. No significant differences ($p < .01$) were observed for the media sample. Ratings of two candidate characteristics differed for the public sample between the 1988 and 1992 surveys: That the candidate should be male ($t[44] = 2.04$, $p < .01$) and faithful to one's spouse ($t[439] = 4.60, p < .01$) were less important characteristics during the 1992 campaign than they were in the 1988 campaign.

## Party Affiliation and Ratings of Candidate Characteristics[2]

In the 1988 campaign, importance ratings of four of the nine candidate characteristics differed significantly by party affiliation. Data reflecting these differences are presented in Table J.3. A similar pattern appears for all four of these characteristics. Specifically, Republicans, more than either Democrats or Independents (who do not differ from one another), agreed that it is important that presidential candidates be faithful to their spouse ($F[2, 349] = 8.11, p < .001$), a forceful public speaker ($F[2, 347] = 6.74, p < .01$), and male ($F[2, 349] = 42.49, p < .001$). In addition, Republicans felt that it was more important that candidates be energetic and aggressive leaders to a greater extent

Table J.3   MEAN RATINGS OF PRESIDENTIAL CANDIDATE CHARACTERISTICS, BY PARTY AFFILIATION OF RESPONDENT

| Candidate Characteristic | Republican | Democrat | Independent |
|---|---|---|---|
| 1988 survey | | | |
| Energetic and aggressive leader | $4.38_a$ | $3.97_b$ | $4.11_{ab}$ |
| Faithful to the spouse | $4.46_a$ | $3.52_b$ | $3.65_b$ |
| Forceful public speaker | $4.31_a$ | $3.95_b$ | $4.02_b$ |
| Male | $2.92_a$ | $1.74_b$ | $1.88_b$ |
| 1992 survey | | | |
| Faithful to the spouse | $4.02_a$ | $3.38_b$ | $3.27_b$ |
| Younger than 60/65 years of age | $2.63_a$ | $3.14_b$ | $2.79_a$ |
| Male | $2.44_a$ | $1.83_b$ | $1.75_b$ |

Note: Means in the same row without common subscripts differ significantly at $p < .05$.

than did Democrats. Independents did not differ from either Republicans or Democrats on this item.

In the 1992 campaign, party affiliation significantly influenced responses to 3 of the 11 items included in the survey. Specifically, Republicans, more than either Democrats or Independents (who did not differ from one another), agreed that it was important that presidential candidates be faithful to the spouse ($F[2, 288] = 9.97, p < .001$) and male ($F[2, 289] = 7.71, p < .001$). In addition, Democrats, more than either Republicans or Independents (who did not differ from one another), felt that it was important that candidates should be younger than 65 years old ($F[2, 288] = 5.37, p < .01$).

## Sex and Ratings of Candidate Characteristics

Significant sex differences in the evaluation of candidate characteristics are presented in Table J.4. In the 1988 survey, two characteristics differed by sex. Females felt that it was more important that candidates should not have been accused of violating the law ($t[333] = -3.72, p < .001$) and that they talk about problems facing the country ($t[338] = -3.47, p < .001$) than did males.

In the 1992 survey, sex significantly influenced ratings of one of the candidate characteristics. Specifically, males, to a greater extent than females, felt that it was more important that presidential candidates be male ($t[291] = 3.47, p < .001$).

## Age and Ratings of Candidate Characteristics

No age differences were observed in the 1992 survey. Significant differences in ratings of candidate characteristics broken down by age from the 1988 survey are presented in Table J.5. Age exerted a significant impact on ratings of the importance that the candidate have experience in office ($F[5, 356] = 5.92, p < .001$). Scheffé tests indicated that the only differences between groups was that the 18–30 age group felt that this characteristic was significantly more important than did the 31–40 age group. No other differences were statistically significant.

In addition, age significantly influenced ratings of the faithful to spouse characteristic ($F[5, 356] = 3.10, p < .01$). Scheffé tests, however, indicated that there were no significant intergroup differences.

Table J.4  MEAN RATINGS OF PRESIDENTIAL CANDIDATE CHARACTERISTICS, BY SEX OF RESPONDENT

| Candidate Characteristic | Male | Female |
|---|---|---|
| 1988 survey | | |
| Not accused of violating the law | 3.83 | 4.29 |
| Talk about nation's problems | 4.74 | 4.90 |
| 1992 survey | | |
| Male | 2.12 | 1.65 |

Table J.5  MEAN RATINGS OF PRESIDENTIAL CANDIDATE CHARACTERISTICS, BY AGE OF RESPONDENT

| Candidate Characteristic | Age (in years) | | | | | |
|---|---|---|---|---|---|---|
| | 18–30 | 31–40 | 41–50 | 51–60 | 61–70 | 71+ |
| Experienced in office | $4.39_a$ | $3.72_b$ | $4.12_{ab}$ | $3.97_{ab}$ | $3.69_{ab}$ | $2.00_{ab}$ |

*Note:* Means in the same row without common subscripts differ significantly at $p < .05$.

# DISCUSSION

This study examined the views of journalists and voting citizens attending rallies for presidential contenders seeking the Democratic and Republican nominations in New Hampshire in 1988 and in 1992. Answers were sought regarding the existence of differences in the image factors considered desirable by media as compared to the public, differences desired by the media and the public in 1988 as compared to 1992, and party-based differences in the two elections.

## The Media and the Public

At first glance, the amount of disagreement between the media and the public appears substantial. Statistical examination of the data from the 1988 election indicates that the public placed significantly more emphasis on six of the nine questionnaire items, agreeing with the media on only the honesty, age, and experience dimensions. Statistical examination of the data from 1992 revealed more agreement between the media and the public than there had been in 1988, but on 4 of 11 items the public still expressed significantly more importance than did the media.

Such disagreement lends support only in limited areas to those individuals, who, according to Greenfield (1993), assert that the media are a liberal influence in elections. If being less demanding on such social issues as faithfulness to a spouse, support of abiding the law, and morality are indicators of a liberal position, the media were more liberal than the voters.

Similarly, some might also see a liberal bias in the media's support for having solutions to problems. If a conservative position is the support of a free market economy, seeking solutions to problems could be perceived as an activist (i.e., liberal) approach. The media did consider seeking solutions for problems to be an important characteristic for a presidential candidate, but because they did not differ significantly from the public on that item, they would not seem to be leading public opinion.

The fact is that any importance in the differences between the public and the media are diminished when the actual ratings of the individual items are examined. There was agreement, for example, that the two most important criteria for selecting a president were that the candidate should be honest and should talk about the problems facing the country. Although the public rating of agreement on talking about problems was significantly higher than that of the media statistically, mean scores of both groups in both elections reached 4.67 or above, indicating that the difference was occurring within the "strongly agree" range. Although the difference was statistically significant, it should be noted that both the public and the media considered the item an important one.

The two groups also agreed that the least important criteria were the sex and the age of the candidate. Neither considered it important that the candidate be younger than 60 in 1988 or younger than 65 in 1992. Although the public rating of the importance of the candidate being male was significantly higher than that of the media, both groups ranked it as least important. Examination of the actual ratings in 1988 indicate that the public was neutral and the media disagreed with the statement that it was important for the candidate to be male. In 1992, the media and the public concurred in disagreeing with the item.

Statistically significant differences were also found in media and public ratings of four other items. The public, more than the media, considered it important that a candidate be energetic and aggressive, faithful to one's spouse, a forceful public speaker, and a person of high moral integrity. The ratings indicate that the level of difference was that the public strongly agreed with each item whereas the media merely agreed.

Although the media covering the 1988 and 1992 primary elections were not in total agreement with the public attending campaign rallies on the characteristics desirable for a candidate, the disagreements were, once again, in degree rather than direction. The public consistently felt more strongly than the media on those items of difference, but when the public thought a characteristic desirable, the media agreed.

The finding that the media hold their convictions less strongly than the general public but that the two do not differ on the direction of their convictions raises a question. Why are members of the press accused of being "media elites," who, as Vice President Dan Quayle argued in 1992, are so liberal that they are "out of touch with mainstream America" (Wilkinson, 1992, p. A7)? At least in terms of the selection of candidates, the press appear to follow the more strongly held opinions of the public rather than leading them.

One reason why the media might be attacked is that they have a platform to present ideas or even express opinions that individual citizens do not have. When as individuals we disagree with the opinion of others, we are free to assume that they represent a minority or even aberrant view. When it becomes apparent that the press do not support the conservative view, they are accused of being liberal even though their criteria on the desirable characteristics for a president are close to those accepted by most of the general population.

## Consistency Between Elections

The importance of candidate characteristics did not vary greatly between 1988 and 1992. No significant differences were found in the media sample, and only two characteristics changed significantly in the public sample. In 1992, the public placed less importance on the candidate being male and on the candidate being faithful to the spouse than they had in 1988. Some of this might be attributed to sex differences in the public survey in the two elections. The percentage of females in the public sample increased from 42% in 1988 to 55% in 1992. That women considered it less important that the candidate be male is not surprising, but at least three other reasons help explain the public's acceptance of a female candidate. First, a phenomenon begun in 1990 exploded in 1992 when a record 119 women sought and won their party's nomination for a seat in the United States Congress. Second, Barbara Bush was her husband's most important and most visible surrogate during the New Hampshire primary. At rallies throughout the state, the First Lady drew large admiring crowds, and public opinion polls indicated that voters were more favorably impressed with her than with her husband (Dowd, 1992). The third factor was the emergence of Hillary Clinton. During the New Hampshire primary, Bill Clinton talked about a copresidency, telling audiences that if he was elected they would get "two for the price of one." Hillary Clinton was also traveling around the state on her own and drawing large crowds for rallies in which she was advertised as the main speaker. Thus there was strong support for women in the public sample, reflecting its belief that a candidate need not be male to be qualified for high public office.

The Clinton candidacy might also have affected rating of the faithfulness-to-spouse item among the public. Two weeks before votes were to be counted in New Hampshire, *The Star,* a weekly tabloid, released its second story accusing the Arkansas governor of having extramarital affairs. This time the headline was "My 12-Year Affair With Bill Clinton," and its story featured a woman who said she had had a sexual relationship with Clinton and "that there were phone tapes to prove everything" (Miller, 1992, p. 33). As concerned Democrats began to worry that "another Gary Hart fiasco might be in the making" (Miller, 1992, p. 33), the Clintons were offered a segment on the January 26, 1992 edition of *60 Minutes* (which immediately followed the Super Bowl) to talk about the allegations and their marriage. Following their appearance, an ABC poll found that the scandal had swayed only 11% of the voters; 79% said the press "had no business poking through such dirty laundry" and 82% believed that enough had been said about Clinton's personal life (Miller, 1992, p. 34). The results of the ABC poll and this study, taken in approximately the same time period, are consistent. The public did not consider faithfulness to the spouse to be an important characteristic for a presidential candidate in 1992.

A different scenario with a different result occurred in 1988. Prior to the New Hampshire primary, Senator Gary Hart, the Democratic front-runner, was accused of having an extramarital relationship with a Miami model. He reacted to the accusation by challenging the media to prove that such a relationship existed. When reporters from the *The Miami Herald* documented the charge, the intensity of national media coverage completely overwhelmed anything else the senator did or said, eventually forcing him to withdraw his candidacy (Trent & Friedenberg, 1991).

Thus the two situations were very different. Whereas the Clintons were able to create doubt about the accusation and establish their stability as a couple, Hart had been caught and people were unable to separate the issue of marital faithfulness from the questions of a candidate's fitness or qualifications to be president.

A second reason why the public might have viewed marital faithfulness as less important in 1992 than it was in 1988 is that the context in which it was judged was different. In 1992, one issue—the economy of the United States—dominated the presidential campaign from beginning to end. The question of whether or not a presidential contender had violated marriage vows was viewed as insignificant when compared to the country's economic problems. Because no such issue dominated the primary period of the 1988 campaign, issues of a personal nature took on added importance.

Unlike the public, media scores on faithfulness to the spouse in 1992 (3.28) were almost identical to those of 1988 (3.23). Perhaps the media placed less importance both on the instances of unfaithfulness and to differences between the 1988 and 1992 actions and accusations because they had become jaded to stories of politicians' sexual wanderings.

## Party Affiliation

Faithfulness to the spouse was also a distinguishing characteristic for Democratic and Independent as opposed to Republican demands of candidates. In both 1988 and 1992, Republicans considered loyalty to one's spouse to be significantly more important than did Democratic or Independent voters. In this case, party difference might also be interpreted as an indication of candidate specificity. It was a Democratic candidate in 1988 and again in 1992 who was charged publicly with having had an affair. The leading Republican candidate in each year, George Bush, was consistently presented as a family man with a wife whose image was that of a loving grandmother and committed spouse. Republican partisans could not be expected to honor the argument that elections should be based on other issues.

Republicans were also more insistent that the candidate be male in both elections. In addition, in the 1988 campaign, Republicans emphasized the importance of being a forceful speaker and being physically energetic and aggressive. This macho combination of characteristics might also be candidate specific and the reason why one of the main Republican candidates sought to erase public perception of himself as weak or "wimpish." George Bush was seeking leadership of the party's ticket after 8 years of being surrounded with the aura of being the vice president to Ronald Reagan, the great communicator, the aggressive leader of the country's victory in Grenada, and an indomitable survivor of an assassin's bullets. Compared with an array of Democratic hopefuls led by the discredited Hart and the soft-spoken Michael Dukakis, the Republicans' preferences seem to accurately represent their characterization of a president.

Another difference between party members that was apparent in the 1992 election but not in 1988 dealt with the issue of age. In 1992, the Democratic respondents considered it significantly more important that the candidate be younger than 65 years of age. This, too, seems to reflect the differences between the candidates. Bush, the incumbent Republican president and the leading Republican candidate, was 69 years old.

Both Paul Tsongas and Bill Clinton, the leading Democratic candidates, were much younger, and Clinton was viewed as the representative of the "baby boom" generation.

It is noteworthy that significant differences were not found among respondents from different political parties on the two position questions that were added in 1992. Two possible explanations exist. Failure to find a significant difference might indicate that differences do not exist in the importance that members of political parties give to position-oriented characteristics. A more likely scenario is that the respondents did not view the positions that were on the questionnaire as making a real distinction between the candidates. If additional rhetorical themes or positions of a more candidate-specific nature had been submitted, significant differences might have been found.

## CONCLUSION

Although statistically significant differences were found between the voters and the media, the differences were in the degree of convictions about the importance of certain criteria for selecting a president rather than on whether the characteristics were desirable or undesirable. This study supports and expands the conclusions of Hofstetter et al. (1978) that network news reinforces or intensifies preexisting candidate image perceptions and issue positions. When the media and the public start out in basic agreement, the media will not change the direction of convictions but they might affect the intensity of feeling that a characteristic is important in either a positive or a negative direction. Every significant difference found in this study in the criteria of media and the public would indicate that the public begins with more intense convictions than do the media. This would seem to indicate that any effect the media would have would be in the direction of reducing the intensity rather than increasing or reinforcing preexisting convictions about the importance of criteria. Nevertheless, the reinforcement of preexisting positions might still occur if the media presented information regarding specific candidate attributes. Even with the media believing that an attribute such as faithfulness is less important than the public thinks, they might still reinforce the public view if they report that a candidate is unfaithful.

The criteria used by the media did not change significantly between the 1988 and 1992 campaigns. Although there were some changes made by the public between 1988 and 1992 in the ratings of importance of two of the nine criteria used in both studies, the changes might reflect differences in the subject pool. The slight shift toward increased acceptability of female candidates would seem to be a natural consequence of significantly increasing the proportion of women in the audience. Also, the slight reduction in the importance placed on the faithfulness-to-spouse issue might reflect confidence in Hillary Clinton's support and backing of her husband against the allegation of unfaithfulness in 1992 as contrasted with Senator Hart's 1988 fiasco. The alleged examples of infidelity might have created different definitions for the faithfulness-to-spouse issue in the two elections.

With no changes occurring in the criteria used by the media in the two elections and significant variations in the degree of intensity being found in only two of the nine characteristics surveyed in the two elections by the public, there is reason to believe that the criteria used to select a president are basically stable across elections but that characteristics of, and circumstances surrounding, leading candidates can vary the importance that the public places on certain criteria.

Although the political party of the subjects did not make a difference in the importance placed on the criteria in most instances, differences were found in characteristics that relate to the leading candidates of the two parties. For example, there was not a significant difference in the importance that members of various political parties accorded to age in the 1988 election when the candidates seemed to be of the same generation, but in 1992, when the Democratic front-runners were noticeably younger than the leading Republican candidate, Democratic survey respondents thought the issue was more important. And when in both elections allegations of marital unfaithfulness were directed only at the leading Democratic candidate, the Republican respondents found that characteristic to be significantly more important than did Democratic respondents. Again, although there is considerable stability on the characteristics demanded of presidential candidates, attributes of candidates and circumstances can significantly affect the importance that voters of both political parties place on specific criteria.

## NOTES

1. Given the sample sizes in both the 1988 and 1992 samples, small mean differences would be statistically significant at the $p < .05$ level of significance even though these differences would be substantively unimportant. Therefore, the $p < .01$ level of significance is used for almost all analyses.
2. Analyses investigating party affiliation, sex, and age differences were performed with the media and public samples combined. Breaking the media sample by these demographic characteristics would create very small and unstable subgroups.

## REFERENCES

Atwood, L. E., & Jarvis, D. (1976, April). *Media use, candidate image and voting: A test of "new politics" emphasis on television.* Paper presented at the annual meeting of the International Communication Association, Portland, OR.

Czepiec, H. (1976). *The impact of television news and party identification on candidate image adoption.* Unpublished doctoral dissertation, Ohio State University.

Davis, D. K. (1990). News and politics. In D. Swanson & D. Nimmo (Eds.), *New directions in political communication: A resource book* (pp. 147–184). Newbury Park, CA: Sage.

Dowd, M. (1992, January 16). Immersing himself in nitty-gritty, Bush barnstorms New Hampshire. *The New York Times,* pp. A1, A10.

Graber, D. (1971). Press coverage patterns of campaign news: The 1968 presidential race. *Journalism Quarterly, 48,* 502–512.

Greenfield, J. (1992, June 22). Media fume over "elite" label. *The Cincinnati Enquirer,* p. A9.

Greenfield, J. (1993, January 30). Equal opportunity harasses. *The Cincinnati Enquirer,* p. A7.

Harrison, T. M., Stephen, T. D., Husson, W., & Fehr, B. J. (1991). Images versus issues in the 1984 presidential election: Differences between men and women. *Human Communication Research, 18,* 209–227.

Hellweg, S. A., Dionisopoulos, G. N., & Kluger, D. B. (1986). *Political candidate image: Concepts and conceptualizations.* Paper presented at the annual meeting of the Speech Communication Association, Chicago.

Hellweg, S. A., & King, S. W. (1983). Comparative evaluation of political candidates implications for the voter decision-making process. *Central States Speech Journal, 34,* 134–138.

Hofstetter, C. R., Zukin, C., & Buss, T. (1978). Political imagery and information in an age of television. *Journalism Quarterly, 55,* 562–569.

Husson, W., Stephen, T., Harrison, T. M., & Fehr, B. J. (1988). An interpersonal communication perspective on images of political candidates. *Human Communication Research, 14,* 397–421.

Johnston, A. (1990). Trends in political communication: A selective review of research in the 1980's. In D. Swanson & D. Nimmo (Eds.), *New directions in political communication: A resource book* (pp. 329–362). Newbury Park, CA: Sage.

Kepplinger, H. M. (1982). Visual biases in television campaign coverage. *Communication Research, 9,* 432–446.

Lichter, R. S., & Rothman, S. (1981). Media and business elites. *Public Opinion, 4,* 42–60.

Masters, R. D., Sullivan, D. G., Feola, A., & McHugo, G. (1987). Television coverage of candidates' display behavior during the 1984 Democratic primaries in the United States. *International Political Science Review, 8,* 121–130.

Miller, A. H., Wattenberg, M. P., & Malanchuk, O. (1985). Cognitive representations of candidate assessments. In K. R. Sanders, L. L. Kaid, & D. Nimmo (Eds.), *Political communication yearbook 1984* (pp. 183–210). Carbondale: Southern Illinois University Press.

Miller, A. H., Wattenberg, M. P., & Malanchuk, O. (1986). Schematic assessments of presidential candidates. *American Political Science Review, 80,* 521–537.

Miller, M. (1992, November/December). The specter of scandal: Clinton nearly sank in an ooze of allegations [Special election issue]. *Newsweek,* pp. 32–36. All material quoted is copyright © Newsweek 1992, used here by permission.

Moriarty, S. E., & Garramone, G. M. (1986). A study of news magazine photographs of the 1984 presidential campaign. *Journalism Quarterly, 63,* 728–734.

Pike, G. R. (1985, May). *Toward a transactional model of political images: Collective images of the candidates in the 1984 election.* Paper presented at the annual meeting of the International Communication Association, Honolulu.

Sanders, K. R., & Pace, T. J. (1977). The influence of speech communication on the image of a political candidate: "Limited effects" revised. *Communication Yearbook, 1,* 465–474.

Stempel, G. H. (1961). The prestige press covers the 1960 presidential campaign. *Journalism Quarterly, 38,* 157–163.

Stempel, G. H. (1965). The prestige press in two presidential elections. *Journalism Quarterly, 42,* 15–21.

Stempel, G. H. (1969). The prestige press meets the third-party challenge. *Journalism Quarterly, 46,* 699–706.

Trent, J. S., & Friedenberg, R. V. (1991). *Political campaign communication: Principles and practices* (2nd ed.). New York: Praeger.

Wilkinson, H. (1992, June 29). Quayle brings his "traditional values" to Middletown. *The Cincinnati Enquirer,* p. A7.

# Credits

Appendix A: Cynthia A. Cronk and Gary P. Johnson, "An Equity Analysis of Pennsylvania's Basic Instruction Subsidy Program, 1977–80," *Journal of Education Finance,* Vol. 8, Spring 1983, pp. 502–510. Reprinted by permission.

Appendix B: *The Star-Ledger*/Eagleton Poll. Eagleton Institute of Politics. Rutgers University. Press release SL/EP 41-1. November 1, 1992. Reprinted by permission.

Appendix C: Chapter 2 of Richard F. Fenno, Jr. *Home Style: House Members in Their Districts.* HarperCollins, 1978. Reprinted by permission.

Appendix D: "Turnout and the Two-Party Vote," by John H. Fenton, from *Journal of Politics,* Vol. 41:1 (February 1979). Reprinted by permission of the author and the University of Texas Press.

Appendix E: "Conflict with Supreme Court Precedent and the Granting of Plenary Review," by S. Sidney Ulmer, from *Journal of Politics,* 45:2 (May 1983), pp. 474–478. Reprinted by permission of the author and the University of Texas Press.

Appendix F: From *Equal Justice and the Death Penalty: A Legal and Empirical Analysis* by David C. Baldus, George G. Woodworth, and Charles A. Pulaski, Jr. Copyright 1990 by David C. Baldus; George G. Woodworth, and Charles A. Pulaski, Jr. Reprinted with permission of Northeastern University Press, Boston.

Appendix G: "State Population and the Electoral Success of U.S. Senators," by John R. Hibbing and Sara L. Brandes, from *American Journal of Political Science,* Vol. 27:4, November 1983. Reprinted by permission of the authors and the University of Texas Press.

Appendix H: From "Abortion and the Public Opinion Polls," by Raymond J. Adamek. Reprinted by permission of the National Right to Life Organization, Washington, DC.

Appendix I: From *International Organization,* "Evaluating the Impact of International Organizations," Vol. 32, pp. 541–563, by Francis W. Hoole. Reprinted by permission of the MIT Press, Cambridge, Massachusetts, Copyright 1977.

Appendix J: Judith S. Trent, *et al.,* "The Ideal Candidate." *American Behavioral Scientist,* Vol. 37, no. 2, Nov.–Dec. 1993. Reprinted by permission of Sage Publications, Inc.

# Index